INTERPRETING EDUCATION

Frontiers of Education

Series Editor: Ronald H. Stein

Addition titles in this series:

The American University
Problems, Prospects, and Trends
edited by Jan H. Blits

The Courts and American Education Law
by Tyll van Geel

Early Childhood Education
An Introduction: Bridging the Gap
by Hulda G. Berk, Ed.D.

Excellence in Education
Perspectives on Policy and Practice
edited by Philip G. Altbach, Gail P. Kelly, and Lois Weis

Higher Education in American Society (Revised Edition)
edited by Philip G. Altbach and Robert O. Berdahl

Paradigms and Promises
New Approaches to Educational Administration
by William Foster

Teaching Undergraduates
Essays from the Lilly Endowment
Workshop on the Liberal Arts
edited by Bruce A. Kimball

INTERPRETING EDUCATION

ABRAHAM EDEL

PROMETHEUS BOOKS • BUFFALO, NEW YORK

Published 1989 by Prometheus Books
700 East Amherst Street, Buffalo, New York 14215

Copyright © 1989 by Transaction, Inc.

All Rights Reserved

No part of this book may be reproduced or transmitted in any form or by any means electronic or mechanical, including photocopying, recording, or by any information-storage system, without prior permission in writing from the publisher. A reviewer who wishes may quote brief passages for inclusion in a magazine, newspaper, or broadcast.

Library of Congress Catalog Number: 89-62320
ISBN 9780879755546

In memory of
Charles Frankel

Contents

Acknowledgments viii
Preface ix

Part I   Educational Institutions and Philosophical Resources
Introduction 3
1. Education and Schooling in Cultural Perspective 7
2. Grading: Tracking the Philosophical Roots of a
   Specific Problem 23
3. A Philosophical Outlook as an Educational Resource 41

Part II   Bases of Normative Judgment
Introduction 65
4. Current Critiques of the Schools 69
5. Politicized Schools and the Ideal of Impartiality 89
6. Ideals and Their Assessment 107
7. Toward a Moral Agenda for Contemporary Education 129
8. Rationality, Autonomy, Relativism 153

Part III   Teacher and Student
Introduction 177
9. Teacher and Student in the Contemporary World 183
10. Learning and Teaching: Conceptual Problems 203
11. Forms of Learning 221
12. The Pedagogical Encounter 237

Part IV   Some Central Problems of Curriculum
Introduction 253
13. Scientific Knowledge and the Humanities 257
14. Social and Moral Education 275
15. Complexities of the Familiar: Sport and Physical Education;
    Crafts, Arts, and Technology; Basic Skills 295
16. The Confrontation of the Liberal and the
    Vocational-Technical 313

Appendix A. The Social Character of Dewey's Philosophy 325
Appendix B. "Aims of Education"—A Comparison instead
   of a Controversy 331

Index 335

Acknowledgments

Free and selective use, with revisions, has been made of three previously published papers:

"The Contribution of Philosophical Anthropology to Educational Development," in *Philosophy and Educational Development*, ed. G. Barnett (Boston: Houghton Mifflin, 1966). (In chapter 1.)

"Dewey's Educational Vision—Is It Still Viable?" in *A New Challenge to the Educational Dream: The Handicapped*, ed. Jacquelyn Ann Kegley (Bakersfield: California State College Bakersfield, 1980). By permission of the editor. (In one section of chapter 3, and in Appendix A.)

"Value Conflict and the Higher Learning," *Humanist* 33 (March/April 1973). By permission of Paul Kurtz, editor. (In the discussion of student attitudes in the 1960s, in chapter 9.)

Preface

This book was prompted by an interest in the problems of educational philosophy under conditions of rapid social change in the twentieth century; by the feeling that too many of the traditional approaches were set in the effort to delineate a permanent structure rather than to work out ways of handling change; by a concern with the different ways in which philosophy and educational thought have been related; and finally by the belief that we are at present in an interlude in which older "paradigms" and "models" have worn thin and new approaches have to be constructed. I cannot claim that this book establishes a new paradigm, but perhaps its studies will clear away some old confusions and indicate some of the conditions that fresh modes of thought will have to satisfy.

I am grateful (now that the book is done) to Richard Peters, who first urged that I undertake it. The greater part of the book was completed during a year at the National Humanities Center in the Research Triangle of North Carolina. The congenial atmosphere of its first group of scholars (1978-79) provided a happy setting and the year-long Seminar on Ideals of Education proved highly stimulating. I am much in the debt of the late Charles Frankel, then president of the Center, to whom this book is dedicated, for the imaginative character of the arrangements and his warm encouragement, as well as for numerous valuable discussions. His wide experience in political problems of education on both the national and international scenes in combination with his humane sense of democratic values enabled him in unusual degree to put his finger on the practical in the ideal and the ideal in the practical. The seminar not only provided occasion for critical discussion of some of the chapters but also put us in contact with ongoing studies and practical problems in education. For example, an international committee of the Organization for Economic Cooperation and Development, reviewing U.S. policies for education, held meetings at the Center after gathering its materials, and provoked a serious philosophical analysis of the concepts of *disadvantaged* children and *equalitarianism*. I am grateful to Torsten Husén of the University of Stockholm, who was both a member of that committee and a fellow at the Center, for many discussions and comparative ideas based on the European as well as the Anglo-American setting. Another practical issue with which the seminar dealt was the controversy over competence testing in North Carolina;

discussion with psychologists concerned in the construction of the tests stimulated consideration of the role of values in the identification of competencies, as well as problems of measurement. I am indebted to other members of the seminar: to William Bennett and Joseph Beatty for critical suggestions, and to Samuel Scolnicov for a thoroughgoing and insightful review of several chapters and discussion on many of the book's problems. I am also greatly indebted to James McClellan for careful criticism of the manuscript at a later stage and very useful suggestions for reorganization of the material. Most of all, I am indebted to my wife, Elizabeth Flower, who was also a fellow at the Center and a member of the seminar, for her central and continuous participation in the preparation of the book—in making it more readable, in spotting defects in clarity and suggesting ways out of difficulties, in Socratic questioning of innumerable ideas, and in unerring judgment of what was required. Her positive contribution is the equivalent of coauthorship, and if she refuses that status because she began with an existent manuscript, a comparison of it with the final form would show that the refusal was her sole erring judgment. This collaboration was continued in two courses we gave together at the University of Pennsylvania under an Exxon grant for experimental curricular work: one on the relation of philosophy and education, the other on problems of moral education. This enabled us to try out some of the ideas of the book on students as the natural "consumers" of the educational process. As usual, we found that such "consumers" play a productive role, and we are thankful to them for it.

A word with respect to the conflict of values in education, a matter of importance in a period of change. I have tried to make clear the outlook of different social philosophies in relation to their underlying presuppositions and assumptions. I have also tried to state clearly, where relevant, the important value attitudes that I adopt, although often it was not possible to do more than indicate the grounds for holding to them. They concern chiefly the view that the movements toward greater equality and democracy will not be stayed; these are also desirable because they are in line with basic human aspirations. They do not, however, necessitate the excessive individualism with which they are often associated. Significant value issues in education today concern rather the interpretation of these ideas than rearguard battles of elitism versus populism. Lessons about the relation of philosophy to education and ways of structuring their cooperation can, however, be appreciated independently of these basic commitments.

Part I

Educational Institutions and Philosophical Resources

Introduction

Ours is an Age of Criticism. Very few institutions, professions or vocations, modes of life, ways of thought have escaped criticism in the decades since World War II. Some passed a turning point and are moving on, for example in many of the liberation struggles against major discriminations. In others there was a loss of confidence—in government, medicine, psychiatry, business, labor, political parties. Some broke down, for example colonialism or older patterns of marriage and the family. The critics—conservative, liberal, socialist, or Marxist—have themselves been criticized. Even hallowed institutions have not been exempt, as modernization within the church has shown. In the 1960s and 1970s, surprisingly, attacks were levied against education and science and technology—the very institutions that had been looked to in the past to promote progress.

Most of all this was practical critique; social action accompanied theory, though not always with a clearly defined program. Many changes were born of World War II and the rebuilding that followed. Many came with the expansion of industry and technology, the rise of population, the demands for greater equality and democratization, during the third quarter of the century. The two movements that seemed most strikingly to round out the critiques were precisely the ones in education and technology. The revolt of the students in the universities in the 1960s swept country after country; in France it nearly brought down the government. In most places there followed changes of one sort or another in educational administration and programs; at least there was the realization that something was profoundly amiss. About technology, a debate arose in the early 1970s over the limits of growth—whether with overpopulation, depletion of resources, increase of pollution, we were reaching a limit of global support for humankind. To this was added controversy over the disruption that large-scale technology was bringing into evolutionary processes. More directly, conflicts emerged over nuclear energy and the control of the pace of development.

In normal times, when institutions and practices are stable, philosophy may center on controversy over justification because for the most part there is agreement on what is being justified. But when the institutions and practices are themselves at issue, philosophic concern is directions of change. Surprisingly, however, during the period of rising critique (at least from the 1940s to the 1970s), philosophical dealings with education took a strange turn. With the general ferment, with Asia and Africa emerging into the modern world and an upsurge of the disadvantaged everywhere, including the beginnings of the Black liberation movement in the United States, one might have expected a socially oriented philosophical approach to emerge—perhaps a sharper form of the pragmatic philosophy of John Dewey that had been so influential in teachers colleges before the war. Instead, the center of the stage was taken by ordinary language analysis that swept over academic philosophy in the 1950s. The United States was scarcely ready for a revolutionary educational theory. A revived conservative outlook was ascendant, and McCarthyite repression equated intellectualism with near-subversion. Academic philosophy at that time pursued the more technical problems of the philosophy of the social sciences rather than the substantive issues of political and social philosophy. Analytic philosophy sharpened educational theory, but in the long run if the pragmatic approach had demanded more of philosophic work in education than it could deliver, the analytic approach seemed to ask less than education needed. The central question now is what to expect in the relations of philosophy and education.

Older approaches had spoken of "philosophy of education" as if it were the transformation of metaphysical and epistemological and ethical doctrines into mandates for educational aims and methods. The central problem for the educator was then which philosophical system to settle on. The newer or analytic philosophy spoke less of "philosophy of education" than of "philosophy and education," what philosophy could do to clarify educational ideas. Yet it often operated with the same lordly stance—as if there were an independent philosophical laboratory to which educational concepts might be shipped for purely philosophical analysis without reference to what is going on in education, and as if the results could then be legislative for education.

This procedure could be helpful only if the state of educational practice could be taken for granted as constant and its underlying purposes as steady, that is, if education could be counted on to have a stable structure. But the contemporary world knows full well that the educational arena has been transformed by vast material and social changes and that its problems are now inordinately complex. For one thing, it used to be assumed that a few years' schooling would provide the learning that one needed for a lifetime. Nowadays much of the learning is provided outside schooling, the adequacy of the schools is under challenge, and social needs appear to require lifelong learning. Accordingly, the relations of philosophy and education might better be conceived as the intimate interrelations of philosophical resources and educational institutions. The lordly stance has to be replaced by a mutually cooperative one in which education looks in terms of its needs and problems to see what use it can make of philosophical resources while philosophy expects also to learn from the way in which its resources are tried out on educational needs, problems, and experiments.

Among the philosophical resources from which educational thought can draw, the history of philosophy deserves an important place. The conflict of schools that it exhibits (for example in ethics) calls not for alignment but rather for a study of the variety of formulations and constructions it provides, which capture different, often unexpected, ways of looking at human processes; this adds to our intellectual equipment and liberates from the tyranny of any currently established model. Among twentieth-century philosophies, that of Dewey is particularly useful, less for his specific educational proposals that responded to the situation of the earlier part of the century than for his persistent relation of philosophical ideas to the sociohistorical needs and problems in which they arise and function, and for his general pragmatic emphasis on an activist attitude of reconstruction, both institutional and conceptual. Analytic philosophy, as noted above, has been useful in clearing the decks and setting a sharper focus, and in insisting on precision; its concern with finer linguistic texture has provided a counterweight to bold general constructions. From other approaches, perhaps less elaborated in contemporary educational thought, we may draw useful lessons: from Marxian theory, particularly the total sociohistorical development as a matrix for both explanatory and normative inquiries into education; from phenomenology, the technique for broadening the field to include the meanings of practices to all participants; from existentialism, a reinforcement of the primacy of practice as seen in the scope of decision; and, as will be evident, from many other philosophies on special points.

Philosophical reflection on education can also take advantage of the materials and approaches of other disciplines. For example, it can cultivate the sensitivity of the anthropologist to cultural comparison and to the vision of alternative ways of mankind; it will thus be dogmatically less bound by the particular shape of institutions and ways of the time. It can also gain from the historian's sense of complexity—how traditions fashion the present, the demands that contingencies impose on construction as well as the opportunities they offer, and the stabilization of trends or directions in development. And of course it must be aware of the impact of different psychologies on the interpretation of knowledge and human capacities.

The studies of Part I probe ways of relating philosophy and education. Given that the simplistic formulae of the past are inadequate for our time, we make no attempt to offer a fresh, simple, all-embracing formula. Instead, we recognize a great complexity of relations, and the exploration offered is only a beginning to what further exploration may reveal. Chapter 1 aims at unfolding the range of tasks that are to be faced in reflection on education. It does this through a use of anthropological materials and a comparative approach to educational processes. Chapter 2 starts with a single problem in a school system—that of grading—and shows how its analysis leads into traditional issues of moral and social philosophy. Chapter 3 explores how a comprehensive philosophy may act as a resource for education and how differences in philosophy may be turned to advantage rather than pose an issue of selective alignment. Collectively these chapters exhibit the complexity of the relations of philosophy and education and the need to approach those relations in particular rather than wholesale terms.

1. Education and Schooling in Cultural Perspective

The problems that arise in philosophical reflection on education and schooling are larger than the traditional focus on the growth of the schools, their demand for teacher preparation and for guidance in the policies of schooling. Notions of *enculturation* and *socialization* in the social sciences have focused on what is happening to the child as he or she grows into a participant of the culture and a practicing member of society. If the paradigm case of education is still the student in the classroom, that is doubtless because of the heavy investment our culture has made in the school as an educational institution. Reflection on education may start its scenarios with the school, but it clearly cannot end there. And in between in attempting to relate school and culture as a whole it can well utilize directly the materials and mode of inquiry developed in modern anthropology.

To approach issues and tasks in education initially through an anthropological lens has marked advantages. It immediately carries us beyond schooling and by scanning educational operations throughout the whole of a culture provides a comprehensive view of interrelations. It also protects us against a narrowing ethnocentrism in which we think of our own ways as the fixed order of nature, for we see differences not simply as varying items but as shaping up into varied systematic patterns. In spite of discovered variety—perhaps even because of it—we are better able to discern what kinds of common or invariant elements there have been. We can come to understand the different ways in which human beings have tried to do similar jobs, and are prompted to develop criteria for effectiveness in doing these jobs. As a result of such inquiries we develop the habit of looking for the relations of particular human ways and practices to the general cultural setting; we anticipate the complexity of different subpatterns and the interinfluence of groups with different ways; we become conscious of persistent changes and the deeply sociohistorical character of human life. And we become aware of the forms of expression that the human spirit has taken, and come to realize its creative character. On the practical side, this means that we are in fact always choosing among possibilities. On the intellectual side, it makes possible a comparative approach that not merely gives different results but—and this is increasingly central in philosophy today—reformulates the questions asked.

All this contributes to a philosophical view of human beings; it is not just a few lively items suggested by anthropology. Perhaps some of these lessons might not have required anthropological assistance. They might have come directly by observing small differences and extrapolating, by studying historical changes in a single culture and so on. In the ancient world, differences in people's ways were closer at hand. The tremendous growth of Western civilization, with so many underlying uniformities, has tended to obscure them. It has been the achievement of modern anthropology to exhibit extreme differences, to furnish a larger variety of patterns, and so to stimulate analytic and self-conscious comparison. That there are thousands of religions and thousands of moralities has not yet been sufficiently exploited for theoretical understanding. The same holds for educational institutions.

That schooling is not the whole story of education has always been evident. The child learns to walk and talk and use a complex kinship nomenclature, even games and table manners, without going to school, and continues to learn outside the classroom. Nowadays the question is sometimes raised whether with television, radio, libraries, journals, and general social sources of information the balance is not tipped in favor of out-of-school sources. Hence it becomes essential not merely for understanding education but even for understanding schooling to see what schooling is doing to relation to the culture as a whole. This is helped by contrast. In his survey of North American primitive education, Pettitt says,

> In primitive society, which had no school system, we find a fairly complete picture of what a people must do to insure the transmittal of its traditions, beliefs, ideals, and aspirations to the younger generation. Through study of such school-free efforts we may obtain a clearer conception of the manifold ramifications of the process of conditioning children and of safeguarding a culture pattern. With such a conception in mind we are then in a better position to judge whether schools and professional teachers, either in justice to themselves or to the public, should be expected to assume the whole responsibility at so much per month.[1]

When we look in this manner at our culture and the ways in which it is transmitted, one of our first realizations is that in spite of the limited and selective role of schooling, it is in fact doing much more than we are inclined to suppose. We recognize this in the familiar adage that the personality of the teacher counts as much as his or her knowledge of the subject; but then we discount this by saying that some types of personality are better able than others to transmit the subject.

The remainder of this chapter accordingly will consider ways in which the idea of enculturation enriches the notion of schooling. We may distinguish three tasks. One is to elicit in cultural perspective the fuller description of the kinds of materials transmitted in schooling. Such material—in effect a map of what sorts of things the learner learns—constitutes merely a beginning. It does not inform us about the principles of selection that determine the educational focus of schooling. To look for these is a second task that carries us into the functional relations of schooling to culture and society as a whole. While this is an explanatory task, showing what the school is trying to do or happens to do, at the same time it makes us aware of the normative character of educational processes and theories. The significant point from an anthropological perspective is that educational normative judgments are legislating not merely for educational institutions but also—because schooling is related to culture—for the culture and the society as a whole. Thus the third task is to raise the question of such relations in both directions and ask whether the value base of social and cultural decision does not in turn furnish grounds for a value direction in educational philosophy.

What Does the Learner Learn?

How the narrower idea of schooling is enriched by the notion of enculturation can be seen by selective illustration—from content and character to skills and sanctions.

What strikes us first about the schools, of course, is content—whether we are examining skills such as reading, writing, and speaking French, or subject matter such as chemistry, mathematics, or Shakespeare. Often we have trouble distinguishing between a skill and an item of knowledge, and in the case of Shakespeare we may hedge a bit on what we are teaching as we shift from memorization and plot detail to a sense of language or an exuberant outlook. Few theoretical implications might at first seem to follow from the fact that the content of our curriculum has changed over the centuries, or from the comparative fact that, say, the Aztec priesthood schools taught the rituals of human sacrifice. That we take for granted a changing subject matter of teaching is itself a cultural acquisition. We have stabilized the ideal of a *growing* body of knowledge, and it is this central phenomenon of modern society that is taken to give substance to schooling.

It is often taken for granted also that beyond conveying knowledge and skills schools are building character. Here variations are found not merely in kinds of character but in how they are identified and patterned, and the attitudes and feelings that cluster around them. Contrasts are great: for example, of Zuni modesty and reserve with Kwakiutl ostentation and arrogance; of the typical, matter-of-course generosity found in many American Indian cultures with our own dominant self-regard; of the male stoicism of the Plains Indians with the gentle tenderness of the Arapesh males; and so on almost endlessly.[2] These striking differences enter into the very organization of concepts as, for example, a particular Chiga [African] character term will apply both to stealing and to inhospitality as if they were one in essence, just as our own term "shiftless" may fuse "lazy," "dirty," and "poor," although these characteristics are related only under special social conditions. Even more penetrating is the recognition that not only the content of moral attitudes is culturally variable, that is, which acts rouse feelings, but also the kinds of feelings thereby aroused, such as guilt or shame or disgust or some other emotional configuration.[3] Also, the ways of expressing feeling are quite different, as can be seen in the impassivity of the Bali, the more ample gestures of South Europeans, and the alleged British reserve. There are even widely varying attitudes toward such a physiologically common phenomenon as pain—feeling it typically as simply something to be gotten rid of or primarily as a threat because it is a symptom of something wrong in the body.[4] Many of our assumptions about unavoidable attitudes give way in comparisons: for example, the assumed inevitability of stresses and strains in adolescence, which Margaret Mead challenged in her early *Coming of Age in Samoa*. Or the inevitability of anthropomorphism in children's beliefs, which she found absent in the early realism of the Manus child. Or the attitudes toward privacy, which she posed in the striking contrast between the Samoan girl who might say that she slept with a boy but would never tell whether she loved him, and the typical American girl [of that period] who might openly confess she loved a boy but never tell whether she slept with him![5]

The cultural diversity of character and attitude holds equally for social principles. It has taken a long time to realize that our democratic school system has not merely harbored but actively imparted nonequalitarian attitudes. We still do not realize that we are teaching bureaucratic attitudes through the example of the bureaucratic structure of our large educational system.

The subtlety of what we are imparting to the young does not end with content and skills, character and attitudes, and social principles. Hallowell, Redfield, and the Kluckhohns have shown how every culture provides orientations of a basic sort for its individuals—modes of reference for their very selves, orientations to space and time, and direction.[6] For example, in our culture we stride forward through time, so that the future lies ahead of us and the past behind us. In another culture, people may think of the future primarily as the unknown and hence it is the past that is visible in front of them while the future is hidden behind them; time is sweeping up on them from behind. (How startled we should be if told we had a great future behind us!) One people may feel themselves to be a part of nature; another feel the need to confront it. In mechanistic fashion we often think of our bodies as machines with replaceable parts; primitive societies more often stress a conception of organic unity. One society lives in the present; another turns its young to working for the future, postponing gratification, even robbing the present of an intrinsic meaning. (This has been shown to be a middle-class American pattern, which is one reason that middle-class teachers often quite fail to understand the ways of their lower-class pupils.) Often the school imparts overt attitudes to restraint and control. We talk a great deal about leeway for self-expression. The Ashanti sound much more like our conservative critics of progressive education when they say, "When your child dances badly, tell him saying, 'Your dancing is not good,' and do not say to him '[Little] soul, just dance as you want to.'"[7] Beneath overt attitudes to expressiveness or control lie patterns of cultural character that vary both in the modern and primitive worlds.

Again, the mode of teaching produces a second-order learning, what Bateson has aptly called "deutero-learning."[8] At this point concepts of method, of authority, of how to go about things and how to fuse thought and experience are inculcated. Wylie's description of the mode of teaching in a French village school is a good example of this:

> In teaching morals, grammar, arithmetic, and science the teacher always follows the same method. She first introduces a principle or rule that each pupil is supposed to memorize so thoroughly that it can be repeated on any occasion without a slightest faltering. Then a concrete illustration or problem is presented and studied or solved in the light of the principle. More problems or examples are given until the children can recognize the abstract principle implicit in the concrete circumstances and the set of circumstances implicit in the principle. When this relationship is sufficiently established in the minds of the children, the teacher moves on to another principle and set of related facts.
>
> The principle itself is not questioned and is hardly discussed. Children are not encouraged to formulate principles independently on the basis of an examination of concrete cases. They are given the impression that principles exist autonomously. They are always there: immutable and constant.[9]

This is clearly the deutero-learning of a Cartesian rationalism. Contrast it with Anthony Leeds's description of the view of many U.S. educators:

> The *process* of learning itself is crucial and content secondary, if not actually unimportant, since it will be learned by virtue of ingesting the process itself, a process labelled "experiencing" and conceptually derived from a systematic

distortion of the scrolls writ by their culture hero, John Dewey. The neonate is to be put through "experiences" about which he subsequently "intellectualizes." This process apparently prepares him, intellectually or in "life-adjustment," as one of the favorite phrases of American educators goes, for any future exigency in learning.[10]

This concern with ways of teaching is largely a feature of modern culture with large-scale schooling, and more important, with critical ideas about the development of knowledge. Professor Arjun Appadurai has pointed out that in primitive society generally, where materials are agreed on, it is taken for granted that one who knows can teach. The task is simply that of handing over.

There are, of course, many other phases of the learning process that could be examined: for example, who teaches, who is taught, what are the contexts of learning, what the sanctions. In primitive societies often the whole community serves as teacher, sometimes priests or elders. Among us schoolteachers are a specially trained group, yet much that is vocational is learned on the job, and much could be learned at an early age from the neighborhood parental group. In China, Linton reminds us, only nobles attended higher schools, where they learned the six liberal arts of ceremonies, music, architecture, charioteering, mathematics, and writing.[11] The ideal of universal education is so recent that even its partial achievement has called for reassessing the whole character of our schools. (Are we still teaching a kind of charioteering and ceremonies?) As for context, we think primarily of a classroom, and even in considering only the college level we have difficulty in thinking of a library as a learning context rather than a preparation for class—to say nothing of the college breakfast table where students may teach each other some of the things they have been learning in class. Primitive societies exhibit more clearly the parental context, the apprenticeship context, learning on the job, the teaching role of striking ceremonials such as initiation rites, the teaching role of designated relatives such as mother's brother or grandparents. We tend to dump every critical learning onto the schools. (Where *should* a child learn how to drive a car, how to repair an electric switch, how to dance, and the facts and norms of sexual life?) And what of the techniques of teaching? Primitive societies use not only talk but music, folklore, and dance to teach: Driberg points out that animal dances are used to portray the characteristics of animals and how to hunt them,[12] and much teaching is done through myths, folkstories[13] (how late we have come to teaching through comic books), and dramatized ceremonies such as the Hopi use of kachina dolls.

And what of the prime issue of sanctions in schooling? The coercive aspect is often dominant in our educational systems: how many of us still remember the school principal's flat strap for which we were expected to hold out our hand, bravely if not willingly—itself a learning experience? And the truant officer is still with us. Pettitt concludes that among primitive societies corporal punishment is rare, not because of the innate kindliness of these people but because it is contrary to developing the type of individual personality they set up as the ideal.[14] He finds ridicule, praise, and reward more common. Yet shame can work in different ways. Consider the aggressive shaming of pupils that Wylie describes:

> "What is seven times nine, Marie?"
> "I don't know, Madame."
> "Ah! She doesn't know seven times nine. Everyone in this class knows that. Class, what is seven times nine?"
> The class roared the answer.[15]

Compare this with the Pueblo school, in which no child will give the answer till everyone has it, for you must not shame anyone. Of course, in the long run, theory recognizes, the sheer desire to learn would be the very best sanction. (St. Augustine, in the first book of his *Confessions,* looking back on his early sin in preferring Virgil to eternal mathematics, says: "No doubt then, that a free curiosity has more force in our learning these things than a frightful enforcement.") Margaret Mead points out that the shift from learning what everyone agrees everyone would *want* to know, to teaching what some think others *should* know is a differentiating mark between most primitive education and modern complex schooling.[16] Whatever the source of such distinction, once there is this complex, separately existing system maintaining compulsory attendance, the problem of incentives and the discrimination between more and less desirable ones is unavoidable.

These considerations may suggest the ways in which the idea of enculturation enriches the narrower concept of schooling. Note, however, that the wide range of dimensions and the breadth of different possibilities within each dimension only throws open—it certainly does not solve—the problem of choice in educational theory. Unfortunately one cannot, for example, simply cull a set of attractive attitudes and character traits, set them into a beautiful mosaic, and hold them up as a shining model for our school system. We should have, instead, to study the psychological, cultural, and historical depth of our own particular character formation before making recommendations for reconstruction. Anthropology itself quickly passed beyond merely descriptive items of difference to a grounding of difference in the needs, problems, cultural patterning, and historical development of the particular peoples studied. A school system, then, once it has emerged as a separate institution—similar to the political or legal system—has no essence of its own. At most it has a temporal core, subject to change. It has crystallized and temporarily stabilized some aims, methods, techniques, and so on, within which and with which it operates. But it remains bound by a thousand ties to the matrix of needs and causes, and informal processes from which it emerged. Its existence and its values reflect the fuller matrix on which it rests; its assessment and its policies can never be self-enclosed nor divorced from reference to its functions. And so we turn to the second task—to consider the contributions of anthropology to our understanding of the functional relations of schooling to culture and society.

What Does Schooling Do in Society?

Anthropology and sociology developed the idea of function for their own scientific uses, sometimes enmeshing it in larger hypotheses about how cultures and societies are integrated. Here we use it in an ordinary sense. For example, if we ask, "What is the function of a wedding ring?" we are inquiring into what uses people make of it—what its role is in the wedding ceremony, in expressing sentiment, in notifying others of the status of the parties (as "out of bounds"), and so on. We discover this by examining aims and intended consequences and noting social reaction to unintended consequences. Functions of course may be latent as well as manifest. For example, anthropologists have noted how the women of a community may feel dissatisfied when the village well is replaced by water piped into individual dwellings. While their labor has been eased and their families' health probably improved, their daily social life has been ruined; they now have to go out of their way to learn the latest gossip. In the village in which I spend my summers we go for sparkling drinking water to a spring just outside the village. Occasionally I exchange words with a local inhabitant bent on the same errand. But often a number of cars line up—usually with out-of-state licenses—and each person waits in silence, shut off in the car, until it is time to go to the spring. Obviously the latent functions of the village well have changed since the days of Isaac and Rebecca. So, too, the manifest functions of Latin have sometimes been transformed in some educational systems; its latent function is often to confer the prestige of the leisure class associated with the older humanistic education in contrast to vocational training.[17]

Anthropology obviously was not needed to reveal the fact that people have aims that their social practices embody. But precisely because it studied bits of social practice in the context of fuller cultural patterning, it was able to stimulate the *systematic* investigation of functions. When this is done in education, it often reveals unexpected aspects and may quite restructure the mode of evaluation. For example, on questions of discipline—to take a psychological function—Plains Indians are horrified by the idea of striking a child. When they found it necessary to check a very young child's crying to prevent their camp's being located by the enemy at night, they dashed water into the child's face. The conditioning appears to have been effective. But this was necessity, not cruelty. Other people elsewhere—e.g. the Tikopia in Polynesia—strike a child occasionally in anger but not in cold retribution.[18] From an outside observer's view, our modes of corporal punishment may be seen as aggressive, an affront to the dignity of the child.

Again, with respect to social functions, Thorstein Veblen analyzes the latent functions of classical education as an embellishment, with a manifest insistence on its lack of utility, but with a consequent enhancement of repute precisely because it constitutes conspicuous waste.[19] At a later time, in some cities at least, the apparently nonvocational character of liberal arts education, especially for girls, obscured the fact that it was largely preparation for teaching as a career. The role of the nineteenth-century and early twentieth-century school system in upward social mobility for lower-middle-class groups and for second-generation immigrant groups has usually been taken for granted, though sometimes questioned. It also provided a trained personnel for industry and business. Concern with total patterning sometimes makes it possible to elicit the functional profile of a whole school system. Leeds suggests, for example, that the Brazilian school system "is thoroughly tied to the class system and is, in fact, latently intended to support and reproduce its [the class system's] present form. Brazilian education is meant to conserve privilege for the privileged, and to create a manipulable lower class for exploitation by the privileged classes."[20] He supports this opinion by reference both to the multiple types of specific schools for different classes, and to the general ideology of the school system.

Functions become self-conscious when they begin to serve as bases for justification or critique. For example, pure research as long as it had little manifest social function was justified in the individualistic terms of intellectual interest or intrinsic value. When its social functions became clear, it was labeled "basic research" and recommended for support as the long-range seedbed of invention and production. The social sciences also, in past and present, are not without a social role, whether it be in economics or political theory. Michael Oakeshott in his defense of conservatism suggests that Machiavelli and Locke functioned as cribs (or handbooks) for princes and classes that had not been born to power.[21]

Again, as functions emerge, even out of differences, there is often a growing awareness of common human aims. Take, for instance, such an apparently remote phenomenon as witchcraft, remembering that spells and ceremonials and use of herbs constitute a quite sizable part of some primitive education. Here there are functions of medicinal endeavor, psychological assuagement, substitute satisfaction, social techniques of control, especially of interpersonal conflict, and so on.[22] Thus quite different practices may be seen as ways of dealing with aims that are common. This tends to stimulate the development of criteria for more or less effective achievement. It is a strange dialectic by which the search for differences and their grounds becomes a way of discovering common aims of a general sort.

On the other hand, the study of education in functional relation to the community does not always yield simple harmonious congruence. There is not merely complexity but also discrepancy, conflict, and change, especially in a period of sociohistorical transformation. These phenomena take innumerable forms. There is often a simple contradiction between educational lessons and social practices. (Wylie, listening to a lesson in which French children repeat and learn by heart, "Let us be the friends and protectors of the little birds," observes, "In a region where a favorite dish is roasted little birds, where a husky man boasts of consuming fifty or sixty warblers at a sitting, there is little likelihood that this lesson will have effect."[23]) There is often a gap between the culture developed in the schools and that of the parent generation that is obvious in immigrant groups but present also in subtler form in native-born groups because of the rapidity of social change; as well as the impact of class differences in aim and mode of life, often focusing sharply in the public schools. Lloyd Warner points out that [in 1962] school boards are 94 percent upper-class or higher; teachers, 94 percent middle-class; and students, 60 percent lower-class and 30 percent lower-middle-class.[24] And underlying the whole process are the obvious vast changes in technology, industry, economic life, and the social forms of the twentieth century.

The most extreme conflicts arise in cases in which the educational system is set against the dominant culture, not simply against that of a particular immigrant group. Anthropological studies of acculturation in the modern world amply illustrate such processes. Take, for example, the treatment of education in Absalom Vilikazi's *Zulu Transformations: A Study of the Dynamics of Social Change*. The conflict is not something that the investigator need take pains to discover: the people themselves are quite conscious of what is going on. Vilikazi points out that the Zulu distinguish socialization (*imfundiso* or *inkuliso*) from education (*imfundo*). The former equips the child with the values, knowledge, and skills of the culture, and is essentially informal. The latter is education in the western sense of the word and is designed to pass on to the child book learning and Christianity and all the things that are characteristic of western civilization. Its aim is and always was to civilize or westernize. It is a new form of upbringing for a new world whose value systems are diametrically opposed to those of the traditional Zulu world. It now dominates the life of the child during all the years of childhood and carries its influence over the childhood years into adulthood.[25]

The consequences of that educational system are quite concrete. The child, not the parent, is able to read a letter or count money. The old culture tells the child not to be disrespectful in talking to an old person by looking directly into his face or eyes; the school teaches that to look away is a sign of shiftiness or dishonesty.[26] The old culture stresses family, kinship, tribal group; the school points to individualism, to economic power and independence. Of course more powerful than the education provided by the school is that provided by the life around both child and parent as they are drawn into the new forms of work of the society, for example abandoning the field for the city and its jobs. In most African countries outside of South Africa, the revolutionary changes in the 1960s and 1970s set the pace for educational tasks and changes. In South Africa because of deepening apartheid, the schools were the victims of conflict.

The wider conception of education we have been considering involves a clear mandate for educational theory. The properties of schooling—whether aim, process, or outcome—are to be understood as a function of wider social relations. In societies in which there are internal conflicts, diverse complex subpatterns, or basic transformations in process, schooling reflects these variations and conflicts, and educational theory inevitably takes sides or proposes fresh paths. Hence, reflection about education is committed to a fuller understanding of effects and qualitative dependence, and it makes normative choices concerning desirable social development and desirable cultural configuration. If it operates on anything less, it is either partially blind or unconsciously reactive. To this normative aspect we now turn.

Social Vectors and Educational Directions

Insofar as the task of educational philosophy is to help guide schooling, the third major use of anthropology is to bring about the realization that educational theory is irretrievably normative for not merely schooling but the whole culture.

Take so simple and essential an objective as universal literacy. Leeds suggests that mass literacy accompanies large-scale shifts from a primarily agrarian base to a commercial-manufacturing and commercial-industrial base, [27] and that it is also tied to certain dissolutions in social stratification and the appearance of egalitarian ideals. Hence to move toward universal literacy in India, only 16.6 percent literate in 1955, is to steer toward overwhelming economic and social transformation. It would be even more so for any society to move toward "functional literacy," or the ability to relate to the complexity of a society and to participate in its necessary processes.

Take even the theoretical concepts of an educational theory. We often speak of education as transmitting the culture from generation to generation. But why transmit? Why not reconstruct? Is there a conservative potential in the very definition of such notions as education, enculturation, socialization? In her article "Our Educational Emphases in Primitive Perspective," Margaret Mead proposed that "instead of attempting to bind and limit the future and to compromise the inhabitants of the next century by a long process of indoctrination which will make them unable to follow any path but that which we have laid down ... we [should] devise and practice a system of education which sets the future free."[28] The future will set its own goals.

Now even to set forth such an educational ideal is to offer a critique of our culture, a proposal for its reorientation. Yet this proposal is not wholly divorced from our cultural needs and development, for it expresses the ideal of a fully self-reliant, democratic culture under conditions of extremely rapid social change in which the rate of acceleration of change can be expected to rise sharply.

Some educators have at times seemed to thrust upon the schools the burden of total social change—for example, George Counts in his *Dare the School Build a New Social Order?* in the 1930s.[29] Such a proposal may correspond to our cultural habit of piling every problem on the schools and then ignoring the problem elsewhere—forgetting to increase the school budget. But in many respects the schools have followed rather than led in social development: they are under strong traditional controls, they often respond belatedly to social causes and necessities instead of exercising what leadership lies within their power. Further, there is always the risk that the schools in rushing to make changes geared to some temporary emergency may create a situation in which havoc results and the problem is reinforced instead of transcended. Of course we must distinguish the kind of problem involved. Sometimes it is merely a question of doing better what the schools are supposed to be doing in any case; for example, under the spur of competition with the Russian advances in space exploration, the teaching of mathematics and physical science in U.S. schools was rapidly advanced. Or again, it may be a question of righting an injustice in the schools, as in attempting integration after the *Brown* decision of the Supreme Court. But of a quite different sort was the attempt, at the height of the Cold War in the 1950s, to gear teaching to a nationalistic policy of anticommunism, rather than to pursue the long-range goal of global peace. Its practical effect was almost to impose a blanket of conformity.[30]

On the normative side, we cannot rest content with merely upholding general ideals, however attractive, nor with merely solidifying even the best traditions of the schools of the past. To take the frequently discussed examples, we can return neither to the concept of the self-development of the individual of progressive education nor the emphasis on basic subject learning of the traditionalists. Nothing less than a full recognition of the complexity of schools in the contemporary world and their roots in our developing historical situation can begin to do the job. Such an inquiry falls into two parts. The first is determination of a basis for valuational judgment, which is a wider task than education alone, since it is fixing the operative value-determinants for a contemporary outlook in all social endeavor. The second is specifically educational, in applying the basis in the light of the means and techniques of the schools in the present period.

Let us underscore the philosophical benefits of adopting a cultural perspective: the stimulation of a systematic consciousness about the culturally specific character of our historically developed school system; the understanding of variety and alternative possibilities; the view of functional relations and underlying aims; the awareness of the normative character of educational policy for the culture as a whole; and a fuller relation of educational policy to a valuational base that fuses knowledge and value in the given age. Stated abstractly, these contributions may sound bare and truistic, but examined concretely, with comparative cultural detail and in depth, they can revolutionize our thinking and, if applied, transform our schools.

Notes

1. George A. Pettitt, *Primitive Education in North America* (University of California Publications in American Archaeology and Ethnology) 43, no. 1 (1946): 3.
2. See Ruth Benedict, *Patterns of Culture* (Boston: Houghton Mifflin 1934); Margaret Mead, *Sex and Temperament in Three Primitive Societies* (New York: William Morrow, 1935).
3. See Margaret Mead, "Social Change and Cultural Surrogates," *Journal of Educational Sociology* 14 (October 1940): 92-109; also, Ruth Benedict, *The Chrysanthemum and the Sword* (Boston: Houghton Mifflin, 1946).
4. See Mark Zborowski's contrast of Italian and Jewish patients in "Cultural Components in Responses to Pain," *Journal of Social Issues* 8 (1952): 16-30.
5. Margaret Mead, *Coming of Age in Samoa* (New York: William Morrow, 1928), and *Growing Up in New Guinea* (New York: William Morrow, 1930).

6. A. Irving Hallowell, *Culture and Experience* (Philadelphia: University of Pennsylvania Press, 1955), esp. ch. 4; Robert Redfield, *The Primitive World and Its Transformations* (Ithaca: Cornell University Press, 1953); Clyde Kluckhohn and others, "Values and Value-Orientation in the Theory of Action," in *Toward a General Theory of Action*, ed. Talcott Parsons and Edward A. Shils (Cambridge: Harvard University Press, 1951); Florence Kluckhohn and Fred L. Strodbeck, *Variations in Value Orientations* (Evanston, Ill.: Row, Peterson, 1961).

7. R. S. Rattray, *Ashanti Proverbs*, 344, as quoted in J. S. Slotkin, *Social Anthropology* (New York: Macmillan, 1950), p. 526.

8. Gregory Bateson, "Social Planning and the Concept of 'Deutero-Learning,'" Conference on Science, Philosophy, and Religion, New York, 1942.

9. Laurence Wylie, *Village in the Vaucluse* (New York: Harper & Brothers, 1957), p. 73.

10. Anthony Leeds, "Cultural Factors in Education: India, Brazil, the United States, the Soviet Union: Some Problems of Applied Anthropology," in *Contemporary India*, ed. Baidya Nath Varma (New York: Asia Publishing House, 1964), pp. 291-92.

11. Ralph Linton, *The Tree of Culture* (New York: Knopf, 1955), pp. 541-42.

12. J.H. Driberg, *At Home with the Savage* (London: Routledge & Kegan Paul, 1932), p. 242.

13. Walter Goldschmidt points out that educational requirements may be seen to influence primitive folktales in the fact that juveniles are utilized as leading characters. See his *Exploring the Ways of Mankind* (New York: Holt, Rinehart & Winston, 1960), p. 217.

14. Pettitt, *Primitive Education in North America*, p. 161.

15. Wylie, *Village in the Vaucluse*, pp. 84-85.

16. Margaret Mead, "Our Educational Emphases in Primitive Perspective," *American Journal of Sociology* 48 (May 1943): 634. Mead traces interesting comparisons with religions proselytizing on the assumption of infallible superiority. She also points to causal factors such as possibilities of changing status and education as a mechanism of change, political factors such as maintaining national loyalty through inculcating a system of ideas, and so on. For consideration of a wide variety of learning modes seen in the general framework of cultural communication, see Mead's *Continuities in Cultural Evolution* (New Haven: Yale University Press, 1964), chs. 4-6.

17. The depth of this problem as a practical matter should not be underestimated. For example, in France it was found that to enable children to take technical subjects without losing face the best policy was to make the teaching of such a subject mandatory in the last two years of compulsory schooling, and thus give everybody some understanding of the technical world in which they live. (*OECD, Reviews of National Policies for Education, FRANCE* [Paris: Organisation for Economic Co-operation and Development, 1971], p. 116.)

18. Raymond Firth, *We, the Tikopia* (Boston: Beacon Press, 1963), p. 141. See also the interesting suggestions concerning modes of corporal punishment (e.g. use of the kitchen spoon or of the hairbrush) and parts of the body focused on, in Martha Wolfenstein, "Some Variants in Moral Training of Children," in *The Psychoanalytic Study of the Child*, vol. 5 (New York: International Universities Press, 1950), pp. 310-28.

19. Thorstein Veblen, "The Higher Learning as an Expression of the Pecuniary Culture," ch. 14 in *The Theory of the Leisure Class* (New York: Macmillan, 1908).

20. Leeds, "Cultural Factors in Education," p. 298.

21. Michael Oakeshott, *Rationalism in Politics* (New York: Basic Books, 1962), pp. 24-26.

22. For a particular study of this subject, see J.D. Krige, "The Social Function of Witchcraft," *Theoria I* (1947): 8-21.

23. Wylie, *Village in the Vaucluse*, p. 65.

24. W. Lloyd Warner, *American Life: Dream and Reality*, rev. ed. (Chicago: University of Chicago Press, 1962), p. 212.

25. Absalom Vilikazi, *Zulu Transformations* (Pietermaritzburg, South Africa: University of Natal Press, 1962), p. 122.

26. Ibid., p. 132.

27. Leeds, "Cultural Factors in Education," pp. 304-5.

28. Mead, "Our Educational Emphases in Primitive Perspective," p. 639.

29. George Counts, *Dare the School Build a New Social Order?* (New York: John Day, 1932).

30. For a study of the impact of these events on one field of education, see Paul F. Lazarsfeld and Wagner Thielens, Jr., *The Academic Mind: Social Scientists in a Time of Crisis* (Glencoe, Ill: Free Press, 1958).

2. Grading: Tracking the Philosophical Roots of a Specific Problem

This chapter is concerned with the way questions that arise in schooling cannot be analyzed effectively—we cannot get to the "bottom" of them—without recourse to long-standing philosophical issues and resources. This can best be shown by example, and the example here chosen is the procedure of grading that is so pervasive in the whole of schooling both in its lower and its college and university levels. Of course many other illustrations could be taken: for example, who should be educated or admitted to different levels of schooling (a question almost settled in the light of our dominant equalitarianism, but still debated at the fringes); where teaching should take place (comprehensive versus special schools, problems of busing, etc.); extent of compulsory schooling; mainstreaming with special reference to the handicapped; whether to have movable desks; the role of students in the governance of schools. (We have not even touched curricular selection in these examples.) Grading is a sufficiently complex issue to serve our present purpose.

Untangling What Goes on in Grading

A Martian social psychologist (as we sometimes called an outside observer before this symbol was ruined by interplanetary exploration), witnessing the scramble for grades in our colleges, might conclude that the objective of learning was the accumulation of high grades. We should have to explain that the reverse was supposed to be the case, that grading was a process of evaluating and that learning was the objective. The possibility of such misinterpretation—by students as well as Martians—shows that there are serious issues involved in evaluating performance.

Evaluation is the generic process, grading one species. There are many modes of evaluation. Things and activities may be evaluated as means to ends, as parts of wholes, as approximations to ideals, as conforming to principles, as intrinsically good, as better or worse, and in a variety of other complex ways. Different patterns of evaluation belong to different contexts of the educational enterprise, and it does not help much to subsume them all under applying standards and meeting or failing to meet standards.

Hence an important part of our job in this chapter consists in taking grading to pieces and seeing the strands that are woven into current practices.

This is an extraordinarily tangled business. We are by now so accustomed to grading that we take too much for granted. Consider an old-fashioned report card for the child. It used to give not only a grade for each subject from arithmetic to manual training or cooking, for behavior and attendance and punctuality, and often a report on progress (which in any case could be estimated from past cards) but also sometimes a further report on effort. Almost any discernible trait was grist to the grading mill. And there was often a competitive aspect: the report might well give class standing. In some universities, the publicly posted grade sheet at the end of a term would specify, in each subject, not only the familiar letter grade but the exact order of every member of the class. Now at least four separate themes are distinguishable here: success in job performance, competitive position, certification, moral character.

Success in job performance involves of course some conception of the job that is being done, that is, some objectives for the specific participant. The clearest case is where the student has learned what was expected would be learned, and there is evidence of that learning. But of course the nature of the objectives may then become the point at issue. If there are different expectations for a gifted student and for a retarded one, the latter might in some systems get a much higher grade for the work of the period than the former, if the retarded one "worked" more or "progressed" more. Shifting warranted expectations have accounted for shifts in the grading system and experiments on grading at all levels of schooling (e.g. pass-fail, pass-everybody-who-tries, etc.).

Rank ordering is quite a different matter. Why would we want to know who is doing better than whom? It could be to encourage competitiveness on the assumption it makes people work harder. Or it could be to teach the lesson that competition is the way of the world, that being good is not enough but that you have to be better. Is it because we assume that without a competitive system there will be less initiative, less discovery of new ways, and the familiar rest of our traditional story? Or is it because we live in a world of limited rewards so that the competition is ultimately for those rewards? If this last, then grading on a competitive basis is a way of deciding who is to get the implied rewards.

In principle we could have a grading system without the competitive element. Some experimental colleges for example have a marking system that simply allows students to go on at their own paces provided a minimum standard is maintained, and makes no higher differentiations. The competitive element may then be displaced to letters of recommendation.

One could even have an Olympics in which the aim is to advance the performance by breaking records. Medals go to any shot-putter or high jumper who breaks the record rather than defeating someone else. In such cases one person's gain need not be another's loss. (Of course it would rule out such games as boxing.) Competition can thus be separated from the improvement of performance.

Certification declares that a person is prepared for some work or kind of work. Of course grading for success in performance at one stage may certify entry to work at another stage—for example, passing an elementary course certifies that the student may enter an advanced course. If the passing were itself purely for certification, the same result could be achieved by an entrance examination to the advanced course. Certification is sometimes for a whole class of jobs or of rewards rather than a specific one. Graduating or getting a degree is a general certification, and it becomes explicit where degree requirements are found in the community for all sorts of jobs.

The quality of character traditionally most subject to grading is a kind of moral earnestness or effort—how hard a person is trying. On the usual assumption that people have different individual abilities in different areas, some may do easily what others find difficult. Obviously the results will not then correspond to effort. The person who did excellent work may have been able to do better, the one who did poor work may have tried harder and on certain meritocratic conceptions deserve greater rewards. It all depends on what the grading is aiming at, or what the particular meritocratic assumptions are. (Abstractly, of course, it is achievement, but what kind?) Effort is different from the other themes, although it may be made the object of competition or of success; effort is also different from progress because there can be unsuccessful effort.

Now, education and even schooling can go on without measuring success or competitive status or certification or moral earnestness. Schools cultivate some kinds of learning without measuring it. In ordinary life language is learned in mutual intercourse, skills are acquired, and of course character is developed, and so on. In cultural institutions—to extend a remark of Paul Goodman's—no examination is required for borrowing a book or record from the library and no proof required of having understood them. The same holds for reading journals, going to movies, watching television, etc. Possibilities with respect to grading range from an intensive use to a complete absence. Its use in any given context thus cannot be taken for granted. Its justification involves appeal to the particular conditions and consequences in the institution in which it is employed and in the broader social context, and to value consequences in the character of people and quality of life. It will not do simply to say that we have a habit of measurement that pervades all living, that we are competitive or status-minded, that we would be lost in interpersonal relations if we could not take the measure of one another. Such realities may, rather, indicate a deep human problem. Even were we to decide that there is some place for this kind of measuring in schooling, it would not follow that we could reach a wholesale conclusion for all of education and its phases, and all of schooling. The conclusion might hold for the schooling of youth and not the continuing education of senior citizens. It might hold for a medical school course in surgery, and not for a music course in a junior college.

These complexities send us to underlying issues. In the rest of this chapter we shall first look at the attempt to settle the problem wholesale, as is often done, by appealing to a *merit* system, and then examine each of the four strands that have been untangled in the grading complex. If we do not reach a definite conclusion about the place of each in contemporary schooling, we shall at least have moved the problems to more fundamental issues, including the understanding of human nature, where confrontation rightfully belongs.

Grading and Meritocracy

It is initially plausible that grading and its concomitant themes are part of a merit system. So concerted a social effort as schooling, carried on at great social cost, requires the best in students and teachers. Why then cavil at the rigorous grading and ranking and rewarding throughout? Grading is an essential part of the idea of wanting the best, and so ethical at its very core.

The meritocratic approach was once in the vanguard of progress. It was prominent in the attack on the old aristocratic elites, serving as a virtuous rallying cry in the fight for equality of opportunity when the able were kept out on discriminatory grounds. But the meritocratic idea cannot live on its past alone. It has taken some hard blows in the contemporary forum. Indeed the whole idea of attaching rewards to abilities has had its moral credentials questioned. Rawls's assumptions in his theory of justice that justice demands equality and that inequalities are justified only if they redound to the benefit of the people at the lowest level of the reward scale is a good example of one way in which ability loses its initial moral claims. This assumption is the gravamen of a conservative attack on Rawls as a subversive "new equalitarian."[1]

That a contemporary philosophy should attempt to jettison the whole relationship between merit and reward suggests that reward is not a necessary part of the meaning of merit, and that their relation is not guaranteed by a moral intuition. Indeed this point was made more than a century ago by John Stuart Mill in his analysis of desert or merit in *Utilitarianism*.[2] If virtue can be its own reward, why should not the exercise of ability be its own reward? Why expect the natural advantages, which are not themselves earned, to be ipso facto rewarded? The rewards that some natural advantages get rest on a socially installed system; society has opted for it in the same sense that it may at a given time decide for pay by the hour as against pay by piece work. As Mill pointed out, reward for *merit* says that the reward has been *deserved*, that it is *due*, in effect that it is *earned*. Why, then, should the exercise of abilities of certain sorts—not every ability exercised is honored with reward—be a process of earning? The answer is simply that society has need of those abilities.

The traditional arguments for rewarding the exercise of some natural abilities differ little from those for economic profit. The arguments are cast in individualistic terms: the exercise of abilities involves sacrifice and hard training, and so the profits are social compensation. Or else they are cast in terms of public need: only by reward can a society get the training and exercise of the abilities that it requires. Merit thus becomes simply a conceptual route for judgments of social utility. That merit ought to be rewarded is no more self-evident or informative than the old formula for justice as giving each person his or her due. The vital question is what is that due and why. And once the issue becomes a matter of instruments for social utility, then the empirical factors become especially prominent, for example in such questions as the following: Should rewards be kept to the minimum that will do the job? (Cf. Are high profits required to stimulate investment or could enterprises be carried out by public nonprofit methods?) To what extent is the opportunity to exercise interesting abilities itself partial reward? (Should we expect to pay less for the self-rewarding work of artists, teachers, athletes, and pure scientists?) And even if, in the present state of our society, higher rewards are required to encourage ability to make its contribution, should it not be a temporary expedient under given social conditions? Should not the meritocratic idea be regarded as an unfortunate compromise rather than a moral demand?

The meritocratic concept, apparently resting the worth of a person on abilities and their exercise, is also in conflict with the basic tenet of our traditional morality that every individual has intrinsic worth. This objection can be understood from sociopsychological theses that it involves. The idea of *conditional* love—"mother won't love you unless you do this or that"—has been attacked as setting a background of basic insecurity in which accomplishment is a necessary ground for love. Conditional love is sometimes seen as part of the old puritan syndrome of the pressure for success. Once put in this way, it becomes associated with the history of accumulation in the Western world and the so-called Protestant ethic of driving oneself in the period of scarcity for constant accumulation; the result is a personality that calls for constant reinforcement of success to have a secure self-identity.

Whether such sociopsychological analysis hits the mark or not, it still is evidence of the widespread and basic character of the revolt against grading the person. Work can be graded if necessary, if grading is indeed the best way to get necessary work done, but not people. This challenge to the meritocratic idea, not suprisingly, came to the fore after World War II, when great hopes of an equalitarianism rested on the expansion of production and beliefs in the possibility of abundance. Once established, this moral equalitarianism is able to resist even the intensity of present problems of overpopulation, scarce resources, and unemployment.

One misunderstanding is to be avoided. When a meritocratic idea is rejected as universally applicable or as necessary throughout, a tendency may remain to think that some other principle of reward is being accepted in place of exercise of ability. Distribution according to need, for example, may be felt as a reward for need, or even as a reward for inability! But obviously this is an intellectual hangover. Yet tendencies of this sort are sometimes extraordinarily subtle. One who is quarantined may regard oneself as punished; restrained one is, but not punished. In the legal theory of torts it took a long time before a clear distinction in vicarious liability (holding one person responsible for another's, e.g. an agent's, action) was made between responsibility for fault and the kind of responsibility that meant simply the person had assumed the risks of any accidental happening. The common ethical view that virtue is its own reward suffers from the same confusion. It is an erroneous way of saying that virtue, having intrinsic worth, requires no reward. The point is simply that the absence of an external reward does not imply the presence of an internal one. The category of reward may not be pertinent at all. Yet so ingrained is our reward attitude that when all get the same we tend to say all are equally rewarded.

Evaluation of performance in education is thus not inherently tied to reward and so a fortiori not to grading, which is only one species of evaluation. Whether grading is desirable on other grounds remains to be considered as we examine the four themes identified earlier. If it were to prove neither necessary nor desirable, evaluation is not thereby eliminated, but it would have to take some form other than grading.

Credentialing and Its Discontents

It is well to begin with *certification*; the most serious problems arise from this role of the schools. If indeed the pervasiveness of grading rests on the need to certify the student for later employment, then the aim of preparing the student for the job market is being allowed to overshadow the various other aims of the educational institutions. After all, the schools are supposed to prepare the student for life in the modern world, to equip him or her with the rudiments of culture, to prepare for participation in modern social and political life, to develop interests and individuality, not merely to find and hold a job. If there are serious distorting effects on the character of education from the emphasis on grades as against the concern with subject matter and its interest (a problem every teacher is aware of), then reconsideration of the relation of the schools to the tasks of certification is overdue.

Such reconsideration has to examine the basic presuppositions, not merely summarize the advantages and disadvantages of competing proposals. Now the first impression is that certification in the schools is directed to the whole *person*, not to the *job*. This raises a serious moral and social problem. When Plato propounded the division of labor (in the *Republic*) and offered as the principle of justice that each do that for which he or she is best fitted,[3] a major task of his educational system was to develop those who had the capacities to be rulers and administrators (the first two classes) as distinct from the mass of the people who were to be farmers and producers (the third class). The three classes corresponded to the natural differences Plato took to characterize people, in whom different parts of the psyche were predominant. Thus the credentialing was of the person, and the area of assigned occupation was fitted to it. Within each class it might not matter much if a person with tailoring ability tried ineffectively to be a cobbler. But to cross major class lines was different: it would be disastrous if a carpenter or a rich property owner (belonging to the third class) tried to be a ruler, for neither would have the proper psychic constitution. The modern situation asks for something quite different. Modern division of labor is a division of jobs, extremely varied and specialized. In a democratic society people can go from one job to another; they are not set in one job or even in one job area for life. Hence the jobs are divided, not the people. Moreover, in a rapidly changing technology, jobs go out of existence so that the ability to change jobs itself becomes an asset, and indeed the ability to deal with a wider range of jobs is one of the points for credentialing.

The credentialing that the schools still do is reminiscent of the older grading of persons. Perhaps it is not so intended; grading may be directed rather at a general level of attainment and skill thought relevant for a whole range of jobs. But if so, on the modern scene, the instrument has become too gross. For example, some studies suggest that success in jobs is positively correlated with a college degree but not with differences in grade level. In that case, grading within the college could be reduced, unless that interfered with motivations. Such a decision could reflect the picture of the time and the pattern of motivations and possibilities of changing patterns. Again, where it has become clear that certain ranges of jobs or careers require specific education, students heading toward such careers could be freed from a credential orientation in other areas.

The more far-reaching question is whether schools ought to be concerned with credentialing at all. Special career schooling or special vocational education aside, the schools are expected to provide general education and general skills and competencies. They are not engaged in job preparation as such. The competencies and general education they offer are far removed from the specific and changing job market. When they examine and grade there is little thought in terms of jobs and job qualifications, and so there is little ground for making refined distinctions in grades the basis for job certification. If, nevertheless, the total results of these chance grades should happen to point to some ordering in the ability to succeed in some unspecified job, the question still remains whether the cost of doing it in this way is worth it. The cost is a heavy one paid by the educational system in the distortions produced by the inevitable overemphasis on grading.

The greatest of these distortions is the diversion of student concern from an interest in the matter to grade achievement. Motivations of prestige and success may replace motivations of understanding and learning. In the earlier years the aim may be not to learn but to satisfy the teacher. Often the criterion in actual inquiry will be not what the subject demands but what the teacher wants. Examinations are passed but learning drives are stunted. With motivations of prestige go fears of failure. Sanctions and punishments may rise to the surface. For example, there is the case of the fifth grade teacher who gave every pupil a star at the beginning of the class; it was to be taken away when a sufficient number of infractions accumulated. There is the high school graduation technique (an actual one in a European country—I do not know whether it continues) of notifying the students who passed and who failed only at the last moment, when the parents and friends are gathered outside to celebrate the ceremony; the announcement is made by the principal, who, walking down the line of the assembled students, shakes hands with all but those who failed.

In colleges today many refinements in grading have as their purpose only to inform graduate schools (or employers) about credentials. I recall that undergraduate students once refused a change in regulations allowing pass-fail grades in a portion of their courses; they said that classes were too large for them to get to know their professor well enough to get individual letters of recommendations for graduate or professional school without grades.

Illich and Reimer argue that the credentialing function of the schools and colleges serves to perpetuate an unjust system of establishment power in that the educational system simply selects middle-class heirs for the next generation.[4] They want a constitutional amendment prohibiting an employer from asking a person's educational background just as the employer is prohibited from asking for religious background. This would force credentialing to be provided by a testing system related to the job. Relevant abilities or skills could be shown without relying on previous certification. Without tying the issue to their background argument, the proposal that certification for employment or for professional or graduate work be separated from previous educational work is worth considering on its own. It would shift the center of gravity from preparation for something beyond to present learning. Even within a college some advantages would accrue in certain areas from having examinations for entry into an advanced class rather than on finishing an elementary class. It depends on the kind of class, the purpose with which the work is undertaken, the motivation for doing what is being done.

There are of course other social costs in such a major change. Fresh credentialing institutions would no doubt have to be built up, and the question is how overmechanized or bureaucratic they might be.

Competition and Credentialing

A decision on a large-scale shift is not wholly independent of the fate of the motif of *competition* in education. If grading is to remain in high gear to support a competitive pattern, then it might as well do the credentialing job. Hence an evaluation of the competitive component is unavoidable. Here there are two distinct factors. One is the sharp competitive cast in the culture as a whole, and the question is whether the schools should accentuate it or mute it. The second stems again from the connection with job orientation. Given the vicissitudes of the job market under contemporary economic conditions, competition is severe. Should the schools train for competitive struggle?

We may appropriately call for some retrenchment on traditional competitiveness. (See chapter 7.) Our culture has been too aggressive, too self-centered, too self-destructive, and too destructive of community, whatever historical contributions competitiveness may have brought. The critical lessons of ethical evaluation and comparative and psychological study need not here be recapitulated. And even if competitiveness still maintains itself to a large degree in the culture as a matter of fact, the weight of education should be pitted in the other direction to develop a basic cooperativeness of human beings in facing their common problems. The schools have often found themselves in a contradictory position, attempting to instill team spirit (including both cooperation and playing for the sake of the game) and individual competitiveness at the same time. They have allowed a come-out-on-top-at-all-costs atmosphere and yet have been surprised at the spread of cheating and its acceptance in the student moral outlook. Certainly from both a moral and a practical point of view the separation of grading as judgment of competitive success and as judgment of task achievement is of the greatest importance.

Doubtless the competitive factor in grading insofar as it depends on the race for jobs cannot be effectively diminished without drastically removing the direct connection between education and job orientation. The overclose connection in the public mind has given education a narrow focus. In a time of economic prosperity the situation was let slip. But in recession it became clear that the more usual situation is that if the schools are regarded as preparing students for jobs, then the schools are always producing a regular proportion of losers. Indeed, the setup is such that the schools are (in part) a natural scapegoat for the defects of the economic system, and are blamed for not having succeeded in preparing those who finished school and did not get jobs and those who dropped out on the way. In any case, in a society in which there are jobs only for a small proportion of those being educated with the skills for them, there will be inevitable disappointment if the whole educational system is sharpened for the job hunt. Particularly with the broadening of admissions, the competitive element has little place remaining within the educational system. It can at least be put outside so as not to ruin education for the larger group.

It is not always realized how far the competitive element has been allowed to permeate educational procedures. For example, marking on a curve indicates a determination that some shall be branded as lower because they are comparatively below others, no matter how good objectively they may be in task accomplishment.[5] The same is true of much testing, where the norms are established in terms of the average of large groups. There is thus no immediate translation between low test result and low ability. To be small in a society of giants does not make one a pygmy.

Perhaps the schools are too sunk in competition to have this motif removed entirely at one blow. As a general direction, it would be highly desirable to diminish and move toward minimizing it. If this were made a policy, the question of an external shift in certification could be put on the serious agenda of educational deliberation. Educators could not, of course, bring this change about by themselves, for it involves other institutional changes. And it would need to be gradual, with experiments taking place to test the costs and feasibilities. The schools could make a start by shedding certain responsibilities. For example, there is no reason that they should be called on to make fine gradations in a range of abilities where all that would be required is a basic competence. The schools are not giving the jobs nor are they committed to any specific meritocratic principles. If they are, then they would have the obligation to investigate job specifications and to prepare students in all dimensions that jobs require—human relations as well as intellectual development, ethical understanding as well as individual drive, and so on.

Let us take an extreme case to illustrate the point that the criteria for job assignment lie outside the scope of the school and may turn out to have little relation to the abilities for which the school prepares its students. Hence grading should not be attuned to the job situation. Suppose a class of jobs, semimechanical in nature, is reserved for retarded people who could do them quite effectively. The reasons for reserving them are that these are the only jobs the retarded could do, and the intellectually gifted could do many other jobs more enjoyably; the work would add to the self-respect of the retarded; they would pay taxes instead of being idle and supported by the public. Would the claims of the gifted that they ranked higher on the examinations and so were entitled to the jobs (because of a recession) be decisive? A society might very well make its decision on utilitarian criteria here rather than a rigid one-principle meritocracy of intellect. (In fact, no job rests on qualifications of intellect alone.) In some fields, where the jobs are unitary ones of limited duration, rotation principles among the group of the qualified are sometimes employed. In others there could very well be use of a lottery on the assumption that decision that looks for fine points as a basis beyond a certain degree of refinement is no better than chance anyhow.

The schools prepare students for jobs only in the sense that a fundamental education prepares them to face contemporary life and gives the knowledge and skills basic to a large variety of undertakings, cultural as well as vocational. More than that should not be expected of schools, except insofar as special schools are developed for special vocations. There too, how general or how specific the preparation should be depends on the state of the field in which the career is to be carried out and the rapidity of change within it. Even attempts of the schools to attune their development to social trends often prove disastrous when those trends prove short-run. The schools do better to keep their eye on the more permanent objectives of human development in the confidence that an educated people is the best natural resource of a society.

There remain the two more substantive bases of grading: moral earnestness in trying, and success in performance. How far do these require a grading system?

Grading and Effort

Trying, as a moral matter, does not submit readily to grading and measuring, in spite of Benjamin Franklin's strenuous efforts in *Poor Richard's Almanack*. Sometimes to grade trying looks like consoling the student for lack of achievement. Students are praised for trying though they did not succeed, or they are praised for the progress made or the effort exerted. On the other hand, doing well without effort may sometimes be looked at askance, as if success had somehow to be earned. Nevertheless, there are fairly definite conditions for work and achievement that can be measured and so become indices capable of entering into grading. Traditional examples are time spent in homework, time spent in the library, care in preparation of reports, and so on. An excellent example of moral earnestness rising into a mass movement is found in the campaign launched by the Reverend Jesse Jackson among Black students and parents to take schoolwork seriously. Blacks, lifting themselves by their own efforts in the current conditions, would break through the controversies over the causes and cures of their social plight. Among the measures employed in the campaign were pledges by parents and students that students abstain from using the telephone and watching television for two hours weekday evenings to do homework. The campaign aimed at a new attitude toward learning and the mastery of knowledge.

We may conclude therefore that in normal times trying and effort may be a ground for comment, praise or blame to the persons concerned; in the case of young children, consultation with their parents may be needed as to why they are not trying. Only under unusual conditions would it be necessary to use a grading system of an organized sort for this dimension.

Grading and Achievement

Finally, we face the question of success in achieving the task itself. To what extent does grading as a measure of progress help progress itself when stripped of certification, competition, and effort? In one respect, at least, some kind of grading will be necessary in a teaching situation in which the teacher cannot work intimately with all the students. (Quite bluntly: if a professor has no time to write comments on several hundred essays, he or she gives them grades instead.) This is of course a compromise; if the relationship were a one-one tutorial situation, this grading would be unnecessary because the extent to which the tasks were being achieved would be evident. Clearly too, the situation varies for different fields of subject matter. If the task is to learn to speak and understand a foreign language, the student would readily be able to judge accomplishment. In a course devoted to music appreciation or drama, the aim may be to secure exposure to an experience, and any grading may be an artificial intrusion. At the very least, the use of grading could be more finely tuned to objectives.

The underlying issue, however, is whether grading is necessary to task achievement and whether it really helps or has a diverting effect somewhat analogous (though perhaps less harmful) to the distorting effect of competition.[6] Criticism of grading along such lines takes this form: Grading should be minimized and replaced with other types of evaluation, such as task-oriented criticism rather than constant measurement of progress or success. The latter, which is the essence of grading, is not an inherent part of learning as task achievement but an external imposition adding a surplus motivational factor that distracts from the desirable orientation to the subject matter. The learner's interest is diverted, perhaps even distorted, becoming an interest in the achieving self rather than in the material or subject. This may be appropriate for games, but learning is not a game. A self-oriented interest is only a step removed from an interest in the prestige that competition brings; it is less harmful, indeed, but less worthy than a genuine learning orientation. From a social point of view too, it is desirable that people have a primary interest in what they are doing, not in what's in it for them psychologically or otherwise.

The Comparative Stance

Against any diminution of grading for achievement, two claims are urged. One is that comparison is natural: the idea of better or worse attends any doing of something serious; that is the simple extension of doing it well or badly. The second claim, to be considered in the next section, is that inherent in all our action is the drive toward the best, toward the perfect; hence the measure of our progress is simply the consciousness of our success or achievement. Both claims are fairly common attitudes.

To take a comparative stance about every activity, far from being natural, reveals a passion for measurement and a definite type of modern consciousness. In ancient thought, the good differs for each form or species and is defined by that form; better means a greater completeness in achieving that form; and best is equivalent to the complete. The linear habit of ordering everything as good, better, or best did not take over the ethics. Only modern thought (a Bentham as against an Aristotle) proposes a universal scale such that anything can be compared with anything else, and the things or events compared summed up as a whole. To manage such a scale Bentham had to assume that there was a common aim or a common property to which everything was contributing, namely to maximize pleasure over pain. But if so, then we can always ask, when grading takes place, what is the common aim involved, or—in more general terms—what is the context that generates the comparison. This contextual presupposition is generally forgotten when it is claimed that grading follows from the natural tendency to judge the better and the worse. What characterizes the modern as against the ancient world is that it provides contexts that generate comparison more widely for people generally.

Take the common saying when we refuse to make a comparison, "It's like comparing oranges and apples." When do we actually compare them? If we are offered fruit and both are before us, we choose by the preference of the moment. If we are in the market shopping for the family, we may choose by the taste of the family, by looks, by price, by vitamin needs. If we are fruit growers, it may depend on the climate of our fields. But if we are directors of a conglomerate investing in agricultural companies, we choose by profitability. In many contexts today people can compare disparate qualities in terms of monetary values. Again, in many countries people have greater choices in occupation, travel, marriage, location, and the like, than most people had in the past. Given also the rise of some degree of political participation, there are more basic judgments to be made. Better and worse loom larger in modern life as categories of thought. This is the basis of the prominence of grading. But its meaning and criteria are properly tied to the contexts that make it relevant. One has only to look at modern advertising to see how the category of the better is exploited in a meaningless, often numerical, way with all the paraphernalia of measurement, to impress and seduce. Curves rise colorfully and top competitors' curves, products are 42 percent better (simpliciter), and so on.

The conclusion is not that judgments of better are not vital and central to modern life. Choices have to be made in terms of comparisons. But there are no general shortcuts through general formulae or general grading processes to substitute for specific consideration of where and which grading processes should be developed and where they are unnecessary, where certification should be located and where it is intrusive, and so on.

The Ideal and the Demand for Progress

The second claim about the drive toward the ideal or the perfect inherent in all action might be said to be only a modernized form of the ancient view left untouched by the first discussion. If "better" is taken in the Aristotelian sense of further along on the task or more completely achieving the form, then it suits admirably the situation in education where success or task achievement is what is being graded. There is always a specific ideal of perfection set by the particular subject; only occasionally does a Cecil Rhodes set an all-around ideal for his scholarships, but this is not the usual grading problem. The difference between the modern notion of the *ideal* and the ancient notion of the *form* lies in such factors as the openness of the former, its distance, and the possibilities of endless movement toward it, hence the possibilities of progress. Perhaps greater value is attached to the fact of progress itself. Grandgent, the Dante scholar, jestingly made the point that in the *Divine Comedy* the modern reader is not interested in the endless bliss of paradise nor the endless torment of hell but, rather, in purgatory, for there people are moving ahead, making progress.

To assume that measuring progress is an inherent part of our action carries with it the view that where we settle on anything less than the best, where our goal is less than to optimize, it is because we compromise or because the existent situation is such that further precision will make no practical difference. Thus an engineer may carry a calculation out no further than two decimal points as sufficient for his purpose, whereas a mathematician may feel it too gross an answer to his problem. Sometimes an employer will hire a person who can do the job and is on the spot rather than spend the time and money necessary to investigate many applicants. The satisfactorily workable is sometimes to be preferred to a search for the optimal. If a romantic man set himself the ideal of marrying the most beautiful and intelligent woman in the country he would remain unwed; falling in love may be nature's method for avoiding the optimizer's pursuit of the ideal.

The traditional view of such exceptions would be that they are compromises due to necessity. Of late, however, the suspicion has arisen that the ideal may not really be the object of human devotion after all. For example, the new developments in electronic recording of music make it possible to put together an almost perfect performance on tape, taking out the imperfect parts and replacing them by more and more perfect ones. And yet, it appears, the results seldom have the appeal of a recorded concert performance with its roughnesses. Similar possibilities loom for representational art and for artifical environments.[7] It is too early to tell what a study of such phenomena may yield.

Comparison of the human brain in its operation with the technical perfection of computers and automata may make a similar point. (The use of the computer in the context of human goals is another matter.) Pugh takes the workable rather than the optimal to be the functioning criterion for the brain in the context of evolutionary-survival processes.[8] He interprets fundamental human values as surrogates for survival serving as marks in testing what is workable. To pursue the optimal choice directly would not be feasible. At each step too great a number of alternatives would have to be scanned. Judging in terms of values is rougher but saves time and cost.

In general, human affairs are laden with the historical, the chance, the adventuresome, the developmental; at each moment possibilities lead in alternative directions. In a particular situation we may not always prefer a given ideal when its simplicity is purchased at the price of lost options. Perhaps we value only some progress in its direction, while at other times we cherish the historical, even the sheer existent, the potentially many-directional.

These considerations do not imply that grading for achievement or success is unnecessary but that it cannot be postulated as necessary and that the conditions of its desirable use have to be specified. Grading is an instrument for explicit ends, which must be justified and tested to see that it achieves them. It presupposes that an explicit task can be approached in definite stages; that there are no objections to grading on other grounds; that it will not affect motivations badly but may even act as a spur. Grading itself admits of all sorts of shades, just as examinations do. (An examination may be chiefly a review or stimulus to review, as practice examinations are in many places.) A degree of sophistication would be reached if in a single course, for example, a distinction were drawn between parts that were gradeable and parts that were otherwise evaluated; for example, just as punctuation or style may be criticized in a paper in history without grading it, so parts of work in any subject might be criticized without grading.

On the whole, if the analysis of grading has been going in the right direction, grading for success or achievement should become a subordinate part of the educational process once the other strands are removed or diminished. We may suspect that its strength and prominence have come from them. It could probably be merged into other processes of evaluation more directly oriented to task accomplishment, that is, forms of constructive help in learning.

Notes

1. John Rawls, *A Theory of Justice* (Cambridge: Harvard University Press, Belknap Press, 1971). For the conservative attack on Rawls, see the analysis of Nisbet's *Twilight of Authority* in chapter 4 below.
2. In John Stuart Mill, *Utilitarianism*, ch. 5, as part of the analysis of justice.
3. Plato, *Republic* 434 a-b.
4. Ivan Illich, *Deschooling Society* (New York: Harper & Row, 1971); Everett Reimer, *An Essay on Alternatives in Education*, 2d ed, Cuaderno No. 1005 (Cuernavaca: CIDOC, 1970).
5. Benjamin S. Bloom, "Mastery Learning," in *Mastery Learning, Theory and Practice*, ed. James H. Block (New York: Holt, Rinehart & Winston, 1971), points out that the normal curve describes the outcome of a random process, whereas education is a purposeful activity and so should be expected to yield a nonnormal

curve (p. 49). He suggests that we regard a normal distribution as the mark of unsuccessful educational effort. For the assumption in mastery learning that students are teachable in a much higher degree than ordinarily assumed, see below, ch. 6, n. 4.

6. The careful distinction of different components in grading and different modes of evaluation is here essential if judgments are not to be too sweeping. Compare, for example, Anthony Flew, *Sociology, Equality and Education: Philosophical Essays in Defense of a Variety of Differences* (New York: Barnes & Noble, 1976), part 2, ch. 6 ("Teaching and Testing"). Flew's position is that "assessment and examination in some form are essential to systematic education as such" (p. 91), that there is a "logically necessary connection between sincerity of purpose and readiness to monitor progress, or lack of it" (p. 92). He even charges "it is a mark of insincerity of educational purpose to propose either as an educational ideal, or as an educational policy, the abolition of all assessment, and all examinations" (p. 97). No careful analysis is given of what precisely is involved in assessment—what properties are being evaluated for what purposes—nor why assessment is being conjoined with the single instrumentality of examinations in so general a manner. Compare the treatment of the question in Robert Paul Wolff, *The Ideal of the University* (Boston: Beacon Press, 1969), part 2, ch. 1 ("A Discourse on Grading"). Wolff distinguishes criticism (analysis for correcting faults and reinforcing excellence), evaluation (measuring against an independent standard of excellence), and ranking (as comparison). He finds only criticism to be inherent; evaluation is for professional purposes; ranking is for a situation where places are scarce. When such distinctions are made clear, there would obviously be no insincerity of educational purpose in proposing an ideal of criticism only (as in a purely tutorial system), a use of evaluation (in Wolff's sense, not in the generic one used in our chapter) only for professional preparation, and ranking only in actual job recommendation where the specific criteria of the job are known. Argument about such proposals would concern desirability and feasibility, not the discernment of a logical connection.

7. Cf. Mark Sagoff, "On Restoring and Reproducing Art," *Journal of Philosophy* 75 (September 1978): 453-70.

8. George Edgin Pugh, *The Biological Origin of Human Values* (New York: Basic Books, 1977).

3. A Philosophical Outlook as an Educational Resource

What kinds of resources for education do comprehensive philosophies offer, and is it necessary to make a choice among them?

In a dialogue, "Philosophies for Sale," the ancient satirist Lucian has the god Hermes serve as auctioneer, advertising the wares of each philosophy. When a buyer expresses an interest in Pythagoreanism and asks what its specialist knows, the ready answer is "Arithmetic, astronomy, charlatanry, geometry, music and quackery." Democritus (father of the atomic theory, called the laughing philosopher) and Heraclitus (the apostle of change, called the crying philosopher) are offered in a single bundle, presumably to serve opposing vicissitudes of life. Now we can imagine an educator wanting a philosophy that would take students away from the pressures of daily life, or one that would plunge students into its mainstream; or even a harassed contemporary school teacher who would want a philosophy that might ensure a quiet classroom or at least a peaceful if hummingly active one. Granted that the choice of a philosophical outlook rests on more serious and basic criteria of value and knowledge, is the educator to be faced with a demand to choose? What is the educator's own *responsibility* in the matter?

A prior question might be how professional philosophers regard their own responsibility in their commitment to one or another philosophical outlook. Actually there is great variety. In the early twentieth century it was commonplace that a philosopher belonged in a given school and both developed it and argued against opposing schools. Then shortly before midcentury, as philosophers began to regard their discipline as technical analysis rather than Weltanschauung, they cast aside school presentations and concentrated on specific problems. Textbooks ceased to be written in terms of realism, idealism, naturalism, and the rest, and were replaced in U.S. colleges by books of selections dealing with specific epistemological and analytic issues. But methodological questions now moved to the center and soon crystallized around different methodological approaches: behavioral, phenomenological, linguistic-analytic, existentialist, structural, hermeneutic, etc. And in the end it mattered little—at least with regard to the demand for a choice—whether the controversy was assigned to old-style metaphysics and epistemology or to new-style method.

The rapidity of such intellectual changes only shows more quickly what is apparent to any careful historian of philosophy: that all schools of philosophy change in response to the growth of knowledge and the alteration of conditions of life. (Indeed a case could be made for the view that a modern materialism and a modern idealism are closer together than the modern and ancient forms of each of these philosophies.) Hence, though professional philosophers work within a specific philosophical outlook in their research, at the present stage of sophistication we should not expect them to be dogmatic about philosophical assumptions. They are in effect experimenting with these assumptions to see what consequences they have. Philosophy, like science, is continually trying out specific formulations and theories, in the hope that they will be refined, revised, and even reformulated in major respects. The crux comes, however, when we ask what are to be the criteria of a satisfactory outcome. Here we find no simple answer, rather a retail accumulation of specific marks of problems solved in highly different contexts. There is a sense then in which philosophical progress is being made, but also a feeling that the selection of marks of satisfactoriness may embody different philosophical outlooks that were initially being put to the test. The whole process has therefore a kind of circularity, but of the nonvicious kind found in science too, in which fresh experience revises theory and fresh theory points out lines of selective experience; in their interaction progress occurs but differences are not wholly eliminated.

The question of specific philosophical commitment is thus altered. It remains possible for particular philosophers to continue along one theoretical limb of the tree of philosophy and ignore the rest because—for whatever reason—they regard it as the best way to work or even just their way to work. They may have confidence that the future will see its value, and should other philosophers in another tradition climb along another limb, let the future decide who reached a dead end or whose limb collapsed.

Can educators take same the same nonchalant approach to their own philosophical commitments? Educators are responsible to an ongoing practical enterprise; they have in some sense to judge which ways of doing philosophy will fruitfully guide their theorizing. They have therefore to keep their eyes with understanding on different proposed approaches, look to educational implications, uses, and consequences, and bring to bear criteria of value that stem from the specific contexts of education. Their responsibility is not as urgent as the doctor's to a patient; the doctor cannot ignore another possible cure that might be better than the customary prescription or favored line of theory. Nor is the educators' responsibility as urgent as a psychiatrist's decision to use on a given occasion a psychoanalytic treatment rather than an organic or a surgical one. The educational responsibility may be parallel to that of the philosophic psychiatrist advancing a conception of the mental such that one or another avenue of research becomes the exclusively preferred direction. Or it is like the philosophic study of medicine or bioethics providing a coherent redefinition of "death" that may guide decision whether to withdraw life-supporting mechanisms from certain kinds of patients, or offering a meaning for "rights" that determines the possibility of application to the unborn and so helps steer policy for or against the practice of abortion. Or, to take an example from a problem we shall shortly meet, analyses of "equality" play a significant part in the acceptance or rejection of specific programs of affirmative action and so shape the character and quality of education for Blacks, women, ethnic minorities, and the handicapped.

It follows that the philosophical education of educators should be broad enough to enable them to exploit for their work the variety of ideas in different philosophies, the multiplicity of modes of analysis and formulations of problems, and the alternative hypotheses of basics in human life and thought. For example, in chapter 4 we shall see the kinds of philosophical assumptions that underlie typical criticisms of contemporary schooling, as well as the way these criticisms can themselves be brought to the bar of critical judgment. In later chapters we shall examine how a multiplicity of conceptual tools culled from different kinds of ethical theory can add to our formation of standards for value guidance in contemporary education; or how philosophic interpretations of knowledge can help diminish the conflict of ideologies, or again establish continuities between science and the humanities; or how interpretations of human relations can give guidance in teaching and learning. Our concern is not wholesale philosophic panaceas for educational problems but the cautious and retail appropriation of philosophical resources for specific educational problems.

What follows attempts to clarify by selective illustration aspects of this tolerant attitude toward the relations of education and philosophy. We look first at the way in which basically contrasting philosophies can be examined for their strengths and the conditions of applicability in spite of their apparent opposition; for this purpose we consider Plato and Dewey. Then we examine why even where a philosophy has proved helpful in some educational concern, the results achieved should not be frozen, for the same philosophy can be associated with different educational recommendations under different and changed social conditions. The illustration here will come from Dewey's treatment of the vocational and the liberal in the early part of the century and what his general approach would suggest under the changed conditions of the contemporary scene. And finally we take examples to show both the special searching light that may be thrown on a problem when it is considered from the standpoint of an explicitly formulated philosophy (not just throwing up philosophical issues as in our study of grading) and at the same time the special limitations that may result from isolating consideration of a problem in terms of one philosophy.

Contrasting Philosophies and Their Educational "Implications"

Plato and Dewey are particularly apt choices for contrast of rounded philosophies, not only because they differ on so many fundamental issues of metaphysics, epistemology, and ethics but because they have played such prominent roles in educational thought. Each deserves an initial vignette.

Plato's basic philosophy expresses the convergence of insights in many different fields of knowledge, discourse, and action. What science we have aims at universals and laws in terms of which we try to explain particular phenomena. Mathematics in both arithmetic and geometry is the supreme example that knowledge is directed to the ideal objects of the intellect, not the changing objects of sense; numbers and lines are abstract entities whose properties we discover by sheer thought, not by experiment with things. The same holds for logic, which gives us standards for reasoning. Language itself consists of terms that are general in essence, and to understand them requires a grasp of meaning rather than an indeterminate pointing to the particulars; even when we point, the object indicated has to be interpreted as of a kind by the mind. In general then, a basic distinction has to be drawn between knowledge that looks to the eternal and the unchanging and the reality (what *is*) and mere belief that deals in the shadowy and changing and material flux. The intellect is the faculty that turns to the real; the senses grope in the particular, the transient, the world that comes and goes. Our very notion of truth is of what is, not of what changes.

Plato thus attempts to give coherence to our consciousness of our experience by his theory of reality as eternal and universal. The real lies in objective Ideas or Forms, which are the prototypes of all that we are aware of. Our knowledge quest, then, is to leave the particular and the changing behind and ascend to the immutable and necessary Forms. Indeed these are what gives meaning to our very experience: the ideal of justice to our conduct and social organization, the ideal of beauty to our art in both creation and appreciation, the ideal of love in our human relations. Ultimately, the story of life is this quest of the individual soul to rise above the material and the sensible to the divine unity of all things.

Insofar as Plato uses a basic model for the interpretation of experience, it is clearly mathematics. His reliance on the intellect as primary, his enthusiasm for its creative breakthrough to the apprehension of necessary truth, his disparagement of sensory experience as at most suggestive (as a shadow is of the object whose shadow it is), his elevation of abstract truth over particular instances, all express the character of mathematics as he knew it. The same mathematical model lies at the heart of philosophic Rationalism when it is invigorated in the seventeenth century by rise of physical science (the Book of Nature is written in the language of mathematics).

Dewey focuses on the changing and the particular. Aristotle had said of Plato that he was convinced by Heraclitus that everything is in flux, and this, Plato concluded, meant that the physical world could not be the object of knowledge. Therefore knowledge had to be of the Forms. Dewey is not a complete Heraclitean: change is a primary feature of our world, but there is repetitiveness, and stability as well as precariousness. Knowledge emerges from the lessons of experience, which insofar as they rest on generalization from the behavior of particulars in the past cannot be absolute. Whether in science or in history funded experience is projected in what ought to be an experimental spirit toward the understanding of the future and where possible its control in light of human values. Such broadly experimental method holds for all fields, whether of theory or practice. Knowledge and discovery have both intrinsic and instrumental value, and no sharp dualisms of knowledge and belief, of reality and appearance, of intellect and sense experience, of intrinsic ultimate ends and lowly means, are to be found in Dewey's philosophy. There is a basic continuity, and distinctions are relative to specific purposes and hold only for specific contexts.

In contrast to what Dewey would regard as Plato's reification of mathematics, Dewey wholeheartedly accepts the Darwinian revolution and its implications. Humankind is a part of the natural world, its biological and social evolution has enhanced its power of survival and broadened areas of possible control. Its complex brain and powers of thought do not cease to be practical in the development of mind. Consciousness itself is an active process that arises when uncertainty or conflict is present and the smooth continuance of habitual reactions disturbed. Hence there is a problematic structure in the situation in which thought, planning, deliberation, and action take place, and intelligence in both practical and theoretical reaches is guided by the criteria of resolution implicit in the particular problematic context.[1] There is no sharp dualism of theory and practice, but there is a vital difference between unenlightened and enlightened practice.

It is worth comparing Plato and Dewey briefly along some important dimensions: the relation of the social and the individual; the theory of politics and social control; and of course the guiding purposes of education.

At first reading of Plato's *Republic* and almost any of Dewey's ethical writings, one would think that both fall on the social side of the great divide in the contemporary world between an individual and a social model in the study of human affairs. To understand justice Plato constructs a whole society, with careful formulation of principles that articulate the common good; and Dewey never fails to remind us that the society and its institutions mold the moral habits and ideas of its people. Yet at a deeper level they part company. Plato is well aware of social power in controlling people and in developing their habits; however, his explanation of the shape that the society itself takes is in terms of the psychology of the individuals, what forces in the psyche are dominant, and the statistical distribution of the psychological types within a given population. (His analysis of the psyche in these respects will be presented in the context of social philosophies in chapter 4.) Ultimately too, his view of human life is that of the individual soul trapped in a body and seeking in its life to prepare itself for salvation. His religious theory is equally individualistic: the soul if successful after many incarnations is released from that round, and its blessedness is found not in an absorption into the divine but in eternal contemplation of the divine. Hence behind the social face of Plato's philosophy is an intransigent individualism. Dewey, in contrast, treats individuality as the outcome within the person of a cultivation through appropriate institutions, a cultivation that enhances creativity and gives expression to the individual's powers and helps develop interests.[2] He rejects the idea of an atomic individual whose will is the source of value, so that all social goods would have to be built up either out of the composition of individual preferences or through the process of contract.

On the contemporary scene, both in social science and in ethics, an individualism is so entrenched that a social approach becomes regarded as one of coercive outside imposition on the individual, hence as risking totalitarianism. The distinctive point of Dewey's view is that he refuses to start with the dualistic opposition of individual and social. A fuller analysis of Dewey's sociohistorical approach in terms of institutions and change is given in Appendix A.

In politics and social control, the contrast between Plato and Dewey is again marked: Plato's approach is elitist, Dewey's democratic. In his own time Plato took the endemic struggle to be between oligarchic rich and democratic poor; rejecting both, he wanted a ruling elite who governed in the light of the good. In brief, politics was to be a science and its practitioners were to exercise the authority of knowledge, not to express an arbitrary will of the governed. He often employed a medical model: doctors and not patients prescribe what is to be done. Dewey also wants knowledge to govern decision, but in his view knowledge is probabilistic and corrigible; it calls for broad participation and constant intelligent critique. Plato's problem is how to secure an elite body of rulers who will not themselves become corrupted. Dewey's problem is how to secure widespread reflective intelligence and initiative.

Both invest strongly in education, but again with a difference. For Plato the guiding purpose of education is to select the best of the youth, to fashion habits and controls that will release a vision of the good among the highest of these and acceptance of authority among the rest. Education thus is to produce the rulers (policymakers) and auxiliaries (administrators and warriors) of the future. A democratic touch is found in the fact that education is initially open to all, girls as well as boys—but that is because there is no predesignated way of determining where ability lies. If in the contemporary mood democracy is accepted as the best form of government, then Plato's conception could be described in the way Robert Michels (in his *Political Parties*) actually defines democracy: a ruling class open from below. It is illusion to think that there can in reality be rule from below. Dewey, on the other hand, is bent on securing the broadest participation; education is a process of growth in which the capacities and interests of people are given full expression in a development in which they actively participate. Education is not a preparation for a definite mode of life, except incidentally. It is growth in living itself.

Given such complexity and manysidedness in the two philosophies, any approach to them as an educational resource may turn to many different emphases. A very different kind of Dewey is the product if stress is largely on an enhanced freedom in the classroom—this often yields the caricature in the popular view of "progressive education" as sheer permissiveness—or if attention is directed to the social need for large-scale institutional reconstruction to provide a more congenial setting for human development. Similarly, one Plato appears when emphasis falls on the total control of the human environment with stern censorship of stories and arts to support a preconceived model; a far different Plato if the spotlight is on the passion of the intellect and the exaltation of reason.

An excellent illustration of the perennial recurrence of the Platonic theme is found in the twentieth-century Great Books movement, though actually cast in Aristotelian-Thomistic terms—man has a rational nature and the purpose of education is to draw it out. Robert M. Hutchins, as dean of Yale Law School at a time when socioeconomic conditions led to rapidly changing legislation, decided it was futile to teach a law that would scarcely outlive a student generation.[3] He concluded that even professional schools should leave vocational detail to practice and apprenticeship and deal instead with rational fundamentals. He carried this revised educational theory into his presidency of the University of Chicago, stimulating far-reaching curricular changes. In the similar revision of the liberal arts curriculum at St. John's College, the full program became the study of the Great Books of the intellectual tradition, philosophic, scientific, literary. It is the Heraclitean character of the practical world that turns theory to the fundamentals of the intellect in the hope of achieving more serious guidance of human affairs.

This appeal to the intellect, however, glosses over the crucial question of different interpretations of mind, theory, and the most effective modes of education for securing guidance. It is here that the differences between Plato and Dewey emerge most strongly. Take, for example, the shape that the teaching of mathematics takes in our two philosophers. Plato wants to awaken the mind by turning it away from the worldly and the changing. The rules and axioms of arithmetic—not only that two plus two equals four but also that things equal to the same thing are equal to one another—and the axioms and theorems of geometry are intellectually attained truths. They may be suggested initially by experience of objects and their combinations but they are grasped by the mind, and proofs are carried out by logical reasoning, not by experience and experiment. Plato goes so far in his interpretation of mathematics as dealing with the eternal that he even objects to the geometric language of "producing a line," for there can be no production or motion in the ideal. (We should rather say that we are attending to a longer line that contains the previous one as part of it.) Dewey, on the other hand, regards the mathematical as abstractions that come from reworking the objects of experience and fashioning instruments of broader scope for handling the things of the world.

In the actual teaching of mathematics, therefore, Plato deals with ideal numbers and ideal equalities, not the manipulation of things by comparing and measuring and putting rules to use. Dewey, on the other hand, looks initially to operations by which we apply arithmetic and geometry. Mathematics can be approached in early education through building and fitting things together and even through making change in the social handling of money. He is not, of course, thrusting aside pure creative mathematics, but he is sensitive to the philosophical use of the dichotomy of the pure and applied to fashion a Platonic dualism. Dewey's approach implies that no matter how far pure mathematical ideas are developed, their role is that of organizing experience.

This brief (simplified) contrast enables us also to see another fundamental point: the decision of which approach to teaching mathematics proves most successful is not made by either of the philosophies. It is not a case of a correct philosophy's commanding and education obeying but of education's appreciating both hypotheses and trying them out. Thus it may prove that one of the two approaches is more successful at an earlier stage and the other at a later stage; or one fits certain personalities but the other a different personality. The controversy of recent decades between the "new mathematics," which tried to begin with ideas of sets drawn from logic and set theory as a basis for teaching arithmetic, and the "old mathematics," which stayed with familiar processes of counting and other applications, bears some resemblance to the issue between Plato and Dewey, but the desirable path in teaching certainly cannot be certified by simple appeal to the philosophies. And of course the way to interest children in doing and not being fearful of mathematics is one thing and the analysis of the relation of mathematics and experience in scientific work is another. Even more, one may well accept on educational grounds the view that the best way to advance learning is to kindle a burning intellectual interest, without commitment to Plato's theory of reason and the nature of the soul. On top of all this is the influence of the general cultural milieu. If the new mathematics loses out as a procedure in the schools of our present culture it does not follow that it may not prove its worth in our society when newly devised children's games are built around logical ideas or when "computer literacy" permeates the common intellectual and practical milieu.

Such complications in the relations of philosophy and educational practice serve to undermine the attitude that one had first to settle on a philosophy and then carry through its implications for education.

Philosophical Outlook and Educational Policy under Changing Conditions

In his preface to *Democracy and Education* (dated August 1915) Dewey says that the book aims "to detect and state the ideas implied in a democratic society and to apply these ideas to the problems of the enterprise of education." We want here to examine what Dewey says about the relation of liberal and vocational-technical education and how far it fitted the social conditions of the early part of the century; then to look at the changed conditions of the late twentieth century and ask whether Dewey's own outlook and values would call for a changed educational policy. (A fuller normative treatment of the liberal and the vocational-technical will be found in chapter 16.)

In the early part of the century Dewey was writing to a predominantly agricultural-rural society in which the direction of growth was clearly to the industrial and technological and urban. The contrast between liberal and vocational-technical, he finds, has covered a variety of antitheses.[4] One is between education for a life of leisure and for useful labor; this he takes to reflect a social division in which the inferior class does the useful work and the superior class is supposed to have the ideal interests. A second antithesis is between theory and practice or pure knowledge and applied knowledge. A third is between learning what is of intrinsic value and what is instrumental or useful. Now Dewey finds no conflict nor any ultimate dichotomy between liberal and vocational, work and leisure, theory and practice, intrinsic and instrumental value. He is bent on restoring the continuities: any content can be liberally studied or narrowly studied, from Shakespeare to engineering. It is not then a subject-matter contrast. Any activity can occupy leisure if it is self-fulfilling; the activity that enters into work should be made as self-fulfilling as possible. (It is the social conditions of labor that generate the contrast, not the nature of the pursuits.) Theory is best learned in its relations to the problems of practice that stimulate and express interest. The intrinsic quality is the attractiveness of the pursuit and the purposive energy it summons; it is not tied to lack of utility.

An interestingly contrasting view at that time is found in W.T. Harris, the founder of the St. Louis Hegelians, who later became U.S. Commissioner of Education and dominated education in attitude and power. Harris strongly favored spreading liberal or cultural education.[5] But this involved a special understanding of its meaning. As Thomas Davidson, at times associated with the St. Louis movement, formulates it, education is self-making and the building of a world in feeling and consciousness.[6] (Davidson played an active part in stimulating labor education.) Harris even argued—in a little pamphlet, *Art Education, The True Industrial Education*—that the best education for work is a general cultural education in the arts; it is more helpful than learning about tools.[7] He offered economic statistics to suggest that exports will increase if the products are beautiful!

Dewey's educational recommendations seemed more realistically to fit the era of technological expansion that was getting under way and the expansion of schooling that was in the offing. Actual classical-cultural education was narrow as well as limited to the upper stratum of society, and preparation for trade and various forms of work had been introduced as an inferior kind of education. What needed educational development and liberalization were engineering and agriculture and the various professions. Dewey sought to fashion an integrated education for an integrated life, not only through broadening the concept of the liberal and upgrading the vocational but by further breaking down the separation.

In our day, conditions of life have altered in most significant respects. Perhaps in some countries the older situation lingers; for example, until recently in France it was difficult to get high school students to elect technical subjects because of the tremendous prestige of the classical culture as an entry to the elite. But in the United States the relation of liberal and technical-vocational has been reversed; the technical and professional schools are in the ascendant, and even liberal education has come to be conceived as preparation for professions, including teaching and research. The content of the liberal arts and sciences has been increased by the place given to pure science, but even this—as well as the social sciences—tends to be practically oriented. While much remains to be done in working out the relations of liberal and practical, and Dewey's job is not yet rounded out, a good case can be made for the view of the St. Louis Hegelians now, but on Deweyan grounds.

This is less a paradox than it seems, for the material and social conditions have changed over the century. The revolution now being wrought by computerization is evident to all. A shorter workday brings more widespread leisure, and the mechanical character of much work is being lessened by the automation and robotization of industry. Changes in production require greater knowledge in processes and the alteration and updating of skills. Basic research takes on greater importance, not merely as aiding different applications but as generating science-based industries; and technical education becomes more liberal precisely because shifting technology makes narrow preparation no longer viable. And in all areas of society, social as well as political, there is a greater democratic demand for general participation in the determination of social policy. The very operations of society now require the constant advance, not simply the wider sharing of what already exists, in knowledge and culture.

The relation of basic research to the varied fields of its utilization may be seen as paradigmatic of what education now requires. It is a growing lesson of the history of science and technology that basic research overleaps the problems of specific technology, even though technology itself is intimately related to research, for example in developing its instrumentation. And so, although the lesson of the interrelation of theory and practice is essentially correct, it is not incompatible with the need for an independent pursuit of basic research in the light of its theoretical problems. (Clearly there is no advantage in directing research narrowly upon the problems of a specific technology when that technology may be swept aside—for example, devoting all theoretical efforts to the problems of existent nuclear energy when solar energy might supersede it.) This paradigm may be generalized for education. Once liberal education is properly conceived, there is no inconsistency in seeing the multiple relations of liberal and technical and yet calling for a strong liberal education for all, for the creativity that is required to advance knowledge and culture and the arts itself demands a freely exploratory education carried through at leisure with primary interest in the materials and traditions and inner problems of the sciences and the arts and the humanities.

In short, the Deweyan outlook calls for fresh examination of changing conditions to furnish intellectual instruments for institutional and theoretical policies appropriate to the conditions of an age and the directions of its movement.

A Philosophy as a Source of Light: Benefits and Cautions

A philosophical outlook that is approached as a resource for reflection on education obviously serves many functions; for example, it helps reformulate problems, calls attention to facets or dimensions of significance, provides modes of analysis, suggests criteria for evaluation. A good general metaphor would be that a philosophy sheds a strong light. Now, the benefits of a source of light are evident: primarily it makes clear the substance and structure of what lies in its path. The cautions required are likewise obvious: the light may shine on only one side of the object leaving the other in the dark, and the light may itself project a shade of color. To exhibit the benefits and the cautions required, let us take two contemporary educational problems: mainstreaming and compulsory schooling.

Mainstreaming

Mainstreaming is the name given to a policy in the placing of different kinds of students. The question is one of tracking or streaming for different categories, usually dichotomously expressed: regular students and retarded students (where "retarded" may cover both lower ability and learning disability produced by emotional disturbance or similar cause); regular students and gifted students; normally healthy students and physically handicapped students (particularly deaf and blind). At various times the categories are adventitious but practically important, like part-time and full-time students, day and evening students, teenage and adult students. Mainstreaming is the policy of the comprehensive school and the common classroom where at all possible. The most interesting shifts and the ones giving rise to the greatest controversy today have been taking place with respect to the retarded, gifted, and handicapped, largely under the impact of ideals of equality and community. Earlier tendencies had stressed special services and special care, with separate classes for the gifted and retarded and special institutions for the deaf and the blind.

On so vast and far-reaching a problem, inquiry naturally looks for some philosophical resource rather than a few ad hoc arguments. We should expect that resource to help address the ideals involved and what they call for; the locus of responsibility; how to regard distinctions among people and what conceptual reconstruction may be required; some criteria for the possible and the feasible.

Now what kind of philosophy might we turn to as a possible resource? We recognize, of course, that underlying previous practices there was a philosophical outlook. It tended to see special abilities as individual gifts of fortune, and disabilities as individual misfortune. It had doubtless shed older philosophical strata that thought of the distribution of gifts and burdens as reward and punishment explained and justified in some theological framework. But its ideals tended to separate the two groups: one was directed toward individual achievement and success; the other toward resignation and acceptance. The responsibility of the community at large was support for one, compassion for the other. The distinction between groups was hardened by conceptual labeling—the normal, the gifted, the handicapped—strengthening a discontinuity in the way of looking at people. Finally, as for the possible and the feasible, traditional outlooks reflected the age-old views of scarcity and the limited means for radical change in human ways.

Because proposals of mainstreaming call for sharp changes in traditional ways, we need to examine them in the strong light of a philosophy that will bring out their structure and theses and so enable us to proceed to critical evaluation. Let us look to the resources of a contemporary naturalistic humanism. In viewing humans as part of the evolving natural world it allows of greater control of human life through the expansion of knowledge and collective action. Its humanistic democractic ideals stress the community and the relatedness of people, and its sociohistorical attitude toward change makes a place for large revisions in social attitudes and comprehensive social reform. Let us sketch briefly the contours of an investigation of mainstreaming in such perspective.

The ideals embedded in mainstreaming are of course highly general, but they have an immediate pertinence in what they rule out. Democratic ideals of respect for all persons, equality, and community signify that everyone *counts* in the educational process, and no one is to be rejected simply in terms of differential ability or special misfortune. The ideal of community is of special significance, for tracking separates and makes special-interest communities while mainstreaming hopes to cultivate the human community and mutual sympathies. Hence it may be thought that the child would be better off in a community of children of all kinds, all with their differences and all their difficulties; sympathy and understanding are likely to develop and would more than compensate for any slowing up or greater effort involved on the way; the gifted might stimulate the regular students, just as these might help the slower learner; in a well-organized class, as contrasted with the older lockstep type, each could advance at his or her own pace; the gifted would be spared the overintellectual pressure that has so often in the past created a gap between their intellectual and social development.

A naturalistic humanism insofar as it analyzes human affairs in terms of their sociohistorical development is prone to call for a recognition of social responsibility. It faces the problems of the handicapped not as an individual matter—the individual does his or her best and should be resigned to losses—but as a social task calling for innovation in working out appropriate techniques and institutions. A society that has already projected health care and education as social responsibilities has to take a broader responsibility for the integration of the handicapped. (It is not surprising that the movement for the liberation of the handicapped followed so closely on that of Blacks and women.) Social responsibility is satisfied not by simply providing financial aid but by fashioning institutions that combine resources, growing knowledge, and technology, as well as material support and human services, and all infused with inventiveness.

On the handling of differences among people, such an outlook is wary of discontinuities and fixed essential types. On that kind of view the gifted become a separate elite (as in the Platonic picture). The recognition of differences among people does not entail such discontinuities. When some parents object to their children's being labeled "gifted children," it is not because they are displeased at learning of their children's abilities but because they do not want their children set apart from their fellows as a special group. The simple fact in the recognition of their abilities is that they can advance in certain kinds of work with greater rapidity and that their performance will have higher quality. To see them as having opportunities for *advanced* work along certain lines, whether or not it may involve some of their work being done in separate groups is one thing; to make them an elite group by name and type of school life is quite another. A realistic attitude to differences has regard to performance and quality, to serving needs and interests. Students with an ability for advanced work should have the opportunity for it. Students with greater athletic ability are, through the institution of school teams, given the opportunity of special coaching. Students with special psychological problems are given the opportunity of psychological counseling, others of remedial work. All of these can be seen under the same rubric as efforts in different ways to serve needs and advance quality.

The case against discontinuity in the handicapped is of the same sort. We have come far from the classic illustration of separateness in the old view of leprosy with its essentialist branding of "the leper" and an isolation expressing fear and ascription of guilt, as well as hopelessness. In reaching the present point of the current movement with respect to the handicapped, there is the whole historical advance of knowledge, inventiveness, social change and aspiration, increased resources. There has always been some human sympathy, if not just the there-but-for-the-grace-of-God-go-I feeling. It is a genuine advance to see even benign neglect as discrimination and inequality.

To break down isolation and build community, as mainstreaming intends, is to refashion attitudes to differences. The traditional tendency has been to make fixed groupings out of them: the handicapped, the gifted, the retarded, the normal. Each accumulates stereotyped properties, and these in a strongly competitive and meritocratic culture have become the basis for rewards and, de facto whether intended or not, punishments. Numerous conceptual changes would have to be made in education to permit special treatment, special work, special remediation, without making special categories of persons out of any necessary and desirable processes. It is significant that there is at present a liberating dissatisfaction with the concept of the handicapped itself. It is of course an omnibus term, and the differences within the category are immense. The unity of the concept has been practical; just as crime is something to be punished and property is something to be protected, so handicaps are something to be overcome or neutralized. If the category has paid its way in securing social advances it has an initial merit. But it risks generating a dichotomy that overlooks a basic human continuity. It is not surprising that alternative conceptualization is today being sought. One suggestion has been to distinguish between "the disabled and the temporarily abled." Another is that instead of speaking of "the handicapped" we speak of "the challenged." It is well to be reminded that abilities are temporary good fortune in a world of chance and illness and aging, that we are all challenged though in different ways. In brief, we are all of the same materials, all more or less in the same boat, and we would do well to pull together, even though chance differences make for different abilities while they last. Such differences may, for relative purposes, differentiate, but there is no human reason that they should divide. Attention should fall on the variety of problems and the extent to which they admit of solution or amelioration. Here is enough to offer endless scope to our ideal energies.

The question of what is possible and what is feasible does not seem to be one for which we should look to philosophical resources; it seems, rather, a practical matter. But philosophies do have markedly different attitudes toward action, which are important for guidance. A naturalist-humanist philosophy is fundamentally an activist one. Faced with doubt about a valuable objective, it would rather test the possible than be held up by the doubts. In some respects action on the question of the handicapped in the United States has already conformed to this attitude. Legislation is passed and general policies adopted without asking how far the means toward their achievement are actually available. Loud complaints are then found throughout the country that vast sums will be needed to make transportation available to the handicapped, or that teachers are being given the burden of mainstreaming without adequate financing of the schools for their fresh burdens. No doubt this is the case, for we are generally more generous with legislation than with material support. (Some might urge waiting for the accumulation of resources before making reforms mandatory, but then—because emergencies always come unexpectedly—they are likely to keep postponing the change.) Nevertheless it is an advantage to dwell less on resignation to the inevitable or acceptance of fate or "practical impossibilities" and instead to welcome the invigorating effect of action. At the least, it puts on the agenda what otherwise might have been an indefinitely postponed dream. Even if temporarily it creates chaos, it is a wholesome chaos, for it summons all our energies to remedy it, not to retrace our steps. It shifts the burden of proof about delay and lack of accomplishment from the positive ideal to the practical effort. It stimulates remarkably our effort and inventiveness; certainly the current breakthrough in physiology, in genetics, in electronics, in microengineering, in various branches of medicine, encourages the hope of massive improvements and multiple remedies and aids. And it encourages inventiveness in social instruments. Thus a class devoted a single day to learning a system of supplementary symbols that enabled a deaf child to participate fully in its proceedings. The respect for persons and the sense of community redounded to the whole class, not just to the advantage of the deaf child.

Where do we stand when the philosophy whose resources are being tapped has made its proposals? Certainly it does not provide a definite solution to the problem of mainstreaming. Even those who initially accept the naturalistic-humanist approach have to see how its formulations and proposed policies work out in educational practice, what its costs are likely to be, and whether other ideals will be jeopardized. A long path of evaluation in practice with the elaboration of criteria for assessment in terms of the particular contexts of practice still lies ahead. And those who are not committed to a philosophical approach would certainly want to explore other approaches and compare the results. What we have gained in any case is a richer view of formulations, ideals, conceptual instruments, and attitudes to practice. Deliberation and experiment can accordingly be much more fruitfully pursued.

Compulsory Schooling

Compulsory schooling has long been regarded as a mark of advanced civilization, and the higher the school-leaving age, the better. Only recently has a moral critique been directed against the compulsory feature. For example, Krimerman, in a paper on the subject, starts by citing Clark Stewart's novella "Auriana," in which everyone who has reached the age of fifty is forced for a ten-year period to spend a large part of every day (except Monday) in recreational games and contests organized for them by younger people.[8] The parallel is made to the schools as a kind of imprisonment for one's alleged good. Even indoctrinated acceptance, it is argued, does not justify the compulsory aspect or make it less than slavery.

The philosophy that underlies Krimerman's paper is not explicit in the paper itself. We have to conjecture it, with possible unfairness to the author. From the strong and exclusive attention to liberty, it is probably an ethical theory cast in terms of individual rights and with a marked libertarian individualism. (In chapter 4, two such individualistic philosophies—libertarianism and anarchism—will be discussed.) The mode of argument employed is largely, after establishing the immoral character of compulsory schooling by analogy with compulsory recreation, to show the inadequacy of defenses in terms of important ends to be achieved, suggesting in some cases that there are other ways in which such ends might be pursued. Yet what is striking about the essay is that there is no consideration of the historical development in which compulsory schooling became viewed as social progress, nor the situations and alternatives in which this technique was instituted, nor again the consequences that would follow if the compulsory aspect were now dropped. In short, the strong light of libertarian individualism provides a moral critique of compulsion but does not light up the full matrix of the decision. It furnishes the valuable ideal of diminishing compulsion as far as possible but has little to say on what is possible. Let us explore this aspect a bit further.

That conditional compulsion attached to specific objectives is morally permissble in the light of social needs and conditions is doubtless not questioned. If I want to drive a car on public roads, I must learn how to drive and I must pass a driving test to secure a license. School taxes are compulsory for childless persons and can be justified in terms of social gains from which in general such persons also benefit. An important enterprise can advocate compulsory contributions from freeloaders when its costs fall unduly on voluntary participants if it is a necessary enterprise even according to free-loaders and would fail by only voluntary contributions. Again, what is compulsory is not the end, that is, the child actually learning. If that were so, the parents could do their own teaching and the child pass an examination. The argument would probably be offered that more than the straight learning is involved. A definite social interest is at stake in everyone's sharing at least to a minimal extent in the culture, and this is accomplished through the school. Society has a right to demand this participation categorically, as it has a right to demand (hypothetically) examinations for licensing certain professions. It is doubtful if this argument will hold up. No such demand is made of those who join the culture as adults, or who attend special private schools (unless it is assumed all schools are sufficiently alike). A more probable justification is paternalistic: anyone who is to live in contemporary culture has to have certain knowledge and skills and would eventually regret not having them, but it would be too late (the period of schooling is a kind of imprinting). Yet if this were so, there is much in schooling beyond what is necessary for such purposes, and much in the procedures that could be liberalized. Colleges have come to recognize this. They used to be just as strict about the unity of their four-year program but now they are tolerant about intermittent education (dropping out and coming in again), they allow considerable part-time work, they are ready to certify alternative life-experience where it genuinely corresponds to experimental social or field work, and so on. Only lack of imagination and failure to experiment stands in the way of many alternative procedures for high school as well.

The moral critique of compulsory attendance is only beginning. We are making a 180 degree turn. Libertarian critiques show us a perspective in which what was regarded as a moral achievement becomes viewed as an immoral enslavement. And ten years of compulsory institutionalization thought of in the light of contemporary critiques of the schools does seem formidable! But then we have to recall that this is in terms of a theory of contemporary institutions that (largely under libertarian and anarchist insights) is highlighting their repressive character. We have to balance that with a historical examination that will also show what problems the schools solved and what interests they advanced in their development. Thus compulsory attendance assisted in the solution of a social problem: it helped eliminate child labor at a time when many children were subject to familial exploitation. It has continually served a psychological function: it gets the child away from the intimate family and so advances the child's independence, which would be delayed if the child continued to be educated at home. It serves a cultural function: it gets the child into a cross-section of contemporaries, among whom the child will lead his or her life. And so on. Now, many of these roles change in time. Child labor was eliminated by law. Nursery schools and day-care centers took the child away from the family, and in any case many women work. Most children would go to primary school whether there were or were not compulsory attendance. The justification for the feature of compulsion is that it was introduced with definite purposes of getting a population to have the rudiments of schooling, which it might not otherwise have gotten; that enough interests were served by compulsion to keep it going; that the schools gained in momentum so that, as they expanded, the compulsion went along with the expansion; that compulsion and expansion served to keep the upper high school group out of the labor market; and so on. The point at which compulsion now causes most trouble is in the upper high school years, and here the question is larger than merely compulsion. Those who advocate abolishing compulsory attendance seldom reckon all the consequences—for example, the effect of present age restriction on work, disadvantages in the labor market, and so on.

Clearly conditions have changed sufficiently so that it is time for reconsideration. The problem is what kind of change. If the model of slavery fits, then the moral problem is simple—the children are enslaved and abolition is in order. This seems, however, tremendously oversimplified. The likely result would be to leave the urban young on the streets adding to the unemployed and to the already high degree of chaos. If there is to be organization and pressure to make the schools the desirable sort of place where the young would go without compulsion, or to develop alternative forms of a more congenial sort, this might as well happen before the added chaos.

While the present conditions and consequences need fuller study, some principles concerning compulsion may be stated. Ideally emphasis should fall on making institutions so useful and attractive that attendance need not be compelled. Where compulsion is necessary, it should be attached to ends rather than to the means to achieve them. In specific decision where to compel and where not, liberty should be valued more highly than mere social convenience in any trade-off. If the problems that generate the resort to compulsion occur chiefly in one part of a system, experiments other than compulsion should be tried in that part of the system rather than generalizing compulsion.

Compared to the breadth of naturalistic humanism in considering mainstreaming, individualist libertarianism is very limited, investing as it does almost totally in the ideal of liberty. Further resources are therefore needed to deal with other aspects and even to analyze in other possible ways the idea of liberty itself. It is the restricted scope that brings into play the cautions noted at the outset as attending the use of philosophical resources.

There remains the final question that arises at the end of all our discussions in this chapter. Educational practice and educational experience are called upon to assess the help that philosophical resources have given, and it is expected that the outcomes will in turn contribute to the refinement of the philosophical outlooks invoked. What, however, are the criteria of value and adequacy that govern such an assessment? It was suggested that these are provided in the contexts in which the initial problems arose that prompted going to the philosophical resources; there was no simple general value formula. The comparison was drawn to the doctor's assessment of different lines of treatment by their effect on the health of the patient. This appeared satisfactory because we have fairly obvious marks of health: absence of pain, ability to function, some degree of vigor, no familiar disease. In fact, however, the criteria of health are continually being refined, revised, and increased as we learn more about our bodily requirements and even about the long-range effects of what appeared to have been successful short-range treatments. In the end, our norms of health rely upon the total knowledge of bodily processes in their interraction with the conditions of our environment. Comparably, the assessments carried out by reference to our educational practice and experience use the criteria embedded in our current judgments of educational success—that learning takes place, that appropriate skills and attitudes are in fact developed, but that all these too undergo modification in the expansion of knowledge of human life.

At this point we meet again the broad circle noted earlier. Our present criteria for judging the help we get from philosophical resources obviously themselves have a philosophical background: there are values and methodological ideas presupposed in our use of the criteria themselves. In going to philosophical outlooks for educational resources are we really back to Lucian's "Philosophies for Sale," that is, simply doing what Santayana says of historians—that they write history like a man looking over a crowd to find his friends?

Perhaps a fairer way of describing what is happening is this: educators are indeed not without a philosophical background. When they go to the resources of various philosophies in dealing with educational problems they are putting their implicit philosophy also to the test. They fail in their responsibilities if they simply grasp at one that pleases or simply confirms their initial prejudices. In short, to go to varied philosophical resources is to put oneself into a position of possible growth. How this takes place, what are the components of the process, is equivalent in our present context to asking how the criteria for normative judgment in education may move from initially prereflective judgments of criticism and objectives to revised and systematized standards. That is the topic of the whole of part II.

Notes

1. For a general account of Dewey's thought in which the implications of this analysis are examined, see Elizabeth Flower and Murray G. Murphey, *A History of Philosophy in America*, vol. 2 (New York: G.P. Putnam's Sons, 1977; Hackett, 1979), ch. 14.

2. Cf. John Dewey, *Individualism Old and New* (New York: Minton, Balch, 1930).

3. Robert M. Hutchins, *The Higher Learning in America* (New Haven: Yale University Press, 1936).

4. See especially, John Dewey, *Democracy and Education* (New York: Macmillan, 1961; originally published 1916), ch. 15 ("Work and Play in the Curricu-

lum"), ch. 19 ("Labor and Leisure"), and ch. 23 ("Vocational Aspects of Education").

5. W.T. Harris, *Psychologic Foundations of Education: An Attempt to Show the Genesis of the Higher Faculties of the Mind* (New York: D. Appleton, 1898), pp. 283 ff. (work and play and the significance of play), pp. 317ff. (child revelation through play), and p. 331 (manual training).

6. Thomas Davidson, *A History of Education* (New York: Charles Scribner's Sons, 1900), p. 5.

7. W.T. Harris, *Art Education: The True Industrial Education*, 2d ed. (Syracuse, N.Y.: C.W. Bardeen, 1897).

8. Leonard I. Krimerman, "Compulsory Education: A Moral Critique," in *Ethics and Educational Policy*, ed. Kenneth A. Strike and Kieran Egan (Boston: Routledge & Kegan Paul, 1978).

Part II
Bases of Normative Judgment

Introduction

In this part we are concerned with the ways in which evaluation of educational institutions and processes takes place, and how they can be improved. The notion of evaluation has a spurious simplicity. It seems a ready matter to react to something, to like or dislike it, to take an attitude for or against. Yet when we try to say precisely what in it we are accepting or rejecting, what reasons we have for the attitude, what criteria or standards we are employing and why we think them relevant, the story becomes inordinately complex. Then we grasp at the kinds of concepts of value that have played a part in the historical drama of moral philosophy.

Most often we try to state our goals or purposes, distinguishing *ends* and the *means* by which we hope to achieve them. Sometimes, however, this distinction does not work well and things do not divide comfortably; for example, liberty seems to be both a means and an end, or perhaps something different, and the same holds for knowledge or enlightenment or virtue. Some (Aristotle and J.S. Mill, for example) have regarded virtue as a part or a constituent of happiness rather than as a means to happiness. In such cases we may think of a whole desired *form or way of life* and its *parts or constituents*. This is an organic view of the good rather than a dissection into means and ends or independent goods. The relation of a person's career or profession to his or her pattern of life is more readily construed in such terms. And out of this latter mode of evaluating often arises the notion of *ideals* as having a structural role in the conception of a good life taken as a whole. To ask whether democracy or individuality or justice or liberty or knowledge or virtue is a means or an end may get a philosophical analysis started, but these are hardly adequate terms in which to frame an eventual answer.

There are other directions in which we might move. When we deal with isolated experiences—what can be experienced almost wholly by itself—we are likely to ask whether an experience or its activity or object are *worthwhile*, whether the value involved is *intrinsic* or *extrinsic*. This division is often assimilated to the means-end mode, as if anything worthwhile would be an end in itself. But this assimilation refers to a different context, namely, that in which we have decided to pursue the object or experience that was worthwhile. The notion of means-end has reference to a situation in which purpose or production is involved. If we ask whether beauty is an intrinsic value, we are not dealing directly with our pursuit of it but its own character. (In some of the current notions of education, education is defined as initiation into worthwhile activities.)

Evaluation can also take place by reference to authoritative *principles* and *rules*, as in the familiar idea of conforming to moral laws. This is found particularly when we are dealing with questions of justice, for these tend to be formulated in universal terms and in systems and subsystems of rights and duties.

Sometimes in evaluation we are not assessing items in isolation, nor in limited intervalue relations, but as parts of a cultural whole, as fitting into *value patterns*. Moreover, because a society and its culture are undergoing change, questions of equilibrium and disequilibrium become relevant. We begin to think in terms of changing values and emerging value patterns.

In ordinary life we employ all these modes for evaluation. We organize our values at different times and for different purposes in the varying ways. We appeal to goals or ends, look for effective means, invoke ideals, line up principles, justify in terms of the intrinsically valuable, refer to our traditional way of life. We ordinarily find no problem in turning to one or the other in different contexts, and even set up jurisdictions—for example, sometimes ruling out ideals as inappropriate in business and politics, or declaring the irrelevance of the principles of justice ("all's fair") in love and war. What is more, we expect that our standards of judgment will sometimes take the form of principles, sometimes of ideals, and so on.

The history of ethics is an insufficiently exploited resource for studying these various modes of organizing values. This may be because each has been embedded in a particular school, and the contemporary study of values usually tries to steer clear of school conflicts—until its analysis turns into a fresh school. If we approach the inquiry in a comparative spirit, there is some cumulative gain from this specialization of schools, for each provides an intensive analysis of the mode on which it has fixed. Each mode of organization turns out to be a subtle structure with refined ways of treating the phenomena and well-developed moves to meet problems of classification and decision, and is usually set in underlying assumptions about the sources of value in human beings' nature and action. Thus the means-end mode of organization has to work out ways of dealing with the interaction of means and ends and with conflicts of ends, as well as criteria of choice among means beyond the usual measures of their efficiency. This mode gives a central place to desire and purpose in its account of sources of value and to rationality in their organization—a teleological outlook like Aristotle's is the classic instance.[1] The outlook that develops part-whole on an organic model, in which self and ideals are related to a totality, is best seen in the self-realization theories of the neo-Hegelians, for example the idealist philosophies of Bradley and Bosanquet.[2] The subtlest elaboration of intrinsic value (in Anglo-American ethics) is in G.E. Moore's *Principia Ethica*, in which all ethical formulations are reinterpreted in terms of that single notion.[3] The most serious problem is how the intrinsic value of a thing or action is itself to be determined, and by what technique confusion with relations and instrumentalities can be avoided. The juridical mode of organizing values into moral laws faces problems of conflicts in processes of application to cases (the old issues of casuistry) and the basic problems of relating the phenomenon of legislating to the human good and attitudes to law. Kant's moral theory is the most notable modern attempt to treat self-legislation in universal terms as the mark of autonomy and the basis of morality. Finally, the mode of organizing values that focuses on changing patterns and emerging values—for example, in Marxian ethical theory and in evolutionary ethics[4]—faces problems not only of identifying patterns and historical or evolutionary trends but of relating history and value without submerging evaluation in the automatic acceptance of directions of ongoing change.

Of course the mode of organizing values need not remain identified with the school that happily provided us with its subtle exploration. Modes can be extracted and lined up as conceptual tools, resources for possible use where found relevant. Here we have to face the difficult inquiry into criteria of relevance and conditions of productive use. The sociology of ethics can be of help in relating the modes to the conditions of practice. In general, the conditions can almost be read from the ethical modes that are prominent at a given time. When practical life is stable and not too complex, people can guide their lives by a kind of situational familiarity, and not much use of general standards is to be found or needed; they know what is the right thing to do in business, in family, in social relations, in education, whether or not they conform. With greater complexity the ordinary rules become entangled in conflict and interpretation; people appeal to principles or to broad ends and varied means. If the level of complexity and instability makes such appeals ineffective, the spotlight falls on methods of resolving problems and conflicts. When even methods fail to guide securely, change and conflict reign, emphasis may fall on general ideals or guidance be sought in emerging directions in which the good can take fresh definite shape. When the realm of practice becomes intensely complex and unstable, hence highly indeterminate, the focus shifts to ultimate attitudes: people are told, as if this were the last and only lesson of ethical wisdom, that life is serious, that they should think in whole-life terms, or face life with courage.

The studies of part II attempt to put these resources of moral philosophy to use in clarifying and improving normative judgment in educational practice. There is no commitment to any one way of organizing evaluation as against all others. The various ways constitute a collective tool chest of conceptual instruments.

The first study (chapter 4) examines the variety of criticisms of schooling as a way of taking hold of educational evaluation at its apparent simplest, but it finds that criticisms, captious and impressionistic as well as profound, are likely to express an underlying social philosophy whose assumptions in turn require exploration. This is carried out for the range of social philosophies from types of conservatism and liberalism to types of anarchism and Marxism.

The second study (chapter 5), with its theme of ideology, indoctrination, and politicization of the schools, deals with the wider contours of establishing basic value positions within educational institutions. It explores alternative possibilities.

The third study (chapter 6) examines how ideals in education and schooling can be evaluated and shows both the complexity of criteria and the way in which (in sampling the problems that arise in the current pursuit of equality) ideals and conditions of practice have to be integrated in determining social policy.

The fourth study (chapter 7) examines how historical conditions and problems give special relevance to selected ends and ideals at given periods. It attempts to formulate a "moral agenda" for education today.

The fifth study (chapter 8) broadens the moral agenda to include the need for more adequate analysis of theoretical concepts with basic value impact in education today. Those considered are: the ideal of rationality, the demand for autonomy, and the (often disruptive) notion of moral relativism.

Of course others of the modes of evaluation discussed here will prove useful in later parts of the book—for example, part-whole organic concepts and ideas of intrinsic value in relation to the value of knowledge and the humanities, and juridical concepts of principles and rules in considering moral education.

Notes

1. Teleological theories may of course take markedly different form depending on the end set up. The most prominent modern teleological theory is Utilitarianism, with pleasure or happiness as the end in human life.

2. E.g., Bernard Bosanquet, *The Principle of Individuality and Value* (London: Macmillan, 1912).

3. G.E. Moore, *Principia Ethica* (Cambridge: Cambridge University Press, 1903).

4. In the original Marxian writings, see, for example, Friedrich Engels, *Anti-Duehring*, trans. Emile Burns (New York, International Publishers), chs. 9-11, and part 3. For an excellent example of a rounded evolutionary ethics, see T.H. Huxley and Julian Huxley, *Touchstone for Ethics, 1893-1943* (New York: Harper, 1947).

4. Current Critiques of the Schools

Constant criticism of the schools and of our educational practices generally is a favorite preoccupation of our times. We start with criticisms of current institutional practices, allowing questions of aims and objectives to emerge in particular contexts. Comparison of typical criticisms will point toward a kind of value assemblage from which the normative bearings of education can be more systematically disentangled.

The advantage of beginning with where the shoe pinches is that it provides an immediate criterion for incorrect size. No doubt in the long run a theory of size requires a fuller measure. Too often we know what is wrong without having a systematic set of criteria to offer a theory of what is right or a standpoint of criticism. This has frequently been noted in psychology and ethics. There may be disagreement about the nature of pleasure, but physical pain is marked and sharp. Happiness may be difficult to identify, but not unhappiness. Even where psychologists proceed boldly to investigate, distortions and neuroses get the full treatment rather than the successful sublimations in the normal personality. In questions of right and wrong, the total weight of intuitive reaction can often tell us that one path is wrong even though we are not sure exactly why, nor which of other possible paths is right.

Yet criticisms cannot be simply piled up without some organizing scheme. For instance, it used to be said that the schools should go back to teaching the three Rs and not waste time on "fads and frills." Some critics, such as Illich,[1] have been almost ready to do away with the public schools and start over again in a different way. Shall we put these two criticisms together simply because one cuts down the work of the schools to a minimum and the other cuts it out almost entirely? We have only to probe into the reasons given to see that they are poles apart. The one stems from a strong conservatism that limits public education to bare essentials, the other from an anarchism that stresses individual self-expression. They thus reflect quite disparate social philosophies.

Criticism remains impressionistic if we do not go beyond particular and isolated items. Broudy suggests that much of current criticism shows simply that adults are unhappy with particulars: when Johnny can't read they say the schools should go back to basics, and when Susie doesn't get enough dates they say that the schools should pay more attention to personal growth.² The significant issue, however, is why a reaction to the particular takes one general line rather than another. When the Soviets first put a Sputnik into orbit, U.S. schools were criticized for an insufficient emphasis on mathematics and science. This seemed a natural criticism because of the competition between the two countries in the Cold War. A Soviet breakthrough in a cure for cancer probably would not have led to a similar criticism of the teaching of biology because it would be a blessing, not a threat.

Criticisms of the schools need to be seen in terms of the state of the schools themselves at the given historical period and in the particular community in which the criticism is being offered. In the United States, for example, school enrollments between 1930 and 1960 rose about 50 percent for elementary school, doubled for secondary, and tripled for higher education; and the decade of the 1960s was one of almost breakneck expansion. Schools were crowded; the shift from rural to urban centers resulted in overcrowding. There was great variety in different communities—urban, suburban, rural—and in different states. Criticisms valid in one place would not apply to others. Again, the criticisms usually involve not isolated items of dissatisfaction but general attitudes toward the schools and the role they play in the mode of life (including any aspirations) of the subclass or subcommunities involved. Contrasting community attitudes makes this point clear.³ An upper-middle-class suburban community may look to the schools to carry through their children's socialization toward further upward mobility and participate actively with favorable attitudes in supporting the schools. A working-class community with specific religious and ethnic background may not want schooling as an instrument of social mobility but simply as a good education without "frills"; it may be worried about rising tax rates, and be doubtful about college for its children. Often a mixed community is the scene of controversies about the character and proper service of the schools. Of course the most serious criticisms were directed against the "center city" schools or "ghetto" schools in impoverished areas of large cities, often predominantly attended by Blacks or by recent Hispanic immigrant groups.⁴ In the 1960s and 1970s these schools were frequently characterized as custodial rather than educational institutions. Reactions from community and students were hostile and the belief was widespread that the schools had in effect given up on their educational task.

Criticism of the schools during this period tended to fall into definite patterns.⁵ For example, to the criticism of the failure of the ghetto urban schools was added the general outraged attitude of the young who sought education as an experience in growing and understanding but found themselves harnessed by the demands of the establishment. Thus higher education, instead of the liberation of mind and spirit, became the "rat race" for grades and a competitive place in the "knowledge industry" to furnish minds and hands for industry generally, adapting itself to a corporate structure and coercing masses of young into a procrustean frame. In the United States such attitudes reached a height during the youth protests against the Vietnam war and were integrated into an antiestablishment mode of thought. This atmosphere of the 1960s and 1970s raised distinctive questions of educational research. Greater emphasis was given to studying the "hidden curriculum" of the classroom, the attitudes developed in the students by their school experience that included learning to obey unquestioningly, to compete with others and be resigned to failure, to be punctual and carry out the day's work in mechanical bits, to curb spontaneity, to be constantly evaluated and shamed, to accept a structure of external rewards rather than intrinsic values. Historians went back to earlier days and reassessed the beginnings of the public schools. They asked, for example, who had opposed the schools' introduction and what interests were at stake in local battles (suggesting that the schools had helped the factory system displace local crafts), and whether the schools had really done all that had been claimed for them in assimilating immigrants into work and society. Social theorists reinterpreted the overt and latent functions of the schools (sometimes cast as their "real" functions) to replace the stated functions of giving students knowledge, skills, and attitudes for living, for understanding and facing their world. Among these reinterpretations are the following: The schools furnish people with the preparation that industry requires in its work force. The schools keep a sizeable part of the population out of the labor market for an extended period. The schools inculcate the virtues for a restrained subordinate population. The schools are a method of selective certification for jobs in a job market that is not wide enough to accommodate all, and on grounds that are largely irrelevant to the work that is to be done. The schools teach the poor to be resigned to their place (a great many drop out on the way and so become convinced of their unworthiness). The schools are just another self-perpetuating business that operates to preserve itself.

Several strands have to be distinguished in these criticisms. Some questions are obviously matters of history, and others involve social and psychological theory. Integrating the multiple functions of an institution, latent as well as overt, into an intelligible pattern is no easy task. And the complaint that what learning takes place is geared to harnessing students into the establishment and violating their genuine or basic needs raises the difficult issue of basic needs. Similarly, the view that students are "turned off" from education and revolt against it in forms that range from primitive vandalism (now increasingly widespread) to drugs, in effect accusing the schools of systematic distortion of our children, of course presupposes a theory of distorting processes. The relatively simpler claim is that the schools are not succeeding in what they purport to do. This is usually accompanied by suggested alternative procedures, which may vary from different methods of teaching or organization of classroom or school to an alternative type of school.

When we distinguish such core issues we find that there is little agreement even in the negative criticism of the schools. Some of the criticism emanates from a liberal devotion to freedom and self-expression, which hopes that the schools can be reformed. Some of it draws on a neoconservative libertarianism opposed to state encroachment on the individual. Some of it comes from an anarchistic resistance to any curbing of individual freedom and creative mutuality by institutional power as such. Some expresses a Marxian view of contemporary institutions. There are profound differences here in theoretical views and in value judgments, as well as in proposed solutions. Accordingly we now attempt to work out some more systematic understanding of educational criticism by recognizing that attitudes to the schools and to education generally are part of attitudes to the institutions of society. These can be synoptically presented in the more or less standard social philosophies from conservatism to Marxism and anarchism.

There are further advantages to using social philosophies to organize educational criticism. Their long philosophical history furnishes us with excellent profiles. Their close association with practice and policy reveals how assumptions of human nature and social theory are used and integrated within value outlooks. And they roughly correspond with constellations and subconstellations of educational criticism. The philosophies themselves have, however, been undergoing transformation; none is monolithic, all have inner differences in response to change and conflicts in the contemporary world. A comparison will show the variety of emphases, as well as the conflicts of theory and the differences of value. The comparative approach here prepares the way for a more systematic conceptual instrument for normative judgment.

Conservative Critiques

Many of the repeated discussions of the schools have a conservative ring in the popular sense of the term: they call education back to the "good old days," the path from which under all sorts of liberal ideas it has strayed. Education should go back to the three Rs and drop "fads and frills," it should prescribe with authority what pupils should learn and not set out cafeteria offerings of learning for pupil choice, it should instill a sense of discipline by a rule that is stern if necessary, not permissive. Its content should be the fundamentals of knowledge, not the varieties of applications. As for intellectual temper, it should recognize the tried and true, the basic principles, rather than promote uncertainty with an experimental attitude. With basic principles go the basic values of our civilization, which conservative philosophies often construe in a quasi-religious vein. Current education is sometimes criticized for its confidence that everyone is capable of making intellectual progress and for its disastrous refashioning of the schools to make room for everyone at the higher levels. An intellectual-moral elite with a sense of obligation to the country has sometimes seemed to be the objective of a conservative program for the schools.

To discern a pattern underlying these criticisms we have to see them in the light of the traditional conservative philosophical outlook. This is composed of different historical strata, with varying strengths at different historical periods, particularly before and after the emergence of democratic forms in the Western world. The essential philosophical ideas that stood out in the earlier conservatism and have set a perennial attitude consist in a theory of human nature, a consequent theory of the masses and of the requisites of social order, a justification of authority in terms of a theory of the mind and of human knowledge, a theory of political governance, and an estimate of the possibilities of progress. The theory of human nature was set forth in bluntest form as early as Plato's *Republic*: humans have a basic appetitive part (the dragon), a rational part (the human), and in between a spirited part (emotion, volition, ambition, symbolized by a lion). The operative idea is the conception of the dragon. For Plato, and for most of the conservative tradition (and for that matter, Freud), appetite is blind, impulsive, driving, and aggressive, unable to control itself, and in need of constant external restraint; reason furnishes that control, aided by an educated emotion. The dragon cannot be domesticated, and if given any leeway grows greater in its aggressive desires. Education is a process of ensuring the mastery of the rational insofar as it is possible. The masses in society correspond to the dragon. Hence they should be subject to authoritative control by the wise or the experienced or whatever elite is available. Burke holds that if there are any natural rights, the chief one is the right of people to be protected against themselves.[6] Human nature thus calls for an authoritative order of values and a corresponding social order; if education opens the door to individual choice, particularly by the immature, education should not be surprised to see worldly appetites and passions boldly walk through and gain in power over the love of learning and the search for wisdom. The order that is to be authoritative is embodied in tradition, in religion, in social distinctions.

The justification of this general scheme requires some account of the mind and its ability to grasp truth, as against being misled by the senses. In Plato this is explicit and elaborated into a rationalistic epistemology and a metaphysics of the eternal. In religious conservatism there is a divine revealed truth that enjoins obedience. Conservatism generally takes it for granted that authority follows knowledge; rule, whether in society, politics, or education, falls properly to the wise and experienced, just as surely as the doctor, not the patient, writes the prescription. Burke's basic concern is with the fragility of the habit of obedience. A respect for authority is fundamental; he would rather accept any vested interest of nobility, religion, or tradition than strengthen the habit of change that dilutes respect. Education thus has the twofold task of preparing leaders for all fields of life and cultivating appropriate habits of acceptance and respect in the mass of the people. In human affairs progress is possible in instrumentalities, material and social. But the battle about the fundamental moral order remains with us, for the dragon is always within us and constant vigilance is the price of morality and social order. When democracy finally becomes too established to be condemned, it is interpreted to be a check on the possible corruption of the rulers; it is not rule by the people, but a veto periodically exercised on their rulers by the people. Division of powers, checks and balances, and indirect election of restraining bodies are all seen as ways of preventing the mass of the people from forming a unified faction with a unified rule, for in effect that would be putting the dragon into power. An elitist continuity is thus maintained throughout the changes of political pattern.

In later conservatism the historical component stands out more strongly. Tradition and community are set off against the future orientation and the individualism of the liberal approach. Room is found for change and progress but they have to be worked out slowly, and in conformity with traditional values, not by sharp breaks. The specific pattern of conservative social and economic programs varies with time and setting. Britain, with older traditions, can hold to more traditional ways; in the United States, with a dominant capitalism and classical liberal political forms, conservatism in politics and economics is in effect a right-wing historical liberalism, while in education it takes more traditional forms. Since World War II, every social philosophy has had to make some accommodation with equalitarian and democratic aspirations by extending educational opportunity. Differences of interpretation concern the type of equality and the character of education itself. Conservative critiques are often concerned with preserving traditional educational values against neglect and corruption.

Let us take examples of modern conservative critiques of a comprehensive sort. In the United States, Robert Nisbet's *Twilight of Authority* poses the contemporary crisis as the waning of historical forms of political community.[7] Western man has made a religion of the state and it has crumbled. With the combination of individualism and despotism, militarism, deletion of all vital forms of association that fall between individual and state, the social bond has been impoverished. Finally, the ideal of equality has been extended from equality of opportunity to equality of results, and the power of the state has been assigned the tasks of equalization. Nisbet takes this as the ruin of education as well as of culture. It has been a long process, foreseen by Burke and Tocqueville. He finds some hope in current movements that revive the local and the plural, pursue the creative without regard to the state, and stress social bonds. Significantly, he regards inequality as the essence of the social bond: "The vast range of temperaments, minds, motivations, strengths, and drives that exists in any population is nothing if not the stuff of hierarchy."[8] The stress on the nonpolitical community is, of course, a strong point in conservatism. For example, when Quintin Hogg presented the Conservative program in Britain immediately after World War II, he took it for granted that an important part of education, namely moral education, is the business of family and church, not the state; that the state is to provide equality of opportunity in primarily secular education, "the things that will help a boy get on in the world, to play his part as a citizen, and use his skill for the benefit of others."[9] In contemporary conservatism the state is no longer cast as the all-embracing and unified form of life, as it was in neo-Hegelian conservative British political philosophy of the late nineteenth and early twentieth century.

While Nisbet strikes the traditional notes of conservatism and keys them into the contemporary mood of opposition to the extension of state power, Michael Oakeshott distills the quintessence of the idea of tradition itself.[10] His is by far the most coherent and persuasive philosophical formulation of contemporary conservatism. Human beings inhabit a world of meanings, they respond in terms of what they imagine and wish for, engage in performances, and enter into relationships. Being human is precisely the recognition of participation in such relationships, as understood and felt. And all these are historic in character and come to be only as they are learned. Education is a transaction between the generations in which the young learn "to look, to listen, to think, to feel, to imagine, to believe, to understand, to choose, and to wish. It is a postulant to a human condition learning to recognize himself as a human being in the only way in which this is possible; namely, by seeing himself in the mirror of an inheritance of human understandings and activities and thus himself . . . acquiring the ability to throw back upon the world his own version of a human being in conduct which is both a self-disclosure and a self-enactment."[11] And this, Oakeshott adds, requires belief in the worth of what is transmitted. Education is thus an engagement with what is worthwhile and constitutes an initiation. The tradition into which it brings the young is not something external but the very stuff of their selves. The relation of teacher and student is distinctive; in the teacher, some part of the inheritance is alive and active. School is a historic community of teachers and learners; it is "a serious and orderly initiation into an intellectual, imaginative, moral and emotional inheritance."[12]

Oakeshott derives immediate consequences for the curriculum from this analysis. For example, learning to read is different from acquiring information, for it is concerned with rethinking and recognizing fine shades of meaning. He concludes that one may learn to read with care only from writings "which stand well off from our immediate concerns: it is almost impossible to *learn* to read from contemporary writing."[13] He also justifies the pluralism of the curriculum by the plurality of modes of experience.

Even more sweeping are the consequences Oakeshott draws for a critique of contemporary educational tendencies. His idea of school is that of a personal transaction between teacher and learner in which some part of the inheritance alive in the teacher is imparted to the learner and renewed in their transaction. Contemporary tendencies either corrupt education or abolish it. Education is corrupted when the self-expression of the child is substituted for the transaction. Oakeshott brands such self-expression as "an arena of childish self-indulgence" in which impulse is master and what is learned is totally unforeseen and completely indifferent.[14] Education is abolished when it is made into an apprenticeship to adult life, a process of socialization for the tasks of living, so that ultimately the school will be no longer separate from society. Oakeshott points out that such vocational and technical education, originally for the poor, was expanded in early nineteenth-century England as an alternative form of education to prepare for commercial and industrial society. It now threatens all education.[15]

Some of the issues involved here will be considered subsequently, but the educational impact of Oakeshott's basic conservatism needs to be underlined. The idea of tradition is not of something external but of something constitutive of ultimate value components in the selves that are developed in human processes of growth. Humans are historical beings; here conservatism and Marxism share a common view. For Oakeshott, however, history is held together not in a material and social system but in the consciousness of humans, and it is activated in their educational engagements over generations. (There is no dependable determinism to ensure the continuity of tradition.) Hence, in spite of the allowance for change, education is oriented toward the past, and the values that are ultimate are primarily the perennial ones of the past. No criteria are suggested for comparative evaluation of differing value systems in different cultures; perhaps it is felt that no comparative evaluation is needed within each culture. The outlook offers little guidance in situations of possible drastic change. This may not affect a society in which continuous adaptations are possible without noticeable effect on basics. It is another matter with, for example, a society like the Iran of the late 1970s, where the traditional values, the traditional education, and their hold on the self may be part of the very problem that generates national and social crisis—international politics aside.

Oakeshott elsewhere says that the attempt to formulate a conservative philosophy is already a sign that its rule has been questioned. In this sense, too, conservative criticism of the schools is less a summons to return to the past than a reminder of the strength of the past within us. Because conservatism has been in possession of the field, it calls for the maintenance of traditional values rather than the achievement of fresh ones. At its best it warns us to retain what has been worthwhile as we move through a time of change.

Liberal Critiques

Many critiques today seem to say that schooling is fundamentally engaged in the proper enterprise but needs sharpening, refinement of purpose, extension of scope. Education reaches too restricted a part of the community—illiteracy, though reduced, should be declining faster, and though more Johnnys can read, too many cannot read well enough. Again, school does not interest the students sufficiently, they have to be dragooned into learning. There should be greater appeal in the subject matter to things that will take a hold on their interests. Some complain that the curriculum does not have enough practical relevance, it has not been brought in line with modern needs.

Compared to the conservatives, liberals have a greater faith in the people. Human nature is either originally plastic, in which case the schools have ample scope to cultivate character, or it is affiliative. The dragonish tendencies are not unavoidable and instinctive but are reactions to traditional and social frustrations. The ideals of progress, of individual initiative, of liberty and equality and fraternity, and the rest of the intellectual apparatus of the eighteenth-century Enlightenment are still the bedrock of liberal thinking; even when liberalism becomes less hopeful under modern pressures, unfavorable conditions are the cause, not a loss of faith in the nature of man. The dynamics of human life is ultimately provided by people's becoming clear about their values and exercising their freedom to achieve them as much as possible. Education, particularly public education, is on the right path only when it is helping fashion individuals to think, explore, and correct their ideas as they go along, and providing the knowledge for the kind of life they want then to fashion. Education in its public (that is, community) school form is still relatively young, and it has much to overcome on many fronts. Liberal critiques tend therefore not to be unsympathetic with the schools, but to press against inadequacies, stupidities, and maladministration—the attitude is in many respects comparable to that in politics.

The central thrust of liberal critiques is thus expansive. It provides the intellectual dynamic for the tremendous extension of schooling. It grapples with the questions of the scope of education—how early to begin and how late to go, with the extension of facilities for adult education and the elderly, with problems of the education of hitherto more or less excluded minorities, with the balance of the vocational and the liberal, with the broadening of opportunities for higher education, and so on. A militant liberalism battles on issues of the encroachement of religion in the schools, on attempts of extremist groups to influence and control what goes into teaching—for example, pressures of right-wing extremists on textbooks and the promulgation of a blatant nationalism in the elementary schools. Liberal critiques therefore, both on the defensive and the offensive, are protecting and reconstructing the schools to bring them more in line with liberal ideals.

Yet in the United States at least, liberalism turns out to be in an anomalous position. Thought to be the reigning philosophy of the schools, it is often charged with the weaknesses of the current schooling. In fact, few of its ideals, whether of structure or discipline or self-expression or attitude to knowledge are really to be found in general practice. The structure of the schools is authoritarian and bureaucratic, administration is centralized even in dealing with curriculum. Discipline is largely strict and punitive. In spite of complaints of permissiveness, there is a dominant spirit of the repressive. It is significant that on the legal front a paradigmatic liberal organization like the American Civil Liberties Union has to engage in constant litigation to defend the rights of students and parents against bureaucratic administrative arbitrariness as well as to defend the schools against attacks such as attempts at book censorship or teacher dismissal and intimidation. Although the breakdown of discipline in schools is popularly blamed on liberal "progressive" education, there is scant evidence that allegiance to progressive education has been more than nominal. And in spite of all the idealism that has gone into teaching, the obstacles have been so great, the weight of tradition, bureaucracy, and budgetary limitation so intense that—given also the prevalence of discriminatory class and racial attitudes—the schools have largely failed in crucial tasks of education in the inner city. Now the criticism of such failures falls within the liberal approach, but it gets readily taken up into the more radical philosophies, both Marxian and anarchist. Here liberalism with respect to education is in much the same position as liberalism with respect to political life: it seems unavoidably tied in with the status quo so that its criticisms appear to be almost criticisms of itself.

Liberal critiques have spoken with a clear voice in the name of the traditional values of liberty and individualism. Equalitarian values have been voiced too, but with some indecision, as to how far to go beyond the traditional equality of opportunity. Even so, large measures of "compensatory education" have been advocated to overcome prior discrimination and its effects or simply to overcome the obstacles in the way of the "disadvantaged." Of the old trio of ideals of the French Revolution—liberty, equality, fraternity—fraternity has been largely neglected. Liberalism's conception of individualism has been voluntaristic and has verged on willfulness, allowing competitive success at times to become indistinguishable from grasping acquisitiveness, while education for community has been overshadowed by education for mastery. The difference between conservatism's emphasis on community and liberalism's lack of such emphasis is marked. Perhaps it is related to the future-orientation of liberalism and its readiness to apply its values to change and reform and practice. This turns it away from the sense of the past that, with its view of a common history, has often been a great source of community.

Anarchist Critiques

The anarchist strain has been strong both in total condemnation of the schools and in experiments with free schools. The ready conclusion that schools run by the state will not succeed is understandable in terms of traditional anarchist theory, for the twin pillars of that theory are a zealous individualism and a total opposition to power in the state. Accumulation of power anywhere is regarded as corrupting, and the state is the modern form in which it is most concentrated. Hence in the anarchist view the state cannot be reformed nor should it even be captured for beneficent use (as other revolutionary theories might hold); it should be entirely broken. This will give scope to mutual sympathy and natural tendencies to mutual aid; people will work out ways in cooperative association to satisfy needs and arrange economic life. The individual is the center of all that is good and constructive, but not the egoist that power institutions make of him or her. The individual's natural tendencies are to be trusted.

While not necessarily accepting this whole social outlook, many current educational criticisms bring the same kind of assumptions to bear in education. There is no point in trying to reform the bureaucratic public school systems; it is better to get rid of them and begin again on an individualistic basis. The trust in natural tendencies is seen directly in the kinds of experimental schools attempted: for example, the Ferrer schools in the earlier part of the century, and the Summerhill school later in the century. The teacher's role is not to impose but to provide opportunities for children to do what they want to do. The children's interest is the source of their learning.

On the contemporary scene, Ivan Illich has been especially prominent in attacking all monopolistic compulsory institutions, the medical profession as well as the teaching profession.[16] Interestingly, he arrived at his criticism of educational methods from observing language teaching; he found that the students were not learning to speak Spanish from the way the university taught it, but they did learn when native speakers were utilized in the classroom. In general, the literature of similar critiques asks persistently: Why is it that children who have learned so much in their first few years— to recognize the surrounding world of things and people, to talk, to walk, to live in relation to the family—suddenly stop learning effectively when they go to school? Why does their learning power not increase?

Illich would start by divorcing all work certification from educational background and making it a function of independent testing with respect to the job; it should be illegal to inquire into educational background, as it is to inquire into religion or race as a condition for employment.[17] Attendance at public school no longer being compulsory, the public money now spent for this would be available to individuals at any time of life for education on their own initiative. To replace or supplement the schools, Illich would provide several opportunities for learning: access to such centers as libraries, museums, farms, factories, and the like; exchange of skills among people who are learning; a system involving the use of computers for matching people who have educational needs and those who can satisfy them; a system of advertisement for those who offer to teach their skills. The fundamental method is thus self-help and mutual agreement, motivated by interest in learning. Liberal critics have strongly attacked such schemes as sure to produce chaos and as lacking in guidance; accepting many of the criticisms that Illich makes of the schools, they still believe these point to a need for inner reconstruction. Here differences between the liberal view of the state and institutions and the anarchist view are central. Illich, like Paul Goodman, sees the schools as isolating the young from life processes in which learning could occur, and so impossible places for reform or reconstruction. To try to improve them is to add to their distorting powers.

Goodman, in the more traditional anarchist vein, looks less to contractualist processes than to spontaneous communal processes for sound education.[18] He regards the great evil of contemporary education to be—especially on the college level—its seizure by administrations to bring it under state and social control. He wants, rather, to restore communities of teachers and learners, the latter being those who want to do the kind of learning that constitutes the liberal scientific-humanistic culture. Special learning belongs in appropriate practical contexts. Goodman attempts no large-scale scheme, as Illich does. With a strong historical sense, he realizes that the same formal aim may have quite different historical content at different times. For example, he contrasts Jefferson and Conant, pointing out that both plan the whole system from grade school through college and professional school and both want to meet national needs.[19] But the national needs are differently conceived. Jefferson is building a new nation with an open unadministered society to be as international as possible, with students free of rules and policing and the faculty untrammeled by administration, with democracy depending on an electorate progressively enlightened, and people learning by making decisions, including making mistakes. Conant is "seeking to mold education merely to bail out an overmature, overcentralized, venal, and conformist *status quo* in the final epoch of the national states: hurriedly to train 'scientists' to wage the Cold War, to man the existing and monstrously growing corporations with apprentices and technicians, and to dampen the 'social dynamite,' as he calls it, of unemployment in the city slums. These national needs he never questions, but he often expresses his impatience with philosophers of education."[20]

On the whole Goodman, like anarchist theory generally, and particularly in the period of the 1960s in the United States, was more effective in criticism than in the elaboration of constructive forms. Perhaps the greatest strength of anarchism lies in its moral force, the fact that it challenges the whole existing state of affairs irrespective of entrenched powers and often without asking the cost.

Neoconservative Libertarian Critiques

In the United States, conservatism has had a complex career. Given the strength of individualism, the dividing line between conservative and liberal politics tends to be that between a laissez-faire and a welfare capitalism. The traditional configuration of conservative social philosophy remained in the background, only to take shape at times against an aggressive democratization. (Extreme right-wing thought argued that this was a republic, not a democracy; even centrist thinkers inveighed against tendencies toward direct democracy.) Occasionally elitist movements appeared in literary or cultural humanist circles. After World War II, in the 1950s, a neoconservative movement arose by that name, with the traditional conservative symbols, attempting to ride the crest of a reinvigorated capitalism.[21] It was off the beaten track. The conservatism in power still spoke the language of individualism, and began to sound more like Herbert Spencer than Edmund Burke—though variations that might reflect corporate developments were the subject of thought experiments. With the vast expansion of state functions and the contemporary loss of faith in politics, a strong strain of libertarian thought has emerged on the political Right directed toward reducing the state and its institutions to a minimal role, and extending individual initiative and contractual forms as far as possible. As represented, for example, by Milton Friedman in economics and Robert Nozick in political philosophy, it is often regarded as a latter-day Spencerian defense of free enterprise in a growingly socialist or welfare-state world. In educational critiques of the schools, there is often little difference between the faults that it finds and those that liberals and anarchists complain about. The differences emerge in the underlying principles and motivations.

Friedman first worked out the voucher system for education.[22] Calculating the amount spent on education by the state per person, people could then get vouchers for sums to be spent on education that they could cash in, either in public schools or in competing private schools or in contracts. In this competitive market there would be greater encouragement for a better product. In short, Friedman has complete faith in the free market to produce the best commodities and the best results all around, and to provide the widest choices. He attributes the present evils to the near-monopoly of the compulsory state-controlled schools. The governing value of the reform is increased liberty: variety of choices, greater span of time (no compulsion to cash in the vouchers at any given time), and presumed better quality as a result of the competition. In line with the general tradition of individual liberty, he does not question the individual's preference or attempt to evaluate it. It is worth noting that Friedman similarly proposed the negative income tax—in effect a way of guaranteeing a minimum income to every family through the income tax system—to replace social security and the welfare system. This too would get rid of controls over people and diminish complex bureaucratic procedures, the internal revenue system being much more impersonal and automatic than the welfare system.

The extreme emphasis on liberty and on the kind of character that this value reflects appears to assume that everything else essential to an ongoing society will take care of itself through free market mechanisms—the central point of controversy.

Marxist Critiques

Marxist critiques of the schools belong to their general critique of bourgeois culture as part of the institutional superstructure of the capitalist world. They rest on an analytic picture of the operations of social systems in relation to the economic base of a society. What is going on in the schools (or the family or the church or art or philosophy) reflects the needs, demands, and pressures of a number of basic processes: the character of production in the given society; the relations of production, that is, the mode of distribution, control, and operation of the economy; the array of opposing classes and the forms of their conflict; the particular historical traditions in the specific institutional field. In each of these too, one would have to distinguish between the general long-range character and the needs that are decisive for specific stages of development. For example, the schools would not be expected to have the same character in the United States when the economy was still largely agricultural and rural, even though agriculture was taking its shape increasingly in a capitalist market economy; nor would the schools remain unaffected by the shift to greater mechanization and automation in industrial production; nor again, in the changes in balance or power as labor unions grew or as a secure capitalist class found itself confronted on the world scene by a growing socialist sector.

Marxist analyses take the public schools to have developed largely because of the need of industry for a better trained labor force, and also in response to the pressure of the working class for some greater share for its children in the opportunities of the advancing society. Education for the masses thus remained always as minimal as it could be kept, as vocationally directed as was needed, as unliberating as the dominant classes could keep it. The great dichotomies of society that reflect the basic split are the rural-urban and the brain-brawn. The operation of these dichotomies was widely recognized in social thought, beyond Marxian theory. For example, John Dewey's *Democracy and Education* (1916) derives much of its criticism of both liberal and vocational education from the need for overcoming the habits of thought engendered by the fundamental social split between the elite and the masses.[23] The comparable exploitative character of the basic male-female distinction as a social dichotomy was not brought to general consciousness until the women's liberation movement of the late twentieth century.

Much in the Marxian mode of analysis has become commonplace in understanding educational trends, in relating social forms to economic needs, social demands, and political necessities. For example, as we have seen, much of the recent large-scale expansion of higher education clearly reflected factors such as demand for scientists and engineers in the expanding post-World War II world economy; U.S.-Soviet competition, particularly after Sputnik; pressure for wider mass opportunities intensified by the deprivations of the war; and growth of scientific research and development, even basic research regarded as an economic asset.

Two different lines of criticism are found in the contemporary Marxian critique. One is negative, pinpointing the respects in which education is restricted and repressed by virtue of its control by the dominant class, and suggesting an ideal of a well-rounded education that would overcome the one-sidedness of human beings and fully develop their individual and social capacities. Or else this view has been put in a paradoxical fashion: against the contemporary complaints that the schools have failed in their tasks, it is said that the schools have performed their tasks admirably. They have done what the capitalist system expected of them—trained a supply of workers, taught them to be disciplined and properly motivated, to be obedient and resigned, kept them from rebelling and flooding the market, and so on. There are difficulties now but they are contradictions within capitalism, not primarily within the schools.[24] We only say that the schools have failed when we think of other tasks that we assign to them; but the tasks of institutions in a society are those that correspond to the needs of the dominant economic productive processes of the society and the way they are organized.

The other line of criticism taps a different facet of Marxian historical analysis. It takes a view over a long span and sees how the schools brought opportunities to the laboring classes and compares their condition and education in the contemporary world with that in the nineteenth century. It contrasts the present ideals of equality and universal opportunity and participation with earlier tight class lines. Stress falls now on the gains that the rising class can make in the course of vigorous struggle and the concessions it can force. The schools, in spite of their manifest defects, are looked upon as part of the gains labor has won that are to be extended and reconstructed in human advance toward a better social order.

The realistic question becomes, for the Marxian analyst, what can be done in an institution like the schools, which are part of the superstructure, to secure improvement; or whether anything short of a fundamental change in the social order will make this possible. No a priori answer is possible; it requires an analysis of forces in the particular society, the degree of flexibility or leeway and the extent to which progressive advances can be made in various institutions, and—in the Marxian conception—whether a peaceful transition to socialism is possible.

Marxist critiques have the virtue of paying close attention to the dynamic flow of social situations. They take values for granted and so are less attentive to them than liberalism, but they relate theoretical analysis to practice more intimately.

In considering the criticisms of schooling, we have been looking at some of the important social perspectives that confront one another in evaluating institutions. Generally, we have made no serious attempt to assess these perspectives but have emphasized how each makes sense of a host of criticisms that otherwise might appear to be isolated and *ad hoc*, and we have noted in a comparative way some aspects of their theory and values. They do not exhaust social perspectives; in any case the reader does not here have to make a choice among these. Growing up in the Western world, he or she has probably absorbed parts of several of them by a kind of selective contagion. They show the sorts of issues about human nature, community, history, value, theory, action, and society, that will require decision in an organized way in making critical judgments about schooling and education in general.

Even at this preliminary stage a few lessons for education may, however, stand out from our discussion. We cannot take for granted that institutional forms characterizing our educational life will be perpetuated. They have already undergone great changes and the possibility of total as well as partial reconstruction is not to be ruled out antecedently. There is need of a thoroughgoing normative base in terms of which we can judge what kind of reconstruction is needed and how far it should go—whether it should be total in character as the anarchist view insists or a basic shift in orientation as the Marxist and the conservative would have it (though in different directions), or a shift in spirit within the body of the present institution as the liberal wants it. There are real choices—or real compromises—to be made, and these appear to depend on the direction marked out by our ideals. Because, however, there is a conflict of ideals in the different social philosophies, our next chapter faces the general impact of social conflict by considering contemporary issues of politicization versus impartiality in the schools. And because we need a systematic way of assessing ideals and their educational implications, chapter 6 attempts to provide criteria and to see them at work.

Notes

1. Ivan Illich, *Deschooling Society* (New York: Harper & Row, 1971).

2. Harry S. Broudy, *The Real World of the Public Schools* (New York: Harcourt Brace Jovanovich, 1972), pp. 43ff.

3. Cf. Elizabeth Eddy, *Walk the White Line: Profile of Urban Education* (Garden City, N.Y.: Doubleday, Anchor Books, 1967).

4. E.g., Jonathan Kozol, *Death at an Early Age: The Destruction of the Hearts and Minds of Negro Children in the Boston Public Schools* (Boston: Houghton Mifflin, 1967).

5. For presentation of the kinds of criticisms here indicated, as well as some historical studies and some proposed reforms, see Ronald and Beatrice Gross, eds. *Radical School Reform* (New York: Simon & Schuster, 1969); Colin Greer, *The Great School Legend: A Revisionist Interpretation of American Public Education* (New York: Basic Books, 1972); P. W. Jackson, *Life in the Classroom* (New York: Holt, Rinehart & Winston, 1968); Samuel Bowles and Herbert Gintis, *Educational Reform and the Contradictions of Economic Life* (New York: Basic Books, 1976); Allen Graubard, *Free the Children: Radical Reform and the Free School Movement* (New York: Random House, Pantheon Books, 1972); Martin Carnoy and Henry M. Levin, *The Limits of Educational Reform* (New York: David McKay, 1976).

6. Edmund Burke's *Reflections on the Revolution in France* (1790), written in the early period of the French Revolution, set the main lines of a conservative outlook for the nineteenth and twentieth centuries.

7. Robert Nisbet, *The Twilight of Authority* (New York: Oxford University Press, 1975).

8. Ibid., p. 217.

9. Quintin Hogg, *The Case for Conservatism* (Harmondsworth: Penguin Books, 1947), p. 144. In the somewhat shorter revised edition—now Viscount Hailsham, *The Conservative Case* (Harmondsworth: Penguin Books, 1959)—the chapter on education is omitted.

10. Michael Oakeshott, "Education: The Engagement and Its Frustration," *Proceedings of the Philosophy of Education Society of Great Britain* 5(January 1971): 43-76.

11. Ibid., p. 47.

12. Ibid., p. 48.

13. Ibid., p. 49.

14. Ibid., p. 52.

15. Ibid., p. 62.

16. For a brief sketch of his criticism of the schools, see Ivan Illich, *Celebration of Awareness* (Garden City, N.Y.: Doubleday, 1970), ch. 8.

17. Illich, *Deschooling Society*. This position is also expounded by Everett Reimer, *School Is Dead: Alternatives in Education* (Magnolia, Mass.: Peter Smith, n.d.).

18. Paul Goodman, *Compulsory Miseducation* and *The Community of Scholars* (New York: Vintage Books, 1962, 1964).

19. Ibid. (1964), pp. 217ff.

20. Ibid., p. 218.

21. Cf. Russell Kirk, *The Conservative Mind from Burke to Santayana* (Chicago: Regnery, 1953).

22. Milton Friedman, "The Role of Government in Education," in *Economics and the Public Interest*, ed. Robert A. Solo (New Brunswick, N.J.; Rutgers University Press, 1955), pp. 123-44.

23. John Dewey, *Democracy and Education* (New York: Macmillan, 1961; originally published 1916), ch. 19.
24. Herbert Gintis, "Toward a Political Economy of Education: A Radical Critique of Ivan Illich's Deschooling Society," *Harvard Educational Review* 42 (February 1972): 70-96.

5. Politicized Schools and the Ideal of Impartiality

In chapter 4 we began the long march toward normative criteria for the schools with specific criticisms of schooling. This quickly led into the variety of social philosophies and their value attitudes. It was clear that social philosophies differ and indeed are often in conflict. They differ in their assumptions about human nature and tradition, about attitudes to freedom and restraint, about change and its controls, even about basic values. And this leads to differences about how the facts of difference and conflict are themselves to be faced. In the schools this is an extremely important matter. Ideals of the search for truth or for the better as against the worse may traditionally occupy the front rank—"Search for truth and the truth will make you free." In the pressure of claimants, however, and in the recognition that the asserted truth of one age is replaced by the fresh truth of another, an ideal is attuned to process rather than result. The free play of ideas and the impartial investigation of contending hypotheses becomes the aim; it is assumed that in the free conflict of views the true and the better will eventually win out. Where, however, conflict drags on and becomes even more intense, and each view proclaims its own truth and its own better—or at least fights for its own—truth and the better not only recede into the background but may even be jettisoned as excess cargo. What we are left with is the battle of opposing programs. Here ideals of civility in process and compromise in outcome take over; they are supported by the bare struggle for survival and the fear of civil war. This is a precarious balance; for one thing it rests on some parity of opposing forces, for if full victory is in sight or if civility and compromise weigh more heavily for one side than the other, the more powerful may press on for full conquest or the less powerful take refuge in guerrilla action.

On the theoretical side, the situation is much more complex than we have envisaged. Particularly in the transition from the free contention of hypotheses to the compromise of warring outlooks there has intervened the theory of ideology in the sociology of knowledge and the theory of relativism in epistemology and ethics. The former denied the possibility of a truth resolution of conflicting outlooks and the latter stressed the ultimacy of disagreement.

In its earlier history the concept of ideology began as an attempt to correct distortions in belief that justify domination or exploitation. It was essentially an unmasking of views by showing their social motivations. In U.S. history, for example, slaveholders countered criticism at one point by arguing that Blacks did not have souls. Not all ideologies are exploitative; they can be protective, for an exploited group may regard itself as a chosen people whose sufferings mark its mission. Theories of racial intellectual inferiority have been offered frequently and revived long after they were disproved, as grounds for restricting immigration and for justifying cheap labor or inequality of educational opportunity. The 1970s witnessed a major educational controversy over the use of intelligence tests; it was claimed that rather than measuring intelligence, they measure the likelihood of success according to middle-class criteria—an ideological use of "intelligence." This whole concept of ideology and its unmasking rested on the contrast of ideology and science; an ideology was not merely opposed by a conflicting ideology but by a more accurate or more adequate account of what was going on. We may think of this view of ideological distortion and the possibility of its correction by scientific knowledge as the *corrective* view.

The corrective view usually proceeds by taking ideologies to pieces and evaluating the components. Objections are sometimes raised that this faith is not warranted, that really comprehensive ideologies are rarely corrected in direct confrontation; historically they are, rather, replaced as different ideologies win out. Even more, the appeal to psychological and social science and history in unmasking one ideology may be simply bringing in a competing ideology which is safely ensconced in the science of the time. For example, with respect to nursery school, the appeal to behaviorist psychology or to Freudian psychology at various times against current practices had the effect of substituting one or another set of values for the ones that were being exercised. There is no general touchstone of knowledge or reason by which to conjure away ideology.

The corrective view does not, however, depend on a wholesale criterion and it need not deny that there has been a great deal of ideology within the psychological and social sciences and history to which it appeals. In fact the hard sciences themselves, both in their earlier stages and even in the twentieth century have had inner ideological conflicts—for example, biology in the development of genetics. But the progress of knowledge has been a fact, and there is no reason that this should not hold for the study of human beings as well. No appeal to a general criterion of knowledge or truth is involved. It is a retail, not a wholesale business. It can deal in better and worse among specific items, or in degrees of objectivity.[1] It is just as in the case of health. There is no general touchstone of what is healthy.

Knowledge gradually accumulates in field after field of what in food, water, environment, exercise, mode of life, and the like is conducive to health, and the idea of health grows in the process. So too every unmasking of an ideology appeals to specific and detailed knowledge that makes that particular unmasking possible, and thereby extends the list of specific empirical criteria for distinguishing ideology or separating fantasy from realistic behavior. To show that hypochondriacs are disguising certain anxieties as symptoms of physical illnesses, there must be ways of showing that they do not have those illnesses and that they have those anxieties. Similarly, to call the Nazi outlook ideological implies knowledge that Hitler's racial biology is false, that he is using the technique of the "big lie" (which he expounds himself), that falsehoods are spread on wishful or purposive grounds; that the avowed aims of the movement function to disguise its practical strivings. To understand what is going on in the public that accepts the doctrines requires historical knowledge of its dilemmas and problems at that time, psychological knowledge of the mechanism of scapegoating, the functions of the authoritarian personality, and so on.

The corrective view has certain strengths for educational purposes, as these are commonly understood. Certainly there are many instances of the kind of outlooks, beliefs, and uses of beliefs that it describes, and they are important in history and social theory and in practical life. In confronting ideology as it does, it preserves the ideal of objective knowledge that is so central to the educational enterprise. It underscores the long process of accumulating knowledge and the concrete rather than the quick-and-easy way of dealing with outlooks. It is trying to extend the scope of rational inquiry in human affairs. What is more, its technique of confronting ideology, being essentially critical, can make us self-conscious about our own ideological outlook and so help us inquire into it. This brings before us the explicit ideals that may be extricated from our outlook, so that we can face them and try to evaluate them directly.

On the other hand, the corrective view does rest heavily on the assumption that scientific knowledge of human beings, not merely of the physical world, can be increasingly expanded. The critique of this outlook as itself ideological became the basis of the development of a quite different view of ideology, which we may label the *relativist view*. It had its start in the generalization of the previous concept, most notably by Karl Mannheim in *Ideology and Utopia*.[2] When Marx unmasked liberal bourgeois ideas as expressing their property interests, argues Mannheim, he was doing it from the standpoint of the proletariat and its interests. The unmasking can itself be unmasked: in social theory, to look for the disappearance of ideology in an eventual victory of science is a transparent use of the liberal ideology of rationality. Truth in social theory is not like truth in physics, says

Mannheim; it must be understood as relative to the social position of the theorist. If intellectuals seem to have an impartial view, it is deceptive; they have simply a broader view because they usually fall between two social classes and so have a foot in opposing camps.

The relativist view of ideology leaves us in a quite different position than the corrective view. The disparaging note is gone. There is nothing to unmask, even though the relations of different outlooks to different social groupings can be traced. Everybody has some ideology or other. The more serious large ideologies tend to be monolithic and impermeable. The supporters of an ideology may take it to be true but this is not. from the standpoint of the relativist concept, the significant feature because their mode of establishing it is internal to the ideology. A comparative historical view sees a procession of ideologies for different social groups under different historical conditions. Systems of ideas in the human field are expressions of inner demands, social groupings and conditions, cultural diversities. To a great extent they serve functions rather than reveal truths. Ideology, on this relativist view, designates a more or less definite ideational-affective-motor cluster. An ideology because it is affective and dynamic is more than a system of ideas. Because it involves pattern of ideas it is more than an abstract ideal. It is an existent outlook of existent people. This general use of the term "ideology" is fairly widespread today. People may speak of their ideology as they do of their property—it is distinctively "theirs." Even more than property, it becomes part of their identity.

Compared to the corrective view, the relativist view has different strengths for educational purposes. It does not break an ideology into bits, and so captures as a whole the unified outlook of a group and sees the way the outlook operates as a dynamic ideational cluster. Such a stance focuses on the opposition of ideologies rather than on their mutual criticism, but in doing so it constantly calls attention to the value aspect, the implicit difference in perspective that underlies criticism as well as opposition. No neutral assessment is possible, even allegedly scientific criticism is also from a given perspective.

A fully developed relativist view need not be bound by the separation of the human and physical sciences. All scientific thinking, physical as well as social, expresses the practical function of human thought and of rationality itself, which is to make possible human beings' survival and comfortable establishment in the world. The very methods of science express a pragmatic base of human purpose, and particular purposes under different social and cultural conditions enter into any type of inquiry. Extremes of this view have sometimes headed toward irrationalism. They have even welcome the revolutionary advances in the study of human beings as revealing the basic irrationality of human beings. Thus Freud and Marx are taken to have revealed the nonrational bases of allegedly rational operations of thought. In showing how cultural differences permeate the thought and values of a people, anthropology is taken to have proved common understanding across cultural lines almost impossible. Paradoxically, these are claims of the proved irrationality of human beings made by offering the evidence that scientific rationality has established.

Other extremes of the relativist view press the concept of ideology to an absolute limit, and all beliefs as the work of a mind that selects in terms of its value attitudes are ideological. Movement in this direction has even permeated the history of science, as seen in Kuhn's picture of scientific revolutions, where the succession of scientific paradigms seems almost to take place on sociological grounds. But the use of "ideology" in so comprehensive a way that a;' belief could be called ideological would lose its interest; the important thing then would be to distinguish its types, so that we could tell the "rational" ideologies from the "irrational," the secure and dependable ones from the ones that breed conflict and confusion. The relativist concept need not be bound by such extremes. It may make concrete distinctions, work out criteria, so that ideologies will become recognizable phenomena for study and analysis, differentiated from ideals on the one hand and ordinary scientific information on the other.

In looking at the two views about ideology from an educational standpoint, we have to recognize more than a difference in usage or a difference in interest. The corrective view is definitely taking a scientific stance and assuming that ideologies purport to tell us about what the world is like and how human strivings and awareness interlock with it. All this can be judged in terms of an ideal of knowledge or truth or correctness. Philosophies may differ about the analysis of correctness (for example about whether there should be a sharp separation of fact components and value components or not), but in some sense correctness means establishing the sort of objectivity in dealing with human affairs that science has advanced in the study of the physical world. The relativist view rests basically on a skepticism about this assumption. The view admits of variations, as we have noted. Sometimes it draws a line between the physical world and human affairs so that the sense of truth or correctness is different for the two. Sometimes it counterattacks against the scientific stance by seeing it as itself an ideology. Sometimes it simply describes the phenomenon of intransigent or impermeable differences in human outlook without commitment on how far they can be resolved by some systematic method. In facing this confrontation of views about ideology and choosing what it finds congenial in both, an educational perspective is at the same time articulating its own conception of knowledge and truth. This is refined in the way ideologies may be studied.

If an educational perspective still has some commitment to an ideal of advancing knowledge, then the study and critique of ideologies has to be brought within the scope of increasing knowledge about ideologies themselves. From the relativist conception it gains a sensitivity to the search for values embedded within any knowledge quest itself, but from the corrective view it learns that no ideology can be left simply self-enclosed, that its judgments about the world and even its entrenched ultimate values have to be brought for criticism into the common world. In some respects ideologies may be looked on as bearing the same relation to the moral life that superstition bears to the search for knowledge; valuable elements have to be strained out from competing complexes and the dross discarded. If it is possible to transcend the conflict of ideologies, they might be replaced by a conjunction of clearer knowledge of our world (including human beings) with explicit ideals worked out to govern human aspiration. The knowledge would embody the long advances of humankind in finding its way around the world and extending control within it. The ideals would constitute the lessons of human experience in self-knowledge and self-direction and could provide a common basis for cooperative endeavor. People need not simply enlist under opposing ideals as banners in a conflict. Different ideals represent directions of aspiration that people may understand and appreciate in spite of the fact that the ideals beckon in different directions. Ideals have to be assessed in relation to people's lives; differences invite reconciliation and the effort to achieve a harmony. The shift from conflicting ideologies to different ideals is thus a significant one. Ideals share the dynamism of ideologies; perhaps it is only because they have been kept remote and fuzzy in our ethical theories and cultural traditions that they have been separated from practice and a gap left for an allegedly hardheaded notion like ideology to fill. If we include in an ethical perspective the need for a reduction of conflict, then the study of ideologies should be closely associated with a critique of ideological judgment.

At the present stage, such a critique could be developed fairly comprehensively because we have had experience with a great many ideologies. We could build up, bit by bit, concepts and procedures for the critique, drawing on gradually accumulating knowledge and gradually established values. Understanding could grow about the different techniques employed in ideologies, the different senses and ways in which ideologies reflect interests and purposes and social groups, how they function and shift their roles, what effects they have upon their holders as well as those who come into contact with them. Where there are distortions, it should be possible to work out ways of detecting them, as suggested by the corrective view of ideology. There could be a persistent attempt to detect hidden values even in apparently neutral knowledge, as suggested by the relativist concept of ideology. And this might be done in studying not only others' ideologies but also our own. It is easier to evaluate far-off ideologies—for example, a cargo cult in the Pacific or the Caribbean—but we have by this time had a great deal of experience even with our own conflicting ideologies. For example, the ideologies associated with capitalism (e.g. "rugged individualism," social Darwinism, corporate ideologies, "free enterprise") have been seen under different stages of economic growth and organization, in prosperity and depression, in dominance and in conflict with competing ideologies. Similarly, the ideologies associated with socialism and communism (e.g. ideology of inevitable gradualism or violent revolution, spontaneous mutualism or the cult of personality, total planning, permanent revolution) have been seen in early organization of minority parties, in prerevolutionary and revolutionary struggles, in postrevolutionary organization of whole countries, in interweaving with nationalist tendencies and cultural variations. A critique of ideological judgment systematically fashioned could become a permanent discipline for self-conscious assessment of our ideals and practices.

Up to this point we have been speaking of ideologies and their mode of study. The schools, however, are institutions, with a given structure and character, in a given social milieu. Corresponding to the different attitudes taken to ideology there can be different institutional structures. A school in which a single ideology is dominant and alternatives kept out may be thought of as a *politicized school*, whether the ideology itself be economic or religious or political. A school that makes room for the interplay of different ideologies is *pluralistic*; its structure may entrench ideals of neutrality or impartiality, or of teacher and student academic freedom and freedom of learning, or merely of civility in controversy. If in addition all these ideals are integrated into the ideal or hope of advancing knowledge as the solvent of differences and conflicts, then its pluralism becomes instrumental and it may be regarded as a *cathedral of learning*. Schools in liberal-democratic countries today may go along in a traditional manner and think of themselves as pluralistic, and the question sometimes becomes a heated one as to whether they are really politicized. At times in their formal ideals of academic freedom, they seem rather to be pluralistic. At other times, when attention is paid to the unanimity of doctrine and attitude transmitted, their pluralism is cast in doubt—for example, when a study is made of high school teaching during the Vietnam war about the history and character of that war.[3] Consciousness about the structural character of the schools usually arises in some controversy about the limits of presentation of untraditional views. It is rarely pursued in a systematic way or made a matter of explicit decision except where a crisis arises.

In the remainder of this chapter emphasis falls on the institutional aspects of the problem of ideology and the schools. For this purpose we begin with other institutions—the press, law, the church—and seek clues for the kinds of choices that schools in fact are making or have to make. It may as well be confessed at the outset that the conception of the cathedral of learning seems today out of reach—the very choice of the term was intended to suggest its almost utopian character. But we shall see some grounds for not abandoning it as an ideal even while recognizing that in fact it may frequently operate as an illusion. Perhaps the chief ground is the sad state that ensues if we really look at the institutional forms that take shape if it is abandoned..

We may begin with contrasting forms of the press. On the one hand is the ideal of a fair reporting of the news: facts and claims are presented in the name of the parties involved, the editorial section is separated from the news, and care is taken with the style of presentation as a source of possible bias. This is the ideal of schools of journalism in the United States. It is well illustrated in the professed policy of the *New York Times*, with its old motto "All the news that's fit to print." In France, on the other hand, there is to a large extent the party press. A newspaper in Paris is likely to be the organ of a particular political standpoint, and impartiality is gained through reading conflicting accounts and comparing them. Such partisanship may be defended by arguing that claims to objectivity are generally spurious. The *New York Times* slogan has been caricatured by a college paper as "All the news that fits we print." Yet the ideal of objectivity need not be abandoned just because it is not fully achieved; new devices can constantly be developed to promote it. Thus columnists of different views can be presented on an op-ed page; an editorial note can explain why a story not reported in the news part was omitted as a deliberate matter. The central point is that procedures are developed in concrete detail to promote the quest for objectivity.

Other institutions exhibit the same contrast as the press. While some interpret judicial process as the search for the truth of the case, drawing the similarities between a trial and a scientific inquiry, others frankly see it as a duel between opposing players, a descendant of the old trial by combat with a shift to less brutal weapons. Yet even to see it as a duel may involve a reference to discovering the truth. In trials by combat or ordeal it was believed that God would give the victory to the innocent, and in modern defenses the duel may be seen as the best way to bring out the truth. In psychiatry, where a plenitude of opposing theoretical positions is encrusted in schools, it is not uncommon to have the differences institutionalized in one-school clinics or departments. The alternative would be a spread of varied outlooks in each department, where competing views can rub up against one another. Separate institutionalization is the almost universal path in religion: the "consumer" chooses among the churches, each of which operates separately, as in the case of the party press. We could in fantasy devise a religious institution that services all varieties; for example, in a common church individuals could tune in on their preferred sermons, as in an international conference each tunes in on the language of his or her choice. Imagine a half-hour's social period after the sermons in which the neighbors compare the lessons of the different sermons. Such an institution would demand greater elasticity and less exclusiveness than religious belief and religious institutions have shown. A secular approach to religions as culturally varied symbols for the moral ordering of life might think in such terms if the moral spread were not too great; so too an unusually hospitable religion such as Hinduism might bring other worships under its symbols. A practically minded ancient Roman religion welcomed the deities of conquered peoples into the pantheon if the people were prepared to sacrifice to the emperor, and so pledge obedience to the state. A comprehensive worship center would be like a comprehensive school; it would require an agreement that brought its different practices under an integrated quest, or it might regard its diverse beliefs as different paths to the same goal.

The history of religion does, however, have many episodes and arguments that could enlighten analogous educational situations. To an older authoritarian religion it might seem evident that because its beliefs were true, opposing or dissident beliefs should not be allowed advocacy. (In our century some nations with established religions still proscribe proselytizing by other religions.) The degree of change or difference of belief tolerated within the fold marks the elasticity of the religion. Sometimes, traditional educational institutions have also regarded themselves as repositories of the received truth to be passed on to appropriately receptive students. With varying toleration, to question the educational fundamentals was suspect as the inroad of heresy, and to appeal to worldly needs and social change attacked as politicization.

Religious toleration in England came with the struggle of sects and represented a compromise of mutual toleration. It remained quite limited; thus Locke's *Essay on Toleration* did not extend to Jews, Moslems, or Catholics. Locke's argument against freedom for Catholics was that a religion that was not tolerant should not itself gain from toleration. Tom Paine, almost a century after Locke, asked for religious freedom as a natural right of all individuals. He denied even the state's right to pass a law granting religious freedom because the whole area was none of its business; it would, he said, be equivalent to a law permitting God to listen to the prayers of other faiths. So too, education in democratic countries has gradually come around to the view that individual exercise of political and social freedom must somehow be accommodated within the institutional framework of education.

Arguments about whether a particular school is politicized or is being politicized usually arise when the exercise of political and social freedom by teachers and students appears to be in conflict with entrenched objectives of the schoools. In recent times the arguments have gone beyond the individual action of teachers and students and dealt also with the policies of the schools as institutions, whether they should take official stands for or against social policies, support or not support governmental military activities in training or in research or intelligence. Well-known examples of such controversies have concerned action regarding officer training programs associated with the schools; governmental action regarded as unjust (the Vietnam war in the United States, the Algerian situation in France); biological research for warfare; investment of university funds in munitions industries, or in South Africa. The arguments about politicization take a different form according to the way we understand the educational objectives of the schools. If the competition of outlooks is ultimate, the schools are at best a neutral forum to which those that have a strong enough following have access. A tenuous balance prevails while none is strong enough to conquer the rest; the conflict in the society is also a conflict in the schools. Considerations about politicization are then questions of broad strategy in such conflict. Two forms of neutrality may be found: in one the subject of dispute is kept out altogether; in the other equal access is given to each position for advocacy. For example, there may be a complete separation of church and state so that public education would have no religious instruction, or there may be religious instruction in which each faith handles its own teaching within the schools. On the other hand, if educational objectives are construed in terms of an underlying quest for knowledge and its expansion, then the notions of academic freedom, of students' rights to learn, of neutrality and impartiality can be given clearer sense, and the issue of politicization then assessed.

The quest for knowledge, seen as an educational objective, has come to embrace procedures, attitudes, and practices issuing in institutional arrangements. There are certainly differences of interpretation about constituent elements, but the differences are subject to investigation in the process itself, which is conceived as self-corrective rather than circular. The quest includes abandonment of claims for infallibility; a persistent search for evidence; not merely the toleration but frank acknowledgment of and the serious search for alternative hypotheses; utilization of logic in the relations of belief and evidence, involving refinement of both deductive and inductive and probabilistic argument; exploratory practice, with experimentation where possible, to decide between alternatives; in general, keeping open the road for the advancement of knowledge and a readiness to revise customary beliefs. In the general relations of people, and in education (construed as including research), the institutions of freedom of inquiry (rules of liberty, protection of unpopular views, and so on) as well as the habits of mind requisite for advancing knowledge (precision, open-mindedness, imaginativeness with respect to alternatives, initiative in ideas, responsible testing, readiness to allow inquiry even with respect to most cherished beliefs) constitute the conditions of the search for knowledge.

John Stuart Mill's *On Liberty*, published more than a century ago, made clear the institutional arrangements that the liberal tradition has on the whole accepted for the knowledge quest. It assumes that the best way in which truth can be discovered and knowledge stabilized is through the conflict of different ideas in an atmosphere of assured freedom of inquiry. Complete freedom of thought and expression for all and as large an area as possible of individual liberty of action are the practices recommended. Since that time many experiments in repression have taken place in liberal-democratic countries, especially by using such concepts as sedition, pornography, clear and present danger, and so on. Beliefs that the mass of the people cannot be trusted to reflect and decide for themselves have often underlain repression and even simple paternalism. The results of the experiments have been disastrous. The evidence is overwhelming—both from nondemocratic countries and in such experiences in the United States as the McCarthy repression of the 1950s and the Watergate period of the 1970s—that a self-proclaimed elite, even acting with the best intentions, quickly identifies public well-being with the preservation and extension of its powers. The alternative of free inquiry, with the hope that experience and education will bring a constant improvement in people's powers of judgment, remains, even for those not strictly convinced, the better pragmatic policy. Perhaps Dewey's formulation, worked out in the early part of our century, gets to the heart of these matters most simply. The basic point is the growth of a scientific outlook fostered by the rise of the sciences of nature; people hope to extend a comparable method with comparable results to all areas of their lives, and to institutionalize the habits and attitudes that will allow such an enterprise to flourish.

In the light of such a background, the specific concepts of impartiality, neutrality, and academic freedom will best be understood as context-bound and varying with conditions, not by a set of universal marks.[4] Impartiality may mean not being partial; yet what forces incline us toward discriminatory judgment or behavior, as well as what positive qualities are needed for judgment, have to be learned from the empirical study of the context. Even what constitutes an impartial jury varies with the kind of case and may raise questions of fair-mindedness or the absence of specific prejudices, membership in a given profession or having had certain kinds of experiences, an ability to empathsize with both sides rather than with neither, ignorance about the details of the case as reported in the media. Being an impartial teacher involves encouraging alternatives to one's own commitments (not lacking commitments), being scrupulous in the consideration of evidence with respect to each alternative, not discriminating among students on irrelevant grounds, even avoiding the halo effect in grading student papers. In principle, to determine the marks of impartiality is a matter of accumulating knowledge about specific conditions and specific disturbing or distorting factors. It is at least as detailed a task as determining what makes a careless and what a careful automobile driver: the needed visual acuity, presence of mind, habits of attention and ability to make rapid decisions, temperateness with respect to alcohol and drugs, and no evidence of accident-proneness. An impartial attitude for students means a genuine readiness to investigate opposing views, not being without a view or remaining in a permanent state of indecision.

Neutrality is subtly different from impartiality. Impartiality is quite compatible with reaching a decision on one side or another; after all, if judges are impartial in their deliberations, they do not cease to be impartial just because they decide for one party against the other. Neutrality lies in not taking sides, in standing outside the controversy. A neutral country in a war may trade with both sides impartially; it is not taking part in the war, and it is not called on to decide between the parties. If in its action it decides one way or the other, even impartially, it is not being neutral. The neutral bystander in an argument does not take part in the argument though he may help both sides clarify their positions. An impartial teacher may help and share making a decision in the question under discussion; the neutral teacher would not have to decide at all. It sometimes makes a difference—say, in a class discussion on the arguments for the existence of God or on the merits of the Vietnam war—whether the teacher is neutral or impartial. In the 1920s, the trial about the teaching of evolution in Tennessee posed the question of teacher attitude on the biblical versus the evolutionary account of the origin of humans. Walter Lippmann, with an eye on this episode, attempted to present sympathetically the view that those who pay the piper have some right to call the tune, and decided that teachers should be a kind of gentle bridge between old beliefs and new knowledge.[5] But although teachers could be expected to be impartial in facing the controversial beliefs, they should not be expected to remain neutral toward what they were to teach. Teachers could be impartial in considering the problem whether the content of teaching should be determined by parents in the community or by the teaching profession. But again, they should not be expected to remain neutral toward the answer. Impartial consideration might, in fact, lead them to break up the question and differentiate what in an educational program should be decided by teachers, what by parents, what by students.

Academic freedom concerns teaching; the freedom to learn pertains to students. Conceivably both could be embraced in an extended notion of academic freedom as freedom of the academy. The idea of academic freedom has been extended to protect civil rights and ordinary freedom of the teachers against punitive action within the academy; there was a time when women teachers in some regions were dismissed for smoking or getting divorced, or teachers in general for holding unpopular opinions. The implicit assumption connecting such protection with academic freedom was that intimidation would result from such violations of rights and freedoms, and this would create an atmosphere in which teaching freely would be difficult. At times, more directly, the central issue has been the right of teachers to decide what is taught and to be free in their teaching from coercion by outsiders, or to give their own interpretation of a subject without administrative dictation. At times the appeal to academic freedom has meant protecting the dissident teachers against the rest of the body of teachers and administrators. In all this, the assumption of libertarian setting required for the quest of knowledge is central; academic freedom thus emerges as the interest not of the teacher alone but of the community at large.

The general case for the nonpoliticized school may be formulated as follows: Because the social struggles of a period are most divisive, and because in the modern world the political mechanisms are the central ones for the decision of broad social controversies, politicized schools would mean their use on one side or another of precisely what most needs rational discussion. If the educational aim is to preserve the pursuit of knowledge through open inquiry, then these are precisely the regions in which academic impartiality needs to be preserved. Nonpoliticization is not inconsistent with the participation of teachers and students in political struggles outside their schools. The school by being neutral would remain the common ground of impartial inquiry

Critics of this case need not call for completely politicized schools. Politicization is not an all-or-none affair; it is a matter of degree and variation, depending on the conditions of the schools and of society. To allow for some is not to abandon the educational objectives that guide decision on the problem. On the contrary, only impartial consideration will tell us how much politicization is present and how much is desirable or undesirable under given conditions. Ideally, nonpoliticization would be most desirable if the schools were stable, relatively isolated, and independent free centers of criticism. This has sometimes been approached in the institution of the autonomous university, as in the traditional German pattern. To be really autonomous it would have to be impervious to governmental influence, outside pressure and internal sectarian capture; its methods of appointment would have to be thoroughly impartial. The concept of rationality under which it operated would have to beg no value that tied it to the status quo and made it unreceptive to novel ideas. The German autonomous university certainly did not conform to these conditions, as experience in social crisis readily proved; it is doubtful whether any universities could do so.

Political activity by educational institutions is sometimes dictated by their educational responsibilities. It is therefore not inconsistent for them to engage in political action against measures that would undermine their educational basis, such as laws curbing freedom of speech, or requiring a political oath or affirmation by students as a condition of financial assistance, or restricting freedom of research. Political lobbying to secure the financial foundation or the property of educational institutions rarely invites the charge of politicization—a university advocating a greater subsidy, opposing measures that would cut down its tax exemptions. Perhaps it was regarded as scarcely more than prudence when an Oxford college hid its silver from the king's agents during the Cromwellian civil war, even though Oxford was on the king's side. Yet when students protest the immorality of a university's extension into a neighborhood on the ground that it deprives the surrounding neighborhood of much-needed housing without adequate replacement (especially when it is an impoverished population), this is usually attacked as politicization of the university, in the sense of agitating for social causes.

Vagueness attends the application of the notion of politicization. Activities that at a given time are educational duties may once have been regarded as wildly radical political agitation. For example, any responsible teacher or student would be sensitive today to a history text that conveyed anti-Black or anti-Semitic bias, or that talked of the immigration of Southern Europeans as diluting American stock. Yet in the 1930s teachers who urged the texts be carefully examined for such material and that it be removed or corrected were often taken to be bringing radical politics into the schools. The difference lies of course in the intervening development of moral sensitivity under the impact of world war and subsequent liberation movements. For girls in contemporary schools to demand equal funds for athletics may create controversy, but is no longer regarded as politicization.

A further difficulty in assessing politicization at a given time lies in the fact that the schools may already be highly politicized; a particular political ideology may be in full possession of the modes of thought and categories of analysis. Any challenge to the established ways may then be reckoned as politicization, while the established ways themselves are regarded as nonpolitical. The educational consequences of gearing United States education to the Cold War in the 1950s were a clear illustration of this point.[6] This movement expressed an attitude that had already been growing and was hardened in the McCarthy period of the 1950s by dismissal of radical teachers and the silencing of critical opinion.[7] The basic categories in social discussion became "the free world" and "the communist world." Stereotyped as democracy and totalitarianism, they were turned into simplistic models to make the contrast complete. These categories permeated the teaching of social science in the high schools as well as political science research in the universities. Because these were the categories that governed political policy during the 1950s and 1960s (leading particularly to oversimplified analyses of the Third World and their mass movements), what the students of the 1960s discovered in their experience of opposing the Vietnam war was the already existent politicization of the schools. In their own description, the schools were the tools of the establishment.

That thorough politicization of the schools affects the educational process profoundly is no doubt the case. Raywid argues that it impoverishes educational relationships; she compares the situation to one in which male and female cannot have a topic-centered conversation without everything's being sex-directed.[8] But if the schools are already thoroughly politicized, what may be called for is to bring opposing political policies into explicit confrontation. Unfortunately the situation may then resemble a war, and under those conditions education usually suffers. For example, in the campaign against the Vietnam war students often raised disturbances at college meetings when government spokesmen came to defend the war. Many did not regard themselves as violating academic freedom in preventing the other side from being heard. They felt more like soldiers jamming an enemy broadcast where the government spokesmen had all the heavy ammunition and the government had falsified what it was doing, for example its activities in Cambodia. They were simply defending themselves; the war in the colleges had been started by the immorality of the Vietnam war itself, with disastrous consequences. Conceivably the students might have claimed to be freeing the universities from their existent politicization, but more perhaps regarded politicization as unavoidable and were on the other side.

Ethical judgment of such a situation of conflict cannot follow simply from any general principle about the undesirability of politicization or the conception of an ideal institution. It has to reckon with the existent situation and decide what is best under the trying circumstances, with the alternatives and consequences in full view. Sometimes there is no happy way out. In the Civil War, Princeton fell apart when the faculty was largely Northern in active sympathy and the students were Southern. The most difficult situation within the schools comes when there is uncertainty; different teachers and students go along different paths because of their beliefs about what is unavoidable, what the whole social situation calls for, and what part educational institutions should play in meeting the crises. Some will call for focusing almost all educational activity in relation to the social crisis, some will think that there is still room for intelligent guidance of the course of affairs and so emphasize the impartial analysis of alternatives that an intellectual community may still achieve, and some may even be ready to have teachers as well as the school stay neutral provided they not be interfered with in their customary work.

At such times, the fundamental stance of the educational institutions is not without importance. Precisely because there are and perhaps always will be conflicting social outlooks, the need for comparing, judging, and deciding among them is a perennial enterprise. It need not be carried on from some transcendent posture, but it does require internal criteria of knowledge, truth, adequacy, and intellectual refinement in analysis. These, as we have seen, are the properties of scientific inquiry. If this is to have any institutionalization at all, education (teaching, learning, and research) seems to be the appropriate locus. The schools could then be regarded as—to multiply metaphors in Homeric style—not an ivory tower but an oasis of the spirit, not a refuge of "social termites" eating away at tradition but a bastion of reflective criticism for all society, not a "conspiracy to undermine the Establishment" but a "seed-bed of fresh ideas" for social as well as technological change.

Such an ideal seems to be a kind of Kantian regulative principle that must be postulated if knowledge and understanding are to have a continual growth. And if contemporary society depends on such growth, it must have an institutional base. Short of this, educational institutions move back to a stage comparable to the compromise noted in the history of religion whereby relative freedom existed only because opposing forces were relatively equal. The schools would still operate on the basis of areas of consensus—in relation to technology, for example, or professions and administration—while in their humanistic and social aspects there would be constant conflict tolerated because no side has superior power. This is operating on a second best.

Such a second best could readily be given institutional form. As in the discussion of the press, the schools could be redesigned so as to represent different positions rather than a common pursuit of knowledge in all areas of life. This requires little imagination, for it corresponds in part to what is found in education in various countries. Religious schools are the most obvious large-scale illustration. Military schools are another example. Labor schools operate in adult education. Sectional differences, ethnic differences, economic differences, political differences—if they were associated with ideological differences—could become the basis for a whole variety of schools. Segregated schools on the basis of race are far from gone, and separate schools for each sex are still often taken for granted. If the voucher system were adopted, alternative schools might readily assume such a character, drawing apart until what they have in common might be only the teaching of the physical sciences. The variety in one country might be as great as that found among the typical schools in, say, a capitalist country, a communist country, a Catholic country, a resurgent Mohammedan country. The body of existent knowledge, particularly where related to technology and medicine and food supply, might partly prevent students from living in wholly different worlds.

Such speculation, or the view of a partially existent situation, raises the question whether we do in fact have a single idea of what the public school is about. Of course institutionally it is a system financed and run through public control on one or another regional level, but that kind of minimal institutional characterization is not enough. The question, rather, is how the functions of the public school are conceived. The public schools may be the common meeting ground of different outlooks compromising on an acceptable minimum. Or they may be a unified enterprise geared to the quest for knowledge and understanding and committed to the attitudes that promote its pursuit—wherever the chips fall. The difference in approach is fundamental, and it underscores the importance of guiding ideals in the shape of the schools.

Notes

1. No more than this is required for our discussion at this point. We are not entering here into the formal epistemological analysis of knowledge. It is sufficient to recognize the pursuit of knowledge and the understanding it brings as an enterprise that enables us to make judgments that one belief is more warranted than another in specific contexts. Further discussion of various aspects of the knowledge quest will be found in chapters 8 (rationality), 10 and 11 (knowledge and learning), and 13 (knowledge in the curriculum). For a defense of the corrective approach to ideology, see Abraham Edel, *Analyzing Concepts in Social Science* (New Brunswick, N.J.: Transaction Books, 1979), ch. 10, "Education and the Concept of Ideology."

2. Karl Mannheim, *Ideology and Utopia* (London: Routledge & Kegan Paul, 1962).

3. Cf. William L. Griffen and John Marciano, *Teaching the Vietnam War* (Montclair, N.J.: Allanheld, Osmun, 1979). The study includes an analysis of twenty-eight high school textbooks widely used in social studies and history courses throughout the United States, and exhibits their overwhelming one-sidedness.

4. Analysis of these concepts is of increasing philosophical concern. Cf. Alan Montefiore, ed., *Neutrality and Impartiality: The University and Political Commitment* (New York: Cambridge University Press, 1975); Kenneth A. Strike, "Liber-

ality, Neutrality and the Modern University" in *Ethics and Educational Policy*, ed. Kenneth A. Strike and Kieran Egan (London: Routledge & Kegan Paul, 1978); Romulo F. Magaino, "Student Academic Freedom and the Changing Student/University Relationship," ibid.; Robert Paul Wolff, *The Ideal of the University* (Boston: Beacon Press, 1969), pt. 1, ch. 4 ("The University as an Assembly Line for Establishment Men"), and pt. 2, ch. 2, ("The Myth of Value Neutrality").

5. Walter Lippmann, *American Inquisitors: A Commentary on Dayton and Chicago* (New York: Macmillan, 1928).

6. The call for such an educational orientation is best seen in *American Education and International Tensions* (Educational Policies Commission of the National Education Association and the American Association of School Administrators, 1949). The report assumed that we would have before us in the foreseeable future a world embroiled in a cold war between East and West, that is, between Soviet and non-Soviet areas, and it asked education to maintain its part in the cold war. It even spoke of education as "an instrument of national policy."

7. For an assessment of the educational consequences of this episode, see Paul Lazarsfeld and Wagner Thielens, Jr., *The Academic Mind* (Glencoe, Ill.: Free Press, 1958).

8. Mary Anne Raywid, "The Politicization of Education," *Educational Theory* 23 (Spring 1973): 119-32.

6. Ideals and Their Assessment

This chapter concerns the way in which ideals may be assessed, how they operate in education, and whether they are sufficient to furnish a theoretical basis for normative judgment. We elicit criteria for assessment, try them out on the ideal of equality in its historical career, and then apply them to equality as an ideal in educational thought.

There is good reason for dealing first with ideals in general. So-called educational ideals turn out usually to be human ideals that have some special pertinence to the functioning of educational institutions, but this does not exhaust their scope. The ideal of advancing knowledge may enter into the curriculum but it also has a place in scientific institutes and research laboratories in the business world as well as in government departments (health, agriculture, and so on). A composite ideal of the good teacher may seem to be peculiarly educational, but if we divide it into its parts, each of them has a more general scope; a good teacher is one who communicates well with others, knows a great deal, organizes his thoughts well, and the like. We are thus building general qualities into an educational ideal rather than generalizing the latter for broader purposes.

Some philosophies regard ideals in an abstract way as forms of perfection. They are grasped by the mind's eye and set standards for our aspiration. They can be assessed in isolation by the degree to which they attract us, the intensity of our aspiration. Perhaps they could be compared where a choice among them was involved. A questionnaire asking an individual American whether he or she would choose to pursue the ideal of intelligence or beauty or athletic success might yield interesting variations in the weighting of ideals. A more productive approach is found in those philosophies that relate ideals to the needs and conditions of life in which they operate. For example, if a woman responded to the questionnaire by ranking beauty over intelligence, it might reflect a dominant aesthetic interest, but it might instead reflect the stereotype of sex appeal as the key to marriage and happiness or the place of Hollywood in the American dream. If she ranked intelligence over beauty, it might mean the struggle for women's liberation and the image of a career in the professions. Similarly, success in sports has to be understood in terms of the place of sport in the life of the time, and for particular groups, such as Blacks, the way in which athletic ability opens doors to striking success in careers. If we look at ideals in this more concrete way, we have to ask what basis they have in human needs—not merely whether liberty will be ranked above security and a life of striving above that of mere comfort but what kind of opportunities and institutions and styles of life were envisaged with such choices.

Normative attempts in ethics and social philosophy to work out a desirable form of society in terms of ideals—or a desirable form of educational institutions—have to achieve concreteness. Ideals are not assessed in isolation but as they operate in people's lives, organize a life in common, give expression to needs and help cope with problems, and ensure a given quality of life in general. The first step in understanding an ideal is thus to locate individuals or groups attracted by or aspiring to the ideal and examine its basis in their needs and problems. This gives the *basis* or *foundations* of the ideal. An ideal has a career over time in relation to such groups; we may track its birth, its changes, even sometimes its death.

As a category of ethics, an *ideal* is part of the conceptual apparatus of morality, although more specialized than *good* or *obligation*, which are more widely analyzed notions. *Good* is a more generic notion, and an ideal is a specific kind of good; generally speaking, ideals are aspired to, whereas goods are either felt satisfactions or goals that are desired. Ideals differ from such goals in being more remote or far off or more abstract; they are not easily achieved, though progress toward their achievement is possible. Ideals differ from obligations in that they designate states of possible existence, not prescriptions or rules or imperatives. Ideals may overlap other moral categories without coinciding with them. Thus some virtues may be ideals of character: people may set as their ideal to be peaceable and cooperative in all their relations with others. And in the same way, a particular goal that is desired as a good may also serve as an ideal if it satisfies the further special conditions of aspiration—for example, to own a home of one's own may be an ideal to many for whom it is not easily attained. In such a case it becomes clear that ideals also have a functional role: they not merely express and answer to human needs, psychological and sociohistorical, that are basic and long lasting rather than ephemeral, but serve to organize desires and demands in various areas of conduct.

In light of this conception of the ideal, criteria for assessment can readily be elicited.[1] A specific ideal may be assessed for *the breadth of its foundations*: does it rest on transient needs or the needs of a few, or does it rest on permanent and pervasive needs, on the primary needs of many? Numbers affected, importance of needs among other needs, relation of needs, typical problems in the effort to satisfy needs, all contribute to forming a solid base for ideals. When a specific ideal is focused upon, it is no small matter to discern its basis fully and accurately. For example, if the ideal of educational freedom is referred only to the needs of persons who are being educated, it has a narrower import than if it is referred to the whole range of people capable of being educated. In the former case it bears on the quality of their learning, in the latter also on access to educational institutions and the expansion of educational opportunities. Nietzsche attacked the whole category of ideals because he sought their basis only in a will to power and took them to express and be a substitute for weakness.

Because ideals are objects of aspiration, they may be assessed for their *intensity*. If the intensity is very low, they risk not being ideals at all but, rather, specific goals. If the intensity is supremely high, they run a different risk: it may issue in a fanaticism that takes over the whole of life's effort. Such investment in one ideal in a world that is replete with multiple aspirations is understandable in a dire or critical situation in which every energy must be marshaled in a single direction. If, on the other hand, it is actually what is called "enslavement by an ideal," the suspicion arises that there is some distortion in the underlying psychological needs. Between the ideal whose intensity has ebbed and that which enslaves, the large majority of ideals can be assessed initially for their worth by the intensity of arousal they bring with them. This is only, however, a beginning in the assessment; it furnishes an initial hypothesis of worth.

Because ideals share the general aim of ethics—to guide action—specific ideals can be assessed for their *motor power* or *dynamism*. The motor power is greater when the ideal spurs to action rather than simply intensifies consciousness for possible future action, though the latter is also clearly important. Something has gone wrong, however, if the ideal has no effect on behavior—for example, if it serves as a consolation for inaction in a serious situation that the individual himself sees as remediable, as if the demand to do one's bit were satisfied by believing in the ideal. At that point questions might arise about the *genuineness* of the ideal. Such a criterion can be applied to any ideal. If an ideal rests on a basis of needs, to whose successful satisfaction it is in the long run adddressed, then it is like a remedy, and remedies that are proposed and even have high motor power may prove to be illusory; a spurious ideal is like a quack remedy. The subjective sincerity of the devotee is no guarantee of genuineness. In this sense, genuineness is the criterion of adequacy of the ideal for its implicit tasks.

To assess an ideal in terms of *attainability* has sometimes been attacked as a pedestrian criterion. Unattainability or remoteness is taken as essential. This is, however, overromantic. For example, peace on earth is an ideal that might be achieved, be institutionalized, and cease to engage human ideal energies. It is a prime example of an ideal whose death would be welcome once it no longer had any tasks to perform. The most inspiring ideals allow for progressive approximation; distance allows a growth in meaning at successive levels as we advance toward them, even where the effect may be that of a receding horizon. A desirable feature with respect to attainability is therefore sufficient distance to enable the ideal to carry out the function of organizing action for the needs and purposes embodied in the basis of the ideal.

Two ideals may be roughly comparable in genuineness, both addressing common needs and likely, if fully and faithfully carried out, to satisfy needs and provide remedies for the problems addressed. Both may be equally dynamic, yet one may be judged greater in *effectiveness*. It may be more practical than the other, which may even be dismissed as impractical, in terms of possible costs, effort required, likelihood of attracting and holding a secure following, impact on other problems and other ideals. For example, the ideal of world government and the ideal of pacifism may be differently effective in abolishing war. Not infrequently, in a critical social situation where the status quo cannot be maintained, one ideal may call for turning back the clock, another for moving sharply in a new direction. For example, Gandhi wanted to restore village life in India rather than promote urban industrialization. The judgment of effectiveness may be the crucial one in a practical decision.

Where ideals begin to compete with one another, fresh criteria of assessment may be added. Some ideals may be relatively isolated so that their approximation or achievement may not seriously affect ideals or other goods in general. Some, however, may be such that their approximation or achievement is a necessary condition for advancing any other ideal or achieving any other goods. Perhaps global peace occupies such a position in the contemporary world. Such an ideal could be said to have the property of *ethical necessity*. This would give it a high rank in the domain of ideals. If in addition such an ideal appears to have overwhelming forces marshaled on its behalf, if it plays an increasing part in the organized movements of peoples, if all signs point to its victory, it is sometimes thought to be *historically necessary*. This notion of historical necessity has been a subject of controversy in the philosophy of history. Marxism sees the victory of socialism as historically necessary; Nazism in its heyday was called the wave of the future; Islamic fundamentalism today has a comparable faith in its victory. In such cases the assumption often seems to be that what will conquer thereby proves its ideal character. The property of historical necessity we are considering, however, presupposes that the ideal has first passed the other tests, including ethical necessity, and then is found to have overwhelming power. A spurious ideal like the Nazi ideal of racial purity would not therefore be regarded as historically necessary even when it was sweeping the historical scene in a given period.

Isolation and the interrelatedness that underlies ethical necessity are extreme cases. In between lie the relations of ideals that neither go it alone nor stand out in the total web of ideals. Perhaps their situation is touched indirectly in the criterion of effectiveness, for that involves the broadest judgment of the practicality of the ideal and so requires consideration of cooperative forces and possibilities of conflict. Still, it is best to focus directly on the contributions that the pursuit of one ideal may make to the pursuit of other ideals. An ideal may therefore be assessed for its *constructiveness*, that is, how far its pursuit enhances that of other ideals held by the same group. In the broadest sense, with reference to the total economy of a system of ideals, an ideal is constructive insofar as its pursuit enhances the general quality of life.

The several criteria considered will suffice for our purpose, though doubtless more subtle ones can be worked out if the category of ideals becomes more refined and its place in ethics more minutely studied. On the face of it, many general ideals are appropriate for education: equality, fraternity, democracy, individuality, autonomy, rationality, growth and development, maturity, even efficiency. It may be thought part of the educational task to advance commitment and devotion to such ideals in students. The ideals may also have particular relevance to special parts of the educational task. A commitment to equality will promote greater opportunities for education throughout the community, and will help teachers cultivate appropriate attitudes in dealing with students of different origin and class. Liberty may be particularly pertinent in establishing rules of school life that will promote initiative in students and convey the sense of a free society. Individuality, autonomy, and the development of one's powers and capacities combine into an almost central educational ideal. Advancing knowledge and aesthetic appreciation, though extending far beyond the educational realm, are central to it. Much of this is so obvious that it seems to identify a normative account of education with simply a listing of educationally relevant ideals, leaving it to educational experts to work out how best to achieve them or approximate to them in the conditions of our life.

It is equally obvious, however, as the previous discussion of the basis or foundation of ideals made clear, that the content of an ideal has much that depends on its historical context and the needs and problems of its time. No ideal tells its own story. If it did, we would not have the multitude of disputes over what liberty consists of, whether a given case is liberty or license, whether one person's exercise of liberty may be another's subjection to tyranny or exploitation, whether liberty is in conflict with equality, and so on. The historical career of an ideal and the specific content built into it at a given time have to be determined to understand the role that the ideal is playing, how broad its basis and what its intensity, whether it is dynamic and genuine, and in general how it satisfied the criteria that enter into its assessment. Indeed this picture gives us the historical meaning of the ideal in that period, just as the general formula of justice—to each his or her due—requires the rules of the social system to understand what in that system is due to a person.

It is an interesting historical question, too, why a given social demand takes one rather than another ideal form, when both seem possible alternatives. Slaves demand freedom when they might have asked for equality or even justice. Or if it is a matter of one step at a time, why did they not construe the second step as further liberty—the liberties guaranteed by full citizenship, opportunities of education, and so on? The present-day movement toward the liberation of disadvantaged groups has been carried on predominantly under the ideal of equality rather than liberty. Is this a function of the ideal itself in some sense, or does it somehow fit the situation in which the disadvantaged find themselves? For example, a plausible other ideal that might have served may be occupied, as it were, by other movements, other interests, or other problems.

To examine more carefully the way an ideal functions, let us look in greater detail at the ideal of equality.

The Career of Equality

On the face of it, careers as ideals would not have been predicted for such notions as equality and identity, whose bare mathematical meaning can nowadays be expressed in purely logical notation. Yet the ideal of equality has been the flag of many a social revolution and the search for identity today not only rocks the psychoanalytic couches and hits best-seller lists but profoundly characterizes ethical probings.

To apply our criteria for evaluation of equality we have first to locate its foundations, then trace its career. Without such a grounding no ready identification of the phenomena seems possible; we are left floundering among numerous possible meanings of "equality" in current equality demands or seeking a phenomenological essence of equality. Unintentional caricatures of the ideal sometimes result, in which equality appears as a demand for government control over all people to cure every ill that any X may have that any Y does not have, or in which indices are sought for comparing X and Y *in toto* to decide how equally X and Y are being treated.[2]

A search for the base of the ideal also has its dangers. Chief among them is the mislocation of the base, that is, referring the ideal to the wrong needs and problems. Suppose we wonder why people worry about being equal to others rather than about what would satisfy their needs and demands. This intriguing question suggests looking for contexts that would provoke comparison. Nietzsche, for example, located modern demands for democratic and economic equality in a psychological base, the phenomena of envy and resentment, and interpreted these as the feelings of a thwarted will to power. Piaget, on the other hand, in *The Moral Judgment of the Child*, focuses on the feeling of unfairness and explores the appearance of the idea of reciprocity in the child. Others, from the time of Aristotle on, noting the same connection of the ideas of fairness and equality with reciprocity, have turned rather to the context of exchanges as interpersonal transactions; for example, modern anthropology investigates gift giving as exchanges in primitive societies and economic exchanges once markets develop and monetary systems are instituted.

The different inquiries, psychological and sociocultural, call attention to different possible bases with which a notion of equality is somehow associated. The ideal of equality, whose career we are trying to plot, runs through social theories and social movements at specific times in history. The contemporary world knows it well in the demands of different social groups or categories of people who organized to advance themselves or solve definite problems—social classes, races and ethnic groups, women, and more specialized groupings of which the handicapped are a good example. Looking back we find clear cases of explicit invoking of equality. Socialist theory of the nineteenth and twentieth centuries relies heavily upon it: socialization of the means of production and planning economic life are demanded so as to secure a wider distribution of material goods to satisfy needs and enhance more generally the quality of life. At the same time, in liberal-democratic countries, socioeconomic demands are addressed to the state, which is asked to move from merely protective or police functions to what in a broad sense are described as social-welfare functions. The familiar phenomena of this sort are state-organized or state-promoted systems of unemployment insurance, workers' compensation, health care, social security or old-age assistance, child welfare laws, insurance for financial institutions, extended public education, consumer protection. In part, the social movement that struggles for such reforms invokes the ideal of equality, but in large part it invokes an ideal of security. This flags a problem in our search for the foundation of an ideal: the needs that constitute the foundation may find expression in ideals other than the one we are examining. Other ideals may offer different solutions to the same problems to which equality is addressed, in which case issues of comparative effectiveness will be prominent; or else they may point to a different kind of life, and so inspire people in different ways to a different organization of life. In the present example, security and equality were both invoked in the movement for the welfare state, and they overlapped in that the outcome at the same time provided basic security and advanced equality. Security probably was a more effective ideal in that it enlisted wider support for a more limited program, while equality demanded more. On the other hand, a study of the period might show that the ideal of equality was more dynamic. But security might not merely be a step toward equality. It could tie in with a corporate ideal for the society, as in the picture of the Japanese economy and its responsibilities to its workers. Or it could point beyond itself to an ideal of fulfillment of individuality in a common life, bypassing altogether claims to equality. Or it could be associated with a general ideal of balance or harmony of the different groups in society.

In company with demands for economic equality are to be found major theoretical battles of liberty versus equality. In the nineteenth century they are also spread through the literature of agitation over the political question of extending the vote, as well as over demands for social equality and for extending schooling. The continuity of this theme with contemporary arguments about the coercion that equality requires is evident. But there are also counterinstances to the antagonism of the two ideals. Many of the contemporary movements invoke indifferently liberty and equality; for example, women's demands for equality with men is also seen as a women's liberation movement. And early in the emergence of the two ideals, we find them comfortably side by side in the French revolutionary slogan of "Liberty, Equality, Fraternity." It follows that a search for the foundations of an ideal and the study of the career of an ideal cannot focus on that ideal in isolation. We need to examine the whole network of ideals that are related to the same base; their overlapping may be chance, or they may have settled into a divison of labor with each depending on the other to handle part of the underlying problems. Only a joint study will show whether they fit well together or point in different directions of social policy.

The career of equality shows many historical strands before the demands for economic equality. Once they emerge they persist as strata in a growing concept. Equality as a demand for political democracy reaches back in England to the Levellers in the midseventeenth century, who claimed that every man should have a vote because he had one life to live. In the United States it reaches forward to refined legal applications in the twentieth century when the Supreme Court rules on the size of election districts so that every person's vote would have comparable weight; or that there be proportionality in the punishment given in different states to the particular crime. Equality of opportunity is a different stratum: as the "career open to talents" of the French Revolution it opens the activities and vocations of a society, with their benefits, to all without discrimination. Legal barriers that reserved occupations for entrenched classes are wiped out. It is hard to say whether this is to be seen as liberty or equality or both, and it scarcely matters at that point, for neither ideal is yet preempted for special institutions and special interpretations. Procedural equality comes in with the legal removal of special status: the poor are to be treated equally with the rich before the law, the peasant with the landlord, the debtor with the usurer. In time this has come to include assignment of public defense counsel to impoverished defendants, and hosts of attempts to equalize treatment in trials, prisons, and so on. (Many of these are helpful; many nevertheless leave the situation as Anatole France's *mot* epitomized it: the law "in its majestic equality" forbids the rich and poor alike to beg and sleep under bridges.)

Roughly in the latter part of the eighteenth century and early part of the nineteenth century, moral philosophy articulates a fundamental stratum in the equalitarian ideal: every person is to count equal with every other. The unanimity on this found in the two opposing theories of ethics—Kantian and Utilitarian—is striking. Kant demands that no person be used as a means alone and sees every person as an autonomous legislator; Bentham affirms that in reckoning happiness everyone is to count as one and no one as more than one. In the theory of natural rights, which Bentham attacked, persons are born equal and endowed by God with inalienable rights. Whatever these rights turn out to be, whether life, liberty, and the pursuit of happiness, or Locke's life, liberty, and property, or later lists of human rights agreed on in the United Nations, or proposed fresh rights that come pell-mell in the contemporary period, there is no going back on the postulate that if they are rights they are everyone's rights.

Of course back of the recognition that everyone counts is the long religious tradition in which all persons are equal before God. We seem to come close to the beginnings of equality when the Reformation has every person face God directly instead of through an authoritative intermediary. In the regnant ideals of the feudal period, still idealized in Dante, there is no room for equality; everyone is to stay in the fixed place to which he or she was allotted. Still there are precursors: the religious equalitarianism of early Christianity, which attracted the poor and the dispossessed; the glimmer of a universalism in the Stoic view of human beings; an occasional suggestion in a slave revolt. No doubt there are precursors for any ideal. Social movements with explicit social theories are another matter. Again, some demands do not at first get formulated under the ideal of equality, though they may fit comfortably later on under rights that as a matter of course are ascribed equally to all. Religious freedom and intellectual freedom or freedom of speech and expression are two striking instances. Perhaps it would have made no sense for religious sects to demand equality with the established religion, for they often sought to eliminate establishment. Perhaps too, intellectual freedom was too new and there was no one to be equal to. Yet something like "Everyone is a king in his mind" might have been teased out of an analysis of thought, just as the sanctity of the home appealed to "A man's home is his castle," a kind of common man's equal treatment with the barons. A genuinely historical study of the career of these ideals is required if we are to understand the conditions under which demands take the shape of liberties as contrasted with entering the lists under the banner of equality. Perhaps it has to do with the extent to which the activity under consideration is already entrenched in the community and needs only to be extended to others; liberty would then be a typical way for a fresh activity to break in. Or, more likely, freedom of thought would not be construed in equalitarian terms anyhow because there is no problem of distribution involved. If freedom of thought is taken to involve access to libraries, then villages could be thought of as demanding equal freedom of thought with cities. Such demands would, however, fit more readily under equality of opportunity.

If we now look back over the career of equality that we have so summarily explored, it stands out as a broad ideal held by groups in a society addressed to their need to count or attain membership in the society, to have access to the activities of the society, to share in the material and cultural progress of the society. The social movements that invoked the ideal have been largely those subject to one or another kind of discrimination. The ideal admits of indefinite approximation, and as it was pursued fresh levels came into view giving the ideal a broader scope. From full membership as against lesser status, the ideal moved to provision of opportunities. Political equality became the focus of the ideal as the state became the broader instrument of social control. Political equality expressed both full membership and the opportunity to advance toward greater share in the goods of a common life. With the growth of industry the focus shifts toward principles of the distribution of goods and burdens that will ensure the greater spread of material and cultural progress. This demand is spurred by the tremendous technological development of the last half-century, by the breakdown of colonialism and the expansion of an international society, and by the unwillingness of people conscious of the tempo of development to be put off by temporary obstacles and repeated excuses.

If these are the foundations of the ideal, then it has tremendous strength because it is integrated with almost all aspects of human striving. The intensity of the ideal may be gauged from the persistence of its pursuit; equality seems almost at times to become an intrinsic value, or at least a structural feature of the good life, though in calmer moments this can be seen as reflecting the momentousness of the total issues at stake. The ideal is highly dynamic; it owes this probably to the fact that its satisfaction would also be instrumental to other needs tied in with its foundations. As to being genuine, its opponents constantly accuse equality of being a spurious ideal and give it such senses that its demands will be for what is impossible or self-contradictory. But if it is interpreted with a strict eye on its foundations, the removal of any of the great discriminations would, if achieved, answer to a significant part of its foundational problems. The scope of the ideal makes it difficult to attain, but ample room is allowed for approximation, as can be seen from the gains of the poor and disadvantaged over the last two centuries; and what is more, it is the kind of ideal that at each step of approximation broadens out with a richer meaning.

The judgment of effectiveness is the most difficult, and here the contemporary theory of equality appears to be at a parting of the ways. The question is whether, even given the high positive evaluation on the preceding criteria, further action toward achieving equality is practical and will in fact solve the underlying problems to which the ideal is addressed. One view holds that equality has gone as far as it reasonably can when it has established respect for persons and political democracy, removed serious discriminations, and ensured equality of opportunity. Of course, the argument goes, there may be improvement in equality of opportunity; some room exists for remedying significant disadvantages that individuals still have before they go out into the struggle of life, but the struggle and its rewards should not be removed by further equalization. This is the traditional meritocratic conception, with the assumption that rewards belong to the successful exercise of ability. If the ideal of equality demands more, it overreaches itself, for beyond that point it loses effectiveness. This is because it crosses too many other ideals and frustrates too many other necessary instrumentalities. Any further reforms needed to address unresolved problems in the foundations should be left to other ideals, such as security, liberty, and more modest ideals such as benevolence or compassion. The opposing view, more thoroughly committed to the effectiveness of the struggle for equality, questions the assumptions of meritocracy. It gives too much weight to chance advantages; they do not entitle people to rewards, only put them in a strategic position to bargain for rewards when the particular skills are in demand. The meritocratic principle belongs to the period before the higher organized production of contemporary technology was possible, and represents a less human outlook that turned person against person, isolating and alienating people from one another. Our complex modern life itself necessitates fuller participation. The further struggle for equality will mute the competitive tone of our culture and engender a deeper sharing attitude. What the expansion of equality thus demands is a set of institutions that channels the goods of social production and spreads the burdens equitably for enhancing the common quality of life and cultivating the individuality of all people, not for selective individual aggrandizement.

This dispute about the effectiveness of the ideal of equality in turn affects the judgment of ethical necessity. Both sides could agree that, given the unlikelihood of enjoying a good life without adequate material conditions, the ideal of equality will have the property of ethical necessity, although pictures of the good life may differ. The view that looks forward to an extended appeal of the ideal, however, will assign it greater ethical necessity because it deems the ideal imperative for dealing with specific problems and working out new principles and practices as changes continue to take place in our complex life. Equality seems also to have a kind of historical necessity, at least as a general ideal. Few ethical theories now oppose it. Even theories that once opposed it in the name of liberty are now inclined to accommodate themselves within an equalitarian approach and to express their values in terms of one version of equality as against another. Progress within the ideal itself—the meritocratic concept was once the radical front and is now the conservative rear—is a mark of its necessity.

Clearly such claims for historical necessity proceed from a theoretical view that sees the rising equalitarian demands as unavoidable, expressing major efforts of large masses of people all over the world. For example, the call from Third World countries for a greater sharing of resources and a transfer of technology is cast in the mantle of equality as well as justice, and equalitarian assumptions permeate those of justice. If the ideal of equality has so great a reach in linking with other ideals for mutual support in the struggle for advancing well-being, then it has high constructiveness. On the other hand, if equality as an ideal has reached a limit and is rounding out its career, it is quite possible that the demands in its foundations may turn to other ideals and speak directly in terms of specific ideals of human well-being and community. Or else equality may become settled as a component ideal in the broader ideal of democracy, with its demands now shaped by the unity of a federation of ideals.

Equality in Educational Theory

We turn now to the relevance of this story to education. As may be expected, different strata of the ideal are involved in connection with different problems. Some concern broad approaches to educational change, others help establish the working rules of individual practice, and some propose experiments in educational practices and institutions.

The whole expansion of education during the past half-century has its manifest dimension that was a response to the ideal of equality. While the expansion answered the needs of technological change for a more educated or better trained work force and for wider participation, at the same time it brought secondary and higher schooling to vast numbers and whole classes that had hitherto had little schooling. Moreover the equalitarian ideal operated within schooling itself in the many movements to remove status distinctions in school structure. For example, in Britain there was a struggle over the comprehensive school to replace different schools that rested on typing abilities at an early age—the grammar, the technical, and the secondary-modern schools. In the United States a comparable tracking had existed in the separation of academic and vocational high schools. Of more special character have been the problems of discrimination against particular groups. These are problems of equality in general, and sometimes they are dealt with by specific interpretation of the meaning and conditions that support equality. Thus the 1954 decision of the United States Supreme Court that overturned segregated schooling for Blacks rested on the interpretation that "separate but equal" systems could not in reality provide equality.

Such operations of the ideal of equality are not to be seen as simple applications of a principle. In light of our analysis of the ideal, they express the effort of a people to meet its needs and problems in working for a better life, and constructing institutions to promote and support a better life. There is always then a background to refer to in deliberating about different proposed formulae of equality and different formulations in terms of which an issue is raised, as well as in assessing equalitarian proposals in relation to other ideals their implementation may affect. The many controversies that have centered around comprehensive schools or methods of integration are not to be reduced to meanings of "equality" nor to deductions from a rule of equality.[3] They always involve issues about the kind of life people are trying to live and toward which they aspire. Ultimately that is what being an ideal is about.

The working rules of individual practice often draw on equalitarian notions. These embody traditional ideals of fairness and ways of securing it. For example, a good teacher, like a good judge, is not biased in his or her relation to students, marks examinations blind, and so on. But the equalitarian approach goes beyond such standards into the context that they express. It inquires into the relation of teacher and student and asks what kind of authority is itself consonant with the ideal.

On the frontier of educational experiment, the ideal of equality can guide inquiry and critique, suggest alternatives worth trying out, and furnish a direction for evaluating the results. For example, if a contemporary equalitarianism has reservations about the meritocratic conception, it may be led to question the intense individualism of the current classroom. At present it is taken for granted that generally all individuals are working for themselves: they are learning individually and when they finish one lesson they go on to learn the next. Even the progressive idea that people should go ahead at their own paces is directed to enabling pupils to develop their own interests and abilities without loss of time or interest. (What one does for the group or the school is likely to be regarded as a duty, and of course one learns that one must do one's duty.) Now suppose the experiment is tried of recasting the whole approach, by thinking in terms of a group effort rather than a lone individual effort. Perhaps a class could work on the whole class's learning something, and as soon as some learned it they could devote themsleves to helping the rest learn it; helping others learn it could be an integral part of class procedure (just as reviewing a lesson and taking a test on it often is), and the class might operate as a group feeling responsible for everybody.[4] It might take a little longer, or again, it might turn out to take less time. Perhaps in any extra time a few other things would be learned: to be interested in classmates and their well-being, how to teach as well as how to learn, what kinds of troubles people have in learning and how to overcome them, how a group can work together, mutual sympathy for others with problems.

If we compare the two patterns, the self-regarding and the sharing, we cannot say that the one is equalitarian and the other not. The self-regarding emphasizes maximal opportunity for each to achieve what each one can. The sharing adds the emphasis on everybody's achieving something; it certainly does not intend to diminish the learning that the swifter learner achieves, although the exact effect of the changed procedure would have to be evaluated in practice. The self-regarding might get a similar learning result by being conjoined with a remedial program to bring everyone up to a predetermined minimum; this would achieve a floor equality. The sharing pattern has added a different dimension to equality, for different attitudes would develop and perhaps a different kind of individualism that could make a contribution to the quality of life that the equalitarian ideal expresses and is promoting. The sharing is not just adding fraternity to equality; it is giving equality itself a richer meaning.

The feasibility of the particular experiment would, of course, have to be determined in the first place, and its results evaluated. It might not advance the intended objectives; it might bring confusion and resentment instead of learning and mutual sympathy. If the objectives were advanced, the further question is whether it would have consequences inimical to other goals and ideals. The issue is not very different from the ones that have been debated concerning separate classes for highly gifted students. A strong case has been made for keeping the highly gifted within the general classes, in part because they raise the general level and in part because they are themselves saved from growing up in a hothouse atmosphere. It is thought better for their own social development, not a sacrifice simply for the sake of the average students. On the other side it has been argued that a greater intensity and a greater inventiveness would come from their constituting a separate group, that although it might tend to set them off from the rest, the returns to science and art and social thought would in the long run be better for society itself, particularly in view of the immensity of today's problems. Such an argument is directed to the external costs of application of equality in a particular direction; it further suggests that the costs will frustrate or at least retard the solution of the very problems to which equality is addressed.

Different moves are possible in such a complex evaluation. Some stay within the ideal of equality: for example, the problem may be divided by keeping gifted students within the general group in their early years and then separating them in their later years. The dividing line could come when learning turns to systematic subjects rather than general skills and projects. Even separate groups throughout could be regarded, on the argument given, as a compromise, just as a democracy compromises out of military necessity when it has a nondemocratic structure within the armed forces. On the other hand, the evaluation may bring the confrontation of different ideals, or at least a problem of weighting values in holding to both ideals. Thus the defender of separate classes for gifted children might argue that knowledge and its advance are of greater weight than social sympathy. If this is proposed as the basis of decision, then a fuller analysis of the ideal of knowledge, comparable to that we have attempted for equality is required (cf. chapter 13). The base or foundations of both have to be examined to see whether there is overlap in problems and underlying needs, how far common objectives can guide the evaluation, what the consequences of different proposed practices will be. A continual theoretical refinement and exploratory practice is directed toward the relations of the two ideals, with the hope of diminishing points of conflict. No crucial experiment to decide between them in general is envisaged, nor are we called on to make a comparable general decision between two different forms of equality.

A strong temptation is found in contemporary educational controversy to oversimplify evaluation by formulating the present frontier in the move to equality as a choice between two conflicting principles labeled *equality of opportunity* and *equality of results*.[5] The former, as a stratum in the development of the ideal of equality, and its relation to the meritocratic concept have already been considered. The latter is a general notion suggesting that the mass of the people, finding that equality of opportunity has not given them the benefits they hoped for, demand those benefits directly irrespective of the character of the process by which the distribution is achieved. In economic matters it has a possible interpretation in programs for transfer of income through taxation to secure redistribution: some social welfare institutions redistribute in favor of the disadvantaged; tariffs and subsidies to industry and agriculture can be seen as income transfer to industrialists and farmers. Education too may be seen in economic terms as a redistributive mechanism, not only in the greater earning power it makes possible for some but in the initial costs of schooling. Studies of the distribution of public funds for higher education suggest that there is an income transfer from the working class to the middle class, for the proportion of middle-class students in the colleges and universities is very much greater. (Whether and where income transfer is a useful general category for economic descriptive analysis is a separate question.)

The current contrast of equality of opportunity with equality of results somehow suggests that a finite store of achievable results in education is being raided on behalf of those with lower abilities—with disastrous consequences. The educational phenomena pointed to are changes in educational practices: the movement to advance every student through the school system whether he or she makes the grade or not, to do away with tests and testing, to open all doors wide, to relax standards, eventually to regard any judgment as good as any other if it is sincere. Sincerity and voluntarism replace ability and knowledge, it is claimed, just as in the history of politics voting and the will of the majority replaced confidence in the ruling class as knowing what is best for the public. This shift, it is argued, may have some justification in matters of public policy that affect people's whole lives, but in education the basic concern is with objective truth and standards of quality in scholarship that cannot be settled by voting. Education thus seems to be called upon today to choose between a guiding ideal of equality of opportunity and one of equality of results.

Each of the items in the list of phenomena under consideration is, of course, a serious one: automatic advancement, criticisms of testing, criticisms of traditional standards, the place of authority. The crucial question is whether the particular issues are fruitfully formulated by being lined up under the rubric of wanting to make all persons equal. There are limited areas in which getting a similar result for all may be the objective: for example, wiping out illiteracy for as great a part of the population as possible. This is not necessarily conceived as equality of results. It may be thought of as providing a necessary condition of opportunity for whatever race a person is to run in a complex society, and therefore under equality of opportunity. Or it may be conceived as getting rid of a great social evil, on a health model, comparable to wiping out measles or smallpox. In fact such analogies played a part in the thinking of U.S. government officials in funding educational experiments for compensatory education for the disadvantaged in the 1960s. It does not follow that because it is applied to illiteracy it will also hold for learning to play some musical instrument: there the equality may lie simply in every child's being exposed to music as an experience, or even in those with a special gift not being kept by poverty or discrimination from getting appropriate training. Of course there may be particular points at which a choice can be subsumed under the opposition of opportunity or results: for example, if there are competency tests given at graduation, one approach may bid farewell to those who fail; another may want to give a second or third chance, with public support for remedial work. Actually, depending on the analysis of causes of failure and costs of remedial work, this could follow on an opportunity approach as well. So we have here a particular experiment rather than an automatic subsumption under a general philosophy.

Grouping together the various phenomena under the single rubric of guaranteeing results without regard to the ways in which the results are achieved may contain a useful warning not to neglect the encouragement of ability. This is, however, a separable criterion relevant to any educational practice. The general opposition of the two types of equality is reminiscent of the nineteenth-century battles of liberty versus equality and is probably the twentieth-century heir of this conservative-liberal conflict. If we have analyzed correctly the way in which ideals are evaluated and the manner in which different stages in the development of the ideal of equality enter into educational practice, any attempt to force a general choice between the principles or slogans poses a trap for educational practice.

If our way of looking at the evaluation of equality is to prove fruitful, it must not merely help dispel misleading formulations but also help toward resolving impasses in practice. Let us look in conclusion at a specific controversy—that of affirmative action—in which the meaning and application of equality are involved.[6]

The practical dilemma of affirmative action, when posed as a question of the conflict of individual rights, is a familiar one. A program is formulated to eliminate the discrimination that has characterized the treatment of Blacks, or women, or some ethnic minority, to remove the consequences of the previous discrimination and help the designated group assume the place and participation it should have in the affairs of the society. As long as this effort consists only in providing training to bring people up to the level at which they may compete for positions—whether admission to professional schools or appointment to positions—there is likely to be little objection. When granting of any preference to the group constitutes part of the program, this is seen as reverse discrimination against Whites, men, etc. Faced with two individuals, A and B, is it equal treatment for A to have the benefit, other things being equal or equally satisfactory, simply in virtue of A's being Black or female or of a particular ethnic group and because the group as such has suffered under past discrimination? B claims now to be discriminated against—B has lived and prepared for the future under normal expectations, which are being violated by the reverse discrimination. The social result is a dilemma. If preferential consideration is construed in this way as reverse discrimination, then the only way in which the members of the designated group can gain entry is by winning out in individual competitions; in short, those who have had lesser opportunity in consequence of discrimination are compelled to be better to gain a place. This is even clearer in the labor situation where layoffs are taking place in reverse order of seniority: those whom discrimination kept from entry until recently, and who are therefore in a junior position, can keep a place only by being senior.

Of course there are many other controversial points, but this brief statement shows the impasse that follows from a formulation in terms of an individualistic model. When, however, equality is understood in the terms that our study is developing, then the initial problem is the social one of the entry of the excluded group into the full life of the society, and the provision of institutional arrangements and specific practices to ensure the result. The use of preferential consideration, where the question is not begged by seeing it from the beginning as reverse discrimination, is a familiar social instrument. Veterans' preference in employment and education, preference in college admissions for those with athletic skills, draft deferment on a variety of presumably socially important grounds are ways in which social practice routes benefits to some rather than others. They are no different in principle from the routing of jobs and profits that follows from tariffs and government subsidies. Indeed, the whole of college education when supported by the tax fund rests on the taxes of vast numbers who do not go to college; it can been seen as preferential consideration for a selection from the youth on presumably socially beneficial grounds. There can thus be no initial objection to practices that will secure the social objective of bringing the group hitherto discriminated against into full participation within the society. That some people will lose out in the process follows from the fact that there is preferential consideration. Morally and socially this is not essentially different from a segment of the community losing out by each act of the legislature that creates benefits to some in a special way. As far as expectations are concerned, a person's expectations of a teaching job or a medical training may be frustrated by inflationary pressures or economic recession wiping out the position or contracting admissions. If steps are warranted to compensate those who lose out, this is a social decision like the one to help groups that are particularly affected by a specific measure. Even more important, however, is the exercise of social imagination and inventiveness to reconstruct the situation, to break up problems and work out fresh techniques, conceptual and institutional alike, to diminish the burdens of change. Such initiative is less likely to flow from an approach through the conflict of individual rights, for it keeps the major conditions of discrimination in place until a creative solution should be discovered. The social approach, on the other hand, sets the reconstruction going and shifts the focus from a struggle over rights to action for resolution.

The analysis of the practice adopted in a particular corner of the field is to be carried out in terms of the history and needs and problems that impinge on that corner. This touches even the kind of model to be used in that area. Just as there is no contradiction in using a strict individual-rights approach in criminal justice and a more collective approach in determining the rules to govern automobile accident claims, so there is no contradiction in using the former approach for problems of dismissing teachers and the latter for rules governing appointments. It is simply that general welfare considerations weigh more heavily in one context while individual rights do in another—and both these policies are decided on the long-range well-being of the society. Preferential considerations for women in college appointments would not be in conflict with even preferential consideration for men in nursery school; the latter might be justified by psychological considerations and the present desire for greater participation by males in the care of children—the well-being of the children being a serious point at issue. So too, the role that a greater proportion of Black doctors could play in meeting the problems of the society might justify preferential consideration of Blacks to entry in medical school; or the size of a Spanish-speaking population in a U.S. community, the preference for Spanish-Americans in police appointment and retention; neither is different in type from cutting down the number of teachers in one department (whether by transfer or attrition) to appoint more in a newly opened department whose creation was socially and educationally desirable.

The use of general rules of affirmative action is, of course, a gross instrument, likely to work hardships on many. It is accordingly to be used only where no better way can be found. In contemporary practice it is resorted to when voluntary measures have failed to signal improvement and when the situation becomes one in which nothing otherwise will be done. Its justification is accordingly in the same social terms as are found in any serious social problem. Sometimes, as after a natural disaster, we have a declaration of a distressed area that entitles the area to special funds, attention, altered regulations, and the like. It is a mistake to seek some principle of eternal justice for the particular kind of disaster. So too it is a mistake to invent formulae of correct proportion, such as that 50 percent of the jobs in any area should be held by women, or a similar proportionate share by each ethnic group. Any use of formula in affirmative action can only be as a shock to achieve a breakthrough, not to establish permanent ratios. Once the discrimination and its lingering effects are gone, the needs of the position and whatever chance distribution of abilities there may be could operate freely.

To approach the problem at every point in this way gets rid also of the claim that when affirmative action is resorted to it should be used for every single group that can show discrimination. The use of remedying instruments is also a function of the concrete sociohistorical analysis. Some groups may require only the lifting of discriminatory barriers to make their way to full participation in some fields. Some require only special stimulation in addition. The decision as to which instrument to use is as plainly an instrumental one as deciding strategy and tactics in campaigns of politics or wars or road building. Affirmative action is a moderately severe instrument. It is no more severe than compulsory schooling or high taxation or turning over an occupational field to union hiring halls when the entry to the union is limited. The importance of affirmative action, compared to these other cases, is that at the present time it is concerned with the frontier of the movement toward greater equality. Its moral force comes from that enterprise in which it is engaged.

Notes

1. For a fuller treatment of the criteria in assessing ideals, see Abraham Edel, *Method in Ethical Theory* (Indianapolis: Bobbs-Merrill; London: Routledge & Kegan Paul, 1963), ch. 15.

2. Illustrations can be found in some of the positions presented or discussed in the following papers: Aharon F. Kleinberger, "Reflections on Equality in Education," *Studies in Philosophy and Education* 5 (Summer 1967): 293-340; John R. Perry, "Equality and Education: Remarks on Kleinberger," ibid. (Fall 1967): 433-46; Kleinberger's reply, "Equality and Educational Policy: A Rejoiner," ibid., 6 (Spring 1968): 209-25; Robert H. Ennis, "Equality of Educational Opportunity," in *Ethics and Educational Policy*, ed. Kenneth Strike and Kieran Egan (London: Routledge & Kegan Paul, 1978). Cf. James Coleman, "The Concept of Equality of Educational Opportunity," *Harvard Educational Review* 38, no. 1 (1968): 7-22.

3. For an illustration of the philosophical controversy, compare David Rubinstein and Colin Stoneman, eds., *Education for Democracy* (Baltimore: Penguin, 1970), and Anthony Flew, *Sociology, Equality and Education: Philosophical Essays in Defense of a Variety of Differences* (New York: Barnes & Noble, 1976). For a general study of the effect of selective systems and comprehensive or inclusive systems, see Torsten Husén, *Talent, Equality and Meritocracy* (*Europe 2000*, Project 1, Educating Man for the 21st Century, vol. 9), (The Hague: Martinus Nijhoff, 1974). Husén's overall conclusion (p. 124) is that the comprehensive system "is a more effective strategy in taking care of all the talent of a nation." For detailed studies of the two systems in the production of mathematicians, see Torsten Husén,

ed., *International Study of Educational Achievement in Mathemetics: A Comparison of Twelve Countries*, 2 vols. (New York: John Wiley & Sons, 1967).

4. A less drastic change, which stays within the individualistic but not competitive motivation, is found in experiments with "mastery learning." Cf. *Mastery Learning, Theory and Practice*, ed. James H. Block (New York: Holt, Rinehart & Winston, 1971). The fundamental shift in perspective is to assume that most students are capable of learning and that aptitudes predict the rate at which a person could learn a given task. Hence the burden is thrown on the other factors, such as quality of instruction, use of supplementary methods, ensuring listening comprehension. The essential procedure is to break up learning tasks into well-defined units (e.g. two-week units), employ systematically arranged materials, and proceed to each later step only after the earlier is achieved. (Pupils who finish a step earlier spend their time in enrichment study of the topic.) It relies in part on the development of techniques in programmed learning. An important factor in the shift of perspective is to use ongoing "formative" evaluation, which directs what to do next, rather than "summative" evaluation, which reports on total success or failure. The approach attempts to shed the grading that places people in relation to others, which is seen to have affective consequences deleterious to learning.

5. Robert Nisbet, in *Twilight of Authority* (New York: Oxford University Press, 1975), ch. 4, launches an all-out attack on equality of results. He centers the attack on Rawls's theory of justice, interpreting it as giving the fullest expression to this principle. Christopher Jencks and others, *Inequality: A Reassessment of the Effect of Family and Schooling in America* (New York: Harper, Colophon Books, 1973), a widely discussed study in the mid-1970s, does not advocate a systematic equality of results in educational policy. Its point is rather that the schools do not overcome the basic inequality in the society, and so those who want to achieve greater equality would better do this more directly by governmental income transfers.

6. For a fuller discussion, see Abraham Edel, "Preferential Consideration and Justice," in *Social Justice and Preferential Treatment: Women and Racial Minorities in Education and Business*, ed. William T. Blackstone and Robert F. Heslep (Athens: University of Georgia Press, 1977), pp. 111-34. Reprinted in Abraham Edel, *Science, Ideology, and Value*, vol. 2, *Exploring Fact and Value* (New Brunswick, N.J.: Transaction Books, 1980), ch. 15.

7. Toward a Moral Agenda for Contemporary Education

This chapter has to do the heavy work of providing a moral agenda for contemporary education, or at least show how to get it. Now, a moral agenda differs from simply the mass of ideals, goals, and values that may be invoked as relevant to education. It differs in its selective character; it spots those among all these ideals, goals, and values that have a special pertinence to time and place and current problems. It talks of the relation of values to probable trends, necessities and unavoidables, likelihood of attainment, what is urgent or postponable. It does not simply attempt to rank values in general in some hierarchical order—for example, that beauty is higher than physical exercise or that ends are higher than means. Moral philosophers have often pointed out that the requirements relevant to safety and survival, because they are most pressing, enter more compellingly into our moral obligations than do the higher values. If we have to choose between removing the lead or asbestos in a classroom environment or acquiring beautiful pictures to hang on the walls, our duty will be, *ceteris paribus*, the former first.

To determine what goes on the moral agenda obviously requires criteria for selection. Writers on education have often thought that such criteria could be readily determined by inquiring into education itself. For example, if we could only get clear about the *aims* of education we should know what to steer toward; we would have an intellectual sieve through which to strain proposals. However, there are controversies not only about aims but even whether education has aims. (Cf. the controversies in Appendix B.) Another proposal is to convert the large bills of aims into the small change of all that people (parents, children, teachers, citizens generally) *want* out of the schools. We would have then to look at motives, efforts, concerns, interests—a helpful and interesting sociological array, but more likely to provide a mass of values rather than a basis for critical evaluation. A more subtle suggestion sends us on the roundabout route of defining "education" or "an educated person" on the assumption that we will then have a view of the process or the end state with the basic value components spread out. This may have the merit of taking us eventually to the particular values or things worthwhile that we associate with education. However, it still leaves us to explore why such worthwhile things should be sought through these special processes and why other worthwhile things are not invoked.

It is much more likely that a search for a set of criteria to provide a moral agenda for contemporary education has to begin with the needs and problems of the community and then go to the special relevance of educational processes. In dealing with educational ideals (chapter 6) we found it best first to go to human ideals and then ask which had a special appropriateness for education. The same lesson applies to any major proposal for reorientation of work in the schools. Suppose it is proposed to shift significant resources to computer education. How would this be justified in comparison, for example, with the demand that we upgrade the teaching of foreign languages? We would have to explore the emerging role of the computer in the whole range of contemporary technology, industry, and life in general. We would have to reassess the need for a wider knowledge and use of foreign languages in relation to our political and social life in a growingly interconnected world, as well as the cultural benefits that would result. Then we would have to examine how far these needs could be met by social institutions and practices outside the schools, and whether it is better to turn the schools in these directions.

If such inquiries are to be carried out systematically, we have to look for a conceptual tool that will help us establish priorities and guide policy decisions in ethics. Let us call such a tool a *valuational base*, to mean a basic set of constituents (needs, values, instrumentalities, and so forth) that can furnish criteria for judgments of policy. (This concept was proposed in *Ethical Judgment: The Use of Science in Ethics.*)[1] In the remainder of this chapter we shall examine the constituents of such a valuational base, how it is constructed, and then how it can be utilized to provide a moral agenda for contemporary education.

A Valuational Base for the Contemporary World

At least four constituents play a part in a valuational base: universal needs, perennial aspirations and major goals, central necessary conditions, and critical contingent factors. These provide neither a full inventory of the good nor a scheme to be applied mechanically with a built-in solution for every problem; they function primarily as a basis for critical judgment. They embody an interlocking structure of knowledge and striving. Even what appear to be its nonvalue components already have interwoven or fused values: a need is such because if not satisfied certain goods will be thwarted; and even contingent factors incorporated into the base are critical because they threaten a mass of values (for example, the danger of the ship's sinking or a nuclear war's breaking out). In constructing the base we may also expect that the human sciences play an increasing role. As knowledge grows and changes there is refinement and modification, just as the existent body of scientific knowledge at any time is altered. Similarly, as human problems are shown in experience to take new historical form and human aspirations shift in specific direction, the valuational base may be reflectively reconstructed to conform to the results of continuing value experience. It is no substitute for the creativity that human valuation involves but helps to guide it.

Two questions may be asked about the construction of a valuational base: why fix upon these four factors, and how do we decide the content under each? These questions may be answered together, illustrating with content first from the midcentury and then with changes prompted by the experience of several decades. In general, factors are qualified by being the dynamic and problem-generating aspects of life at the time. Universal needs can be counted on, if correctly diagnosed, to be always present and operative, sometimes directly and sometimes in distorted form when direct expression is thwarted. The reach of such needs in the disruption nonsatisfaction creates and in solving or eliminating widespread problems can be best seen in cases where they are freshly discovered—for example, that for vitamins among biological needs and that for affiliation or affectionate warmth among psychological needs. (For the latter, see below on the mandate to mute the competitive character of our culture.) Perennial aspirations and major goals are those among people's ideals and purposes that have or acquire a pressing or dynamic character from being intertwined with a vast array of objectives and values; the career of the ideal of equality discussed in the preceding chapter is an excellent illustration. Central necessary conditions are precisely the ones required for a broad achievement of values, however diverse these may be; peace, internal order, employment, education are obvious examples in modern times, and the need of a country to industrialize has generally been taken to be a pivotal one. Here again the correct means may not always be read off from prevalent beliefs; for example, the devotion of all effort to military victory over others has often usurped a place in this factor, and only bitter subsequent experience has shown that the problems at which the means were directed have not disappeared. Finally, critical contingent factors are those emergencies that demand attention because of the ramification of problems they generate: for example, drought or plague at some times and places, the need for land reform in some countries, critical overpopulation in others.

In some respects a valuational base constructed for a given period may be compared to a party platform, if the latter is taken in a serious and not a demagogic sense. It is not supposed to be just bait to different interests in the country to enable the party to win an election but a presentation of major and central diagnosis and policies to meet the pressing needs and problems of the country. It is intended to guide conduct and action and act as a base for evaluating results while itself being tested by the general satisfactoriness of the results. Of course any particular construction of a valuational base may be strongly ideological, but the purpose in the construction (and certainly it presents itself as such) is to achieve a *correct* analysis and to incorporate the best available knowledge of the time. It does rest on shared values but not in all respects, for some of the claims are about what is required no matter how diverse the values involved.

The transformations in our mode of life in the twentieth century show the need for the kind of systematic reconstruction that a valuational base offers. We have moved from a world that was local and isolated in its outlook to one that is worldwide in its perspective. From being centered in one culture, we have become aware of many cultures and their interaction; from thinking of one religious tradition, we have come to acknowledge the varied and the secular. A basically agricultural world has moved in many regions toward an urban and a posturban society. In spite of innumerable problems, a rapid extension of technology first opened up a vista of abundance and then intensified the problems that would limit such a vista; hence the tasks posed by technology are among the most serious. Our world has witnessed the rise of the masses demanding a share in power and strong enough not to be gainsaid, even if not organized enough to win out. As a result, the older ideal of acknowledged authority is replaced by an ideal of democracy, whose clarification becomes a pressing need. A world of established inequalities and discriminations has been forced by an apparently endless succession of liberation movements to focus on an ideal of equality. Confidence in a stable pattern has yielded to an expectation of change, perhaps even to a worship of change.

Such central changes locate where we have to look for important elements in constructing a valuational base. We need not, of course, accept every change as good. Indeed, sometimes a powerful trend may be seen as a critical factor that requires summoning all our energies in confrontation. But one way or another we have to reckon with it. On the other hand, some changes may be continuous with age-old aspirations, as a global perspective is continuous with humanity's long dream of universal kinship. After centuries in which it had the status of an impractical ideal, it may now be included in the valuational base because realistic material grounds make it relevant to the solution of pressing problems.

That the contents of a valuational base are subject to further critique and refinement, with possibilities of disagreement, may be illustrated from the changes of the last quarter of a century. With the development of nuclear energy and the expansion of technology after World War II, a governing moral ideal was the expansion of abundance, the industrialization of the underdeveloped parts of the world, and the provision of basic security for all peoples. With the tremendous growth of population, the promise of nuclear energy turning sour, and the discovery of the dangers of pollution and exhaustion of resources implicit in operating large-scale technology, the general idea of limits has permeated the intellectual horizon to put in jeopardy long-standing assumptions of progress. In reconstructing the valuational base we have therefore to decide whether a central ideal should be sober planned advances or belt-tightening and resignation. This involves such questions as: How much of the present concern with limits is ideological in character reflecting present economic-political struggles? Will the not-too-distant course of science provide a source of clean energy (e.g. solar) to remove a central trouble source in present basic difficulties? How far have present difficulties come from our traditional institutions and practices rather than from physical and environmental sources? The interrelation of scientific knowledge and fundamental value policy in the base is evident.

Similar inquiries are needed for the continuation of technological development and the expansion of equality and democratization within the valuational base. A decision to include or retain technological development as a central demand would have to deal with the attacks on technology in the contemporary milieu and successfully distinguish the kind of automation in which the machine becomes an extension of the person from the kind in which the person becomes an extension of the machine. It would have to work out a concept of technology that freed it from one particular form—for example, large-scale centralized technology—as the only viable possibility; and it would have to distinguish between technological necessities and associated possibly changeable institutional forms in which technology has been embedded. It would have to consider the impact of technological necessities on the mass of values and discern alternative possible effects on the way we live.

With respect to both equality and democratization, the last quarter of a century has provided increasingly stronger grounds for their place in the valuational base. In the case of racial equality, we have moved from acknowledgment of its necessity and the condemnation of remaining pockets of apartheid to the realization of the vast effort required to make a reality of a thoroughgoing equalitarian program. Sexual equality has moved into the foreground, and the demand is not only for its achievement in obviously practical ways but also for the sensitive exploration of the scope of discrimination in innumerable aspects of thought and feeling. Demands for racial and sexual equality today occupy a large part of the moral space.

Democratization too is far less challenged today than it was a quarter of a century ago, but it does not thereby drop out of the valuational base, for its acceptance is still narrow in practice and often only verbal in allegiance. The ideal still demands detailed practical clarification as a guide in the welter of controversies about increased participation in controlling policy and determining the forms of associated living.

Finally, we should note that the orientation of the valuational base itself involves the same kind of inquiry and validation as its constituents. Even now there remains the choice whether it is to be constructed as a valuational base for limited groups, such as nations, or a common-human base for humankind at the present stage of its development. Grounds for the latter rest on the degree of integration of the world in material conditions and communications, as well as in the emerging proportion of national interests that depend on common programs. With this are of course associated the age-old conceptions of the unity of humankind, and the growing scientific knowledge of the common-human tasks that have to be carried out for the preservation of the species. Both a sober realism and a mature idealism seem to dictate a global rather than a national perspective, with the requirements of the more limited groupings to find a place within the total ethic.

The development of a valuational base for the contemporary world clearly remains a gigantic ethical task. It is not, however, the subject of this book, and to pursue it would postpone immeasurably our educational considerations. In proceeding now to a moral agenda for contemporary education, I shall therefore assume certain conclusions about the valuational base: it will be a common-human one in essentials; it will include, in addition to familiar perennial goals and basic needs (some of which will be discussed in what follows), the special requirements of technological development, equalitarian expansion, and democratization; also, these are set within a scheme of decision in which judgments can be made about enhancement of the quality of associated living.

Normative judgments in education embrace perennial elements long established and novel elements. The former are likely to find expression in educational statements about helping students acquire the knowledge, skills, and attitudes that will enable them to develop their abilities and lead satisfying lives in the modern world. By this time such educational statements will have in mind three areas: knowledge and skills pertinent to science and technology; the management of individual and social life; the engagement of cultural life. In the case of schooling, the specific content of these areas—the kinds of values involved and their interrelations—should guide the determination of curriculum. Some general aspects of this will be considered in part IV. The novel elements can best be discerned when they serve as guides for specific reconstruction over a wide range of educational activity. Of the eight topics that are here considered, some deal with familiar material and can be briefly sketched. Others, however, involve important tasks of reconstruction and require more extended treatment. The themes that give rise to mandates on the moral agenda are: global perspective; expanded equality; more thorough democratization; sensitive response to modern technological economy; second look at our competitive culture; cultivating a sense of community; restoration of humanistic quality; and reassessment of the institution of schooling. Chapter 8 will suggest three further items of a different sort for the moral agenda.

Cultivate a Global Perspective

A morality in which everybody counts (not simply the members of some partial grouping like kin or village or race or nation) is an old story. It is a minimal morality of the kinship of humanity, not requiring that beyond this mutual recognition all people share the same morality. It reaches back to parts of the Old Testament, to the Stoic philosophers after Alexander's conquests broke out of Greek parochialism, to the universal fellowship of the New Testament and early Christianity. It scales new theoretical heights in the eighteenth-century Enlightenment. In ethics both Bentham and Kant then speak for all people, different as their moral philosophy may be in other respects. Bentham has every person count as one and no more than one, and Kant's goodwill legislates for all humankind in its moral decisions. (Indeed Kant ascribes this to every rational being, not just to humans—if somewhere there be rational beings that are not humans.) In the linguistically oriented moral philosophies of the twentieth century, universalization has been built into the very moral language: part of the meaning of "ought," we are told repeatedly, is that if I ought to do X, then everyone else in the same situation is also obligated to do X.

It is easier for such an equalitarian "brotherhood of man" (or perhaps we ought to say "siblinghood of humankind") to conquer theory and language than to take over human reality in conduct and policy. But the evidence of history is at least a sign of deep-seated aspiration that gives a moral quality to the ideal of human kinship. Sociological scanning of history can note how the in-group grew in extent from the earliest days in which only the kingroup constituted the moral community and the stranger or outsider was fair game, through the territorial unifications of city and country, up to the growing interrelations of economy and communication that now give a strong appearance of one world. Yet the nineteenth and the twentieth centuries have unleashed the most serious forms of nationalism and the most virulent forms of racism.

In spite of these recessions in the growing ideal of human kinship, the pace of interconnection in the globe gives the extension of the moral community to include all human beings the character of an imperative on the moral agenda of our time. It may be premature to state it in a way that overrides all narrower moral claims—the legitimate claims of family, friendship, locality, nation, and other less than universal groupings. Perhaps these can be stated as exceptions or countervailing considerations under universalization formulae; or perhaps differences in the context of application might reconcile conflicts. At the very least, the consequences of any social policy or program have to be worked out far enough to see what they would do to others throughout the world. (Country A cannot simply claim the right to dam the upper part of a river that runs through country B as well, and so ruin B's agriculture for A's own benefit.)[2]

How would a global attitude as a moral imperative affect, say, the more familiar aspects of our schooling? Geography would be taught from a cosmic-global perspective, culture more from a comparative anthropological perspective, history from a world rather than a Western view. Even familiar books on philosophical history would no longer be called "A History of Philosophy" but (as Bertrand Russell called his book) "A History of Western Philosophy." More crucially, the way national patriotism has been imparted in the past to the teaching of civics in text and ceremonial would certainly require many changes. It would mean learning to look at ourselves, in part seeing ourselves as others see us. It would no longer be, as the old slogan had it, "My country, right or wrong" but with the addition that Carl Schurz provided (in 1899), "When right to be kept right, when wrong to be put right." And part of the right or wrong would be the effect on humankind at large.

It is easy to put a global perspective on the moral agenda. The task is to work out its implications in all corners of educational practice.

Expand Equality

We have seen in a previous chapter what the movement for human equality entails as an ideal, how in the last two centuries it has summoned the deepest moral energies of people and in our time has issued in one liberation movement after another. Little argument is needed to see the removal of the remaining discriminations on grounds of race, color, class, sex, ethnic origin, religion, and so on as high among the tasks imposed on present generations.

The discriminations to be removed run through the whole of society and its institutions—business, labor, political life, family, and associations, as well as schooling. While much of the task of removing discrimination involves legal and political action, a pervasive part falls to the lot of education. The battle against discrimination has to take place in the media (newspapers, journals, movies, television, radio) and in the variety of cultural forms. Much of it is properly carried out in political campaigns and in the internal conflicts within unions and associations. In all these education is closely tied to manifold forms of social action.

The schools have been a particularly central scene of conflicts about discrimination, not only with respect to the character of teaching but also with respect to policies of admission and treatment. The attempt to provide schooling for all the young is itself a fairly recent one, and given the growth of population, it has required tremendous expansion in the last half-century. In many countries, the idea that the masses should be educated is itself a novel one. Moreover, the idea of equality has meant that the same type of education should be open to all, not a first-class education for the upper class and some substitute for the poor, say, some immediately applicable job training.

Expanding equality is constantly relevant also because implementing it is a long and difficult task. It will take decades to complete educational integration of Black youth, primarily because economic equality, upon which educational equality depends, is not sufficiently advanced. Everywhere the movement for equality of the sexes in education is only in its infancy; even where it has been formally granted, old habits linger and much discrimination of which we are unconscious remains embedded in theory as well as in practice. And so on for other forms of inequality and discrimination.

The heritage of the past in unequal treatment is often a welter of present problems for which present solutions may be difficult and involve conflicts of interest. There have to be sacrifices and compromises and experiments. In some cases the outline of a solution may even be unclear. One of the most serious involves ethnic pluralism. In some countries one ethnic group's dominating and repressing another is the source of grievance and rebellion. In others, such as Canada and Belgium, a policy of dual cultures is found. In the United States, assimilation was for a long time the approved policy (except with respect to Blacks). Now almost everywhere a vigorous pluralism seems to be the order of the day. Of course the phenomenon requires separate exploration in each context, and perhaps for each ethnic group. In one case it may be a long-standing isolation on the part of a group, in another a response to special outer pressures or a revolt against second-class status. Now a schooling policy like bilingual education, currently found in the United States, may be a transitory device whereby students who do not know English are taught in another language (e.g. Spanish, Korean, French) until they learn English. Or it may be the beginnings of a dual school system, that would support a linguistic-cultural pluralism in enclaves where there are large ethnic groups speaking a different language. Discussions about ethnicity have tended largely to stress the values of rootedness against assimilation. They have looked backward to preserving different traditions in isolation but not forward to consider the kind of common life that a pluralistic society can have and how different traditions that are preserved may share in a common culture. This remains a philosophical task and there is no easy answer.[3]

The variety of problems in education that invoke equality as a guiding principle and their scope throughout the school system guarantee that this standard will have a busy time in the next few decades. Its theoretical clarification in terms of human moral and historical aspirations can be brought to bear on the educational problems, but the educational issues and results can also contribute both understanding and data. It is important to know whether traditional cultural materials can have universal appeal, as has been assumed; in what ways equal treatment improves learning; whether full equality of treatment of the sexes is sufficient to remove the restricted self-image that unequal treatment has imposed on girls; and so on. We may expect that the meaning of equality will be enriched as it is applied to specific educational problems.

Deepen Democratization

That some political and social form will belong in the valuational base as a necessary condition for social organization is to be expected. The long lessons of human experience combined with the history of ethical analysis of political life point today to democratic forms, whether regarded as means or as containing elements of intrinsic value. We need not recapitulate the evidence of the failure of reliance on wisdom of the few, from whatever walks of life; of the growing powers of control in modern life and the dangers of a manipulated closed society; of the growing conviction that an open society with an increasingly enlightened citizenry controlling its own destiny still remains the best alternative among available political-social forms. On such an assumption, education gets the general assignment implicit in the notion of *a responsible enlightened citizenry.*

If the concept of democracy were perfectly clear, this assignment would rank among the perennial tasks of education rather than a principle of contemporary reconstruction. What reason is there, then, to put deepening democractization on the agenda? The answer can be read from the history of democracy in the twentieth century. Seen as the wave of the future in the period of World War I, it was thereafter attacked as weakness and chaos by fascism and as a bourgeois facade by communism. It recovered confidence during the 1930s in the development of welfare functions on the economic front and in the successes of World War II. The political development of the Third World brought the lesson that there were cultural conditions requisite for the operations of democracy; it was a cultural, not a native product. Growing sociological and psychological studies of attitudes and group formations and personality structures added to the view that more than politics was involved in the functioning of democracy. And fundamental to the story was the internal drive to democracy in the whole history of its growth: democracy had been fought for not only because it meant freeing people from previous shackles but because it promised a structure and character by which people could move forward into what they hoped would be new and more satisfying ways of life. If existing democratic forms failed to achieve this, then people would seek an extension of democracy or else abandon it. Thus in the nineteenth century when political democracy did not lighten the lot of the masses, we see the beginnings of social democracy and of socialism viewed as the extension of democracy into economic life. Twentieth-century debates still go in such terms, and in liberal democratic countries of Western Europe today intermediate experiments are advocated and attempted in various forms of worker participation in economic management.

The concept of democracy itself has long reflected these historical processes. It has moved from a narrower political sense to a broader sense in which it designates a social outlook. As a restricted political form, it is rule by the people as against rule by the few. A detailed account of it would concern mode of rule, minority rights, direct and representative forms, and so on. As a social outlook it would include ideals and principles, attitudes and character, and method, as well as fundamentals of government and control. This wider sense is usually intended when we speak of education for democracy or democracy in education. The traditional ideals are liberty or freedom and equality, with occasionally nominal deference to fraternity, and all against a background of individualism. The attitudes and character traits are those that fit these ideals and principles, for example a sense of responsibility, readiness to participate, individual initiative, deliberative or rational discussion and decision, with civility and a readiness to cooperate as contrasted with a ready resort to violence.

While this broad outline of democracy is now clear and generally accepted, its implications and presuppositions need further exploration. A deeper analysis is required for its ideals, a more historical and functional investigation of its governmental principles, and a more sensitive assessment of its character values. In general, the question has not been fully faced whether democracy as a way of life expresses a specialized cultural setting in which highly individualistic values are prevalent, or whether it can be generalized over widely different cultural forms. While this might seem to be of more immediate concern to India or China in their modernization than to Western Europe or the United States, it would be a mistake so to regard it. The same kind of questions have to be answered to know whether our democratic individualism is, for example, tied to free enterprise economic forms, whether a democratic socialism is possible, whether a transnational corporatism is reconcilable with an intranational individualism, and so on. The program for theoretical work is therefore large. On the practical side, the dilemma of democracy can be read from daily events. We are told that there is a general disillusionment about electoral processes and a loss of confidence in leadership. A growing tendency bypasses the legislature where possible to put an important measure to direct initiative (especially in California), and it is debated whether this is more or less democratic. Similarly, the question is argued whether complete publicity is a mark of democracy.

Another aspect of increasing importance is the attempt to apply democratic ideas not only in politics at large but within the operation of institutions. For example, even where agreement exists on the general aim of more democratic governance within universities, questions arise about the role of students, junior faculty, senior faculty, administration. What weight is to be given to the longer-range commitment of faculty as compared to the shorter-range commitment of a student generation, to the experience of research faculty as compared to the numerical weight or often the fresh though untried ideas of junior faculty, to the practical experience of laboratory assistants and service personnel? The idea of a community with different functions but without elite ordering easily gets into oversimplified shortcuts (such as reliance on simple majority voting) and calls for greater exploratory practice with a strong measure of goodwill. Comparable problems arise in many other institutions, and most seriously in those such as business and corporate bodies in which strict hierarchical patterns and conflicts of interest between workers and managers have been traditional.

While some remains of older antidemocratic outlooks are to be found gloating in the chaos that sometimes results, the dominant evaluation tends to be a positive one. Deepening democracy belongs in the valuational base because it is seen as carrying through the hopes that the introduction of democracy brought into the Western world but did not sufficiently achieve. The diagnosis of the failures of democracy have been not that democracy failed but that it was not sufficiently tried, that it should be extended into institutions other than the narrow political ones in which it was introduced, that the same powers that were driven from politics were left in control of economic life, education, and the remaining social institutions. Hence education has not merely the perennial task to create a responsible enlightened citizenry but the task to forge the special reconstructive standard by which to judge its work, a more thorough democratization.

Just as in the case of removing discriminations, education for and in democracy belongs in all the institutions and cultural media of society. Vital learning about democracy and competing conceptions comes in political struggles, in the fashioning of union policies, in the experience of domination in the workplace, in the controversies found in the media, and so forth. But the centrality of public schooling as an institution has given a special status to its curriculum and operation, so that the slogan of teaching for democracy and cultivating democratic attitudes is usually referred to the schools. Some points have been obvious, such as concern with the individual child in programs of progressive education, or the changed attitude toward students and the rights of students that replaced the older notion that the teacher stands *in loco parentis*, which used to prevail even in higher education. Some questions were tackled systematically under the rebellion of the 1960s, such as the place of students in the governance of schools. In general, much of the older authoritarianism is on the way out in educational theory, but it is still entrenched in the habits of practice. This lends a special importance to projecting further democratization into the moral agenda for education. Some additional consideration of the problem will be found in chapter 9.

Shape a Responsible Technology

Technological development underlies the possibilities of a more satisfying life, however different people's aims may be and their specific values, and however varied the interpretations of the technology and its social conditions. And of course an important part of the technological development lies in the requisite scientific and technological knowledge and skills. Education responded historically to the growth of industry and its numerous demands for a work force and diverse skills and attitudes; the spread of schooling came in this context, and many of the criticisms of education were directed at this orientation.

The development of a responsible technology is central not simply because it is important to human welfare on a wide scale but because of its ramifications and the multitude of tasks it imposes. Education is needed to counter assumptions about technological development that have occupied the scene without possibly more humane alternatives having been considered. For example, the image of technology has been that of a larger and larger system that imposes its demands on all people and coordinates their life to these demands. This is only beginning to be challenged by ideas of "intermediate technology" or "technology with a human face." (Technological changes may themselves help in this; for example, robotics allows of greater flexibility compared to the straitjacket of mass production techniques.) Again, technology has been associated with sprawling urbanization and with overcrowding and pollution; these problems are now beginning to be better understood and alternatives envisaged. The popular strength of the environmental movement is evidence of the need for bringing ideas of the quality of life to bear on judgments about technology. Similar questions arise about the association of technological advance with any one economic system, such as capitalism; or with any one philosophy of history, such as continual growth or the view that anything technologically possible must be produced and if produced then used; and so on. Again, the rapidity of change in technology has tremendous social consequences in employment and the obsolescence of skills, so that readjustments are needed and should be anticipated wherever possible. Moreover, the social and moral consequences of technological changes should be followed up lest we be caught unawares, as our society was with the development of the automobile or again with that of communication and the media, where we discovered the effects belatedly. Because of all these ramifications and the need to monitor them and not to abdicate moral judgment of technologies, and yet because of the importance of technological development to our lives as a whole, the imperative of a responsible technology is definitely on the agenda.

One phase of the development of science and technology is often neglected. We are accustomed to their rapid advance and to fresh problems at each stage; the solution of the problems usually requires fresh invention. A responsible technology thus has to include a mandate to advance knowledge. That this has not been systematically provided for in the uncontrolled workings of our economy does not change the fact that we often count upon the results. This is most dramatically evident in agriculture, when an unexpected insect form threatens a crop, or in medicine when some new disease demands a new form of antibiotic or vaccine.

Education thus receives as its standard of judgment with respect to technology not merely to provide knowledge, skills, and attitudes that science and technology require but to make a sensitive determination of the kind of response needed. In one respect, education is very fortunate nowadays: the rapidity of technological advance makes it no longer feasible to educate for specific jobs, so there is less reason for education to be torn in different directions. Nevertheless, serious issues remain between so-called liberal and general education and so-called vocational education (chapter 16). And there are problems also about the extent to which the schools should keep an eye on preparing students for employment, and if they do, what this does to their educational programs and their educational objectives (chapter 2). Whatever shape the educational response takes, because technology has changed the face of modern living, one of the fundamental tasks of education whether in the schools or out is to provide the skills, attitudes, and knowledge necessary for understanding and responsibility in steering one's way around a world so transformed. And this requires much more than it did only a short time ago.

Mute the Competitive Character of Our Culture

An assessment of the competitive character of our culture is obviously required because our competitive outlook has broad consequences in the moral development of the young. In fact such an assessment has been going on for some time and evidence has accumulated. We have to decide how far competition is desirable or undesirable, under what conditions and in which areas, and how far if it is too rampant it should be muted.

Competition has obviously been at the root of our economic institutions. In effect, to succeed or win out has meant overcoming the competitor. It is clearly intensified when, in modes of thought and feeling, it comes to be central to the individual's sense of achievement. And it is even more intensified when, in an increasingly anomic atmosphere, almost any means becomes tolerated. The story is played out for all to see today in the familiar field of sport. Where traditional moral education talked of team spirit and cooperation in a competition of "good sportsmanship," we find now the massive inroads of the star system and competitive violence often reminiscent of gladiatorial combat in ancient Rome—at least in ice hockey!

In the psychological investigations of the midcentury a major and far-reaching thesis was the existence of universal human affiliative needs, alongside the familiar biological needs whose satisfaction contributes to survival and health. The latter, because of their familiarity, had no difficulty in gaining moral authority as modern biological and medical knowledge revised traditional ideas. Thus it showed what specific ills are escaped by the inclusion of vitamins in food supply, and recently even what the baby's food requires to avoid dangers of brain deficiency. Widespread starvation and malnutrition today would in itself be sufficient to give a high priority to food, health, and shelter, but the extent of contemporary knowledge about how to provide what is needed and the onrush of scientific and medical advances intensify the moral obligation. Questionings and conflict come where the moral dictates cross entrenched habits and interests, largely on pollution problems and such issues as the hazards of smoking, but here, from a moral point of view at least, the economic motivation of the opposition is transparent.

The thesis of affiliative need cuts deeper in its threat to dominant cultural modes. Accompanying it was the evidence of distortions produced in human feelings and behavior when this basic need is thwarted. Our understanding of aggressive and competitive behavior and the corresponding human character, especially in the exaggerated forms of our culture, is changed as a result. Instead of being seen as a natural expression, or else even as one of the alternative forms in which a plastic human nature is readily turned, these patterns became understood as an extreme development, often a distorted form, in which our search for identity and emotional security is cast under highly competitive social conditions. The evidence for such an interpretation came from studies of infant needs and response, child development, pathological behavior, relations of frustration and aggression, the social psychology of scapegoating, family structure and different kinds of personality, authoritarianism, and so on. Widely accepted conclusions were that the extremes of aggression and competition, although built into economic life and national rivalry and patriotism, as well as into popular conceptions of manliness, are the source of suffering and harm in interpersonal relations and in the inner life of people.

The outcome of such psychological and social investigation and the moral consequences are of sufficient scope to raise the question of basic reassessment as a moral imperative, primarily for education because the subject is a basic development of the young. A reassessment requires greater conceptual refinement in the notion of competitiveness and related ideas. The notion of success is part of the traditional work ethic, but its casting as winning out over others is a specialization that is not inherent. In simplified grading terms, suppose you are on top with an "A plus." Need that involve that nobody else gets a similar grade? Only if your sense of winning is geared to winning over others rather than object-oriented, that is simply to the achievement of excellence. The critique of the place of competitiveness in our culture may thus take shape as an effort to restore excellence as the interpretation of success rather than overcoming the other person. The changes that such an approach would bring in familiar aspects of the schooling process were examined in the discussion of grading (chapter 2).

The tie-in of competitiveness with the system of economic free enterprise ensures that any grappling with it in our society will invoke serious and difficult issues. Yet a reassessment of competitiveness with respect to education may not be decisive for competitiveness in economic life; it may rather pertain to the degree to which the habits of that domain are to be permitted to shape habits in other areas of our culture. A limited outcome could be that education has the job of redressing the evils that competitiveness produces—bending back the stick, as it were, to straighten it out. If the school stressed the cooperative, the communal, excellence rather than outdoing others—if it were able to do so successfully—then the cultural impact of economic competitiveness might be limited or muted. It might also force a realization that competitiveness is a tool for achieving ends, and that different areas of life—family, friendship and association, work, leisure activities, sport—have the task of determining independently where it is a useful and where a harmful tool, and there need be no single answer for all fields. Even within economic institutions there would be no requirement of a uniform answer—in the familiar debate between free enterprise and socialism some blend or contextual distribution could be a possibility.

Build a Sense of Community

If for no other reason, building a sense of community would gain an important place in the moral agenda because its loss is so widely and intensely lamented. A sense of community embraces an awareness of belonging to a group, some feeling of loyalty to it, the presence of moral bonds beyond self-interest, civility to others as fellows rather than outsiders, a relationship that enters to some degree into one's selfhood. On the moral side communal membership involves obligation that is not subject at every point to the reckoning of "what's in it for me"; the obligation is more commitment than external imposition, and the commitment is found within oneself rather than through conscious acceptance. The typical illustration of such community is the family, where family ties have not crumbled and where they have not become too crushing. The more extended kin group, the village or hometown when people lived their lives in one place, the church where it played an integrating role in its members' lives, perhaps the school or college of one's youth (in recollection at least) constituted such a community. Beyond these were the manifold groups of friends and associates in a diversity of cultural relations that combined stability and commitment. Such groups are often bound by a common objective, sometimes an ideal that unites the members.

The contrast with communal bond is the voluntary choice in the pursuit of one's interests. The historical prototype is the business company, which in spite of an occasional ideology of loyalty is primarily a matter of individual profit and loss. Its tie, in legal terms, is essentially one of agreement or contract, that is, the joining of individual wills in a particular acceptance. The inroads made by such "contractualism" in Western society and European thought from the sixteenth century to the present is a commonplace of intellectual and sociological history. Its assumption is that obligation to others issues from individual exercise of will in agreement between individuals, and its high point was the theory of the social contract in which political and social organization were construed in individualistic contractual terms. Moreover, the spread of contractualism was itself regarded as progress; few maxims have been invoked so frequently as Maine's when he identified as the movement of progressive societies that from status to contract.[4]

This growth of voluntaristic individualism was conditioned historically by profound social changes: the shift from a feudal society with fixed position and fixed bonds to the open society of individual commercial and later industrial expansion. As we have seen earlier, the ideal of individual liberty gained its strength in the critique of existent institutions and fixed forms, in the pursuit of a more ample life. The unshackling of the individual unavoidably broke communal bonds as specific forms of community were shattered or swept away. For example, mobility that industry engendered broke older local bonds; the growth of the nation and its demands put into the shade lesser loyalties, and our century with its move beyond the nation has even weakened national bonds; the extended family shrank into the nuclear family, and even there the mobility of children and the greater incidence of divorce have accentuated the voluntaristic element; secular society has meant a loss in the communal role of the church; devotion to craft and vocational groups has evaporated in the rapid shift of technology.

The challenge of individual liberty was not initially intended to undermine all communal bonds; critique and change were directed only at points of stress. In the seventeenth century when Locke advanced the theory of the social contract, he directed it not at social bonds generally but at the political relationship and the divine right of kings. The theory was to explain and evaluate *political* organization; outside this, the state of nature still contained a full morality of human bonds and rights. But the idea of contract could readily be extended to other bonds, and indeed Hobbes had already denied the existence of morality outside all contractual organization. The "individualistic model" in which individuals are the atomic units of social organization and their choices or preferences are the primary data for explaining and evaluating social forms became and still remains a staple intellectual instrument of Western social science.

The history of modern ethics also reflects these changes, at least in Anglo-American theory. The eighteenth century dissolved moral bonds into feelings and classified them neatly as self-regarding or other-regarding; the latter were generalized as sympathy or compassion. Instead of the older roster of virtues that expressed the variety of human relationships, the central moral problem was focused as egoism versus altruism. And eventually, in spite of nineteenth-century attempts to find a stable basis for altruism through logical analysis of rationality or metaphysical analysis of transcendence, the choice between egoistic and altruistic conduct fell firmly on the individual. In contemporary ethics the individual, wrapped in liberty in almost all domains, has the glory—and the burden—of choice and decision.

The loss of community is thus the dark underside of individualism and liberty; it cannot be remedied by the inclusion of fraternity, as in the slogan "Liberty, Equality, Fraternity." To some extent close attention to the historical conditions that brought about the situation can help us avoid making an absolute of the individual to the extent of permanently banishing community, for it can show us how each liberty in its time arose as a critique of specific existent forms of community; it was a call for the opportunity to bring about conscious changes. Liberty cannot mean the total withdrawal of human beings from the matrix of social bonds. Thus the loss of community, felt as alienation or rootlessness of the individual, cannot be overcome by theory alone, nor for that matter by turning back the clock to authoritative moral imposition. A sense of community can be cultivated only by rediscovering community of purposes that still exist in a common life, and by throwing sufficient light upon them to guide institutional reconstruction and give it organizational shape, opening the way to the growth of greater or stronger communal bonds.

The role of education in such a practical task is to devise ways in which the experience of community, with its natural and intrinsic appeal, can take place particularly among the young in the period of their growth, so that they may come to appreciate its quality, experience in which each person ceases to be an outsider to every other.

Restore Humanistic Quality

In our remaining two topics we turn more directly to moral demands for education that stem from the overall present situation. Clearly the restoration of humanistic quality cannot be a perennial task, for to restore implies something has been upset. It is thus a demand generated by a critical present contingency, like overcoming a malaise or removing a widespread alienation that has somehow settled upon people. Now, it is not surprising that the vast changes in so short a period of the twentieth century have had serious effects on the quality of life everywhere. Even where improvements have taken place in the material conditions of people it has been in the most developed countries, under conditions of mass production for private profit, resulting in uniformity of product and often of taste, a mixture of the shoddy with the useful, and an advertising that whetted the appetite for the novel and the trivial. It is not surprising that the expression "quality of life" has begun to compete with "the greatest happiness" in ethical discourse, for the latter has become tied in with a hedonistic reckoning and hedonism with the accumulation of pleasurable goods and situations as they appear in contemporary presentations of what the man and woman of distinction will wear and possess and use and experience.

Of course "quality of life" refers to much more than temper and taste. It reflects the order and safety, or their opposites, of the urban streets; the calm or anxiety, the successes or failures, of daily life; the regular functioning or malfunctioning of institutions; the presence of some leisure; the absence of driving needs for drugs and the like; the variety or dullness of cultural opportunities. Philosophers and social scientists have begun to think that a measure of quality of life would be an important index of the well-being of a society, perhaps more so than gross national product.

We are not here concerned with analyzing the causes of the malaise in the quality of our life—whether it has come simply from the rapidity of change or the extreme urbanization or the character of our economic system or the violence of world wars and social struggles. It is enough to realize that the restoration of a humanistic quality is a major effort, summoning great moral energies, to place it as a standard for judging human projects in our time. We should not, however, overlook the implications of the notion of restoring. It suggests that there was a time when life did have the kind of quality we are seeking. A continuity with the past is thus provided for the effort to secure the humanistic quality. It is not something entirely new that we have never understood or appreciated. Now, it is possible that there are ideological elements in this notion. Certainly the search for the natural has sometimes been used in that way, and turning to the past has also been a typical conservative attitude. But this simply means that we have to distinguish the ideological use of the notion from the nonideological, not to throw out the notion in a wholesale way. In many different contexts it is true that the quality of life has deteriorated from what was previously felt satisfactory, while in others (for example in health) it has improved.

The complex problems set by this theme are particularly relevant to education. The rapid changes we noted in the schools during the last few decades unavoidably brought a certain disruption, and education suffered in the process.[5] There is no single reason for this, rather a convergence of many factors, on the whole familiar ones: rapid expansion without adequate provision; often lack of preparation of the new entrants; difficulties of teaching larger groups; lack of confidence in the new groups affecting their performance; continued patterns of discrimination with respect to minorities; relaxation of standards; changes in requirements sometimes sidetracking students into vocational paths; general confusion. In spite of all this, great advances were made in the spread of education, both secondary and higher. But there were also qualitative changes. Specialization became more intensive. The shift to the "useful" or what appeared such was overwhelming. The gap between the scientific and the humanistic became greater. In their isolation the humanities became almost as specialist as the sciences. Democratic tendencies in education were confused with a kind of voluntarism where mere choice or preference was its own justification. In part this came from being cut off from the older tradition in each field, which had provided disciplined standards. Change had been so rapid, so much was new—from the automobile and the airplane to nuclear energy and electronic communication in scarcely more than half a century—that the young felt one could not learn from the past. In the 1960s even young college instructors argued this thesis. Perhaps too they were reacting against the use of the familiar appeal to tradition as part of an elitist argument. In any case, education suffered from the generation gap. It was almost as if the young were out to discover the world anew and had cast off the past.

Without specifying the detail at this point, it is clear that one of the central tasks of education in the contemporary world, as well as a serious standard for judging its success, is the restoration of a humanistic quality that at various times in the past it has had but that has been disturbed in the many transitions. It is necessary to be absolutely clear what this recommendation is not. It is not an adulation of older aristocratic classical education. I am talking of what education was at its best—in the sciences, mathematics, classics, literature, and language, not a particular school. Nor should any shade of elitism be involved; it is essential that the notion of quality be separated from any elitist flavor. The reference to restoration also involves a philosophical conception of the relation of past and present that has to be explored in considering the role of history in the curriculum. We also find involved conceptions of the nature of man, of spirit and nature, of genius and thought and appreciation. And so in education it concerns the relation of knowledge and history, of culture and science, of the outstanding thinkers or artists and the mass of people who respond to their works. The restoration is essentially a restoration of continuity.

The restoration of quality should be seen as parallel to the expansion of equality. The latter is essentially a principle of distribution. It makes sure that the opportunity for entry and participation and thereafter for sharing in education is widespread and not reserved for a small group. But just as in economics, alongside of distribution there is production, in some respects prior to it. It would be a sad state of affairs if the education that was made available on the successful expansion of equality was a thinned-down version of the education that had existed before. Indeed, the quality of production should not only be restored but improved beyond that.

Reassess Schooling

In chapter 4 we have seen the variety of dissatisfactions with and criticisms of contemporary schooling. This attention is directed upon the public schools, so long in public consciousness the basic educational institution. Criticism that underscores present evils, that in some cases calls for turning back the clock and in extreme cases for abolition of the institution, at least shows that a reassessment of the total character of contemporary schooling is on the moral agenda.

This is not peculiar to schooling. We saw (in the introduction to part I) that all contemporary institutions have in the last half-century come under severe criticism. The one point needing special emphasis is that critiques of the schools, like those of other institutions, need not yield a single overall formula for reconstruction. It may prove wise to detach some of the present functions of the school and hand them over to other institutions, yet at some points the question may arise whether to add functions. To take obvious examples, should public quasi-professional competitive sports be removed from the college and centered in independent community or private athletic organizations? Or again, should nursery schools be attached to the public schools or constitute separate, more local institutions, and if so should they take over some of the current kindergarten and early elementary school tasks? And similar questions have been raised about continuing education. Again, questions of educational theory and emphasis in the schools—for example, whether the vocational orientation should be advanced or diminished—and questions of support and improvement of material conditions are quite different ones. Another serious issue is what to do when we bring to light the "hidden agenda" of the public schools in consolidating class divisions. Of course the general matrix that makes reconstruction necessary is the whole change in contemporary life, with its technological and social transformations, equalitarian and democratic aspirations, and proliferation of cultural institutions that may carry an increasingly larger share of the tasks of education. In the introduction to part IV we shall note the problems of reconstruction in schooling that become involved with philosophical issues, and some aspects will be discussed in the several chapters of part IV.

In this chapter we have tried to indicate moral demands that appear on the agenda for educational thought. They concerned social changes and fresh turns in moral outlook. Beyond these, in chapter 8, lie the development of some fresh modes of thought and reanalysis of venerable concepts.

We should not be surprised at the variety, and doubtless work oriented toward fashioning a moral agenda will increase rather than simplify the complexities.

Notes

1. Abraham Edel, *Ethical Judgment: The Use of Science in Ethics* (Glencoe, Ill.: Free Press, 1955; paperback, 1964), ch. 9

2. Cf. Oscar Schachter, *Sharing the World's Resources* (New York: Columbia University Press, 1977).

3. Cf. Mary Anne Raywid, "Pluralism as a Basis for Educational Policy," in *Educational Policy*, ed. Janice Weaver (Danville, Ill.: Interstate Printers and Publishers, 1975), pp. 87-99. Raywid concludes her critique with a warning about the fragmenting character of the movement: "In short, it is hard to overstate pluralism's ramifications for education's future direction, organization, and control. And in making the related decisions, educational policy-makers will be going a long way towards choosing society's future as well." Cf. also, Richard Pratte, "Cultural Diversity and Education," in *Ethics and Educational Policy*, ed. Kenneth A. Strike and Kieran Egan (London: Routledge & Kegan Paul, 1978). pp. 147-67.

4. Henry Maine, *Ancient Law* (New York: E.P. Dutton, Everyman Library; London: J.M. Dent & Sons, 1917), p. 99.

5. In the case of higher education, see, for example, Organisation for Economic Cooperation and Development, *Towards Mass Higher Education, Issues and Dilemmas* (Paris, 1974); these studies were prepared for the Conference on Future Structures of Post-Secondary Education, Paris, 26-29 June 1973. See also Martin A. Trow, *Problems in the Transition from Elite to Mass Higher Education* (Carnegie Commission on Higher Education, 1973), which traces clearly major educational consequences of the expansion.

8. Rationality, Autonomy, Relativism

In this chapter we continue the moral agenda for education, but with a possibly surprising turn. Whereas the eight mandates considered in chapter 7 were transparently moral and social, to rethink three concepts is a patently intellectual task. Why should it be part of a moral agenda to develop a sound idea of rationality, of autonomy, of relativism?

The classical tradition would have found no difficulty in this demand. Because the human being was taken to be a rational animal, and ethics was concerned with the development of the human being's humanity, what were called intellectual virtues—the proper development of intellectual capacities—had as stable a place in ethics as what were called moral virtues. Certainly the first two of the three concepts are of great importance in the educational development of the person. An ideal of rationality sets the guidelines for the way in which reason is to be shaped, and that is how our reflective thinking is to proceed. An idea of autonomy sets the guidelines for shaping will, choice, decision—as Kant had it, how reason is to become practical. (Indeed, autonomy is often set in contemporary educational thought as a supreme goal in personal development.) The idea of moral relativism seems more removed, though its inclusion might be excused because of the veritable din of argument about it on the contemporary scene. The ground of inclusion is, however, more direct: moral relativism is argued over because it seems to make arbitrary the ultimate basis of obligation and commitment, hence to bring turmoil into the fundamentals of moral education. It is therefore a fitting member of the trio.

Toward a Reconstructed Conception of Rationality

Moral philosophers since the time of Kant have pinned great hopes on somehow extracting the basics of morality and even the essence of personhood from what it is to be a rational being.[1] Without rationality, freedom tends to sink back into some kind of arbitrariness; self-discipline may become repressive or fanatical; autonomy may become sheer willfulness. Even more seriously, the very notion of the advance of knowledge may be rendered incoherent. This problem was touched in considering the politicization of the schools (chapter 5). If there is no notion of the advance of knowledge, there remain simply different points of view and little or no basis for declaring one better or more correct than another. The question is not, of course, one of absolute knowledge but of ideas and beliefs that are corrigible in the advance of experience, and that can act as a basis for assessing conflicting ideas and hypotheses. We would not thus be left simply with conflicting ideologies and the view that knowledge is merely the ideology of the intellectual.

The false step that leads into an ultimate status for ideology is to expect some simple or wholesale way of distinguishing what is ideological and what is scientific. Instead we have at best the retail accumulation of results and methods that enable us to judge in detail the comparative correctness of views and hypotheses and so distinguish the better and the worse in way of knowledge.[2] This minimum shall here be taken for granted. There has been, in contemporary philosophy of science, a revolt against earlier positivist ideas of verification; greater place has been assigned to theoretical considerations and preferences that seem at times almost political and sociological rather than scientific. But even with some relaxation of criteria to give a wider place to theoretical controversy in the procession of science itself, the denial of better or worse in scientific results seems self-defeating.

Advancing knowledge and rationality are correlative notions. The former concerns the object of thought and the latter the capacity for thought. Moreover, the notion of rationality is continued into the consideration of practice or conduct; rational decision is a problem for action as well as for belief. We are thus led into an analysis of rationality.

To attribute rationality to a person is to say—at least this is one common notion—that he or she exercises reason or that in thinking and deciding is reasonable.[3] To unpack the concept of rationality in this sense is to explicate the character of reasonableness as it is found in thought and action. Comparative method in the history of philosophy is helpful for this: the different content philosophers have packed into the concept of rationality suggests its complexity and some of the changes it has undergone. It stands out as a concept that has grown throughout the history of philosophy, that has different strata added as philosophy advanced, beginning with the early definition of the human being as a rational animal. These additions reflect largely the growth of knowledge and experience, and the stabilization of purposes. A contemporary concept of rationality should embody the outcome of this development.

The minimal requirement of rationality is that of consistency, the absence of contradiction. But even when Aristotle stated this, his account included more than that logical demand. It included semantic features arising from a concern with discourse and communication. Aristotle insisted that rationality entailed some stability of meanings; words could not change their meanings every moment, as some of the Heracliteans had suggested.

The concept of rationality gets applied also to action. What a reasonable person will do or not do provides criteria for rationality that extend the notion. Reasonable persons will not pursue contradictory or inconsistent aims. They may cling to inconsistent objectives in the hope that some way will be found to encompass both, or to opposing distant ideals because each appeals to a different interest; but where the aims or ideals cannot be achieved together, they cannot pursue both and will be deeply frustrated if they try.

Two courses are open to us. We can limit the idea of consistency to propositions and speak of incompatible aims instead. Or, letting the idea of a reasonable human being and reasonable action be extended, we can say that "contradiction" changes its meaning as we move from propositions or beliefs to aims and desires. In the latter case, which seems to be the path generally followed as the concept of rationality is extended, we begin to introduce fresh criteria. Rationality in action is then said to demand a coherent pattern of means and objectives or some degree of systematic organization in action. Different fields may add to the criteria, often in specialized ways. For example, we often find rationality involving ideas of utility; it is stripped down to the efficient pursuit of means to the proposed ends, where the criteria of efficiency will include least wasteful, least costly, and so on. A familiar usage in economics identifies rationality with maximizing preferences. This formulation is not without implicit value choices; for example, where it refrains from interpersonal comparisons it in effect makes existing interests privileged, and the idea of maximizing will involve a value choice between different strategies, such as minimizing risk or maximizing gain.

That lessons of experience get cumulatively incorporated into the concept of rationality can be seen throughout its long history. The move from logical rationality to empirical rationality incorporates criteria of scientific verification—how hypotheses are tested in experience, what elements of sensory experience have proved stable and reliable confirmatory signs, what are reliable states of observers. We tend to take these for granted by now and have sometimes defined verification principles in terms of sensation as a matter of course. (But, note, why not satisfactions? And why do we insist on a cool observer rather than a passionate observer as the best condition for accurate observation?) The reader may justly smile at this extended treatment of the now obvious. But the point is important. If the concept of empirical rationality is the product of long experience whose results got built in, why cannot further experience in other areas get similarly built in when acquired? Should not the concept of rationality be constantly expanding as our knowledge grows? In a way, it does, through our judgments of what a reasonable person would decide. These are the empirical judgments we make, and after they are sufficiently established we can incorporate their lessons into the definition of rationality, much as in a familiar example the electrical properties of copper, after they were established, may be incorporated into the criteria of what copper is, or even into a revised definition of copper.

An excellent example of this development can be seen in the growth of our knowledge of psychological mechanisms. As we have learned of the inner mechanisms of self-deceit, or more generally of self-defense, or of "rationalization," we may say that it is a mark of rational persons that they look out for and discount such tendencies in themselves; persons who typically yield to such distortions in their thinking are to that extent less rational. Similarly, for what we have learned of social ideologies: now that we have come to know the influence of social perspective in fashioning a point of view, we would say that persons who try to understand things from other points of view, whether or not they agree with them, are more rational. Again, as our knowledge of history has made clear the difference between understanding in the short view and in the long view, persons who see things and formulate policy only by weighing immediate consequences (apart from the question whether the particular policy is right or wrong) are being less rational than persons who incorporate and bring to the situation also an understanding of the long-range view; or at least we develop the notion of the appropriate temporal perspective for different contexts and problems. Comparably, given our knowledge of the world today, for the national and the global perspective: it is very likely that on many questions such as energy and pollution and weather and air and ocean, it will soon be irrational to take less than a global perspective. The conclusion about rationality thus suggested is that the concept embodies the best of our knowledge transmuted into method and some of the most pervasive of our values that are crucial. Let us now look at the value aspects.

The value components in rationality do not stop with the demand for consistency in action and the avoidance of frustration. The idea of system as a theoretical demand is rich enough in its requirements of simplicity and fruitfulness as explored in the philosophy of science. The parallel notions of unity, harmony, and systematic order found in philosophical accounts of rationality in action, especially when accompanied with ideas of the authority of reason, are ample enough to fill out whole social philosophies. Clearly the concept here acts as a kind of intellectual magnet to attract and shelter ideologies, and a great deal of critical analysis has been required to rescue it from them. The lesson is not that the concept is without value content; rather, that we must be explicit in recognizing and grounding the value content we agree on building into it. For example, there is a strong tendency in moral philosophy since Kant to argue that a criterion for the rationality of an action—and thereby a test as to whether it ought to be done—is its universalizability. (To take Kant's negative example, if I am tempted to make a false promise to get myself out of difficulties, I know it is irrational and that I ought not to do it because I cannot consistently will that everyone in these difficulties should resort to such a device.) Some philosophers have taken the element of generality to be directly a part of the meaning of "ought"; others argue instead that "ought" contextually implies that reasons can be furnished for the judgment, and reasons are universal in form, so that generality enters by this side door. In either case, a conceptual partnership is formed: rationality, obligation, and generality become linked and an all-human morality is fashioned: moral prescriptions become addressed to a community of all rational beings, not anything less, such as nation, kin, race, village, or group. If obligation has grown in meaning by this linkage with what was hitherto a largely logical idea of generality, so too rationality has extended its domain by its linkage with obligation and generality. It has built in the values of an all-human moral perspective.

Obviously concepts cannot conjure values out of themselves; their analysis reveals what human beings have built into them in thought and development. As we suggested in discussing a global perspective, the all-human perspective in Kant comes with the awakening of the Enlightenment and the universal outlook of the bourgeoisie in breaking down the old order. Little study of the fuller Kantian writings is required to see that his conception of reason is an intellectual response to the historical development. Even more, contemporary moral philosophers, who find the element of generalization well installed in the meaning of "ought" and see it as the mark of rationality and claim to be simply explicating ordinary English usage, are certainly doing that, but they are overlooking the fact that the universalistic morality has had a long time since the eighteenth century to get thoroughly built into contemporary thought and language. It has not been time enough, however, in spite of the growing unification of the world in economic relations and communication, to get built into moral action. Whether a strict universalization or something more limited belongs in the concept of rationality (as some element of disinterestedness clearly does) or only in certain contexts appears to be an unsettled problem.

What has been shown here is only that we have a growing concept of rationality, that both with respect to increase of knowledge and stabilization of value commitments it may become richer and more rounded, function with greater determinateness and reliability, and be open to refinement. The significant educational problems are then whether rationality can be taught, how rationality can be learned, or to what extent it is fostered to some degree in today's typical experience of the young and so has only to be elicited and sharpened.

It is worth suggesting some directions in which our idea of rationality may grow. For example, it may prove useful to distinguish in morality between microethics and macroethics (somewhat as economics does between microeconomics and macroeconomics) purely on the basis of type of problem and methods of analysis required, so that there would not be the need to impose on all moral problems the individualistic model of starting from individual desires and values.[4] Rationality in morality might well add criteria for differentiating the appropriateness of micro- and macroapproaches, just as rationality in science would help us decide where it is reasonable to expect reduction of systems and where not. Again, in morals it might add criteria for the conditions under which an activist attitude is appropriate in formulating questions, rather than a purely contemplative attitude. Various moral philosophies have been working toward this for some time. Analytic schools have differentiated the reportorial from the participatory attitude. Existentialists have insisted on responsibility as against the explanatory determinist approach. It is perhaps too early to incorporate criteria for an activist outlook as such. That would require the lessons of a richer philosophy of history that would tell us where human intervention is likely to be effective and where people's ideas of a share in determining the course of events tend to be ideological or illusory. The extension of a concept of rationality in this direction is something to be looked for eventually.

The present concept of rationality is thus a historical product. It sums the lessons of knowledge and the values of human effort; fact and value are not sharply separate but, rather, ways in which the same materials are ordered for different purposes. Education, in attempting to understand the moral development of the child, looks within the individual and finds it has to deal with the operations of the whole society. Thought makes sharp distinctions but experience shows continually how to qualify them. Because there are few beginnings and no endings and because we are constantly in the middle of things, we have to attend to relations within the system as a whole, refining ideas for the direction of fresh experience and revising directions in the light of experience structured by those ideas. Such is the nature of rationality.

A Reconstruction of the Ideal of Autonomy

The popular idea of autonomy is a twentieth-century variant of traditional individualism. There has always been some conception of what makes a person (or a self or an individual) to act as a channel for judgments about how the individual is to be handled through socially educative influences. Early (Platonic) ideas of reason focused on the repression of the appetites. Medieval elaboration centered on free will as the basis of responsibility. Self-realization doctrines of nineteenth-century idealism turned to the growth of the self and its structuring of knowledge and conduct. Autonomy as a kind of self-rule or self-determination had a Kantian basis but blossomed in twentieth-century discussions of the extent to which the mature individual is the proper center for ultimate decision about himself or herself, and the extent to which educational processes should carry this back to ways of child growth. It fed on issues that had previously debated individual freedom and social liberty, the authority of external standards, the efficacy of reflective thought, and a host of kindred problems. Because of this scope and these interrelations, the analysis of autonomy wins an important place on the moral agenda of education.[5]

Sometimes when it is said that we want to educate for autonomy all that is meant is that we want a person to be able to make up his or her own mind and not to lean on somebody else all the time. But the notion of autonomy has been applied not only to persons but also to morality as such. The two uses are connected, and it is best to examine the autonomy of morality first. Kant held that a system of morality was *heteronomous* when its idea of duty depended on some outside notion, such as the idea of God in religion or that of happiness or pleasure in psychology. He freed morality from a dependence on religion (in fact he quite reversed the roles) and in his sharp is-ought dichotomy he sundered morality from science. Then he went on to explore the inner character of the ought and of morality itself. That it turned out to yield a self engaged in universalizing the maxims of his or her action or in a kind of self-legislation meant that the person who was the center of morality was an autonomous person, quite literally a self-legislator.

The autonomy of morality since then has meant largely the struggle of morality as a field not to be subordinated to some other area. In the nineteenth century there was psychological ethics, metaphysical ethics, biological evolutionist ethics, historical materialist ethics, and so on. In each case, the ethics was shaped as a consequence of the picture of humankind and its conditions and career as seen in the particular field. Many of the proposals were oversimplified, many were ideological, but some were rich and insightful, breaking through old stereotypes that bound people to outworn institutions. At the beginning of the twentieth century, G. E. Moore, in *Principia Ethica* (1903), reasserted the autonomy of ethics. He used the concept of *good* or *intrinsic value*, to which he reduced all other moral concepts, including *ought*, and maintained that this was an indefinable notion. He cut all bridges between ethics and any state of existence, insisting that ethical truths were true whatever the nature of the world might be. In short, neither science nor metaphysics furnished the meaning of ethical terms and neither scientific evidence nor metaphysical evidence furnished the ground for ethical truths. To define "good" in terms of any metaphysical or natural property was called "the naturalistic fallacy," and the intrinsic goodness of any contemplated object or situation was a matter of direct intuition. Such an extreme conception of autonomy was rather isolationism than independence, and ethics was thereby deprived of any serious assistance from the advancing fields of human inquiry all around it. If the autonomy of morals had meant instead not the isolation of the meaning and evidence for value from all knowledge but the refusal to bind it to any one branch or to any one model or interest or state of a field, to keep it open to the growth of knowledge and the development of human beings, then it would have been quite another matter.

The autonomy of the individual does not differ from the conception of a free person. An autonomous individual is not one who is isolated and from whom decision issues. The character of the person is involved. The person acts from knowledge and uses reason. It is free action, not impulsive reaction. What then does the label of autonomy add? The currency of the concept and its occasional advantages stem from three factors. One is that the concept of freedom or the free person got too enmeshed in controversy, and a new term added fresh possibilities. Particularly, the tie-in of notions of freedom with liberty (and the conflict of concepts of negative freedom or liberty and positive freedom or liberty, involving often the confrontation of different social philosophies) was scarcely conducive to conceptual clarity. A second advantage is etymological: *auto-nomy* is literally self-rule. By calling attention to the self, autonomy could lock into the considerable psychological material on inner forces and distortions that thwart self-expression and decision, which was also obviously part of the empirical interpretation of a free person. And by calling attention to *rule*, it could lock into the work that was being done in philosophical psychology to distinguish human *action* (as contrasted with behavior) as essentially rule-governed. The third advantage is that the typical obstacles of the age come from the intrusions on the individual by large-scale organizations—corporate formations, work organizations, political organizations—whose mass effect is to produce individual alienation and helplessness; here the concept of autonomy seems to have borne the standard of revolt in the pale realm of the categories. When there is a sober recognition of the state of affairs and the various concepts are analyzed in their historical development, and particularly when that of freedom is restored to some intellectual utility, perhaps autonomy can be relegated to its more limited contextual role. But then the greater weight bears on rationality and freedom.

Perhaps a few comments are thus required on freedom, at least as it enters into moral and educative contexts. Here it is usually invoked as a basis for justifying praise and blame, holding responsible and imposing obligations. Now, Dewey has argued that praise and blame are best seen as prospective rather than retrospective (a view with some antecedents in Priestley and Adam Smith): we praise a child for doing something even when the child has not yet become aware of what he or she is doing, and similarly we may even blame the child in such a manner. We are in effect helping the child to isolate and identify his or her act as having certain kinds of desirable and undesirable consequences for future recognition.[6] To hold persons responsible for their acts is thus a social way of teaching and supporting the web of learning. Dewey's view is often taken to be manipulative, but that is so only on a narrow behavioristic theory of the learning process, which of course is not his view.[7] The emphasis is on the activity of the subject, who is learning of the competing claims and has to decide what to do. Through this learning in relation to others the subject becomes sensitive and forms habits that fashion character, and in this way a self grows and is developed. Those cases of being held responsible that are accepted as responsibilities may become incorporated into the structure of the self and so, far from inhibiting freedom, enter into the marks of what is compatible with freedom later on.

If freedom is identified with the capacity for learning, and seen as increased by learning that establishes a firmer self with stable and well-organized habits, it is a particularly appropriate concept for educational theory. It is compatible with a number of different psychological and philosophical analyses of freedom in the historical tradition of that problem, though not in the sense of an arbitrary indeterminism. Obviously it would fit a Freudian theory in which the ego makes inroads on the superego by furnishing insight and bringing a wider range of reactions into consciousness. It would be consonant with an evolutionary theory in which humankind gains greater control over its environment, social and political as well natural, and is able to stabilize the conditions of its survival. It would most readily express the idea of freedom in the pragmatist and naturalist philosophies in which, freedom not being opposed to causality, people are free to the degree that they have achieved knowledge of the world (including humankind and society) and are able to apply that knowledge for the advancement of human values. And it might fit philosophical idealism or even transcendent metaphysical theories for which this would be the worldly or phenomenal picture.

How then, we may ask finally, can the concept of autonomy be reconstructed to play a fruitful role in evaluation? One possibility is to focus more carefully on its social and historical development as the conceptual counterpart of modern individualism. Seen in this light, and not merely in terms of the liberation of morality from domination by one or another outside discipline, and not merely in terms of its relation to freedom as a psychological exploration of human learning capacities, it becomes the intellectual vehicle of humankind's social experimentation with the scope and limits of individual decision. So, far from having a complete meaning antecedent to social experience, it becomes the expression of that experience and its lessons. Let us trace briefly the outlines of this experimentation in the last three centuries.

It is commonplace that individualism in the Western tradition made its entry in religion and in economic life. Early Protestantism went through a stage in which the religion was determined by the prince or national powers, but eventually it blossomed in individual freedom of religious conscience. Granted the causes included different sects fighting themselves to a standstill, yet eventually the lesson accepted was individual decision in matters of religion. In economic life the story is even more familiar: from the onward plodding of the individual trader to the establishment of laissez-faire as a social dogma. Meanwhile other experiments in individualism are tried out. Freedom of thought and expression moves from a demand for freedom for intellectuals to freedom everywhere to try out in the marketplace of ideas. Mill's *On Liberty* as the classic nineteenth-century statement is even ready to have the individual experiment with different plans of life. Freedom of thought and expression does win out in the aspirations of liberalism and remains today the star liberty in battles against repression. Political individualism meanwhile grows as a relatively separate strand. Won by revolutions and subsequent agitations, it is experimentally extended to different social strata and is still undergoing testing for different instruments or techniques.

Less-advertised individualisms are readily apparent once we look at them not simply as freedoms but as areas of activity in which the individual can make his or her own decision: freedom of movement, of residence, of marriage (parentally arranged marriages yielding to romantic individual love), of selection of work or vocation, of education, and so on. We still find places where each of these is absent, and in which the absence is stoutly defended—in short, we are not without controversy in assessment of the experiments. But this is also true of some of the recognized basic liberties.

Experimentation advancing individualism into new fields continues apace. Individualism is being expanded in matters of sex and the family (sexual relations and sexual orientation, divorce, family planning, contraception, abortion); individual conscience has entered the bailiwick of patriotism in recognition of conscientious objection and in some measure civil disobedience (particularly on war and revolutionary agitation); new forms of individual rights are promulgated (welfare rights, rights of children). Now there is no reason that continued evaluation of the new moral claims should not take place as well as of the old established moral claims, in the same manner that we can read history for the way the entry of individualism in each of the previous domains was evaluated. For example, the question of limits was eventually raised in the evaluation of economic individualism—limitations on usury, the rise of labor organization as a major balance, government regulation on health and welfare, even an alternative ideal of socialism. A variety of limiting concepts were used with respect to freedom of speech—arguments over the line between advocacy and present danger in action, sedition, pornography, libel—with varying refinements. So too with individual choice in marriage (requirement of health certificates), travel (passport regulation), and so on. Now, in all these, and kindred evaluation processes, there are many points of interpretation, of comparative evaluation, of synthesis, that still need much further experience. Yet some lessons are definitely learned—for example, the impact of an extreme individualism in alienation and the loss of a sense of community, the havoc that results in a complex social organization, the need for some limits, the recognition that at some points individualism serves as a covering ideology for specific group aims. In an age of unavoidable change we have to act without waiting for the definite solution of problems and act under risk, with the hope that we will learn from the results. The lesson of social change has been that even to act from established traditions under changing conditions has risks as well.

The proposal here offered is that autonomy be analyzed as the attempt to apply the sociopsychological lessons drawn from the experiments to the understanding of what it is to be an individual. We expect the outcome of the historical experiments to help us shape the theory of autonomy by revealing relevant facts, conditions, consequences. The chief mistake in analyses of autonomy is that they try to give a completely antecedent idea in relatively bare and abstract terms, as if the analysis of the notion (or of freedom or self-expression) could provide sufficient criteria to give a green light or a red light to decision. On the contrary, the task is to construct a concept that will embody the lessons of success and failure in the vast experimentation with individualism that has occurred in the past few centuries and is still going on. Our intellectual difficulties with the concept reflect practical difficulties in evaluating institutions' functioning, as well as insufficient development of knowledge in psychological and social science, and more immediately insufficient attention to the criteria of evaluation.

What can we ask of the psychological and social sciences? From the former we want a reliable theory of the development of a self and its capacities and its formation of patterns, and the psychological costs and benefits of different patterns. These would be helpful in making judgments of pathologies of decision, of times and stages in personal development that admit of greater leeway in individual decision as contrasted with occasions where serious missteps are possible, of the strains and limits of different patterns. From the social sciences (including historical lessons) we should want reliable analyses of curbs on individual decision that have been tried out—for example in the twentieth century, the successes and failures of army rule in different countries, the outcomes in individual life of the Nazi episode, the impact of collective control of production, the social and cultural consequences of the Iranian turnabout against modernism. And in the opposite direction, we should want the full sociological study of the expansion of individual decision, as in the liberal countries of Europe and the United States. This is of course asking a great deal, in areas so subject to social and ideological conflict. If the results are likely to be somewhat conjectural, at least we will come to understand what questions have to be answered in a quest for autonomy, and that there are few shortcuts, if any.

The crucial issue is, of course, the criteria of success and failure. Some of these can be elicited from the history of ethical thought. The hopes and fears when experiments in greater individualism were initiated will give us the criteria we need. Criteria for success might include the higher incidence of thoughtfulness in reflection, sensitivity in feeling, participation in social action, inventiveness. Mill's desire for a preponderance of the active over the passive and his evaluation of political forms by the educative effects on people, as well as Tocqueville's admiration for the resourcefulness of individual Americans are both near the mark.[8] And Carol Gilligan's reminder that such criteria are dominantly attuned to male images[9] should lead us to elaborate sensitivity in feeling into greater incidence of care and love and mutual respect. Criteria for failure would be the contraction and lesser incidence of those itemized as success. Outstanding among these would be the entrenchment of egoism and the spread of anomie. It is true that egoism has at times been offered as an ethical theory, and a distinction must be made. Take the parallel case of pleasure theory as advocated by the Cyrenaics. If a person just does what he or she feels like at any moment, that is not an ethical theory. But if he or she reflects that life is too precarious to admit of planning and it is best to follow momentary impulse, then it is an ethical theory whether or not it proves adequate. So too the egoism that has any pretension to ethics appeals to a rational self-interest or a cool self-interest and offers preestablished harmonies that turn each pursuing his or her own into higher productivity and general welfare. These are quite different from greed and acquisitiveness. To engender and promote sheer egoism is a criterion of failure in an institution. As for anomie, it embraces the chaos and disorder that ensue socially where any means goes provided it achieves the egoistic end—violence, dishonesty, and the rest.

Of course to evaluate an institution's functioning by such criteria is no easy task. Subsidiary hypotheses might purport to explain why a favored institution went astray under special conditions. And there are often conflicting values. Some may still argue today that the first experiment in individualism—the break in a unified religion—was a failure because it generated dissension and helped the growth of nationalism with consequent wars; perhaps to maintain even dogmatic unity would have been better. But on the whole, given the fact that the individualistic tendency promoted individual effort, the growth of science, and major social gains, religious individualism proved a benefit. Such controversies about the results of the social experiments of individualism are not likely to hamper seriously long-range decisions about the value of results. Again, even before general decisions are made it may be possible to define limits for the particular individualisms. For example, usury laws presuppose limits to individual decision about interest rates; laws forbidding prostitution limit areas of sale; compulsory education limits individual decision about extent of learning; welfare legislation embodies the lesson of experience that a social net is required to limit the consequences of economic individualism; current controversies about removing life-support systems for severe and incurable illness are attempting to determine the limits for individual decision about ending one's life.

All such determinations are profound ethical answers in the light of accepted human values. They come together in a view of a good life and individual participation in it. In so doing they help outline what a self is like that participates in such ways. The outcome underlies the construction of a general concept of autonomy and its conditions. Like all knowledge, such a concept is open to correction and revision with the growth of knowledge and experience. That a reconstruction of the concept of autonomy is on the moral agenda for education in the contemporary world thus expresses the demand that we evaluate the individualism of our culture in the history of the last four centuries, as a guide in contemporary decision. It is a demand not for adulation or condemnation but for sober assessment of the individualistic trends in our institutional life.

The Issue of Moral Relativism

The issue of moral relativism remains a serious block to devising a program for moral and social education. By acting as a popular and wholesale whipping boy, just as the issue of permissiveness does, it suggests that the only way to have moral education is to affirm dogmatically some form of absolutistic morality. Moral relativism is thus equated with the view that morality is in some sense arbitrary. Moral education would have sad prospects if its choice were between a dogmatism of moral absolutism and an arbitrariness of moral relativism. The thesis advanced here is that this is an epistemological sideshow of the real problem of the development of autonomy and the search for the limits of individualism, as discussed in the preceding section. Hence the analysis of moral relativism is an imperative precursor to the later consideration of moral and social education (chapter 14).

The literature on moral relativism in the twentieth century is vast, and there is no agreed-on formulation. The briefest one is perhaps that in the case of opposing basic moral convictions either both can be true (correct, valid, adequate) or that for morality there is no meaning to truth (correctness, validity, adequacy). Such formulations seem to make the issue an essentially epistemological one. To deal with it we have to distinguish first various exploratory perspectives or stances, to make sure that we are not confusing questions across their lines.

The chief difference is between a stance of *giving an account of* (describing, analyzing, explaining) and that of *evaluating*. This is not a distinction of fact and value; it is rather the difference between asking, "What is going on here?" and, "What shall we do about it?" Not only can there be factual and valuational elements in both cases but nothing prevents morality (moral convictions and beliefs) from being the subject matter in both cases.

Now, when a historian or an anthropologist finds that morality differs in different peoples or different times—for example, that one period condemns usury and another finds it normal, or one culture is competitive and another is cooperative—we have so far simply the exhibition of *variation*. The historian or anthropologist could even go on to explain the variety in terms of different conditions and different needs, tasks, opportunities, and modes of thought of the periods or cultures. Explanations can offer handles for evaluation, but neither descriptive variety nor its explanatory accounts precludes the separate and subsequent question of evaluation. On the whole, neither those who attack moral relativism nor those who defend it deny that there has been considerable variety in moral beliefs (codes, systems) of different peoples or periods. It is even conceivable that the globe has had thousands of moralities, as it has had thousands of languages. And in modern times variety has been found not only among peoples and periods but among subgroups in one country at one period and (what has become increasingly important) among individuals.

Let us try to see now how the issue of moral relativity enters over and above the picture of variety. One helpful way is to reflect on the *moral* lessons that the historians and anthropologists are often tempted to enunciate after finding the variations and explaining how conditions contributed to them. For example, Ruth Benedict's *Patterns of Culture* in the early 1930s found different moralities to be part of the different cultural patterns of life of different peoples.[10] She was regarded as propounding moral relativism, but in fact she drew the lesson that we should be more appreciative of what different people under different conditions were trying to do in building a coherent mode of life, and she urged tolerance as a value in facing differences. But of course to urge tolerance is to affirm a moral outlook; in the evaluative stance this meant regarding tolerance as morally superior (correct, more valid, and the like) to the intolerance of racial superiority and hatred that was then being preached.

The morality of tolerance has had to face the same kind of exploration for its limits that we saw characterized the morality of individualism in the development of the theory of autonomy. It was spared a lengthy consideration with respect to tolerating Nazi intolerance because Nazi aggression in World War II rapidly made defense and victory a superior obligation. But the theoretical question of the limits of tolerance still remains both serious and pressing in a number of different contexts. One is the moral attitude to take to a dogmatic system that represses what our morality regards as fundamental human rights—for example, the Iran of Khomeini in the 1970s and 1980s with the militant morality of a fundamentalist religion; or the racism of South Africa. Another context is the moral (and legal) attitude to be taken toward advocacy of such views within our own democratic framework, for example, neo-Nazi and Ku Klux Klan parades demanding police protection against an indignant populace. The significant theoretical point about all these cases, however, is that they do not arise as problems of moral relativism but as particular problems of interpretation and decision *within our own morality*, and the limits of tolerance within it. They are typically such questions as: Does not our morality allow the right of any other people to try out whatever pattern of life they may adopt or have come to, and to learn by their own experience? How far may we try to influence the outcome of that learning, and by what means? What is permissible in being "my brother's keeper"? What are the limits of proselytizing, or of warding off potential dangers to oneself? Such questions usually lead into refined moral distinctions of what we may or may not do against proponents of other moralities.

Clearly moral tolerance is not moral relativism. It does not preclude judgments of better or worse among patterns any more than religious tolerance means that opposing religious views are all equally valid; religious tolerance means simply that we should respect people's efforts and problems for which religious views are answers, and try if we are concerned with them to find out which is more adequate and in what respects. What we have said of tolerance holds comparably for sincerity as a virtue in individuals: we respect a person's sincerity in acting on convictions, but we need not evaluate equally the action in which it issues. Moreover, the scope of action that a society gives to a sincere person need not be limitless. Terrorists often pass the hardest test of sincerity, a readiness to sacrifice life for principle, but we are prone to regard their action as fanaticism or moral arrogance rather than as an individualism that in virtue of its sincerity has the right to follow its convictions.

The objection may arise that we are treating moral variations as moral beliefs and therefore subject to evaluation as more or less true, adequate, and so on. But do we always have the criteria for such judgments? In an opposition of scientific beliefs we do not stay with variety because we have an accepted procedure for scientific evaluation. What corresponds to this in the evaluation of moral beliefs? When we meet opposing scientific hypotheses or convictions we do not say each one is right for its side, but we assume one or the other is wrong, or both are wrong. When we do not have evidence to decide we simply say that. We may not even know how we should decide if we could, or we may imagine situations that would enable us to decide but that we cannot set up. Suppose, however, *we had to engage in action* along one or another of the opposing hypotheses. What else could we say but that each side may at present act along its convictions, even though we expect that sooner or later only one side will turn out to be right—if the formulation of the whole question is not itself changed? Where the conflict of moral beliefs concerns some hypothetical situation we do not now have to face, we can also afford the same luxury of indecision that we can in many scientific matters.

This analysis will seem to make the case in science and morals parallel by fastening on a rare situation in science. But examples are becoming frequent enough in technological matters where there is no disagreement about the values desired: for instance, decisions about nuclear energy, about dangers to the ozone layer, about the effect of increasing carbon dioxide as a consequence of industrial production and the possibility of its raising the temperature of the settled parts of the earth. In the social sciences problems of this type are frequent rather than rare: economic hypotheses in conflict where it is urgent to act, conflicting sociological hypotheses as to how to resolve situations of violence or discrimination to achieve agreed-on ends.

Clearly we do have a model that has scientific instances of importance in human life. How far can we use it in moral situations? The fact that such situations occur more frequently in morals does not constitute a matter of principle; it means simply that in problems of moral decision there is likely to be greater uncertainty or indeterminacy than in scientific questions. By indeterminacy here is meant a difficulty in reaching definite answers, whether the difficulty stems from insufficient information, knowledge of laws, variables too large or complex to handle, too great a rapidity of change, and the like. In this sense, issues of action based on social science have a greater indeterminacy than those based on technology, and issues of action based on morals sometimes greater than either. The usual objection here offered is that somehow in morals the indeterminacy is radical, that in the others we can conceive of possible evidence to resolve the issue but in morals we cannot conceive of what would be convincing evidence. (Of course it does not mean that a belief is stubbornly continued irrespective of evidence; there may still be people who believe the earth is flat, which is not a moral matter.)

The contrast tends to be hardened under interpretations of science that think of verification as simply settled by selected observations. But even where this takes place there is a whole background of theory that determines what will count as verifying instances. To the degree that complexities and differences in the theory enter—as they often do in social science and history—the end result is more or less like that which holds for morality. At least the differences are of degree, not of kind. At this point talk of relativism becomes loudest. Let us then draw some conclusions about the way moral relativism should be understood.

First, the situation in which the charge of relativism arises is one in which there is an indeterminacy that prevents a decisive answer, or yields several different answers. In short, unresolved indeterminacy is the basis of claims of relativism.

Second, moral relativism falls in the class of situations that present a major indeterminacy for action. Of course not all these are moral questions. In the case of scientific indecision of this sort, the comparable issue is not which view is true but acting on which view where action is necessary is right.

Third, in moral matters, we do not find indeterminacy everywhere. The mere fact that people with different moral outlooks may regard the same action as moral—e.g. honesty on a religious ethic of "Thou shalt not bear false witness" and on a utilitarian ethic that dishonesty will be inimical to human well-being or happiness—shows there can be areas of broad moral agreement in action. Hence moral relativism is not a specific ethical theory: it is simply calling attention to problems of indeterminacy that in fact are found in parts of all ethical theories.

Fourth, the opposite of moral relativism is usually taken to be moral absolutism. But there is no moral absolutism that does not present at some points the appearance of a relativism, and no relativism that does not present at some points the appearance of an absolutism. Religious theories that refer morality to God's will are determinate only insofar as they have a way of ascertaining what that will commands. In a religious existentialism in which we have no such certainty, we have in effect a relativism. (The more usual instance is the clash of different religious moralities.) A relativism that says morality is simply people's expression of their feelings turns into an absolutism if one takes the feelings to have a fixed character—e.g. expressive of basic sympathy. The best illustration is the most extreme relativism, that every person's ultimate moral convictions are right for him or her and not open to external question. But this seems to be making the absolute moral assertion that anyone has the right to fashion his or her own morality to act upon! In short, it is the assertion of an absolute moral individualism.

We conclude, then, that what is called moral relativism is something different in each of the two stances we distinguished above. In *the stance of giving an account of* it is an epistemological theory propounding a radical indeterminism for morality; in short, that the indeterminacy will remain particularly for fundamental or ultimate moral judgments irrespective of any growth of knowledge. In the *evaluative stance* it is itself a particular moral outlook of unlimited tolerance (in group judgments) and unlimited individualism (in individual judgments). As a moral outlook it had some force when the typical moral situation was one of dogmatism; but it lost credibility when it got to serious issues at the outer boundary. At that point a liberal morality that embraces both tolerance and individualism may rightly look back on its history and say that it never made absolutes (or meant to make absolutes) out of a tolerance of anything and everything or an individual fiat in which anything goes.

Clearly the more serious relativism is the epistemological. On the whole, most of the a priori arguments that have been given for a radical indeterminacy in morals have not been sustained—e.g. those resting on a philosophical dualism and the distinctive freedom of the will in humans; or upon the assumption that there is an arbitrariness inherent in human feeling. Its strong appeal has been rather to the extent of moral disagreement among people. Much of its prediction of a sustained indeterminacy, however, is like the older laments in science about what we can never know: for example, about the limits of vision in astronomy or the claims for a lower limit in the analysis of matter. Let us then turn to the central issue: in what ways morality can move to diminish indeterminacy by conceiving of knowledge that if acquired would tip the scales with respect to indeterminacy. Illustrations of actual historical cases are not hard to find.

First, there is the growth of factual knowledge that has an impact. For example, people once held that illness was morally culpable because it was punishment for some wrongdoing. Here the knowledge of causes of illness removed the moral indeterminacy and adjudicated between opposing views.

Second, there are cases where the growth of experience makes a distinction in the subject matter of moral judgment. For example, the old argument about whether usury was morally wrong at one point in Western history and became morally permissible at another point lost its flavor of indeterminacy when the distinction was drawn between two kinds of borrowing: the usury condemned concerned loans for consumption by the impoverished, while that found permissible was borrowing for investment and possible profit. Once they are distinguished, there is greater agreement on each separate judgment.

Third, explanatory accounts of the conditions under which certain moral beliefs are held help us understand their character and see them as moral compromises rather than as morally evil. The stock example, taken from the Eskimo customs of the old days, is that they abandoned their parents when the latter were old and incapacitated. Abstracted from the conditions of their lives this is readily labeled cruelty or ingratitude or even killing. In actuality, it was enmeshed in the conditions of hardship: survival of the family required moving on from the given location, and to be burdened by the incapacitated meant the likely death of the whole family. Moreover, we learn that the parents asked for or expected this treatment, and that the culture even had myths to palliate the situation. The situation then begins to look more like an overloaded lifeboat in which some have to get out; it looks more like parental heroism and sacrifice, like our soldiers sent off to die in a war. Indeed many moral disputes will turn out to be disputes about appropriate *moral compromise* rather than sheer indeterminacy of resolution.

Fourth, advance in some whole area of knowledge may throw a fresh light upon some entrenched moral belief that had hitherto condemned alternative ways as morally evil. The growth of depth psychology and theory of ideology in social science has led to the reinterpretation of some such intensely held moral beliefs. The "work ethic" is a good historical example: an important human need was enshrined in a religious theory of salvation and coupled with demands for thrift and industriousness that produced accumulation but at a tremendous psychic cost. It now becomes possible under enhanced modes of production to reassess the evidence for both the need and the cost. *Fifth*, the sociological and anthropological study of the general tasks that every society has to accomplish to secure survival enables us to look at some cultural differences in institutional values and moral demands in terms of underlying functions. Thus a strict rule in one primitive culture that when a large animal is trapped specified parts go to specified kin, an injunction of hospitality in a second culture (so that even the same word is used for inhospitality and for theft), systematic gift giving in a third, and rules of credit and trade in a fourth can all be seen as different ways of ensuring the distribution of the goods of that society under different conditions and cultural emphases. (The first case prevents loss of the meat under conditions of the absence of refrigeration!) Hence it becomes possible to evaluate all these institutions by the common criterion of effective distribution, though it may be crossed at some points by other, e.g. aristocratic or meritocratic, value strands. Sometimes we may even be able to predict the acceptance of one rather than an opposing moral trend on the basis of our knowledge of changing conditions. Over and beyond the impact of growing knowledge, we may anticipate that there may be convergences in moral feeling under common experiences. For example, we do not know what the morality of an overcrowded world will be like, but we may suspect that some components in it will be promoted by the quality of the experience.

Finally, we may revert to the point made in connection with autonomy and the brief historical sketch of attempts to decide on the limits of individualism. We saw there that a definite meaning could be established for long-range experiment or exploratory practice using broad criteria of success or failure. This removes the last theoretical ground for interpreting moral disagreement and the conflict it may involve as necessarily a clash of arbitrariness. It may instead be viewed as a point calling for further and continued evaluation in the light of improved formulation of the problem, deeper understanding of conditions and relations to other values, and deeper understanding of human nature and society and aspirations. Of course evaluation can go on indefinitely, but so can the improvement of knowledge; in both cases there can be progress and growth, and in both cases continued patches of indeterminacy.

Education is a long-range matter and from that perspective there is a tremendous difference between saying that we have a conflict of arbitrary opposites and saying we have opposing hypotheses for long-range evaluation, even though we may have to make a present choice of which to experiment with. The methods, the attitudes, the expectations, and the temper of present conflict become different. It is with this solution to the claims of moral relativism in its epistemological thesis that we shall approach the question of what is to be done in moral and social education (chapter 14).

Notes

1. For some interesting portraits of reason or of rationality from different angles, see various essays in "Reason," part 2 of *Education and the Development of*

Reason, ed. R.F. Dearden, P.H. Hirst, and R.S. Peters (Boston: Routledge & Kegan Paul, 1972).

2. See also above, ch. 5, n. 1.

3. Of course many fruitful distinctions can be and have been made at this point. For example, C.I. Lewis distinguishes intelligence and rationality. The opposite of the first, applied to a person, is "unintelligent" or "stupid"; of the second, "irrational" or "perverse." They are "two different ways in which we may come to choose the worse instead of the better course of conduct." Rationality is tied to the constraints of knowledge. *Our Social Inheritance* (Bloomington: Indiana University Press, 1957), p. 88.

4. This proposal is presented in Abraham Edel, "Toward an Analytic Method for Dealing with Moral Change," in *Exploring Fact and Value* (New Brunswick, N.J.: Transaction Books, 1980), ch. 9.

5. The versatility of autonomy is seen in the diversity of its interpretations. Cf. R.F. Dearden, "Autonomy and Education," in "Education and Reason," part 3 of *Education and the Development of Reason*, ed. R.F. Dearden, P.H. Hirst, and R.S. Peters (Boston: Routledge & Kegan Paul, 1972), pp. 58-75; Kurt Baier, "Moral Autonomy as an Aim of Moral Education," in *New Essays in the Philosophy of Education*. ed. Glenn Langford and D.J. O'Connor (Boston: Routledge & Kegan Paul, 1973), pp. 96-114; Brian Crittenden, "Autonomy as an Aim of Education," in *Ethics and Educational Policy*, ed. Kenneth A. Strike and Kieran Egan (Boston: Routledge & Kegan Paul, 1978), pp. 105-26. Dearden decides that a person is autonomous to the degree that what the person thinks and does on important matters are determined by himself or herself, that is, cannot be explained without reference to his or her own activity of mind (p.71). Baier tries out identifying autonomy with self-mastery, so that it includes self-control, strength of will, tenacity, and resoluteness; each is defined as resistance to something—to the impulse to laugh or sneeze or blurt out; to temptation; to fatigue and pain; to the effects of adversity; to doubt and uncertainty. Moral autonomy is construed as moral self-mastery (pp. 106-7). Crittenden distinguishes intellectual, moral, and emotional autonomy. The first lies in determining for oneself what constitutes adequate evidence and so forth; the second centers on practical judgment and action, and executive capacities for carrying into practice; the third is illustrated by the Stoics, a self-sufficiency detached in relation to others. Crittenden concludes: "In fact, it seems that personal autonomy has become one of those idols in whose name the effort to make liberal education available to as many people as possible is being betrayed" (p. 123).

6. John Dewey, *Human Nature and Conduct* (New York: Modern Library, 1930), part 4, secs. 3, 4; John Dewey and James H. Tufts, *Ethics*, rev. ed. (New York: Henry Holt, 1932), pp. 336-42.

7. That Dewey identifies freedom from the outset with the power to learn from experience is clear if we look at his definition of "plasticity" in the case of a human being: "This is something quite different from the plasticity of putty or wax. It is not a capacity to take on change of form in accord with external pressure. . . . It is essentially the ability to learn from experience. . . . This means power to modify actions on the basis of the results of prior experiences, the power to *develop dispositions.*" *Democracy and Education* (New York: Macmillan, 1961; originally published 1916), p. 44.

8. See especially John Stuart Mill's *On Liberty*, ch. 3, and also his *Representative Government*, especially chs. 2, 3; Alexis de Tocqueville. *Democracy in America.*

9. Carol Gilligan, *In a Different Voice: Psychological Theory and Women's Development* (Cambridge: Harvard University Press, 1982).

10. Ruth Benedict, *Patterns of Culture* (New York: Houghton Mifflin, 1934).

Part III
Teacher and Student

Introduction

It would be comforting at this point to preface our consideration of teacher and student with a formal definition of "education." As the reader may suspect by this time, no such essentialist comfort is afforded us. Instead of unfolding a single concept, let us see why no single analysis of "education" or "an educated person" offered at the outset or even at this stage of our inquiry can carry the tasks of the philosophy of education. Perhaps this is best done in brief compass by comparing a few of the different treatments in different philosophical approaches and drawing the lessons from their variety.

We may begin with Dewey. The first four chapters of his *Democracy and Education* (1916)[1] give an amazingly rich and structured conception. In the first, "Education as a Necessity of Life," the necessity is seen to flow from the facts of birth and death of the members in a social group. Education primarily lies in transmitting the ways and shared experience of the group. Formal teaching arises as societies become more complex in structure and resources. The second chapter is "Education as a Social Function." Education operates through the action of an environment to call out certain responses, the environment involving the social as well as rearrangement of the physical. The use of language in education to transmit ideas is an extension of this, for "things gain meaning by being used in a shared experience or joint action." When a considerable part of the accumulated experience is written and transmitted through symbols, schools as a special environment come into existence. The third chapter, "Education as Direction," and the fourth, "Education as Growth," obviously approach educating from the side of teaching and of learning respectively. With close attention to the underlying psychological process, Dewey has his eye throughout on the children whose nature shapes what the guidance can accomplish. The four chapters collectively give a comprehensive presentation of origins, motivating factors, general possibilities and limits, and dominating normative perspective. And, in the spirit of his philosophy, these are not treated each in isolation but as phases arising out of the problematic context in which humans find themselves in their development.

It is not surprising that such unity disappears in the philosophies of education that grew up after major dichotomies, particularly of fact and value and of the logical and the genetic, began under positivist and analytic influence to permeate the philosophical scene. Questions were thereby raised: is education a descriptive concept, a scientific one, an evaluative one? Let us take some proposed answers in Anglo-American educational thought.

In his *The Real World of the Public Schools* (1972), Broudy interprets "education" directly as a value concept, comparing it to "health" and "social welfare."[2] Like them, it would be an open term, which would become clearer as our values become clearer and better informed and as our knowledge increases. Disputes arise about what education is, just as they do in the case of health—for example, whether mental health should use the same model as physical health. Similarly, should the measure of social welfare be happiness, the greatest happiness of the greatest number, the satisfaction of desires or the satisfaction of needs, and so on. The disputes shift from clarifying education as a concept to the content that would promote the values associated within it.

A similar end result along a different path is reached in McClellan's *Philosophy of Education* (1976). Like Broudy, McClellan regards attempts to give a scientific definition of "education" as pseudoscience: "Behaviorism stands to philosophy of education as nihilism to metaphysics, skepticism to epistemology, or cynicism to ethics."[3] At a minimum, the attempts of social science to give a neutral definition are uninteresting, for the concept is really concerned with "a particular *way of becoming* a person-in-society,"[4] and so with fundamental evaluations at the center of our communal life. Current definitions express different beliefs about the particular process, but because the beliefs are confused we cannot expect a clear definition. McClellan's conclusion is that "when we get our ideas about teaching and learning perfectly straight, the concept of education will take care of itself."[5]

A persistent attempt of a different sort is to be found in the educational writings of Richard Peters. It is of special interest because he develops his ideas as he continues his investigation and is explicit about the reasons for change. In his earlier view, education was initiation into worthwhile activities.[6] It thus included the transmission of worthwhile activities to those who become committed to them; some knowledge and understanding, and cognitive perspective that is not inert; and the exclusion of some procedures as lacking wittingness and voluntariness on the part of the learner. His modified view separates the processes from the outcome, which is the educated person.[7] Thus by attending to different emphases in the family of processes, he is able to accomodate different usages: the widespread equation of "education" with varieties of training, the application of the term to ways of bringing up the young in which little is made of cognitive knowledge (e.g. "Spartan education"), and even the contrasting case of people who, when the cognitive is stressed, say that "an education is not worth it." (Such an expression as the latter could not be used if by definition education was the pursuit of worthwhile activities.) In part, Peters is showing how the concept of education has broken apart under modern conditions. His chief interest appears to lie in the outcome, the educated person. He shows what such a person is like, how knowledge plays its part in sensitizing the student to standards that are intrinsic to worthwhile activities, and what care and commitment are involved in the pursuits.

These few samples suggest how varied the approach may be to the concept of education. Dewey's is rooted in the pragmatic method and his holistic perspective, so that education has to be understood in terms of the full operations of the society. Peters relies on the assumption of intrinsically worthwhile activities that can be set off from the rest of life's goings-on and can be grasped as self-justified. Broudy's approach recognizes that many of our higher-order concepts about human affairs have a substantial valuational content and set standards for human life, and that the questions in their analysis are more clearly tackled if we go directly to the analysis of the standards themselves. But to analyze the standards will bring us either to a relativism of commitments or to a theory of intrinsic values in Peters's sense or to a depth inquiry in Dewey's sense, or—and this is our fourth sample—to throw up our hands in McClellan's sense and say that we have first to get clear the domain that the concept of education governs (teaching, learning, and so on), and education will take care of itself.

Now, it is true that abstract concepts such as education, or democracy, or capitalism, or nationalism, require continual and developing reanalysis. The reason is twofold. In part it is because our knowledge grows as the concept is taxed by fresh situations, and we are led to refine our ideas; and in part it is because the phenomena involved themselves undergo change so that the concepts may have to be reshaped. Obvious historical examples are the way in which democracy developed as the population increased from the face-to-face group to the large group and representative institutions were fashioned, and also changes that took place as modes of communication were altered. Similarly, the idea of capitalism was altered as economies went through different stages from a manufacturing to an industrial to a large-scale technological production and comparably from a laissez-faire to a corporate to an international corporate form. So too, education and its functions changed from its earlier less formal ways with the development of the public school systems, and with the growth of almost universal or mass education, with the development of technical education, and so on. Because there is no definite way of predicting future influences and future changes, there needs to be continuous refinement in the concept, tracing both continuities and changes, with explicit indication of the value shifts and the empirical substitutions. Such an attitude to definition has become commonplace in the philosophy of science in concept formation, and its recognition as the way of dealing with abstractions like education will spare us many analytic worries.

Our brief review suggests that proposals to define "education" in a particular way should be treated as pointers to different aspects of the processes we set off as educational. The path to greater clarity lies through an examination of these processes—the general situation in which teachers and students find themselves, the character of teaching and learning and the organization of schooling. To such questions part III is devoted.

This conclusion is supported by the practical role that "education" often plays, in which it helps set policy and shape institutions. Even terms like "science" or "family" carry this aspect in their subtle shades. For example, to include or exclude grandparents in the definition of "the family" is to take a stand on the shape of the institution, and to make obligations to grandparents either an inner or an outside matter. So too, in the history of schooling, community groups have sometimes attempted to cut down certain subjects (usually in the interests of economy) by labeling them "fads and frills," that is, decorations and not a proper part of education. As schooling has become a complex institution, this policy use of "education" is likely to grow rather than diminish. In the days of the one-room schoolhouse the teacher's job covered everything from subject teaching to keeping the woodstove fired up. Nowadays the "noneducational" jobs are kept separated off, and likely to be more separated off with the addition, beyond custodial services, and psychological and other welfare services, of assistants and paraprofessionals. Keeping records may come to be certified as "clerical" and come under another jurisdiction.

Major questions of policy are likely to be settled under the definition of "educational activities," just as major questions of the American way of life were settled under the definition of "due process."[8] Take, for example, the question whether research is an educational activity. Answers to this may well shape the relation of graduate to undergraduate work in the colleges. Some colleges insist that their primary task is teaching, not advancing knowledge; they are not always consistent in that they sometimes demand productive scholarship as a condition for promotion in their teaching staff. Peters, in his *Ethics and Education*, raises the question in a reverse direction—whether teaching belongs in the university (as distinguished from the college). Clearly we cannot expect to settle such questions by a peremptory definition of "education" that will tell us whether research is included or excluded. We have to inquire, rather, what contribution is made to teaching by a college faculty's engaging in research as against having separate research institutes. If we recognize the policy-determining and institution-shaping function of discourse about "education" and "educational activities," it becomes necessary to track down the components that shape the outcome and the values embedded therein. In that sense we are systematically building up and refining a definition of "education" as we go along; if there is to be a definition it is an outcome, not a starting point. And the outcome is more likely to be a view of a fully constructed educational system, with structure and tasks explained and justified.

Notes

1. John Dewey, *Democracy and Education* (New York: Macmillan, 1961; originally published 1916), chs. 1-4.
2. Harry S. Broudy, *The Real World of the Public Schools* (New York: Harcourt Brace Jovanovich, 1972).
3. James E. McClellan, *Philosophy of Education* (Englewood Cliffs, N.J.: Prentice-Hall, 1976), p. 8.
4. Ibid., p. 14.
5. Ibid., p. 21.
6. R.S. Peters, *Ethics and Education* (London: Allen & Unwin, 1966), ch. 1.
7. R.S. Peters, "Education and the Educated Man," *The Philosophy of Education Society of Great Britain, Proceedings of the Annual Conference* 4: 5-20.
8. A good example of the concrete way in which powers and budget are steered along the lines of what is conceived as an educational matter can be seen in the changes that took place when on the federal level education was taken out of the Department of Health, Education, and Welfare and a separate department set up, with a separate cabinet officer of education and a separate budget. It is interesting to note that of the two chief (and competing) teacher organizations, the National Education Association advocated this step as giving education an appropriate stature, whereas the American Federation of Teachers, allied with the AFL-CIO, opposed it as tending to isolate education and also turning attention to bureaucratic questions of readjustment rather than content questions. Educational activities of one kind or another still continued separately, for example, under the army, in the Veterans Administration, and under the National Science Foundation and the National Endowment for the Arts and Humanities. These resisted coordination under a unified educational department for fear of being controlled in their activities by the interests of the massive school system. The degree of unity in what falls under "education" is thus far from a settled question—even apart from the "political" aspects.

9. Teacher and Student in the Contemporary World

The actors at the center of the stage in contemporary schooling are the teachers and the students; administrators intermingle with both in the exercise of their functions. In the next chapter we shall deal with teaching and learning, at the analytic distance in which today they have to be examined to gain a comprehensive perspective. It is well first to look at the persons in the actual context of the problems and conflicts that beset them.

On Being a Teacher in the Contemporary World

Teachers no longer have the fixed assured role they once had. They react to changes that have taken place or are taking place, and have to choose between drift and an attitude of active reconstruction involving normative judgments. In any case they need a heightened awareness to appreciate what they are trying to retain or to achieve.

What has been the teacher's self-image? I do not mean the image as against the reality, a contrast so often posed in the Madison Avenue manufacture of "images" and the political assumption of "postures," but how the community has looked upon the teacher and how the teacher has looked upon himself or herself. Is the teacher just "holding a job," or being a "public servant"? "A maker of the future," or at least a "special person in the community," or just another citizen "doing a specialized job"? Is the teacher the "community's intellectual," or just a "daytime custodian for the children"? Clearly the teacher is not the only one to exercise these functions. Others hold jobs: garbage collectors are public servants, engineers and politicians make the future, librarians and scientists are custodians of knowledge, parents mold the youth, and in older Russian novels the doctor and the lawyer find their place among the community intellectuals. What stands out in the role of teachers depends largely on the shape these functions take in the particular conditions of the community and its institutions. Almost any of these listed—and others—have somewhere or other been their public image and self-image. The question now is what are the desirable views and role of self, and that means what are the desirable emphases in function? In part these are determined by the nature of teaching and learning as we are to understand them (in their whole cultural and social context), but their particular form is now a problem for social decision.

It is of little help to ask whether teaching is a job, a vocation, or a profession, for these are themselves in flux. If a job means *only* work for fixed hours with no responsibility for the character of the work, carrying out assignments that foreman or assistant principals and department heads prescribe, then teaching has often been just a job like working in a factory, but clearly it should be more. The same point has been made in our time for factory work, and in many parts of the Western world there are attempts to move factory work itself away from simply this. "Vocational education," particularly when contrasted with "liberal education," has sometimes had a derogatory sense, an education merely for a job. But there was a time when the term "vocation" carried the sense of devotion to a calling. Teaching can be a vocation in that sense, just like the calling of a clergyman. Today teaching often is taken to have a place among the professions, with a status in relation to medicine, law, engineering, that depends on cultural tradition and economic conditions.

A profession involves at least the following: having some collective responsibility for determining the *content* and the standards of the work, having some share in determining the *conditions* under which the work is carried out, and being responsible in some measure for the *process* and *results* of the work. In each of these regards the appropriate extent of participation and responsibility of teaching is controversial, as with other professions; the social patterns on these matters are in the making rather than fixed by tradition.

Whose responsibility is it to determine what gets taught? Largely a matter of tradition by this time, the bulk of the content of education on the higher as well as the lower levels of education persists under a standard rubric. New subjects within and across disciplines sometimes slowly emerge; at other times they come with the tone of a revolutionary change, accompanied by justificatory slogans of immediate necessity. In the United States, "It's time the schools did something about it" is often heard about pressing social problems as diverse as typing or driving or sex education. Or demands arise in one country for modernization and catching up with advances other countries have made, for example, in introducing sociology into British universities. Interdisciplinary subjects and modes of teaching may be prompted by experimental programs sponsored by foundations.

The more technical specific subject matters become, the more they are seen as the responsibility of the teaching body; just as curing is left to the medical professions, so teaching is left to the teaching profession. (But this assumes an accepted ideal, parallel to health in the medical profession.)

Outside participation becomes broader in its thrust rather than deeper. There may be financial objections to the cost of programs, ideological objections to whole or partial areas—as in religious attacks on the teaching of evolution or attacks by committees in the community upon the use of certain kinds of textbooks (on grounds of "subversive" tendencies or "indecency"). And of course there are expressions of social needs for the development of fresh areas—whether a new branch of science that is economically desirable, as in the history of the growth of teaching in electronics or automotive industries, or a growing social problem, as in the new recognition of pollution problems. (Even teachers of literature have then to decide whether the romantic London fog shall now appear as just plain smog.) Again, outside pressure with respect to content may become strong when it is believed the schools have neglected or dealt badly or unfairly with particular questions or particular groups—as happened in moves under community pressure with respect to Black studies, ethnic group studies, feminist studies, and the like.

While in general it is clear today that the job of deciding educational content lies with the educational profession, and on the whole no alternative seems feasible, this is believed to be a social trust, with the understanding that the major social needs will have their place. It follows that especially in a time of change and educational reconstruction such as the present, questions about the whole character of education will come to the fore, that the multiplicity of objectives will force a more systematic pattern of consideration, and that the dialogue of basic decision will be between the teaching profession and the community and its organs at large.

At this point the expectations of the community about what education provides become particularly important. This is an old story, about which we can read in Aristophanes's comedies. In his *Clouds* a peasant coerces his son into attending Socrates's school because he expects the son will learn rhetorical argument and be able to help him outwit his creditors. The father is at first puzzled by what is done in the school: Socrates swings in a basket in the air and looks at the stars; the pupils measure the jump of a flea and all that "science." The son does learn dialectical argument, but he turns his new skills against the father in the conflict of generations. Desperate, the father watches gleefully as the irate public puts the school to the torch.

The plot almost fits the way community and professional assumptions about objectives drifted apart in the 1970s. The community assumed that schooling is the avenue to a job, and the profession assumed that education is the awakening of an intellectual and value consciousness that enhances the whole life. They drifted along together in the previous period of economic and school expansion but drifted apart when economic recession followed, bringing increased unemployment in skilled and professional areas. Economic contraction kept the schools from improving quality to correspond to increase of numbers, with the inner-city schools of the large urban centers who needed most getting least. Because the profession had allowed the argument that schooling is a good economic investment to circulate in prosperous times to promote the schools, it was rather awkward in time of recession suddenly to decide that after all education is good for human living and to forget about economic advantages.[1] Moreover, the strata of the population at the bottom of the economic ladder—in this case, Blacks and Hispanics—could very well feel aggrieved that the public schools had proclaimed themselves the road to upward mobility until they come along, and then changed the song. If the end result was not the burning of the schools, as in Aristophanes's *Clouds*, it was at least the cutting of their budgets and increased violence within.

This story indicates that the justifications of an institution are important practically, not only in theory or in rhetoric. Honest communication among teachers, administrators, and community on objectives and limitations, on empirical and essential connections, is requisite to basic understanding and cooperation. To speak of dialogue among the parties, however, raises the question of their organization. This is less critical for administrators because their position is usually one that carries authority and its responsibilities. It is critical for teachers and community. Internal structuring of the profession itself takes different forms. Teachers may be organized in associations that are largely advisory, or in unions having an almost external relation to the processes of decision about school policy. Or again, teachers may have an integral part in the structure of authority within the institution. Here the subject merges with the general problem of governance, and fundamental stands in social philosophy become immediately relevant. One side will stress reliance on expertise in an elitist sense—as in the U.S. structuring of school administration with superintendents on top, or traditional German structuring of university control with the professor as the authoritative head of each department. On the other side is the call for democratic participation and responsibility within institutional structurings. Similar differences arise on the community's participation: there may be centralized or local controls for formulating objectives and evaluation, and there may be determination by bodies of experts or else elected or community boards of representatives.

In the United States broader questions of institutional structure have arisen less over the content of schooling than in struggles over conditions of work. The school was a latecomer to union organization. Major controversies still remain about tenure and job security, salary and hours of labor, class size, and permissible modes of maintaining order. And there are always special problems arising.

Tenure and job security, like academic freedom, are of educational as well as economic concern. Without tenure teachers may be constrained by insecurity in pursuing work and expressing views or teaching what they hold to be the truth. In short, the general justification offered for tenure is that without it the system would have a teaching body of conformists. On the other hand, tenure is said to give a permanent lodging to some mediocrities. In times of overcrowding in the academic world, tenure may also pit an entrenched older generation against an eager younger generation, many of whom may get lost to the profession. Here the rigidity of tenure is related to the planlessness of the wider social scene. Presumably if a society had more varied and flexibly patterned arrangements for its intellectuals throughout its institutions, less rigidity might be demanded within any one institution.

The other matters mentioned turn out to be very complex. Salary, hours of labor, and class size lead eventually, in the case of the public schools, to rates of taxation in the community; permissible modes of maintaining order occasionally end up in the courts when the right to expel a student is questioned. While salary matters seem to deal only with teachers' welfare as workers, experience has shown that worker morale is critical in carrying on a delicate enterprise. Class size is a matter of "production quota"—parallel to production minima in digging coal—but it is also important to the quality of the result. Here the question of optimal class size is rarely the issue; usually it is a question of costs.

Analysis of these issues has on the whole shown that the problems of teachers are not essentially different from the problems of workers generally. During the period in which teacher unions arose and struggled for recognition it was often argued that teachers are professionals, not workers for whom this form of organization might be suitable. As to claims that teachers were exploited, it was argued that whatever was the case in private enterprise, nobody made a profit from the hard work of teachers and so there could be no exploitation involved. On this, it eventually became clear that an indirect route of possible exploitation existed: in public schools support comes from taxation, and so from the society, and a pattern of justice or injustice may be expressed through the tax formulae. The fact that the route of struggle was thus more directly political has affected the history of the growth of teacher unionism, but only in the same way as that of other public employees (e.g. in such questions as the right to strike).

The scope of action of teacher unions has also raised questions of moral responsibilities. Two general directions may be distinguished. One is straight economism: union teachers are workers like other workers, and have to fight for their rights and the satisfaction of their needs against various types of exploitation. The other, not necessarily less militant, sets conditions of the pupils' well-being as a major component of the struggle. Thus diminishing class size is said to be a proper objective for union struggle, for it concerns directly the quality of education. Political programs such as free hot lunches for children are deemed legitimate because an underfed child is not an attentive pupil. Remedial programs are justified by what they do for the pupils, not simply by easing the job of the teacher. The crucial issues between the two directions might concern tactics, such as where a strike would be legitimate; the second tendency might suggest political organization of parents of pupils in a struggle for just wages, with lesser emphasis on strikes. However, these would in large measure be empirical matters; on both views strikes would be last resorts in desperately frustrating conditons.

The opposition among teachers to union organization and to association with labor reflected the middle-class ideology of the distinctive role of the intellectual professions. While the scope of schooling was more limited, it maintained (especially in colleges and universities) the aloofness that seemed dictated by professionals generally. But the vast extension of schooling and the multiplication of numbers in the profession as well as of the economic problems and social problems and their complexity drove teacher organizations to behave in ways not unlike unions, so that the chief remaining question became the benefit of affiliating with the labor movement.

That the existence of a strong teachers' organization, a union or functioning like a union, makes a difference in a school system, is clear enough. It changes the balance of control on many matters, and raises issues of the extent of its desirable scope. It is sometimes asked whether there are educational questions that are strictly outside the range of union deliberation and possible pressure, and whether there are strictly union methods that are not appropriate for educational decisions. This involves regarding the union as in some sense outside the institution, while the faculty is clearly inside. A teacher would thus have to draw sharp lines between acting as a union member and acting as a faculty member or member of a faculty senate. These are issues chiefly where unions are a comparatively recent phenomenon in education and their roles have not been sufficiently determined within the broader pattern of governance in educational institutions.

The question of responsibilities for the process and results in schooling is not wholly independent of the previous ones. Obviously if teachers have no part in determining the content and objectives of their work and are simply following orders for a limited period, and if the conditions of their labor are out of their control, they can have little responsibility for the way the work is carried out and the outcome. They simply have to show, if their work is questioned, that they have followed orders from the appropriate authority. Thus the inner strands of responsibility depend on the structure of the institution.

The extent of responsibilities arises therefore from the extent of teachers' participation and control. For example, if teachers are to educate students into independent responsible persons, and if they are given their way in determining the means of education, then they are responsible for cultivating the best available methods to this end. Suppose it is agreed that this means at a minimum teaching with respect for the students. They are responsible then for inquiry into the teaching directives this would entail—for example, the degree of required permissiveness or repressiveness to characterize teacher-student relations or the limits to regarding the teacher as an authority. One has only to compare present methods, even with all the controversies involved, with the old way of teaching that resorted to use of the cane; and even now there is a shade of difference between a teacher always giving an answer or sometimes saying, "I don't know. Let's look it up."

Recent attempts to hold teachers accountable for their "production" have some initial plausibility: given a large investment, say in automobiles, dissatisfaction would be reasonable if most of the cars proved to be defective; similarly if most surgical operations were failures. Why not accountability, it is asked, if a high percentage of the pupils graduating from high school cannot read or write effectively? (Lawyers are generically lucky, for there is always a winner in each litigation.)

On the other hand, some discount should be allowed for the general cultural habit of blaming the schools, which is a correlate of the general cultural habit of dumping all difficult problems on the schools, In the extreme this neglects the participation of students in their own education and the effects of social and school conditions. For example, during the McCarthy period professors were often regarded as all-powerful sources of what happened to students: a magazine article would portray the self-searching of a confessed subversive on how he or she first went wrong—and it would discover the influence of a particular liberal professor.

When, however, one looks into the matter more carefully, the overall plausibility may disappear. Doctors are not held responsible for a patient's death if nothing could reasonably have averted it. The limit of obligation is doing one's best, given the state of knowledge of the time and the conditions of practice. Just as a doctor cannot use a machine that the hospital does not have, for the purchase of which the community has not provided, so the teacher cannot be assigned the shortcomings of the schools when the conditions needed for learning have not been provided. Again, just as the doctor is not responsible for effects of the patient's neglect of his or her body or society's neglect of pollution and carcinogenic wastes, so the teacher is not responsible for the effects of a student's delinquency and propensity to violence nor of school overcrowding or home slum conditions, though the teacher's immediate daily experience of their effects may impose some moral obligation to enter on some social or political activity with respect to the matter.

What are teachers responsible for apart from doing their best? Nothing else, perhaps, but then the scope and domain of the best becomes the precise issue. Just as doctors are responsible for knowing what new treatments have been discovered for particular diseases, so teachers have a responsibility to keep up to date, not simply to keep on in traditional ways unquestioningly. School systems may then be expected to provide conditions that make this possible, not to discourage new ideas and insist on uniformity in methods. The teaching profession would be responsible for maintaining a general level of competence, just as the medical profession is. There have indeed been attempts to extend the concept of malpractice, as a negative way of doing this, whether directed at the individual teacher or the institution (for example, by a student who was graduated from high school without adequate reading skill). Whether the negative approach, usually through the courts, is the best way of doing this is a serious social issue, especially because it tends to impose a legalistic and rigid caution on educational institutions. Perhaps it is necessary only where congealed habits of inertia or bureaucratic disregard of rights or justice within a profession have thwarted all other modes of redress. Thus it compels the facing of a problem but does not provide a solution, as the contemporary history of malpractice in the medical profession has shown.

The traditional method of working toward the improvement of teaching has been by merit reward through selective salary increase and promotion. This has three defects. It stimulates competition and so divides teachers from one another precisely where they need to work together. (This is, however, a general problem of the culture.) It does nothing for the "losers" who are nevertheless within the system, not outsiders who do not enter it by losing. And the reward, being money, or prestige, has no intrinsic relation to the subject matter, that is, education or learning. To some extent there have been attempts, especially where organization has given scope to teacher energies and released initiative, to provide institutional forms for cooperation on educational improvement. One such form is a teacher center in connection with each school, completely under teacher control, in which new and experimental teaching materials and methods can be exhibited and cooperative exploration of problems constantly carried on.

A strong movement for "accountability" contrasts with these attempts to motivate improvement through enhancing common interest in the objectives and methods of education. Diverse strands run through such a movement. Pressure of economic recession (as in the 1970s) intensifies budget cutting, particularly as inflation pushes up educational costs; the result is a worsening of existent problems. Dissatisfaction with the results of education, such as the extent of illiteracy among high school graduates, instigates a search for whom to blame. And professional inertia often stands in the way of the need for reconstruction, comparable to the inertia of the medical profession under social change. In this atmosphere we have the various suggestions noted in chapter 4, such as breaking the monopoly of public education and through a voucher system giving every individual a limited educational fund to be used as he or she wishes, or contracting with a private system or corporation to be paid according to the performance of the child. The idea of accountability suggests that teachers should be rewarded according to the performance of the pupils taught, that is, the success of the teacher.

The arguments about responsibility given above would seem to hold here too. (If doctors were paid that way, would they take hopeless cases? Should teachers have the opportunity to exclude slow learners and refuse admission to "difficult" students?) General objections can be advanced. Pincoffs, for example, suggests that measuring and testing of performance refers to specific skills or determinate excellences (being a good speller, juggling, making cat's cradles) rather than indeterminate excellences (being prudent, wise, imaginative, considerate).[2] The latter are the objectives in education, and if we go in for accountability, emphasis in teaching will shift to the former. It is just as if the whole term were to be spent in reviewing old examination papers rather than in serious and genuine learning. Thus even were the performance of students improved and teachers paid more, less education might result.

Such considerations raise the general question of motivation within the profession and the extent to which merit systems are useful or outworn (cf. chapter 2). In the end, strengthening the intrinsic appeal of the work may prove the most successful means.

The most serious and intimate responsibilities of teachers have not yet been touched—those arising in their *direct* relationship to their students. Perennial responsibilities stem from the character of the teacher-student bond and the character of knowledge. These have been endlessly discussed and different views about them reflect philosophical differences in analyzing teaching.³ Special responsibilities arising from the particular issues of today's world are largely the problems of the students: increased numbers in an educational system originally fashioned for a select few; girls in a world built for boys; minority groups in a milieu long occupied by whites alone; emerging varied ethnic groups; students with some experience of the world doing work originally intended for youngsters; and so on. Teachers as the educated members of the relationship have the responsibility to see ahead, at least a step, and often do; but many are not aware of the nature of the tensions generated around them. The essential requirement is the cultivation of a broad empathy with different conditions and different strata of the population. Such matters are best seen from the point of view of the students.

Teachers are thus cast into a multitude of relations—to students as learners and persons primarily; to parents and community, to the profession with varying degree of cohesion and conflict with other social groups. Perhaps what is also needed to understand the teacher in the contemporary world is the teacher's inner perspective: the tensions set up by aspirations in the course of a teaching career and its frustrations, the early pressures of training, the slow-moving job lists (in urban centers) and the difficulties in getting jobs, the ideal of working with children and students, the pulls of learning or research or teaching, the conflicting ideas of what is demanded of teachers, the battle with deteriorating conditions (especially problems of violence and discipline in today's schools), the battle with institutional bureaucracy and authoritarianism, the kinds of compromises and lapses into resignation and apathy that are often found. They all explain why the teaching profession is the scene of such struggles of the spirit and why the schools remain a center of social conflict in the modern world. Teachers today in the United States have long passed the million mark, and it is no longer possible to make generalizations that would fit all parts of the country, all levels of schooling, all kinds of persons and temperaments, and all strata that have entered into the profession. There may still be a few places where "those who can't do, teach" or where young women do a few years' teaching between graduation and marriage. For the most part, however, old sterotypes are gone; it is not even always an underpaid profession, as it used to be, that offers security instead of good wages. It has its share of those for whom it is a haven. But a high proportion come into the profession with a strong devotion to learning and a sense of the importance of communicating with the young. Perhaps no other profession, short of medicine, is endowed with so much initial idealism. The surprising thing is how much of the satisfaction lasts in spite of the frustrations. Our understanding would be greatly helped by autobiographies of ordinary teachers, carried out as part of the new oral history. Yet along with the idealism, the toll of the spirit is great. We constantly hear of teacher "burnout"—getting worn out early on the job, showing fatigue, abandoning the profession in large numbers, in short the clear symptoms of alienation. At the same time, given the tremendous store of idealism that has gone into teaching, one may expect increasing struggle for reconstruction.

Being a Student in the Contemporary World

The older generation, even teachers in close quarters with students, has not always found it easy to understand what it is like to be a student in the world of the last half of the twentieth century. This is true at all levels. There are too many barriers to surmount, too many traditional ways of looking at things and people, too great a quickness to assert and not to listen. Empathy alone, while admirable, will not itself do the job. Too often when we put ourselves in others' shoes, it is we, with our traditions and reactions, not they, who stand there. It has taken extended scientific study to tell us about a dog's hearing or a fish's seeing, and a photographer's creative skill and imagination to produce pictures of what the baby's field of vision is like when the adult looms over it. If we can go so far without dialogue and rational discussion, why should not our phenomenological methods, our controlled scientific observation, our social sciences, and our reflective rational discussion enable us to see the social and educational world from the student's point of view? Perhaps the clearest instance of the failure to communicate came in the startling explosion of students in the 1960s. Assuming a paternalistic stance, many teachers and professors declaimed the irrationality of youth and the decline of standards and restraints, and called for renewed repressive efforts. Although the episode has receded into history, if left insufficiently analyzed and its educational lessons insufficiently drawn, some fresh form of it is likely to happen again. For this reason, we include an analysis of the counterculture and its revolt in that period, and the way it expressed the predicament of the older as well as the younger generation.

The two notions most often employed in discussing such matters were the generation gap and alienation. An illuminating conceptual study of the first is to be found in Margaret Mead's *Culture and Commitment*.[4] She compares the generation gap to that between the immigrants coming to the United States from another culture and their children, whom they encouraged to adopt the culture around them—a task that was to a great extent beyond their own powers. The result is a cultural conflict: older and younger generations lead almost different lives, with mutual and inner tensions. Mead sees us all as immigrants in time who have repeatedly to adjust to a new world. The social and technical changes that used to be spread over several lifetimes now are compressed within one generation. This is something most of the older generation in the 1960s could then verify readily; how much of their thinking and how many of their attitudes were cast in terms of the problems and alternatives of the 1930s and World War II, while the younger generation grew up in the 1950s and later. The material technical environment of the younger generation was altogether different: they were at home from the beginning in a world of television, of aviation, of rapid communication (and soon, of computers), each of which was a fresh and remembered change in the world for the older generation. Mead's point is that the young more readily mastered the changed environment because they grew up in it; the older generation had at least the strain of changing its ways. And this holds not only for the technical and the social but for the moral as well—attitudes to sex and work, to discipline and success. Still the formulation in terms of a generation gap may itself be misleading. Perhaps the very meaning of "youth" has changed in recent centuries. The usual dividing line of thirty years of age in the literature of the generation gap can be set alongside the older statistics of life expectancy in which thirty at many places and times was the average life span. This suggests that youth itself is a sociological and cultural category. In the educational world it is used to cover those who are still studying, and so comes in fact to cover graduate students who may themselves be doing a great deal of the teaching in introductory classes.

"Alienation" became popular as a description of the contemporary mood. The term, utilized by Marx in his *Economic and Philosophical Manuscripts of 1844*, applied to a variety of phenomena whose explanation was assigned to the social operations of capitalism. Workers become estranged from productive work and its satisfaction, from nature, and from other human beings. They are reduced to objects, to treating as means of survival what should have been free and spontaneous activity. The notion caught on particularly in the midtwentieth century during a revival of the early Marx. People are separated from their natural surroundings, as in the shift from rural to urban life; a large part of the population loses contact with and becomes even uninformed about the natural and animal environment and the processes of providing the basics of survival. In becoming hired hands, people are separated from the instruments of production and cease to be integrated participants in a total work. An exploitative wall grows up between persons; large impersonal organizations come to control people's lives and hem in their choices. Increasing mobility brings a decline of long-lasting personal relationships. The young are most affected; the older generation has a lingering recollection of more stable relations.

The economic situation of the period also played a part in widening the gap. During the expansion of the 1960s (and until the recession in the

1970s) the younger generation could take opportunity for granted, whereas the older generation had the sense of insecurity born of the Great Depression.

The general effect of the changes was to make a coherent group out of the young not only in mode of life but in the source of their standards. The United States had long been a youth culture, with adulation of youth and strength. Now there was also, as in many countries, the development of what sociologists and anthropologists described as a peer-group domination of standards replacing the authority of elders, and this was intensified in the 1960s. (From an anthropological descriptive view it was not freedom but a change in masters.)

To understand the students of the 1960s even more background is necessary. Our culture is different from others in which the young work and learn alongside older members of society. The separation of schooling from work creates a separate student group isolated from the vital social currents. Because unique historical conditions of a country give it a special cast, I shall, in treating of the counterculture and its educational revolt, deal with the United States alone.

By many thinkers and writers on educational topics, the counterculture and the student explosions of the 1960s (and into the 1970s) were taken to be a breakthrough of the irrational forces of human nature, wholly contrary to the dominant cultural tradition. Calls for repression were common, and even comparison of students to storm troopers were made. On the other hand, the strength and scope of the movement, its influence on the older generation, the fact that among the young it has not since been rejected although the next generation of youth did not follow it up, suggest that it should be given a less hysterical interpretation. Higher education especially felt the intensity of the revolt, which went far beyond the demand for specific reforms and questioned the whole moral and organizational basis of the establishment. It was a kind of total critique of the institution itself.

If we want to see the revolt from the student point of view, we have to look at its themes in the historical and cultural context of the period. It is then possible to see what it was reacting against, what valid elements there were in its critiques, what directions of transformation it was reaching toward (whether sound or not), and the almost revolutionary character of the age in which all institutions were being brought to the test—a fact to which the youth responded even if with theories not well formed. To see this, the several themes in the movement have to be untangled.

The basic theme was a moral critique of the establishment for which the older generation was held responsible. The critique took characteristic shape in the civil rights movement for the rights of Blacks and the removal of discrimination, and it was carried later into action against the Vietnam war. It issued in immediate action, with a sense of moral outrage; it did not reckon consequences, and spurned utilitarian calculations. Especially when it took on the universities, where it seemed least justifiable in the light of their intellectual ideals, and in some cases was accompanied with excesses, the charge of irrationalism took firm hold. But general conditions can be specified under which such a response is not irrational. The conditions include at least the following: (1) There is a major conflict between current ideals and current practice. World War II had been fought in the name of ideals that were now being neglected. (Black soldiers who had fought for freedom in Europe were to go back to discrimination in the United States; the Americans who had condemned genocide in Europe were called on to do something suspiciously like it in Vietnam). (2) Evils are intense and widespread, and pursued in a morally callous manner. The race problem and the Vietnam war were so regarded by a great part of the public. (3) The consequences of nonaction appear to intensify the evil. The youth saw the war on its venal side and the inhumanity of the media "body counts." (4) Events are moving toward a major disaster. For nearly two decades the sense of impending nuclear warfare had given this an apocalyptic character. The younger generation had heard the alarmist discussions over television about deep shelters and perhaps had drills in school. (5) Current institutions seem to be mobilized by the establishment against any resolution, and offer no constructive channels. There was a profound loss of faith in political action: the establishment goes on its way whatever its campaign promises (for example, President Johnson had won an election on not extending the Vietnam war). (6) There is evidence that moral example brings results. The nonviolent movements for civil rights in its earlier phase had launched desegregation.

When such conditions are satisified, it is not irrational for people who see the situation in this way—whether they are right or wrong—to act accordingly. They need not have a systematic theory underlying their action. They may not believe the current theories, or else believe that these theories have been taken over by the establishment, as the counterculture seems to have regarded most of them, whether conservative, liberal, or Marxian. Action is posssible while keeping belief open with respect to theory to allow of growth. The important point in this analysis is that no new ideals were required in the critique. It assumes the convergence of multiple failures of the establishment in the light of the old ideals.

A second theme was the consciousness of the generation gap, whose bases we have considered. The youth felt that its entry into a responsible share of power was being indefinitely postponed. The period of requisite education was getting longer and longer. In the society and its institutions they were kept out of policy formation; they felt they were being kept in line for the goals of a past that they rejected. In simple overreaction, in part a consequence of their isolation, they often proclaimed that nothing could be learned from the past; it was a new world and they had to begin afresh.

Another striking theme, visible in the counterculture, was an individualist-anarchist strain. This individualism, far from being a novel element was, rather, one of the major ideals of the establishment, carried to an extreme. It was a kind of spiritual trust busting, launched against corporate tendencies and the constricting effect of large-scale organization. Nevertheless, this individualism with its pride of craft and its do-your-own-thing without taint of competitiveness helped restore a faith in human beings as against their organizational instruments. It did not answer the hard questions in the theory of self-making, that is how the self is fashioned by the society through its institutions and by the individual through his or her creative action. It revived a kind of romantic individualism, quite understandable in terms of what it was reacting against.

The theme of irrationalism in the counterculture was part of the ground for the charge of irrationalism. Rationality, including science, philosophy of science, technology, and the like, was rejected by some writers in favor of immediacy. But for the most part this theme was a minor note; most found a place for technology and science. Critiques were directed against beliefs that accompanied them, such as constant growth, the inevitability of large-scale technology, corporate forms, and so on.

Religious and ethical themes took several forms. One was the value of immediacy, as against the postponement of value in the traditional puritan ethic. This need not be hedonism, insofar as it involves the suspicion that puritan postponement is inauthentic, that it uses people (including oneself) wrongly. Another strain was the value of love, as against a contractual attitude to community. Man and life are thought of as of immediate worth and not as an instrument harnessed for ulterior ends. However, immediacy, particularly in the drug culture, was also pursued as a way of running out on the world and its problems. It was a demand for instant salvation rather than a disciplined mastery that the ideal may call for.

One of the most constructive themes was the encouragement of experiment in institution-building. Social construction could be done by people themselves without waiting for the totality of social change to put a new order on the agenda of history. There followed such experiments as communes, organization in craft production, familial change. Of course institutional experiment was not a new phenomenon. The cooperative movement was once looked upon with hope in a similar way, while insurance, corporations, Medicare, all began as experiments. The difference between the old and the new lay rather in the kind of institution generated—whether it falls under some central control or is an expression of simply individual spontaneity.

The material and interpretation offered do no more than suggest the need for a phenomenology of the student. For one thing, only a part of the student body was concerned in the activities of the 1960s, but it was influential enough to set the tone of a generation, even to determine the form of reaction against it. So far the rational core has been stressed; but the movement also had the full spectrum of human attitudes always found in any movement. The full story would perhaps have to be written by wise students themselves. Certainly it would contain the sense of a world that was out of hand, whereas in the past it had been believed to be manageable. It would convey a world beyond handling by resignation, a world that called for total confrontation. Religious philosophy provides an analogue. In the nineteenth century, Schleiermacher rested his theology on a sense of ultimate dependence that pointed to the divine. In the twentieth, Tillich could go so far as to equate being religious with ultimate seriousness in facing the world. The shift is significant, for the nineteenth century did not question that it could depend, but the twentieth came to feel that it had the burden of total seriousness on its own shoulders.

If we were to go from this prelude to the actual students of the contemporary classrooms, a first temptation would be to get a student to write this section, but probably no one student would do. Could he or she give the view of male and female, White and Black and many an ethnic group, working class and middle class, and all the other significant differentiations that affect the educational life? Our standpoint perforce remains that of the teacher attempting to understand the student, and to recognize how this understanding should affect teaching. The first obligation—too often violated—is to learn to look and to listen. No escape is possible by a commitment to the subject or matter of teaching as primary obligation, because all the violations of respect for the student, all the discriminations, all the misunderstandings that prevent learning are found in the material perhaps no less than in the interpersonal relations.

Some of the common pressures that operate in students are well known, even though the school has not found the best ways to cope with them or may be in no position to do so. These are the familiar problems of inadequate facilities, student poverty, lack of jobs, aggression and violence, an atmosphere of extreme competition, inadequate approaches to sexual matters and pregnancy, and so on. Schools provide lunches, develop advisory and psychological services, and do what they can. The question is whether the spirit is manipulative or understanding of the young, particularly in the classroom. Our concern has been with the aspects and biases so often overlooked because so deeply ingrained. Perhaps further items can best be indicated in relation to some of the standards proposed in the moral agenda for directions of contemporary educational change—particularly the expansion of equality, the extension of democracy, a sensitive reaction to technological demands, and the restoration of a humanistic quality.

The equalitarian standard is not satisfied merely by greater opportunity for schooling. The liberation movements so characteristic of the contemporary world have only edged into the schoolroom and into the texts. What was it like to be a Black student in a classroom studying U.S. history and find the contributions of the slaves ignored, and their past and history of no interest? Or—to take a well-worn example—an Indian student to be told that Columbus discovered North America and in almost the same breath that Indians were there, as if their presence did not count as a previous discovery? (In time we learn to speak of it as the Europeans' discovery. Would we say that, for example, certain Phoenician sailors discovered Britain, or that they were the first to reach Britain from Asia Minor?) We may also be sure that many of the students have been affected in the past by the way in which immigrant groups have been presented in texts: the disparaging references to South European as contrasted with North European, the omission of the contribution of workers of specific ethnic groups in building up parts of the country, the attitude toward assimilation as the shedding of inferior civilizations to adopt a superior one. And, perhaps most permeating because its ramifications are still not uncovered, the inequality of the sexes. Half of the population of the schools are still hemmed in by external and internal constraints, some of which are recognized and only in part being dealt with. For example, attention to women's sports is under way, and the neat division of carpentry for boys and sewing and cooking for girls of olden days is gone. But the attitudes and expectations with respect to masculinity and femininity, to what is man's work and what is women's, to whose work has priority and who should sacrifice for whom, to what equality means—all still have to be dealt with.

The standard of democratization requires that all students be treated with respect. It is of course a moral attitude due toward all human beings, but often ignored toward the young. Teaching is one of the fields in which the students quite immediately sense it, and an observer can readily see it also. Because authoritarian and paternalistic attitudes have been so prevalent in the past,[5] respect for the young has been unexpectedly rare. It often has a quite revolutionary effect on teaching. The complex aspects of democratization center on the students' expectations and aspirations with respect to democratic conceptions—ideals of individual success, cooperation, community, and so forth. As we have seen, these are in a somewhat conflicting state in our culture. The student comes with opposing tendencies. The school can play some part in helping the development of a coherent configuration, or it can sharpen the internal conflicts. Such issues focus on the topic of moral education (chapter 14).

Student reaction to technological demands poses no comparable problems. On the whole, teachers take it for granted that they know student motivation on these matters. They assume an eagerness for many reasons—preparation for life in general, preparation for work, a desire to be in the front of things. But there are strange crosscurrents both on the side of the schools, where they have lagged in older ways, and on the side of the students and their home environment. In the United States the practical attitude raises little difficulties in expecting the schools to furnish practical preparation for steering one's way around the modern world; the lament is rather likely to be the inadequacy of the results. In France, we have noted, the veneration for the older humanistic curriculum (with Latin as the symbol) made it necessary that a course on technical matters be a required subject lest it be not elected, having only a secondary status.[6] In Britain tracking or streaming served to send a large part of working-class students into technical preparation or general terminal minimal preparation; sometimes where class lines were sharply drawn one would find an occasional reverse phenomenon, that a working-class student's desire for humanistic education would be regarded as desertion of class. In any case, the world is rapidly changing, any classroom anywhere may have students of various sorts, and teachers who will not know their students are teaching with eyes closed.

There remains the standard of excellence or quality. Teachers often make the mistake of assuming that they have to impart a sense of excellence to students, as if students were unaware that activity in all fields has inherent criteria of achievement. But students engage in all sorts of physical activity; they run, fight, play ball, skate, perhaps drive, or repair machines. They know about learning and practice and even disciplined activity and care—in some domain or other. In our culture, given the usual commercialism, they cannot help knowing about the shoddy and what comes to pieces, and what lasts for but a day. The ideas of discipline and practice and learning and self-control have reached ideal, almost religious proportions with reference to sport. The problem is not to impart a sense of excellence in genneral, but to transfer the student attitude toward excellence to cultural pursuits. It is an amazing feature of schooling that this attitude should be so absent from current intellectual and aesthetic education, and that instead criticism should be reduced to simply liking or disliking. The criterion of quality calls for an idea of excellence that will be pure—not corrupted by adventitious ideas of competition or prestige—and that means determined by the nature of the materials that are being learned and whatever inherent tasks they entail.[7]

Remaining questions include that of the direct relation of teacher and student. The kind of relation required by our standards would seem fairly clear from what has been said. But its precise form depends on the analysis of the concepts of teaching and learning, and so must be deferred (chapter 13).

Notes

1. In such an atmosphere it was not surprising to find considerable questioning of the utility of a college education. See, for example, Caroline Bird, *The Case Against College* (New York: David McKay and Bantam Books, 1975).
2. Edmund L. Pincoffs, "Educational Accountability," *Studies in Philosophy and Education* 8 (Fall 1973): 131-45.
3. Teacher-student relations in this connection will be considered in chapter 12, and the different interpretations of the nature of knowledge in chapters 11 and 13.
4. Margaret Mead, *Culture and Commitment* (Garden City, N.Y.: Doubleday, Natural History Press, 1970).
5. How permeating the authoritarianism still is can be seen from the extent to which even serious historical studies of leadership in the schools pay little or no attention to either student responses or teacher movements as part of the phenomena. Even hopes for the future are vested in the quality of administrative leadership, not the concerted and active cooperative participation of teachers and students as well, within a democratic structure. See, for example, David Tyack and Elizabeth Hansot, *Managers of Virtue: Public School Leadership in America, 1820-1980* (New York: Basic Books, 1982).
6. *OECD, Review of National Policies for Education, FRANCE* (Paris: Organisation for Economic Cooperation and Development, 1971), p. 116.
7. Harry S. Broudy, *The Real World of the Public Schools* (New York: Harcourt Brace Jovanovich, 1972), calls attention to the special satisfaction that self-cultivation affords to one who disciplines himself or herself sufficiently to master a skill. He points to the devotion of a connoisseur or a buff in the pursuit of his or her interest (pp. 218ff.).

10. Learning and Teaching: Conceptual Problems

Learning and teaching have been studied in different disciplines; for example, in various psychological theories of learning or in historical and sociological accounts of teacher roles and teaching content. In philosophy, the twentieth century witnessed a marked shift in its study of learning and teaching that corresponded to a shift in philosophical method. While Dewey's broad theory of learning is assimilated to a general analysis of experience and lies at the heart of his philosophy, mid-century analytic philosophy, concerned largely with analyzing concepts, approached teaching and learning as concepts to be unpacked.

Such analytic modes revealed the complexity and inner diversity of the ideas by marshaling the resources of ordinary language along the full line of usage. While they thus escaped simplified single-formulae interpretations, they were isolated by the confident assumption that analysis is carried on with purely linguistic-logical tools without any further material assumptions about the subject matter examined or value assumptions and implicit policies to guide the specific inquiry. I have elsewhere argued that the result is often impoverished as a consequence: conclusions are arbitrary because alternative paths suggested by empirical considerations are not noted, and value presuppositions that turn inquiry in one rather than another direction are not attended to. In short, empirical and valuational factors are integral to the operations of analysis itself.[1] Nevertheless, because educational philosophy carried on in the analytic mode shaped the formulation of inquiry for the latter part of the century, it is better to begin within its conclusions rather than to start afresh. In this way its gains will not be lost while its defects are remedied.

We may begin our inquiry with a number of points about learning and teaching on which there appears to be a consensus:

1. Learning has a logical priority in the analysis of teaching because the purpose of teaching is to get someone to learn something.
2. Because so many different things can be taught (almost anything a person can undertake) and so many things can be learned, educational focus should be on the varied types of learning and teaching in relation

to the varied subject matters and the specific principles or lessons to be gathered from each. General definitions of teaching and learning can be at best general characterizations through paradigms or broad features.
3. Both teaching and learning involve a central feature of purpose or intent on the part of the teacher and the learner. If a learning theory in psychology or a theory of group behavior in social science does not allow of purpose or intent, then teaching or learning cannot be understood purely in terms of such a psychology or social science.
4. Most analyses, though not all, refer to knowledge as the object of learning. It thereby becomes essential to distinguish different kinds of knowing in order that a single model should not be cast in procrustean fashion on the great variety of what can be learned.
5. In spite of the fact that the differences seem to turn out more important than the broad features, the analysis of the general concept is an important act of housekeeping or stocktaking, at least in a negative way, for if the concept is not clear we tend to overlook important distinctions and confound teaching with such activities as conditioning, indoctrination, and so on.
6. Similarly, the conceptual analysis should help distinguish which relations of teacher and student are educational and which pertain to some other human interaction.

Each of these six topics deserves careful and critical consideration. Some may be set in an analysis that assumes possibly outworn formulations and so need revision to articulate their spirit. Others may be suggesting a fruitful direction but miss its central significance—e.g. pose as a logical issue what is in an important sense a value issue. And where doors are clearly opened we may be tempted to follow through boldly, if only speculatively. This chapter will deal with the first three topics in which problems of conceptual analysis are paramount, attempting to go beyond conceptual restraints to trace the involvement of factual and policy issues. Chapter 11 will question whether there are fundamentally different kinds of knowledge that require radically different forms of learning (the fourth topic). And chapter 12 will consider types of teaching and the relations of students and teachers (the fifth and sixth topics).

The Priority of Learning

The priority of learning to teaching appears to be a fairly recent thesis.[2] For the most part, even in analytic studies, interest centered on teaching and its relation to the forms of knowledge; if "teach" was seen as a task word, "learn" was taken to be an achievment word. But if purpose or intent is a central feature of teaching, the very definition of "teaching" logically involves that of "learning." Thus, for example, Paul H. Hirst, after showing that no unified concept of teaching can be elicited from an examination of the activities of teachers and concluding that the concept of teaching is parasitic on that of learning, offers the following account of teaching: "A teaching activity is the activity of a person, A (the teacher), the intention of which is to bring about an activity (learning), by a person, B (the pupil), the intention of which is to achieve some end-state (e.g., knowing, appreciating) whose object is X (e.g., a belief, attitude, skill). From this it follows that to understand what is involved in teaching, one must start at the other end of a logical chain of relations, with an understanding of the end achievements to which everything is being directed."[3]

Surprisingly, the most serious difficulties in this account arise from the general categories employed—the sense in which teaching and learning are "activities," and the one "brings about" the other. With respect to the latter, for example, Thomas F. Green in *The Activities of Teaching*, argues that teaching cannot cause learning because it can occur when learning does not, and conversely.[4] He compares teaching-taking-place and learning-taking-place to running a race and winning it, and teaching-taking-place and learning-not-taking-place to running a race and losing it, and suggests that to see the relation as causal is a category mistake. Teaching does contribute something to learning but probably not in a causal or in a logically necessary way. Hirst instead simply distinguishes two ways of talking about teaching, one of which is that of trying to get people to learn and the other adds succeeding.[5] Learning outside of teaching is attributed to causal processes that produce learning (e.g. hypnotism).

Whether the relation of A's teaching and B's learning is causal or of some other contributory kind depends on how human interaction is to be analyzed. But whether A's teaching and B's learning are to be construed as separate activities is a prior matter in setting up the scheme of inquiry, before questions of influence or priority can be raised. If they are different activities, can they take place at separate times? Can the professor finish the teaching in class and the student do the corresponding learning two days later in the library? Can that learning depend on other things done meanwhile, such as conversations about the last class with fellow students? It looks as if we could set up different conceptual schemes or "models" that would either allow or forbid such possibilities.

Take, for example, the model of process or movement that Aristotle offers in *Physics* (Book III, 3) dealing with the relation of agent and patient in the analysis of motion and change. When any movement or process takes place—and he cites teaching and learning as one example, the doctor curing a patient as another—the action of the agent and the passion of the patient do not constitute two separate activities. They are one and single, differing only as the road from Athens to Thebes differs from the road from Thebes to Athens. Just as the doctor-curing-the-patient and the patient-being-cured-by-the-doctor are a single process looked at from two ends, so teaching-and-learning is a single unified process in which two persons participate. The teacher is not engaging in one activity that is going on in him or her and the learner in another going on in him or her. Aristotle is offering a distinctive metaphysical theory of action, in which an integral relation is expounded as against two parallel or correlated activities. It is a kind of "transactional" model with the individuals participating in a common activity. (Of course there may be different properties associated with the different directions in the unified activity. The same road is uphill one way, downhill the other; the patient, not the doctor, suffers the pains of the treatment; the sense of novelty may come in the learning, not the teaching.) Aristotle goes on to ask where the activity takes place, whether in the agent or the patient, and decides on the latter because the patient is the one who is changed as a result. The doctor's curing goes on in the patient, and the teaching-learning is manifest in the pupil.

Aristotle seems to be quite aware of the fact that his model is adapted to small-scale transactions. It plays an important part in his physics and his psychology, and when it is pressed hard by large-scale phenomena, such as apparent action at a distance or the fact that sound travels over long distances, he tries to explain things by breaking down the large into a succession of smalls. Some of the attempts in psychology are helpful, while others particularly in physics are simply ingenious efforts to shore up a basically incorrect physical theory. Now, there is no reason that we cannot take the same kind of approach to the educational uses of the models of teaching and learning. The Aristotelian transactional model obviously makes the relation between teaching and learning a logical one because they are logically equivalent descriptions of the same activity. It does not give priority to learning but to teaching, for priority is assigned in his system to the active over the passive and so to the agent rather than the patient. This is clearly the kind of priority that in his *Politics* the ruler has over the ruled and the master over the slave, the male over the female and the father over the child. Now, while this judgment of priority involves a social bias, it is explicitly related in his system to psychological considerations of the presumed nature of human beings and the nature of the child as capable of reason but immature. Moreover, in Aristotle's teleological view the rational nature of human beings provides a goal for education.

In application, the scheme would readily fit person-to-person teaching of the pedagogue and the pupil. There would be little point in asking whether the learning was something separate from the teaching in the ideal tutorial with its constant dialogue. Take the analogy of the ideal democratic town-meeting. If it operates by reaching a consensus, there is no point in asking whether the deliberation is something different from the deciding. But if there is a formal vote after the discussion, or even more if the town turned into a megalopolis and ended up with representative government, the distinction between deliberation and decision might be drawn as to time and place with a separation of activities and a variety of intervening influences. A fresh model would be needed; some people would say that the concept of democracy has been extended, others that it was not democracy any more. So too for teaching and learning. By the time that the multiversity operates with classes of hundreds or more, with varieties of instrumentalities that come between the teacher and the student, with complex forms of programmed learning, with the face-to-face situation playing a small part in the totality of the work that goes into learning, with not only a greater division of labor but even a separation of location for tasks, the unity of transaction has long ceased to fit. The transactional model may still fit or be felt as necessary on the elementary level; it is reserved for only rarer occasions further up the academic ladder. Certainly television teaching would be a clear separation of teaching and learning; the teacher would not even know at the time whether a learner was listening or even whether communication had broken down.

It does not follow from this analysis that learning is not prior to teaching, but only that there is more constructional activity in the analysis than we are prone to think, often presupposed in the underlying categories and concepts, and unless we spell them out together with the assumptions about human psychology and society and about value emphases, we are simply ending up with one among alternatively possible models. For example, to continue with Hirst's definition of teaching in terms of learning, because he treats learning itself as purposive, we are led on to the knowledge, skills, and so forth at which learning is directed. But this is what the older analyses of teaching did. They went straight from teaching to what was taught and what they hoped the learner would learn. Then why is learning central? Why not skip over it in the philosophical analysis and pay attention to the teacher's lesson plans and see whether they are good enough in the light of what is to be learned, that is knowledge and its forms? Aristotle's scheme is able to focus on knowledge without having learning prior to teaching. Perhaps Hirst is concerned whether the ends are properly conceived, but that would be another matter and would not involve the jockeying of teaching and learning for primacy. More likely his point is simply the very sensible one that the learner should not be left out. We should never forget that the purpose of the schools is that the learner learn. But is this all that is meant by the priority of learning to teaching? Perhaps the best way to get the learner to learn is to forget about the learner and concentrate on the teacher and what he or she does. That is what the old-fashioned view of the passivity of the pupil and the activity of the teacher seemed to entail. By separating the learner's activity something much more must then be intended. We have to know concretely what that activity is, what the underlying psychological account of learning is and what the implicit view of the educational and social relation of learning and what kind of intellectual relations are most fruitful. What in short is the "activity of learning" both in and apart from "being taught"?

If we construe the priority of learning in this broader sense, then it is not a recent thesis. It has been around for quite a while taking different forms. John Stuart Mill in his "On Genius" goes so far as to suggest teaching might be reduced to the minimum necessary to start the learning: "The end of education is not to *teach* but to fit the mind for learning under its own consciousness and observation: . . . we have occasion for this power under ever varying circumstances, for which no routine or rule of thumb can possibly make provision."[6] On this kind of view, teaching should constantly be geared to awakening the powers of the learners, until they can stand on their own feet and go their own way. In the early twentieth century the progressive education movement with its emphasis on the activity of the child as against the transmission of a fixed curriculum was focusing attention on the learner as against the set ways of the teacher. The familiar slogan "Teach children, not subjects," puzzling if taken literally, is quite clear in its demand that teaching methods focus on the development of learning powers. It scarcely seems an accident that student revolts and renewed calls for a children's bill of rights come in the same period as analytic formulations ruling out indoctrination and modes of conditioning from teaching. In earlier days these would have been classified as forms of teaching, though criticized for their educational disadvantages.

Clearly what posed as an analytic conclusion from a study of usage was really the culmination of a century's growth of moral sensitivity that revolutionized the place of the child and fashioned a notion of human autonomy developed through learning. But if this is so, then a model of teaching and learning has to be worked out to embody this standpoint and the ends to be envisaged, as well as to allow for a schematic variety that will encompass the new complexity noted in conditions of contemporary schooling. No doubt a model is premature, but some progress should be possible in preparing for one.

We need to give up attempts to save the simple older model with its concept of teaching. It is in fact given up when a gap is in one way or another allowed to appear between teaching and learning. They become separate events. Learning in becoming prior is no longer simply the mark of successful teaching but also of some (usually unspecified) student activity. However, there remain arguments here and there that try to save the old model by extending its concept of teaching. It used to be said that unsuccessful teaching was not teaching, only trying to teach; but failure to teach is different from failure in teaching. Attempts were also made to dispose of learning that had no teaching. Some kinds that are not intentional are dismissed as not really learning but something else that is the result of a causal process. If a person follows a program of self-education that person is said to be his or her own teacher; Langford cites *Jude the Obscure* as an instance.[7] If a person learns from a book, doubtless the author could be regarded as the teacher, although it might be odd to say one was being taught by a writer dead several centuries. This could be avoided by adding some nonformal conditions. The teacher and student would have to communicate in some way—the teacher answer questions, engage in further explanations, and so on. Indeed, lectures to a thousand in the contemporary multiversity scarcely constitute teaching unless indirectly, that is, taken with the professor's office hours or with question-and-answer periods or with the professor's guidance of assistants who run discussion sections. In this sense, teaching could occur with the combination of broadcasting and telephone. The limit would be reached in learning about plants and animals and rocks by observation or in ordinary learning from experience. Would Nature then be the teacher? It is better to face Mill's challenge concretely and recognize that there are two seriously different paths in educational policy involved in the primacy of teaching and the primacy of learning, that such a contrast requires the construction of different models. It must not be assumed that a simple choice will be forced between them; each will involve underlying scientific and valuational considerations, each can be examined for whatever evidence we may have of its educational consequences. But a possible verdict may be that there are also intermediate models, that the different models apply to different portions of the educational field, or that the different ones apply under different social and educational conditions or achieve different ends. Therefore what is necessary first of all is to see the possible variety and understand what is built into each and what are the conditions of application.

Another point suggested by our analysis is that the two concepts of teaching and learning are not themselves sufficient to do the job just indicated. Teaching has been analyzed with respect to knowing and the analysis of learning has involved it as well. (Knowing has to be taken in a broad sense as covering beliefs, skills, appreciation, and so on, not merely the cognitive—if indeed this can be separated at all.) Once learning is treated as a separate activity, the fact that it is a success term, whereas teaching is a process term or a task term, seriously limits its scope. It has some difficulty in covering much that a person who hopes to end up with knowledge (having learned) is doing besides being taught. We may suggest the introduction of an additional major concept, that of *studying*. This fortunately can cover both getting steeped in a familiar field and engaging in inquiries in a fresh field: one can study French as well as the habits of a new species of fish. Studying can cover the acquisition of a skill, as in serious practice in learning to play a musical instrument; or the cultivation of a virtue, as in learning to control one's temper, or again stabilizing an attitude as in learning to listen sympathetically to others. In short, "studying" as we construe it, can cover most relevant activity that mediates teaching and learning. Like knowing, it moves freely over cognition, skill, attitude, and so on.

A further suggestion is that we give up analyzing each concept separately. The separatist treatment tends to solve problems in relation to one concept by passing them along to others, whereas if we deal with them all together we are compelled to face all the problems. We also see what division of labor there is among the concepts, we face frankly any aggrandizing tendencies in any one of them. In general, I am recommending a network mode of analysis on principle as more likely to prove satisfactory in the long run, though probably more difficult.[8]

A scheme that adds the concept of studying is a theoretical experiment. It may not solve our problems but it should help us grasp the complexity that is found in the interval between teaching and learning once they are seen as separate activities. Of course an attempt could be made to reduce studying to increments of learning or to teaching of bits. I doubt whether this would succeed, or do more than gloss over problems. Something is going on in between and if bringing it under a concept of studying is unsatisfactory, then the reader may interpret S (the symbol for studying) as something like stewing instead!

Using the four concepts, then, of *teaching, studying, learning, knowing*, we may approach our second topic of the breadth and variety of teaching and learning.

The Breadth and Variety of Teaching and Learning

Initially we set out to clarify the kind of concepts teaching and learning are supposed to be. Is teaching really a genus (a broad class of activities) or does "teaching" indicate an analogy between quite disparate processes? Is there a clear paradigm, or only a few clear cases with an area of vagueness as we move away from them? Is there the kind of unity in which we could find general laws or principles for teaching and learning, or would we do better to break each up into a variety of kinds, with distinct laws and principles for each?

We know that philosophical experiences with such highly general concepts have not been very happy. Concepts like power or value seem almost to have diverted attention from rich variety in human activities into a fruitless search for generality. Thus political science at one point made the pursuit of power the essence of political phenomena and began to look for the laws of power rather than attend to the diversity of aims in different groups of society (all this was translated into merely "bases of power") so that eventually the science seemed reduced to a branch of psychology. Laws and principles were sought in psychology instead of among the political phenomena. Similarly, the richness of ethics was much diminished when goods and obligations were all treated as simply instances of "values" and expected to conform to a common pattern of verification. Such intellectual processes are comparable to gathering all kinds of "skills" from playing billiards to organizing political machines to doing mathematical puzzles, and expecting a science of skill to yield fruitful results. The question is whether teaching and learning are similarly inflated concepts.

By introducing the additional concept of studying and dealing with the four concepts together, we can get a view of the variety that comes from their general relations, rather than trying to establish the variety in the first place from differences within any one of them, such as types of knowledge. We do not expect substantial results from so distant a view, simply to clear up some issues that intrude on substantial discussion. Because there are four concepts, and each may apply or not apply to a particular situation, let us try out a matrix, using T, S, L, K, for teaching, studying, learning, knowing, respectively—and their negations T̄ S̄ L̄ K̄. The combinations are:

(1) T S L K
(2) T S L K̄   (3) T S L̄ K   (4) T S̄ L K   (5) T̄ S L K
(6) T S L̄ K̄   (7) T S̄ L K̄   (8) T̄ S L K̄   (9) T S̄ L̄ K   (10) T̄ S L L̄ K   (11) T̄ S̄ L K
(12) T S̄ L̄ K̄   (13) T̄ S L̄ K̄   (14) T̄ S̄ L K̄   (15) T̄ S̄ L̄ K
(16) T̄ S̄ L̄ K̄

The universe of discourse is the standard one of the schools with teachers and students and their usual relations, although we may keep an eye out on the broader universe of educational experiences so as not to overlook continuities. The matrix is not constructed with an interest in proof. It is intended to serve as a heuristic tool, adapted for a more holistic exploration than taking the concepts singly.

(1). TSLK is the normal clear case of educational processes, what is hoped for in our schools: the teachers teach, the students study, the students learn, the students know. This makes the nonformal assumptions of our standard universe of discourse. What the students learn is what the teachers intended to teach. This is often not the case: the teacher may teach specific laws of mechanics; the student may learn that physics is hard or interesting or how to learn or to follow instructions carefully. In many contexts of learning the problem is even more complex. Most of our statements about learning what is being taught deal with standard or ideal cases, indeed abstractions out of the mass of differences that occur in actual communication. The teacher and student are different persons with different funds of experience, different perspectives in different stages. What is the probability that there will be genuine coincidence of what is given and what is taken? Literary critics, for example, have worried a great deal about the reader's reception of a work and whether it is worth trying to match it with the writer's intention; some go so far as to find the meaning of the work (particularly in a later age) in the audience's understanding and reaction, dismissing any historical problem of reconstructing the author's mind. Now while the understanding and appreciation of literature and art may lie at one end of the continuum of communication and that of mathematics and science at the other, the differences are of degree, not of kind. Short of pure logic and the rigid precision of computer programming, there are always areas of ambiguity and vagueness. It is well to recognize that in such abstract forms as TSLK we are postulating ideal conditions.

Another point of educational importance is that learning may also be taking place on the part of the teacher, not merely on the part of the student. It may be about the subject matter in the act of teaching or about how to teach or about the diversity of student reactions, and so on. But the K here refers to the laws of mechanics, not all these matters of possible knowledge. Nevertheless, it is generally agreed that the best teachers are constantly learning from their students.

(2). T S L $\tilde{K}$ is the case where everything seems normal, but the end result is that the students do not know. This seems to contradict the fact that they have learned. We have to consider the interpretation of $\tilde{K}$ if we are not simply to dismiss this combination. $\tilde{K}$ could not mean that the students do not have beliefs about the subject matter, as an outcome of the process, because they have learned something. It may mean that unfortunately what they have been taught is wrong. To follow such an interpretation saves the combination but raises the question whether we should call it teaching, and even more call it learning, where what is taught and learned is false. In spite of all the insistence that epistemologically "'A knows that p' if and only if p is true," and learning implies knowing so that learning p holds only if p is true, ordinary uses raise their own difficulties. Suppose A says that in Canada he was taught that United States was responsible for starting the War of 1812, and B says that in the United States she was taught that Britain was responsible, and suppose that both give evidence that they learned their lesson (they got top honors in history). Shall we say one of them did not really learn and was not really taught? Perhaps the best suggestion is that all learning include the tentativeness of statements about the world and the probable character of empirical statements and their relation to evidence. Thus, even where the propositions learned turn out to be false, the students know because they know that the evidence available (or furnished) supports that conclusion and they do not know the conclusion absolutely.

Another way of saving (2) from contradiction focuses on L. We might abandon the strong requirement that "learning" is a success term or an achievement term in all contexts, and allow it to be a process term. This would fit some uses, such as "He is learning French, but can't yet speak it" or even "He is learning slowly" (like "She is teaching badly," which would not deny that she is teaching and would not be equivalent only to "She is trying to teach"). In that case, teaching and studying and learning could be taking place without knowing—yet.

Such moves show that the combination of concepts, even where it does not admit of an easy interpretation, helps us explore and reconsider the implicit rules for the use of our terms. The concepts become clarified in the process.

(3) and (6). In both no learning takes place. The latter (T S L K̄) appears to be a failure of learning (on the assumption that the teaching was properly carried on) because there was teaching and there was studying but nothing crystallized. K may have two senses here: either having beliefs that are incorrect or not having a belief in the area at all (e.g. the student reports after studying that the whole lesson does not make sense). In (3) on the other hand (T S L̄ K) the student knows, but does not learn in spite of the teaching and studying. It has a rather paradoxical appearance but need not be a nonsensical case. For example, if the student happens to have the correct belief but is being taught and is studying the incorrect one, the student will fit the present case if his or her learning does not take hold. The historical picture of the inquisitor trying to convert someone to a false belief where even the sincere attempts of the "victim" fail to dislodge an existent (correct) belief is a dramatic case—for example, the victim cannot see that differing from an official line was wrong; the inquisitorial saving hypothesis is that the inquisitee is internally corrupt. (3) may therefore prove to be a socially important case where the teaching has an indoctrinating character that the students even unconsciously resist.

(4) and (7). T S̄ L K, (4), is the initial case of teaching and learning without studying; it may be the communication of the mature, or else the simplicity of the subject matter. It seems to correspond to what is sometimes called *telling* or *showing*: some things have only to be told or shown

to be learned, or for some people that is enough. T S̄ L K̄, (7), involves the same issues of interpretation as (2) because it has learning but not knowing.

(5) and (8). T S L K, (5), is the ideal case of studying and learning on one's own. T S L K̄, (8), has the same problems as (2) and (7).

(9) and (12). T S̄ L K, (9), lacks everything between teaching and knowing; it would fit teaching a student in sleep or through hypnosis, what for a special definition of the term might be called "unconscious learning." But if we keep to (9) strictly, then such a construct would not be admitted because we have no learning. It seems an undesirable usage in that it is preferable to think of consciousness as characterizing the teaching-learning situation. A different possibility is that there is something special about the knowledge, as in (10) below. T S̄ L K̄, (12), need not be in the same position as (2) and (7) were. It could, in a situation of attempted normal teaching, indicate a complete failure where the student neither studies nor learns nor knows.

The remaining three sets turn out to have interesting features that make it worth discussing them together: (10) and (13), (11) and (14), (15) and (16). T̄ S̄ L K, (11), is clearest; it is self-learning without either teaching or studying. In the broader universe of educational experience it fits ordinary learning from observation that requires no special scrutiny; as such its scope is vast, covering the more immediate or easier part of what we call "learning from experience." T̄ S̄ L K̄, (14), is in the same position as (2) or (7), but because it has neither teaching nor studying, it might refer to learning from experience but getting the wrong lesson. Now, T̄ S L K, (10), appears paradoxical; it goes from studying, without teaching and without learning, directly to knowing. We have to search for a possible meaning; we might take it together with T̄ S̄ L K, (15), where we have a case of knowing without teaching, studying, or learning. (15) would apply to what has historically been advanced as innate ideas or natural knowledge or, in the rationalist tradition, self-evident truths and so on. In that case, (10) makes sense if studying can be taken in the minimal sense of burrowing in the materials sufficiently to stimulate the grasping, for example, what happens when we go to "things equal to the same thing are equal to one another" from puttering with three sticks. Now this is regarded as K rather than as L simply because it is felt as *recognition* of what was somehow known, whereas to learn is to come to know what one did not know before. T̄ S L K̄, (13), is a failure of learning, as (6) was. Finally, as for T̄ S̄ L K̄, (16), nothing is going on there.

The table of combination helps explore possible relations and suggests varieties and problems, prior to a precise determination of the meanings we are going to assign ultimately to the four terms. We see what would happen if we widen the meanings, narrow them, regard them as correlative, or instead as independent. Thus the table quickly brought to attention the question whether teaching and learning implicate each other, by making us face cases of T and $\bar{L}$ as well as $\bar{T}$ L; we have already seen how the concept of teaching would have to be stretched beyond plausibility to ensure mutual implication by insisting that we teach ourselves or nature or experience teaches us, or else the meaning of learning would have to be drastically narrowed. The significant cases of $\bar{L}$ opened up rich problems precisely because of the differences in the other concepts with which it was associated. In (3) the search for a possible interpretation brought us to the question of teaching and studying contrary to a true belief. This not only involves the importance of interpreting K in terms of the relation of evidence and belief and a general "fallibilism" already noted in discussing (2), but could raise the question of further educational consequences for teaching and learning. For example, it suggested exploring the differences in teaching methods where the students have beliefs about the subject taught and where they are without any prior beliefs. (The two interpretations of $\bar{K}$ here refer to quite different pedagogical situations.) Now in (9), where $\bar{L}$ was associated with $\bar{S}$, a quite different set of problems emerged—whether consciousness is a necessary element in learning; some of the ordinary learning from experience that we associated with (11) would not require consciousness. This touches the continuity of learning with acquiring beliefs, cultivating attitudes, and developing habits and skills.

A parallel question is posed for teaching when we wonder whether, in some more subtle sense, there must be teaching in what appear as $\bar{T}$ L cases. A temptation arises to introduce a concept of indirect teaching. Perhaps Socrates's method could be so described, for he raised questions and refused to give answers, letting the participants in the dialogue offer answers that again were met with questions. (Do the practices of the Zen master constitute a type of teaching?) But (10) and (15), where $\bar{L}$ is associated in the one case with studying and in the other with no studying and yet both have K, called our attention to the phenomenon of knowledge felt as recognition rather than as fresh acquisition. Of course an easy way out is to say that the new element is recognition in learning, e. g. that the particular before me is an instance of the universal I knew—that this man is John or that these three pieces of wood are an instance of the equality relation. But the fundamental issue opened up here is whether insight with a sense of recognition is different in other respects from insight with a sense of novelty, and whether any such differences have educational consequences. Certainly in epistemology the problem whether the "product" is to be regarded as discovered (cognitive) or conventional (will-act or commitment) or a turning point in the readjustment of experience and knowledge (pragmatic reconstruction) has been a central issue. Even where nothing appears to be going on, in (16), interesting questions may arise. For example, is there ever a situation in which this combination holds—no teaching taking place, no engaging in any inquiries, nothing being learned, no invoking of the knowledge we have? If we feel uncomfortable with this and say it can only be when we are asleep, that our experience is constantly strengthening or weakening the bonds of our knowledge and so adding to our learning, we have implicitly extended the concept of learning or discerned a continuity between what goes on in the school situation and all experience. Whether our concepts are to be reconstructed to show this becomes a matter of theoretical policy.

The occurrence of $\bar{K}$ in fully half the cases obviously raises the question of what success and failure mean in teaching and learning. Interestingly, none of these cases resists interpretation. It depends on what $\bar{K}$ is associated with; thus some of them indicated a failure in learning, whether with teaching or with studying alone. The need to interpret K was helpful to show that teaching and learning might fail not only because the student got no results but also because the student got bad results. It seemed best at this point not to make an issue of the definition of K in one way or another but to note how education might take place in such a manner as to appreciate the needed correction of our beliefs and the need for improvement in our skills and attitudes. To move in this direction brings in the new question of evaluating the combinations as attuned to different contexts, in terms of educational effect. For example, we might explore where T L is preferable to $\bar{T}$ L, even though it may involve more work. For certain skills that are hard to unlearn—that is, to revise the habits involved—teaching would impart better habits from the outset and there will be less to unlearn in improving the skill (e.g. in swimming and car driving). Perhaps in theoretical learning too, teaching provides significant lessons of what to avoid as well as what will advance learning.

The table may also help us face more clearly the question of the priority of teaching or learning. When we see the interrelation of the concepts and how the consequences may follow not from one of them but how they are tied together, the question of priority itself tends to be relativized. We can envisage contexts in which the spotlight might fall on each of the concepts in turn. Of course the priority of teaching will be as good or bad as the way the teachers conceive their goals; on the other hand, the very assignment of priority may carry an authoritarian or at least a paternalistic attitude. The spotlight on the middle concepts of learning, and even more on studying, is obviously important if the purpose of education is construed as learning; moreover, it embodies a positive valuation of initiative and student self-development and so has a democratic emphasis. If we shift the spotlight to knowledge, then the analysis is carried beyond the educational process to the goals and ideals and ethical relations of what is learned, that is, to the place of education in the good life of human beings. Priority no longer falls to learning; in this context it is on the community of human beings and the quality of their individual and common life that education helps make possible. Now, which context is most significant for a given time and place is itself a question of decision depending on the character of the period and the conditions of life and knowledge. The suggestion was offered earlier that the priority of learning over teaching is thus no merely logical problem; its acceptance (or rejection) is a serious evaluation of the demands that the situation in educational practice today makes on philosophical theory. The further question of whether priority falls beyond education itself is better formulated, as we have done, in terms of the requirements of the valuational base for contemporary human life and its moral agenda for education. The claim for the priority of learning seems to be, in its fuller sense, a proposed answer to this question.

On the whole, the examination of the combinations also strengthens the current view that the main progress in the study of teaching and learning will come through different types and different contexts rather than through general definitions and overriding paradigms. This will be pursued in the analysis of knowing. Whether there is a universal account depends on the general picture of human experience, as suggested in the comments on (16). Here there seem to be two different paths. On the one hand, some growth of behavioral science, cast in terms of causal explanation of human behavior, frequently enmeshes both teaching and learning in the concept of conditioning. Conditioning factors need not be deliberate human actions but can be seen as all those happenings that produce the regularity of determinate responses that constitute habit patterns. Human intervention (or teaching in its various forms) is a consequence of growing knowledge about how behavior can be directed or stimulated so as to produce those patterns. On the other hand, there is a philosophical tradition that is geared more to the standpoint of the individual subject, not the scientific observer who looks upon the individual as object. In this psychology, which in the American philosophical tradition is associated with William James and pragmatism, the purposive element plays a large part in understanding the flow of experience, the selection that shapes concepts and categories, and the theoretical construction of knowledge. Hence learning is (for example, with variations in Dewey and C. I. Lewis) the correction of experience by subsequent experience. Learning is thus a pervasive feature of all experience.

Such general views are not a full answer to the educational demand for precising the concepts of learning or teaching because obviously if we are always being taught (conditioned) or we are always learning (revising experience), the important questions are shifted to specific forms and types. But the general character of the process does provide *specific features* that are relevant both to the understanding of what is going on and to normative judgments about it. We look next to some of the contemporary shapes that controversy has taken in this area.

Purpose or Intent versus Scientific Description of Behavior?

The widely current view that teaching and learning involve purpose or intent on the part of teacher as well as learner tends to be cast as an attack on a behaviorist view of teaching and learning as causal conditioning. And sometimes this reflects a conflict between a scientific view of human beings and an ordinary purposive-moral view of human beings. This is neither historically nor philosophically necessary. Behaviorism initially attempted to replace the concept of purpose with purely behavioral descriptions; to find this unsatisfactory was not always an extrascientific conclusion but a conclusion within other schools of psychology. James's psychology gave purpose and interest a central place, and the pragmatic tradition does not regard the phenomenon of human purposes as outside scientific study, nor need there be a conflict between the causal and the purposive. The situation is complicated by ideological controversies about the place of science in human affairs; what should have been corrections of extremes in scientific pretensions have often been turned into antiscientific obscurantism.

Perhaps the issues involved may be approached in another way. In *The Concept of Motivation*, R. S. Peters criticizes Freud for trying to use a mechanical-causal account to deal with unconscious purpose.[9] There are, he says, two models involved: one for the helmsman steering to port, the other for the moth moving to the light. Freud confuses the two. The difficulty with this sharp distinction that Peters makes is that, while it may hold for the clear cases, there is a large twilight zone that resists such assignment. The suspicion arises that something more complex is going on. A similar situation holds for perception, with the discovery of subliminal perception and multiple other forms of awareness that later affect consciousness but cannot be interpreted as simply causal traces of physical-physiological processes, even though this may be involved. In fact, some psychologists begin to speak of the "registration" of experience without asking whether it is a physical or a mental phenomenon; it is the hard mental-physical distinction that is thereby being challenged. Similarly for the dichotomy between the purposive and the mechanical. The twilight zone may well be one in which *purposes are being formed or emerging* in situations in which both previous purposive and causal factors are operative. The model needed for capturing them might, for example, be one in which there is a selection in causal processes among purposive variations, with a new resultant. (Perhaps "unconscious purposes" are precursors of conscious purposes in the same way that precursor forms of a species are neither of that species nor of the previous species that is undergoing evolutionary change.)

The philosophical parallel to this problem is seen in the contemporary theory of action. Unlike Aristotle, who as we saw above was interested in distinguishing the active and the passive, the contemporary theory is interested in the dichotomy between human *action*, marked by purpose or intent, and organic-physical *behavior*, subject to causal explanation. Hence it tends to be peremptory in its educational treatments, dismissing other ways of engendering beliefs and attitudes—indoctrinating, brainwashing, conditioning, and the like—as not teaching. In effect, this is the older physical-mental dichotomy come to roost in educational quarters. But if the suggestion of a twilight zone, in which purposes are formed or there are purposive capturings of or entanglement with the causal-mechanical processes, has any merit, then there should be a more careful study without the antecedent insistence on dichotomizing.

Take, for example, the conception of reading-readiness in educational literature. On the one hand, it breaks down reading skills on their motor side to see what elementary skills or habits are required to make the integrated reading possible—for example, to distinguish a *p* from a *q* requires the ability to distinguish left-right reversals of the same letter (just as M and W are up-down reversals). There can thus be a sharpening of such more general ability in other clearer contexts (as well as discovering defective perceptual apparatus in some). Again, there are general ideas that have to be captured by the child to make sense of reading—for example the fundamental one that marks on paper symbolize sounds; and so the generalized cultivation of the idea of symbolizing in a purely conventional manner (as even chimpanzees have learned to associate specific colors with specific requests for different things). Now, in all this, there is no sharp adherence to a purely mechanical or a purely purposive. Failures in perception may be traced to emotional and purposive factors rather than to physiological causes. The point is to get a comprehensive picture of what goes on in the whole situation, with its parts articulated whether they are distinctly physical, distinctively purposive, integrated complexities, selective processes, and so on. It will then be possible to determine what patterns can be encouraged in what ways to help what kinds of learning and what the consequences of that kind of learning will be. Specific teaching methods for actual reading—for example, whether flash cards help or harm, whether there should be whole-word reading or first letter-sounding, and so on—rest upon the fuller understanding.

The same approach may be taken to the so-called variant forms of teaching—indoctrinating, conditioning, and so forth—to which McClellan applies the interesting name of *counterfeits* of teaching.[10] They are, he says, types of teaching in precisely the same sense as counterfeit money is called money. But perhaps at this point, especially in the light of the primacy of learning discussed above, it is best to remain with a generic character of teaching as *helping to learn*, and postpone the analysis of the differentiating features. (Of course nonformal conditions are assumed to distinguish external help, such as subsidizing leisure, from more direct contributions in one form or another to the actual studying and learning.) Since we cannot tell how far drawing distinctions of types of teaching may be affected by the sharpness of distinctions drawn in analyzing knowledge, it is best to turn to the matter next.

Notes

1. Abraham Edel, "Analytic Philosophy of Education at the Cross-Roads," in *Educational Judgments: Papers in the Philosophy of Education*, ed. James F. Doyle (Boston: Routledge & Kegan Paul, 1973), pp. 232-57. Also published in *Educational Theory* 22 (Spring 1972): 131-52.

2. Thomas F. Green writes (*The Activities of Teaching* [New York: McGraw-Hill, 1971], pp. 121-22) that learning has been examined "primarily because of its supposed connection to the concepts of knowledge and belief. The central problems of epistemology have revolved about the concepts of knowledge and belief instead of learning, and, consequently, the tradition offers little guidance in asking the right kind of questions about the concept of learning."

3. Paul H. Hirst, *Knowledge and the Curriculum: A Collection of Philosophical Papers* (Boston: Routledge & Kegan Paul, 1974), p. 108.

4. Green, *The Activities of Teaching*, pp. 140-41.

5. Hirst, *Knowledge and the Curriculum*, p. 106.

6. J. S. Mill, "On Genius," in *Mill's Essays on Literature and Society*, ed. J. B. Schneewind (New York: Macmillan, Collier Books, 1965), p. 101.

7. Glenn Langford, "The Concept of Education," in *New Essays in the Philosophy of Education*, ed. Glenn Langford and D. J. O'Connor (Boston: Routledge & Kegan Paul, 1973), p. 8.

8. For a discussion of the need for and character of a network mode of analysis, see Abraham Edel, "Toward an Analytical Method for Dealing with Moral Change," Journal of Value Inquiry 12 (Spring 1978): 81-99. Reprinted in Abraham Edel, *Science, Ideology, and Value*, vol. 2, *Exploring Fact and Value* (New Brunswick, N.J.: Transaction Books, 1980), ch. 9.

9. R. S. Peters, *The Concept of Motivation* (London: Routledge & Kegan Paul; New York: Humanities Press, 1958), pp. 62-71.

10. James E. McClellan, *Philosophy of Education* (Englewood Cliffs, N.J.: Prentice-Hall, 1976), pp. 53-54.

11. Forms of Learning

A prominent thesis, particularly in British analytic philosophy in recent decades, holds that there are radically distinct types of knowledge that determine radically distinct forms of learning and call for correspondingly distinct ways of teaching. Let us refer to this as the *discontinuity* thesis. An opposing view—let us call it the *continuity* thesis—prevalent in traditional ideas, finds all experience to be of one piece: knowledge is pervasively cognitive, no matter how the subject matters of teaching and learning are cut up for special contexts and special purposes. In the present chapter we examine this fundamental controversy. How far-reaching are its consequences will be seen in the discussions of curriculum in part IV.

Development of the Discontinuity Thesis

A well-known path along which the discontinuity thesis emerged on the contemporary scene was Gilbert Ryle's analysis of *knowing*. His distinction between *knowing that* and *knowing how* was generally taken to show that theoretical knowledge was something different from practical knowledge, and so the ways of acquiring information were intellectual but the ways of acquiring skill were somehow practical. Much of the further treatment in educational philosophy, however, stayed on the conceptual level, looking for other uses and counteruses rather than testing the proposed distinctions against a more intimate exploration of what goes on in practical learning. Discussion centered largely on whether the two forms of knowing could be reduced to a single one, and if not, whether still other forms could be distinguished by further search into uses.

Ryle had given the suggestion that knowing-that might be reduced to knowing-how to teach: "Having a theory involves being able to deliver lessons or refresher-lessons in it."[1] This led him to interesting ideas, both theoretical and educational. For example, he wondered whether if arithmetic and chess had come into the curriculum before geometry and formal logic, theorizing might have been modeled on calculations and gambits, and we would have talked of inference in the vocabulary of games (i.e. as participants) rather than of the grandstand (i.e. as observers). Indeed, he thought of logical formulae as licenses to make inferences rather than as laws to be apprehended.

A struggle was accordingly waged on the possibility of reducing knowing-that to knowing-how. On the whole, it was not successful. Perhaps the intellectual tradition was too strong, and for that matter the propositional form too rooted in language, and scientific knowledge too entrenched in the shape of systematic theory. Some of the arguments are revealing. For example, Jane Martin argues that even if the reduction were accomplished, the category of *know-how* would be expanded and itself require a distinction between two different dispositions, one of which had to be learned through practicing, and one of which did not.[2] The former cases of *knowing-that* would not require practice; for example, if I know how to answer the question "Who murdered Y?" I need no practice, but if I know how to swim or speak French, these capacities were acquired through practice. The striking thing about this argument is that Martin has already selected the distinction with respect to practicing as the significant one so as to preserve a division between two kinds of knowing. Other distinctions might be suggested that would arrange the capacities otherwise: for example, a distinction on concern with communication might group the capacity to answer questions with that to talk French as against the capacity to swim. In short, the educationally significant distinction between what requires practicing and what does not has become the basis of the epistemological preference. The conceptual analysis thus turns out to be steered by educational needs and purposes, not by any inherent structure in the subject matter.

There can be no victor in the analytic struggles either for reduction of one kind to another or for the maintenance of a separation. This is suggested by the progress of the argument. Suppose in the attempt to reduce *knowing-how* to *knowing-that* one did construct apparently equivalent sentences such that "I know how to do X" could be transformed into "I know that if I do a, b, c . . . , X will take place." It would be a fruitless victory, for the desire to make a distinction between theoretical and practical knowing could simply move on to a fresh distinction. Could not one know how to do something and still not be able to do it? If know-how is reduced to know-that, then the fresh distinction is between *know-how* and *know-how-to*, with the latter located almost in the nerves and muscles. Now, some such way out seems possible for almost any reduction in any direction. But to give up reduction and stay with a division, one is faced with the plethora of divisions that have come on the scene, as well as those to be found among past philosophers once attention is turned upon the search. Thus Aristotle distinguishes between knowing-that and knowing-why;[3] Russell, between knowing by acquaintance and knowing by description (the former involving immediacy of presentation);[4] James, between knowledge of acquaintance and knowledge-about (mere acquaintance as against the inner nature of things);[5] Bergson, in effect, between inner and outer knowledge;[6] Buber (we might construct from his philosophy), between thou-knowledge and it-knowledge.[7] Again, a more systematic inquiry might add the variations that come from making the cut by distinguishing meanings of "know," from the preposition or conjunctive adverb associated with it, or from the nature of the content that is the object of knowing. Thus in the biblical account when David knows Bathsheba, it is carnal knowledge, and when he knows Saul's intention to kill him it is informational. When we know of, about, how, where, when, that, and so on, the preposition or conjunctive adverb steers us. When we grasp a distinction only as the object of knowledge comes into view, content is decisive; for example, Peters[8] suggests that knowledge of the good is different from either knowing-how or knowing-that. This could suggest a distinction of categories of knowledge corresponding to category words, such as fact, task, value; it would invite a further search for uses to correspond to other categories, such as process, product, explanation (knowing what is going on, know the result, know why).

The outcome seems paradoxical in light of the original Rylean intentions. Ryle wanted to slay the dragon of dualism, not to create fresh ones, and even in his view of the two knowledges he inclined toward a primacy of the practical. If linguistic analysis emphasizes multiple contexts of use, each with a logic of its own, it is in the sense of an open pluralism; it ought not to congeal hastily into a set of sharply distinct forms of knowing.

The full-blown thesis that there are radically different forms of knowledge usually distinguishes at least the intellectual or cognitive, the moral or practical, the aesthetic or artistic. Forms are differentiated on the basis of distinctive concepts, logical forms employed, types of organization of material, ways and techniques of testing and establishing the particular kind of product or experience that characterizes the corresponding discipline. On such grounds some make further distinctions between scientific and mathematical experience, the one being empirical and the other purely logical; or between science and history, the one emphasizing the universal, the other focusing on the individual event. Older theses of this kind used to rest on frank metaphysical ground, for example, that human free will made the difference between the study of human beings and the study of nature, or between morals and science. Contemporary theses more frequently take their departure from an analysis of the forms of knowledge, not merely in the contexts of uses we have considered but also in the investigation of the way knowledge is organized. As Hirst, who himself propounded such a thesis, rethinks the problem: "If one holds, as I hold, that all forms of experience are intelligible only by virtue of the concepts under which we have them, a classification of forms of knowledge provides also a classification of forms of experience."[9] He raises the question frankly whether, given the shift of concepts over time, the distinctions of forms of experience are to be regarded as absolute divisions or whether they may not be expressing a purely contemporary situation. His answer is that change in the forms is conceivable, that rationality involves "developing conceptual schemes by means of public language in which words are related to our form of life, so that we make objective judgments in relation to that form of life," and how far such schemes have an invariant structure has to be determined by investigation.[10] Given flux and evolutionary development, long-range change is possible. But the structure we have defines our capacities and contexts and notions of intelligibility. "Maybe new forms are at present being slowly differentiated out. We can do little but wait and see."[11] He regards his thesis as analyzing the present state of affairs without treating it as transient and relative, nor as the expression of an absolute framework.

The Confrontation of Theses

The continuity thesis is not to be taken as reducing all experience to the intellectual. The cognitive runs through all experience, and differences express the variety of materials, conditions, contexts. Of course experience, like the world, is full of differences, but they are relative to varying emphases, prominence of different aspects, and functional advantages in stressing one rather than another phase of experience for different purposes. They should not be turned into fixed structures. Concepts and modes of organization are too often given absolute formal shape by taking them out of the contexts in which they function, the relations in which they are involved, and the underlying bases that support them. When we are tempted to make such fixed frames out of the scientific, the moral and practical, and the aesthetic, we can restore the continuity by seeking the features of each of these in the others. When we look at science in its fuller operation, we can see the purposive aspects of human practice that underlie it and the imaginative and creative-aesthetic components that permeate large segments of its operation. When we look at moral decision, moral feeling, moral action, policy formation, and human institution-constructing, we see all the cognitive aspects and the imaginative and creative aspects that do not appear in a technical formulation of obligation concepts as either cognitive or prescriptive. When we look into the arts and into appreciation we find a cognitive basis in each context that is inherent and necessary to the quality of appreciation or creation as well as to understanding. Of course noting differences is always in order, but in context and with respect to purposes for which the differentiations are being made.

The issue between the two broad theses is fundamental to educational practice. Certainly during the period in which the Rylean distinction was explored and explained, the educational consequences were often felt to be momentous. For example, T.F. Green writes of forms of teaching corresponding to the distinctions of knowing: "If 'teaching that' is understood to be the more fundamental, then we are likely to view education as more centrally concerned with the transmission of knowledge and the formation of belief. If 'teaching to' is taken as the more fundamental perspective, then we are likely to think of education as more centrally concerned with the formation of ways of acting."[12] He sees the relation between thinking and doing at stake in the decision, and says that quite different philosophies of education may turn on how the relation is understood. Apart from such broad implications, the structure of the curriculum is bound to be affected, possibly less in subject matter than in manner of teaching.

How can we decide between theses of such scope? Three lines of argument may be suggested. The first considers how successful has been the delineation of the distinct forms, whether they emerge as stable under scrutiny and refinement or whether the lines become vague and fresh divisions have successively to be installed. A second looks to educational consequences in teaching on the plans indicated by each of the two theses. A third, much more complex in the philosophical controversies that it opens up, examines the underlying epistemological and psychological presuppositions for each thesis.

How Stable Are the Forms of Knowledge?

How stable or precarious is the autonomy of each discipline associated with a form of knowledge? The discontinuity thesis is committed to the stable independence of the fundamental concepts and modes of organization; that of continuity, to a vista of possible change, reinterpretation, relation, and even reduction, readjustment of boundaries. Both agree that there must be some conceptual structure to be able to operate at any time; they disagree on the fixity and autonomy of the structure. Take, for example, the listing of religion among the forms of knowledge. There are certainly religious concepts (God, grace, sin, and so on) and there are forms of discourse in which they are related in specifiable ways. But the independence of the form depends on the interpretation of the concepts. A naturalistic interpretation like George Santayana's takes religion to consist of symbols, essentially poetic in character, put to work in the moral ordering of human life within specific cultures.[13] This view is worked out in detail for the interpretation of religious doctrines (e.g. heaven and hell), for rituals (e.g. prayer and sacrifice), for religious emotions and attitudes (e.g. piety, charity, resignation). Moreover, it is accompanied with the historical hypothesis that the meaning of religion to the faithful (as distinct from the arguments of theologians) has always been primarily its practical-moral ordering of life. Now, Santayana's is neither a cursory nor an unsympathetic treatment of religion, but on its interpretation, clearly the religious concepts are inherently both aesthetic and moral and function as practical. The concepts as such are not autonomous. Similar points could be made about the autonomy of aesthetic concepts. In certain contexts the distinction between the beautiful and the moral or the beautiful and the useful are obviously clear and relevant. But these may be cases in which the isolation of the object of appreciation has first been secured by the context—for example, the painting may be set off by its frame. But if we think of architecture rather than painting, the instrumental and the technical enter not only through the character of the materials but with greater exigency through the purposes of the construction. Here aesthetic appreciation is not so readily separable from an understanding of function.

A striking illustration of the relativity of a field's organizing categories and their dependence on conditions and techniques in specific contexts may be taken from an exchange between two civil engineers on the contrast between *structures* and *machines*. It can serve as a symbol of our general problem. In "Technology and the Structuring of Cities," Billington sets up a basic contrast between structures and machines.[14] The former are static and usually large-scale, custom-made, and designed to last, for the most part unique. Machines are dynamic, small-scale, and mass-produced, not intended to last indefinitely, and universal in the sense of performing a definite function wherever they are. He offers as a symbolic contrast the dike and the locomotive. This dichotomy he takes to be basic in engineering, and he outlines different laws for each, in the end aligning the machines with science and the structure with art. Now the speculative philosopher, faced with this contrast, may wonder whether a structure could not itself be seen as a machine doing slower or steadier jobs, as the dike is holding back the constantly beating waves. In that case, the differences Billington gives could be seen as simply different practical methods of construction corresponding to differences in speed and stability. This is a mild speculation as long as technological conditions do not allow of significant overlapping. In his response to Billington, Salvadori quotes Le Corbusier, "La maison c'est une machine à habiter," and then points to the case where the outer columns of a building are kept from becoming destructively hot by a permanently circulating liquid. Little imagination is needed today to think of flying machines and space stations as dwellings and factories. In general, then, the concepts of a field and the modes of organization they dictate hold under limited conditions of materials, purposes, traditions of construction, and ingenuity. While they are stable, the majority of cases may be the "clear cases" and serve as ready paradigms for generalizations about the form of knowledge and the corresponding discipline. But with changed conditions, greater knowledge, and newer techniques, more inventiveness, come conceptual vagueness and conceptual shifts. The previously clear cases may be fewer in proportion, as well as lose interest, and even large-scale conceptual alterations become possible.

The actual classification of forms of knowledge tends to follow the existent disciplines. Thus Hirst lists mathematics, physical sciences, human sciences, history, religion, literature and the fine arts, philosophy.[15] It is not hard to discern the unstable elements in this classification. Hirst himself changed his mind: almost a decade after this paper was written, he reassessed the forms of knowledge, and took history and the social sciences out of the list.[16] Parts of the social sciences seemed to him now to be no different in type from physical science, and the remainder, like history, distinguished by their concern with explaining human behavior in terms of intentions, will, hopes, beliefs, and so on. Accordingly the two relevant forms become one concerned with truths of the physical world, and the other with truths of a mental or personal kind. This is almost a return to the older distinction in German philosophic thought between *Naturwissenschaft* and *Geisteswissenschaft*. A different kind of unification for the human side might be found in emphasizing the historical character of human phenomena rather than a mental character; this would imply that the social sciences are less successful if they neglect history. Another unification sometimes proposed is a practical-moral one: to recast the social sciences as attempted answers to human problems rather than model them on the physical sciences. Now, all these could be seen as proposed reconstruction in the light of dissatisfaction with the progress of the social sciences. They need not line up as candidates for a newly discovered form of knowledge and experience. The many reorganizations within the social sciences in the past two decades are evidence of the dissatisfaction—for example, attempts to set off the behavioral from the social sciences. The shiftings within the physical sciences as a consequence of advancing knowledge have also been widespread; they attract less philosophical attention in classifying disciplines simply because physical science had become an established category and what goes on inside it is left to its own management. We need scarcely add that a backward glance over the past two centuries and the attempts to set permanent outlines of the sciences, or to make scientific boundaries coincide with "realms of reality" or, after the consolidation of an evolutionary outlook, "emerging levels of reality," teach us the same lesson, namely, that the conceptual distinctions follow the advances in knowledge rather than set boundaries within which they are to be carried out. Even the concept of philosophy itself is not an exception to problems of conceptual shift.

How Reliable Is Direct Educational Evidence?

In principle, it should be possible to muster direct educational evidence concerning the advantages and disadvantages of the two theses, in their impact on teaching and learning. But this is not easy, for the same subjects may well be recommended for the curriculum on both views. The differences will come in the attitude toward the curriculum and in teaching. Sometimes the evidence reflects the entrenched position of a theory that dominates educational practice. For example, the view that science and the humanities are two distinct cultures may be reenforced by the curricular structure and mode of teaching, so that the immediate educational phenomena would seem to count against their continuity. Only experience with curriculum and teaching structured on the opposing theory would make effective comparison of evidence possible. Hence a revelation of the depth of the cleavage between the two forms—such as C.P. Snow's account of the "two cultures" of science and the humanities—so far from proving separateness may be evidence of bad policy and, as Snow indeed sees it, of a sad cultural situation in which we have drifted. Such questions are perhaps then better considered at present in normative terms of what is desirable for education rather than in terms of what educational practice may still indecisively establish. In the long run we will, perhaps, be able to figure out retrospectively what the educational experience shall have shown.

Underlying Epistemological and Psychological Assumptions

When distinctions alleging discontinuity are made between the logical, the empirical, the practical, and the aesthetic, there looms behind every step the long history of philosophical controversy over the status of logical laws, the nature of experience, the interpretation of practice, and the nature of appreciation. The legitimacy of hard as against relative distinctions has been at the center of the epistemological controversies: dichotomies of formal-material, sensory-intellectual, fact-value, cognitive-affective. Each of these deserves brief comment.

Formal-material. The separateness of the logical and mathematical as formal has been countered by conceiving of them as idealization of empirical distinctions turned into commitments for inquiry. In older dispute, the issue was cast as the dichotomy of the necessary and the contingent; in recent philosophy, it has been rather the tenability of a distinction between the analytic and the synthetic. Perhaps for our present purposes it will suffice to look at the difference in underlying attitude to the formal.

A continuity thesis denies that a satisfactory account can be given of formal properties in any domain without reference to the material that is being organized and structured in the given form. The distinction between form and matter is a relative one, within some purposive context. Hence to understand why certain features are set up as formal requires seeing the way they function, the offices they are carrying out, and the criteria of success on which their stability depends. Thus categories can undergo change and basic concepts undergo change when they no longer successfully carry out their function, just as concepts become altered as more is learned about the materials to which they are related. As we come to understand the material base on which a category or general concept rests, we can think in terms of its refinement, improvement, and even its replacement. We do not just have to wait and see. On such an active approach—consonant with the way an advancing science treats its concepts and the way change takes place on the historical scene—Hirst's patient resignation about the possibility of change of forms of knowledge is in the spirit of Hegel's owl of Minerva that takes flight only in the dusk after action is over.

Sensory-intellectual. The separateness of the empirical is usually secured by setting off the sensory from the intellectual. (The intellectual gets aligned with the logical and the formal). Various epistemological devices are employed to rule out the intrusion of theory or interpretation into the sensory; for example, in older days by a Lockean belief in simple or atomic sensations or impressions and in more recent philosophy by more subtle claims about sense-data. It is not always easy to realize that such notions are *constructions* in the attempt to understand the nature and growth of knowledge, or to appreciate the part that the discovery of techniques plays in stimulating such constructions. For example, if we ask what differentiates the twentieth-century concept of sense-data from the previous Lockean view of simple sensations, it is probably the hope of applying the mode of analysis developed in logical matrices: truth-tables analyze complex propositional forms in terms of the combinations of truth values for the simple propositions, and so a complex empirical sentence is to be analyzed into simple or absolutely elementary statements of sensory experience. (What is more, the logical structure of the world is made to conform to the structure the technique demands.)

In the case of this dichotomy with its contrast of the theoretical and the observational, the current trend seems decisively to be toward a continuity thesis. At least within the domain of the scientific, the distinction is recognized as relative to context, so that what is observational within one context is seen as interpretive and theoretical within another. (This does not yet extend decisively to logic and pure mathematics.)

Fact-value. The isolation of the moral and practical from the empirical has rested on claims of different kinds of experience or else on different concepts (the true and the good). Since Kant it has relied on the formidable dichotomy of the *is* and the *ought* or the more generalized (though originally different) dichotomy of fact and value. Against this the continuity thesis maintains that the distinction is relative to purposive contexts. In recent moral philosophy this has been argued on several grounds. For one thing, the effort even in the analysis of moral language to sort out distinctive forms of expression or establish different linguistic forms has not been successful. Doubtless a prima facie distinction can be maintained between two different stances or enterprises, one descriptive and the other evaluative, but this is quite different from maintaining values and facts as different types of content. Moreover, every descriptive stance can be seen to involve certain values and every evaluative stance to involve certain facts. Indeed all conceptualization and all knowledge may be seen to involve a selective element that is purposive and so continuous with the valuational in all life and awareness. Finally, the question may be raised whether the fact-value dichotomy is not a program rather than a metaphysical or epistemological truth: it assumes that our ordinary experience and our ordinary language admit of the sharp separation of factual and valuational components, just as the isolation of the empirical assumed that we could separate the sensory from the interpretive. It looks as if in both cases it has gone from the assertion of a program to an assertion of its assured success. But the quandaries of experience have brought the whole program into doubt.[17] While this controversy is by no means over, the strength of the claims for the fact-value dichotomy has much receded.

Cognitive-affective. The isolation of the aesthetic has rested on the distinction of experienced qualities (the beautiful, the sublime, and the like), but probably more strongly on claims for the autonomy of feeling. Yet feeling and emotion turn out to have both volitional and cognitive aspects. Emotions are not purely reactive; they are seen to be inherently purposive both in their occurrence and their meaning—one is angry at something, not just angry—and such emotional reactions register and comprehend the situation.[18] Defenders of the view that the cognitive permeates art find support from recent work in cognitive psychology on such topics as language and problem solving, memory storage and retrieval, perceptual discrimination and learning.[19] In general, art becomes regarded itself as a way of seeing the world.

The psychological substructures of these four issues can be seen in the opposing interpretations of human activities in general, over and above the qualitative character of their objects. Philosophical analysis of human activity usually reflects one or another psychological standpoint regarding thinking, sensing, deliberating or deciding, feeling. The isolation of their objects as the formal, the empirical, the practical, the aesthetic appears to be committed to a psychology strikingly similar to the old faculty psychology that separated thinking, sensing, willing, feeling. Such a parallel suggests that one of the constraints to be imposed on philosophical constructions is some degree of coherence with the psychological analysis of the human processes involved. Ryle's distinctions were tied to his rejection of a dualistic theory of mind. If the discontinuity thesis is at bottom linked with a four-faculty psychological conception, even if only in a residual way, then one of the strongest possible arguments for the continuity thesis is to be found in the way in which it is explicitly linked with the kind of integrative psychology that Dewey early advanced and that is finding increasing acceptance in psychological circles. In a basic article in 1896 Dewey had already challenged dualism in a distinctive way.[20] Stimulus and response (or stimulus, central process, and response) are ways of cutting into and analyzing ongoing behavior. They do not refer to separated and isolated acts in sequence. They both involve perceptual and motor features (visual perception is both optical and ocular). What is viewed as a response in one context is to be regarded as a stimulus in another. To reify them is to miss the continuity of behavior. The utility of analyzing into stimulus and response is functional. We may understand analyzing a situation in terms of stimulus and analyzing it in terms of response as respectively analyzing with reference to alternative meanings that present themselves and with respect to alternative proposals of action that are offered. We may pay attention to the latter aspect, as is done in the perspective of the agent; or we may attend to the former, which focuses on the conditions of action, as is done in the perspective of the scientific observer. A full analysis will encompass both aspects in their total relation and to the extent that the agent can be conscious of the fuller picture decision is more comprehensively based, and accordingly wiser. The model that Dewey here offered was generalized by him in the light of his theory of consciousness—the view widely prevalent after the growth of the evolutionary outlook, that consciousness comes on the scene when there is a hitch in the smooth flow of the habitual and in the presence of a problem that brings hesitation and requires fresh selection among alternatives to bring a solution and release action. Dewey applied this model in social psychology as well and in the theory of morality and society and its institutions. Its transactional character distinguishes it markedly from the psychologies that treat separately of the different activities of the human being.

On such a psychological approach a construction that sharply separated thinking from doing would be misleading, set as it traditionally has been in a mind-body dualism. On the Deweyan psychology there is no sheer thought without operational reference nor sheer doing without some role in the problematic situation. Distinctions can of course be offered in different contexts; a more appropriate general one might be between enlightened and unenlightened doing—a relative distinction open to refinement as the criteria of enlightenment (rationality, as we have seen in chapter 8) were themselves extended and refined. The fact-value distinction would similarly be a relative one to be understood contextually with reference to specific conditions and purposes; it might have to be more sharply drawn from the perspective of agency where the criteria for the assessment of a situation have to be initially set up in relation to the problem that is being faced, but not in the examination of conditions and consequences where the criteria themselves would be related to the wider purposes that the context would reveal. And comparably, feelings could be gross or refined, according to their purposive coherence and cognitive differentiation.

The Continuity Thesis and the Social Character of Knowledge

It looks as if the argument leans toward the continuity thesis. There is, however, a special problem that faces this thesis. It seems to involve a commitment to a public or social interpretation that has to run through the whole gamut of knowledge. If knowledge is individual, ultimately private, how could any theses of continuity or discontinuity be settled to reach a common agreement? Doubtless underlying the claims of privacy are dualistic assumptions of inner and outer, familiar enough in the history of epistemology, and their exploration would be even more complex than that of the dichotomies just considered. What we need here is a minimal analysis of what is meant by a social matter and in what sense knowledge can be conceived of as social.

Let us start with the standard example of language. The users of language are, of course, all individuals, and if the last informant for a given language otherwise unrecorded were to die, the language would be lost forever. Nevertheless language is social in several senses. The individual learns it from others in the group, so that the source of his or her knowledge, skill, and attitudes toward its uses is social. Second, its uses or functions are social initially or primarily—the individual employs it to communicate with others in the first place, and then develops it as a mode of self-expression and thought. Insofar as it is an inner or private phenomenon, it is quite literally an internalization of the social that becomes in the individual's development part of the self. Of course there are idiosyncratic elements in this process, and all sorts of chance variations the individual introduces may take hold in the social process of communication. Languages as well as the individual's use of language are constantly changing and these elements are part of the source of change. Finally, the meaning of the words in language and the modes of use are all in a similar way products of a cultural process. The richness of vocabulary in any area reflects the extent of cultural interest in that area, the formulation of ideas reflects the purposive construction of a world of things and events that people of that culture have made in orienting their life and thought in the milieu of their environment and occupations and social relations, and the categories carried by labels guide perception itself.

Now, when a person says, "I know," we may think the person is reporting on an inner state, and much of the analysis of knowing has gone into attempting to see the presuppositions of that state—what the person assumes, what belief the person has, how strong it may be, and so on, depending on the type of philosophy in which the analysis is carried out. But in any case, even if a person carries on reflections, so to speak, within, the person's materials and their meanings are to be found in the tradition that the person is embodying, using, clarifying, altering. To look in the individual is to see the social materials worked on. To look in the social is to see the tradition developing and being modified. When all then is said and done, to insist on the social approach is essentially to correct the excessively isolating individualistic approach, not to deny the significance of individual action. Once the correction is made, a full view sees differences of analytic perspective or focus, not a break into two separate processes, whether isolated from one another or interactive. When we study the whole developmental process the focus is better characterized as social, for we see the conditions of individual action, the relations and influences and meanings. When we are engaged in action, the focus is better characterized as individual, for the individual is the center of deliberation and action, of whatever control is possible and of evaluation. But it is not only mistaken but foolish to think that the conditions and meanings and influences and standards that enter into the individual's decision and action and evaluation are somehow entirely within the individual and require no understanding in terms of their transactional properties. An individualistic approach that looks upon the individual in this way takes away the vital relations that give body to the individual's judgment. Value judgments become treated as simply the individual's arbitrary acts of will, preferences as sheer expressions of taste, and action as just the exertion of what power the individual possesses. When the individual is seen in the full perspective of the social, the individual's value judgments can now be understood as more or less reasonable; taste can be seen as gross or refined, cultivated and discriminating or unlearned; and action as influential or authoritative, not simply coercive.

The same difference is found in approaches to knowledge. If inquiry into the meaning of knowledge is confined to the individual, the knower is regarded as one who deals with inner data and measures their strength and stability. If knowledge is regarded as a public achievement, the focus is on the cumulation of systematic science, craft, and art experience, as well as less formalized bodies of information, and on the shaping of systematic attitude. Cumulation implies also processes of discovery, ordering, conceptual reconstruction. Knowing understood in this light is not a private or inner affair but a relation to the public tradition and its resources. The sense in which knowing and knowledge would then be used for education, that is, for investigating teaching annd learning, would already include giving of reasons, using criteria and standards, and discriminating among practices. The question so often raised, as to how it is possible to have judgments of quality, would not arise as a general question at all. It is the offspring of an erroneous isolation, like asking how a being who had no feelings would decide which of two alternatives felt better. There are enough genuine questions in judging the quality of alternative paths in concrete situations. We do better to study the tradition (and the competing traditions) of the inquiries and practices about which the concrete arises, for if such study does not resolve our problem it will at least show us where a refined creativity is to be exercised.

In the light of such considerations, we are able to go a few steps further on the question (raised in the previous chapter) of how far the correctness of what is taught and learned is assumed in its being "teaching" and "learning." The question is a normative one. It amounts to deciding whether to allow that learning is taking place when less than a certain standard of correctness is achieved in what is taught or learned—usually taught, because the point of responsibility is the teacher. Thus if we used a purely internal standard we might say there was learning if the teacher sincerely believed what he or she was teaching to be true, and the pupil learned it. But where and in what fields and under what conditions would we be ready to entrust our children to schools that were satisfied with such a criterion? Add to that the practical point that to call it learning might be a defense for the teacher against charges of incompetence! This is of course oversimplified, but it should underscore the fact that the issue is one of policy, not sociological description nor linguistic uses. To set the standard for education at a sufficiently high level, probably nothing less than defining learning and teaching so as to include the current advanced level of the body of knowledge is likely to do. Any shortcomings would have to be justified, the obligation to keep up would fall on the teachers and to provide opportunities for this to be done on the school system.

Central to this conception of correctness is of course the realization that the results at any time may prove in the future to have been insufficiently refined and even in some serious respects on the wrong track. This is one of the many places at which we should flag the need for including the *advancement* of knowledge rather than merely the acquisition of knowledge, by each successive generation, as a major contemporary aim.

Finally, the method of stabilizing correctness is itself part of the very tradition that grows and improves in the social process of advancing knowledge. The components that enter into a method of inquiry—theories, laws, observations, interpreted facts, gross facts, types of data, types of insight, different types of logical system—may come to bear on inquiries in varying ways. Teaching and learning satisfy the conditions of authenticity if they convey an understanding of evidence and methods with respect to what is taught and learned—and both with the degree of refinement that the stage of development of the students admits of.

Notes

1. Gilbert Ryle, *The Concept of Mind* (London: Hutchinson's University Library, 1949), p. 286.
2. Jane Roland Martin, "On the Reduction of 'Knowing That' to 'Knowing How'," *Language and Concepts in Education*, ed. B. O. Smith and R. H. Ennis (Chicago: Rand-McNally, 1961), pp. 57-71.
3. In his *Posterior Analytics* 2, 1, Aristotle distinguishes between asking if something is and what it is. The more general distinction is between knowing *that* something is the case and on *account of what* it is the case.
4. Bertrand Russell, "Knowledge by Acquaintance and Knowledge by Description," *Mysticism and Logic* (New York: W. W. Norton, 1929).
5. William James, *The Principles of Psychology* (New York: Henry Holt, 1890) 1:221 ff. Interestingly, contemporary usage almost reverses this. To be acquainted with something is really to know it, while to know about it may be just what we gathered concerning it, for example from reading a book review instead of the book.
6. Henri Bergson, *An Introduction to Metaphysics*, trans. T. E. Hulme (New York: Liberal Arts Press, 1949).
7. Martin Buber, *I and Thou*, trans. Ronald Gregor Smith (Edinburgh: T.&T. Clark, 1937).
8. R.S. Peters, "Education and the Educated Man," *The Philosophy of Education Society of Great Britain, Proceedings of the Annual Conference* 4: 8.
9. Paul H. Hirst, *Knowledge and the Curriculum: a Collection of Philosophical Papers* (Boston: Routledge & Kegan Paul, 1974), p. 91.
10. Ibid., p. 93.
11. Ibid., p. 95.

236   Interpreting Education

12. Thomas F. Green, *The Activities of Teaching* (New York: McGraw-Hill, 1971), p. 23.

13. George Santayana, *Reason in Religion* (New York: Charles Scribner's Sons, 1905).

14. In *Small Comforts for Hard Times: Humanists on Public Policy*, ed. Michael Mooney and Florian Stuber (New York: Columbia University Press, 1977), pp. 182-98. The response to this view is Mario G. Salvadori, "The Aesthetics of Technology," ibid., pp. 199-203.

15. Hirst, *Knowledge and the Curriculum*, p. 46.

16. Ibid., p. 86. See also his remarks on religion, pp. 88-89, and the whole of chapter 6 ("The Forms of Knowledge Revisited").

17. For a fuller discussion of this issue, see Abraham Edel, *Exploring Fact and Value* (New Brunswick, N.J.: Transaction Books, 1980), esp. chs. 2, 3.

18. The critique of the sharp separation of purpose, with its cognition, from emotion has been going on for a long time in different forms. In the 1940s it was a startling challenge when R.W. Leeper offered "A Motivational Theory of Emotion to Replace 'Emotion as Disorganized Response'," *Psychological Review* 55 (1948): 5-21. Psychologists soon came to realize that the theory of the emotions was in an unsettled state. Philosophical schools in their own way moved in the direction pragmatism had earlier projected. For example, Jean-Paul Sartre's *Existentialism and Human Emotions* (New York: Philosophical Library, 1957) rests on the purposive character of emotional expression. Analytic philosophers began to find the Humean separation of reason and emotion, which had been consistently invoked in positivist theory, lacking in cogency. Cf. R.S. Peters, *Reason and Compassion* (Boston: Routledge & Kegan Paul, 1973), Lecture 3. See also his "Reason and Passion" in "Reason," part 2 of *Education and the Development of Reason*, ed. R.F. Dearden, P.H. Hirst, and R.S. Peters (Boston: Routledge & Kegan Paul, 1972).

19. David Perkins and Barbara Leondar, eds., *The Arts and Cognition* (Baltimore: Johns Hopkins University Press, 1977), p. 2.

20. John Dewey, "The Reflex Arc Concept in Psychology," *Psychological Review*, July 1896, pp. 357-70. Reprinted in John Dewey, *The Early Works* 5: 96-109. Cf. Appendix A, Below.

12. The Pedagogical Encounter

This chapter is essentially about what the teacher is doing and what the teacher is like *in the teaching*, and what the learner is like *in the learning*. Is there a distinctive "pedagogical encounter"?

Occasionally an attempt is made to list the activities that go on in teaching, and to present their nature. *Showing, telling, informing* (taken in a purely descriptive sense) seem to have their place; telling sometimes carries the implication of asserting authoritatively. *Explaining* or *demonstrating* are clearly important activities, just as *defining* and *expounding* are. *Convincing* and *persuading* touch more difficult ground; students may appropriately find themselves convinced or persuaded of something after they have learned a great deal about it, but the effort of the teacher, it is generally felt, should not be directed primarily to convincing or persuading. *Training* in the limited sense of drilling in a skill or technique and *instructing* in the limited sense of issuing directives are parts of teaching, but to substitute such training for teaching as a whole is to ruin teaching, while "instructing" ("instruction") as a general term is simply a synonym for teaching. Finally, when we get to such notions as *indoctrinating* and *conditioning*, a moral note enters the discussion, and the substitution of these activities for teaching is generally condemned.

Is There a Place for Indoctrinating and Conditioning?

McClellan, in his *Philosophy of Education*, brands conditioning and indoctrination as "counterfeits" of teaching; they cannot be differentiated from teaching without attending to the kind of learning that takes place.[1] Hirst, as we have seen, holds that teaching is to be understood in terms of learning, so that the approach to indoctrination follows the same route. He raises the problem in directly moral terms: "People are now aware of a range of activities, some of them thought to be morally undesirable, whose relation to teaching is by no means clear: activities like indoctrinating, preaching, advertising, and propagandizing. There are many terms that are as it were in the same logical band as 'teaching', and we are I think rightly getting more sensitive as to whether or not the activities these terms label ought to go on in school."[2] It is interesting to note that each of the dubious activities he lists belongs to a specific profession, so that setting them aside from teaching is equivalent to saying that a teacher is not like a military officer, a minister, a merchant, a politician. Perhaps we would get closer to what is being rejected by following up this institutional clue: what is wrong with indoctrination is that it is *imposing* a doctrine in one or another way; with preaching that it is proselytizing; with advertising that it is selling a belief, too often it is luring or seducing; with propagandizing that it is an organized campaign to win an allegiance. All these show that we have come to see teaching as a pursuit in which the student is to develop independent thinking and become a rational being. This explains also why conditioning is one of the prime targets of attack in listing what is not teaching, for whatever the psychological theory from which it emerges, conditioning is a causal process in which what stands out most prominently is the external direction and control rather than the internal deliberative process. Thus it is seen as manipulative, even where it is for good ends.[3]

Is there anything to be said on the other side—that indoctrination, conditioning, and the like are not altogether ruled out from teaching? For one thing, suppose we hold that all events, human as well as purely physical, are causally related. Then it is not sufficient to set off conditioning as causal to exclude it from the ranks of teaching forms. One would have to distinguish in the results of conditioning where reflective behavior was produced and where unreflective behavior; the conditioning that produced the former could then be accepted as a kind of teaching. The mistaken condemnation of all conditioning as nonteaching would reflect an unnecessarily sharp contrast of the intentional and the causal. We have tended to assume that the result will manifest the character of the process, that because the process is manipulative, the acquired skill or belief acquired must thereafter carry the stamp of manipulation. Skinner overadvertised that view of conditioning; even *Walden II*, which presents his ideal society, has a leader who is pulling the strings. But the situation from the learner's point of view may yield a different picture. We could do worse than start with the jest of the pigeon that said excitedly to a fellow pigeon, "I've just conditioned Professor Skinner: every time I press a lever he gives me a food pellet." If as a result of the conditioning the learner lost a fear that inhibited learning a particular skill and emerged with that skill, then the learning would indeed have taken place whether the learner was aware of the process or not. Human dignity may demand that the learner be told. Clearly too, conditioning may be sought by a subject who wants to get rid of a habit he or she cannot break. Self-conditioning might well bring together the two aspects—the moral and the scientific—that the general contrast of the intentional and the causal have seemed to separate. This was implicit in the earlier discussion of freedom and control in the context of clarifying the demands of autonomy.

Take a specifically educational example. Shortly after the Russian Revolution, it is said, Soviet nursery schools used to furnish blocks for the children to play with that were too heavy for a single child to handle. The aim was to generate cooperativeness and helpfulness among the children. Now, is this conditioning in the nonteaching sense? Or is it teaching because it manipulates not the body but the environment? Dewey, for example, describes teaching as making appropriate changes in the environment so that the student will be active in a desirable way in coping with it. Again, one of the things that much affected U.S. educators in the 1930s and 1940s was the way in which apparently fundamental changes were made in the character of Soviet and German society. Perhaps, they felt, the United States had been too naive in thinking that if children were left alone they turned into democractically minded citizens whereas strict controls were needed to make them fall into alien patterns. Perhaps democratic-mindedness needs to be cultivated quite as consciously.[4]

In some respects the variety of models for teaching raises the same problems. Mechanical models exhibit teaching as almost pressing the right levers and pulling the right strings to get the desired effect. Agricultural analogies at times at least have the virtue of modulating the manipulation: teaching is like casting seeds into the ground, and hoping the plants will grow and flourish. The teacher can help by furnishing congenial conditions, but growth cannot be forced. Perhaps models of interpersonal relations or communication may bring the process closer to human dialogue; much of the influence of Martin Buber's *I and Thou* in educational thought came from the sheer respect for persons that it entailed, and the recognition of the destructive effect of manipulation, even though his treatment of knowledge or science as embodying the standpoint of manipulation and reducing the Thou to It may be open to serious criticism.

The net impact of the critique of conditioning as nonteaching is that teaching is not simply bringing about acts of behavior on the part of another person. It is helping a self to learn. Neither knowledge, nor skill, nor attitude can be broken up into a set of discrete units. Knowledge is not a set of sense-data, nor skill a set of muscular reactions, nor attitude a set of isolated habits. Knowledge involves a theoretical framework, skill an organized pattern of purpose, attitude a motivated self. Because we do not have a fully developed theory of the self, we have to use models and metaphors as theory-surrogates in different ways. If teaching is helping a person learn (though this is only the genus), then any mode of helping is not to be equated with teaching if it relates only to a partial activity, isolates it from an organized self, discounts or ignores the self or reduces it to separate acts.

This does not mean, however, that in separate parts of the complex of teaching there may not be room for some of the questionable processes. Some modes of conditioning may play a useful part in the case of persons who choose to use such processes on themselves for particular purposes (or invite the assistance of others in this respect). What should be acquired in this way rather than be consciously acquired, is a matter for rational decision too. Many of the questions that have been raised in the past about drill, rote learning, mechanical aids, teaching machines, separating and even mechanizing some aspects of a subject matter are of the same kind. (Our discussion of reading-readiness above showed this.) The warning is never to invoke the mechanical aids if they break down the organization that the self should carry. But this is far from asserting that they cannot be aids, that they always enslave. Enslavement can come in innumerable ways; its possibility is not limited to a mechanical conditioning. The attraction of the ideal can sometimes turn into fanaticism, the attraction of a person into a charismatic loss of freedom, and even the magnetism of the divine (as in the angels forever turned to God once they have chosen in the first split second of creation) into a transcending of self. That is when the Miltonic Satan can be readily seen as the hero of anticonditioning, unless all these phenomena be interpreted as the marks of a driven rather than a free self.

We may add that the criticism of the other modes is also an empirical matter. Thus it has often been assumed that indoctrination is necessary in the military establishment because unshakable belief is the only way in which split-second response to emergencies can be counted on. But experience suggests that this is the procedure needed for reliance in an authoritarian framework. Subsequent experience in conditions of guerrilla warfare and the like have shown that initiative may often be required and that, particularly where the motive for participation is strong, a better military can be developed by nonindoctrinating teaching. Similarly, although advertising plays a large part in our competitive profit-seeking economy, much of its force would be irrelevant given a legal context that abandoned "caveat emptor" for some consumer protection. The protection may lie in regulating what can be produced and sold, but it can also ensure procedures of information that enable the consumer to exercise choice. Preaching also differs under different social conditions; for example in seventeenth-century England sermons played a role very much like that which contemporary journalism does in relation to politics.

In general, the study of variants of teaching calls for more intensive investigation into the variants of learning. This might have been expected from the contemporary shift to the primacy of learning, but the habit of looking at education chiefly from the standpoint of the teacher is not easily broken even when teaching itself is analyzed in terms of the learning that is to ensue. The analysis of "counterfeits" of teaching is not sufficiently matched with analysis of "counterfeits" of learning. This seems to be the next important step. A critique of variant forms of studying and of learning should make the student as sensitive to quality differences in these aspects as he or she has become to the responsibilities of teachers. The earlier stages of such a critique may take the shape of ruling out certain activities as pseudoforms: the substitution of note-taking and memorization and the weaving of snippets for integrative understanding, or pursuing the association of ideas for structural evaluation. But in the long run it is less a matter of conferring the title of studying and learning than of seeing the place of different activities within a systematic achievement of the objectives of learning. If the suggestion that has emerged from our consideration of the variants of teaching provides a lead, then studying and learning have to be understood as in some measure self-making. This requires a fuller understanding than we have of the development of the self and its powers and the way it relates to teaching and learning.

Teacher-Student Bonds

In most accounts of teaching and learning the spotlight does eventually come to rest on the interaction of the two central figures in the educational process. This centrality takes different form in theoretical analyses. Sometimes it is put into a definition, as Langford defines formal education in terms of two parties, one of whom accepts responsibility for the education of the other.[5] McClellan puts the *pedagogical encounter* as the first condition to be satisfied if a teaching claim is to be true.[6] As to long-distance teaching, he dismisses it with a quip, comparing it to a long-distance telephone call: "Ma Bell claims only that it's the next best thing to being there, not that it's another way of being there." Oakeshott says, "The idea 'School' is that of a personal transaction between a 'teacher' and a 'learner'."[7] Langford and Oakeshott are thinking of a longer stretch than McClellan; McClellan seems to be focusing on the here-now episode. His formulation does correspond to a prevalent tendency to regard the rest of the educational process as either preparation or support for the educational performance, which is what goes on in the classroom or the tutorial. In any case, any question about the character of teacher-student interaction or the nature of teacher-student bonds must obviously ask first: what goes on in the pedagogical encounter?

The simplest answer, and perhaps the most pedestrian, is that the teaching is helping the student learn. But a more "inner" picture is wanted of what the help consists in. Sometimes, from the habit of U.S. college students of saying at the end of a discussion with the professor (outside class), "Thank you for your time," one might think that the significant feature of the encounter is spending time with the student. A psychologist might be tempted to add that, given the pressures of contemporary schooling and the alienation of students, the mere spending-time-with was important in showing concern, and that a fundamental component of the teacher-student bond is to care or be concerned about the student. But of course this would not distinguish a teacher from a parent or a nurse. Still, the presence of concern may be a necessary condition for other more directly educational bonds.

In the classical tradition, Socrates described his part in the encounter by saying that he was a midwife of ideas. His questioning awakens the mind by leading the participants to discern contradictions in their beliefs or statements. The resulting inner tension activates reflection, and fresh ideas are born. The fellow participants in the encounter often resented the process; contemporary students undergoing such an encounter sometimes feel it as a "put-down." It is certainly not an authoritarian method, for it leaves to the individual what he or she is to say next and does not do more than ask pointed questions. No doubt it offers scope for arrogance and a touch of sadism. But Socrates saw it as a concern for truth rather than for victory in argument.

The actual characterization of the encounter as governed by an impersonal truth is more systematically formulated by Aristotle, who set it in a framework supplied by a theory of thinking and of the human good. Aristotle distinguishes three kinds of association or interpersonal relations.[8] One is for the sake of benefits, and can be studied according to the kinds of exchange carried out. A second is for the sake of pleasure, given and received, whose condition and proportions may be examined. Both of these are directed to the individuals who take part in the transaction. The third, however, is for the sake of the good; here there is a good or ideal with which the parties jointly become identified, so that its demands guide their personal action and deliberation. The teacher-student bond cast in this last mold would express a mutual direction toward the truth or the good and an immersion in the subject matter. Teacher and student would be governed by the object of their study in the same way people are governed by an ideal when they are committed to it.[9] The distinctively teacher-student relation would thus not be a directly person-to-person bond, but a shared experience and a joint commitment to something impersonal. Aristotle actually thought that the highest contemplation of truth was solitary rather than shared; it was a kind of direct communion in which the individual lost all sense of self.

Compare with this Oakeshott's interpretation of the teacher-student transaction. He sees it as a kind of handing on of the spiritual torch from one generation to another. The teacher has a part of the human inheritance that he or she keeps alive in himself or herself. The learner in sharing it is engaged in becoming human. "Education is not learning to do *this* or *that* more proficiently, it is acquiring in some measure an understanding of a human condition in which the 'fact of life' is continuously illuminated by a 'quality of life'. It is learning how to be at once an autonomous and a civilized subscriber to a human life."[10] On such a view the pedagogical encounter is obviously not instrumental but has inherent value. For Oakeshott that value lies in its being a transaction between generations. The continuity of tradition over time, not the impersonal universal truth or good, lies back of his description of the bond.

So marked a contrast between Aristotle and Oakeshott invites the question of the nature of our inquiry. Are these two different interpretations of a common experience that teachers and students have in their transaction, given a different cast when set in differing metaphysical backgrounds, associated with different theories of mind, and different value frameworks—even apart from differences in the phenomena of schooling? Is there a definite core experience of teaching-and-learning, as there may be of nurturing, a basic psychosocial experience that might be extricated so as to reveal its distinctive quality apart from other relations mingled with it or philosophical patterns imposed upon it? If so, one might hope to find a psychological description of the phenomenon in its basic terms. Of course different psychological schools might go about the task in different ways. We expect that a Freudian would immediately look for emotional attachments as expressing the particular processes and problems that are given a central place in psychoanalytic theory. It is a safer bet, then, to try a cognitive psychologist, particularly if he is writing on education. Jerome Bruner, in *Toward a Theory of Instruction*, takes it to be lesson of psychology that intellectual development depends on "a systematic and contingent interaction between a tutor and a learner, the tutor already being equipped with a wide range of previously invented techniques that he teaches the child."[11] The tutor-tutee relationship may be handled by the culture in different ways, and Bruner points to the family, special identification figures, and heroes as well as teachers. The teacher-learner bond is thus not cut off sharply from other psychological bonds. In general, psychologists do not sharply distinguish teaching processes from those of socialization. There is a continuity between them in the emotional sources they draw on. Teaching is a more conscious matter, it developed in institutional form under conditions that required more organized transmission of knowledge and skills and attitudes.

The psychologist's approach is not without its own philosophical background assumptions in the way it understands the human situation and the capacities of thought and experience. Usually it accepts the evolutionary development of the human being, and the factors that entered into the extension of the human being's powers. The teacher-learner transaction is one kind of relationship that, as it developed in different ways, played a role in the progress of civilization. The central points that entered into Oakeshott's and Aristotle's account of the transaction need not be thrust aside on such an approach; they simply are provided a different place in the story. Oakeshott's interest in tradition and the continuity of generations, and the sense in which the growth of autonomy is identified with becoming human can enter into the content of education. For example, Bruner outlines a proposed course on man, in which the theme is what is human about human beings, how they got that way, how they can be made more so.[12] It explores in detail and with varied educational techniques the major humanizing forces—toolmaking, language, social organization, the management of prolonged childhood, and the urge to explain the world. Doubtless students after such a course would have a strong historical sense of culture as handed on from generation to generation, but they would also have a strong sense of cumulative culture as human beings' way of improving their lot in this world. Perhaps both of these would color students' consciousness in teaching and learning. The question might be put to Oakeshott why the sense of the transaction should be one rather than both of these. Similarly, Aristotle's interest in an impersonal object of knowledge that overarches the teacher-student transaction might find its place in the part of the course that examined the urge to explain the world. The growth of the human quest for knowledge would have to include both an idea of a real that determines what is true and the fallibilism and effort at improvement that characterizes the expansion of knowledge. That the teacher-learner transaction should be characterized by both of these would seem to be a matter of educational policy rather than simply a description or analysis of existent pedagogical encounters.

Such an outcome should not be surprising. Supposing we were asked in considering the family, what is the distinctive relation between grandparents and grandchildren. We may be instigating a search for the current patterns of expectations with respect to behavior and feeling. This might start as a purely psychological or anthropological study. If, however, it helped us find out the values implicit in the functions and roles assigned to people who are in such a relationship, then, relying on a wider normative social framework, we might construct a scheme of good relationships and the feelings appropriate to them. The same holds for the teacher-student transaction. Particularly if there is no distinctive core experience—as seems likely—we should have to find out what the bonds are in all their variety, what functions and roles are assigned under varying sociocultural conditions, and what wider framework of values and objectives guides our educational inquiry. The current concept of the transaction would help chiefly in that it indicates the objectives of the transaction. But the interpretation of objectives seems to be precisely the point at which different theories disagree. The concept is itself refined in the inquiry that it helps initiate, as different theories are analyzed and assessed.

Let us see how this would work out in practice. What, for example, should the teacher-pupil bonds be like in kindergarten? Should there be an element of the parental in the attitude of the teacher? It depends on the objectives in kindergarten. If one of the objectives is that the child step out from the home into a wider group, then a parental attitude might make it seem just like a larger family; it would not then constitute a sufficient break. On the other hand, if there are emotional risks for the child in too sharp a break, then some element of the parental may be desirable. (In some nursery schools, where the mother spends part of the time helping out with the group, the difference between the mother's and the teacher's attitude might be shaded significantly.) In short, the answer depends on the developmental requirements, but the objectives of the educational process in kindergarten furnish criteria for decision. Take another example, from higher education. Given the authoritarian atmosphere that has pervaded education, the college teacher has to work very hard to avoid being turned into an authoritarian figure. What the transaction should be like requires subtle attention to the situation, to the existing tendencies, to the dangers of overreaction, and it is guided by the objectives. When we ask what the affective quality of the transaction should be, we are led to the purposes and ideals that characterize the education of the period. This is to be expected because the affections are best described by their objects. Traditionally, the teacher is to be respected for his or her knowledge; the student, for capacities and aspirations. Given the objective of greater democratization, at some educational levels the relationship may be seen more as co-workers in a common enterprise, with a certain division of labor. That higher education has not always resolved its problem about teacher-student bonds has been evident in the past from the phenomenon of intense discipleship in which some confusion of relations is involved. Difficulties today are apparent in the confusion as to what democratization entails.[13]

The way in which different answers are required under different conditions and at different educational levels suggests that no simple or uniform answer is adequate concerning teacher-student bonds. Different theories at best embody partial emphases and are relative to different conditions. This does not mean that an eclectic approach is required; more likely traditional theories could be refined into models to use at different points. Thus the Aristotelian model, seen as an impersonal subject holding both teacher and student to account, may fit advanced fields of higher education, while earlier levels may do better with a model of interpersonal relations oriented to personal well-being. Such complexities suggest a conclusion very much like that reached earlier for ideals. For the most part, the ideals invoked in education were found to be general human ideals. They became educational ideals only when they were applied to educational practices or captured within a strictly educational concept, like that of a good teacher. The same has happened here. The concept of a good teacher includes having certain attitudes toward students. But this does not mean that there is a prior concept of the right teacher attitudes. It is rather a case of working out what desirable attitudes in interpersonal relations have application to what educational situations. Only if there turned out to be unique attitudes for a typical function—as for example, the surgeon may in limited contexts have to treat the patient as an object rather than a subject—does it become possible to speak of the distinctive relationship. And this is the outcome of inquiry, not its starting point.

Such a conclusion undercuts rather than answers any demand for a criterion to distinguish the educational from noneducational bonds in the teacher-learner transaction. Once this is translated into the concrete inquiry into the kinds of mutual attitudes appropriate under different conditions at different levels in the light of stated educational objectives, there remains no special reason for isolating the pedagogical encounter from all the rest of the educational process and seeking a distinctive essence for it. Or perhaps this isolation was itself appropriate under given conditions which now no longer hold.

The theoretical point at issue may perhaps be clarified by analogy. Consider war as an enterprise or institution. Does the pedagogical encounter have the same position in education that front-line battle had in earlier warfare? The contention that the battle encounter in the field or in the trenches is the primary point where war takes place, that everything else is either preparation for it or supporting services for it, that every action related to war should be tested by what it will do to the battle encounter, does not seem implausible. It is not affected by our understanding the battle itself to be a means of victory and victory itself a means to the spoils of war. So too, much that goes on in the way the community makes schooling possible, in the way the pupil prepares and goes to school, in the way the teacher masters the difficult art of teaching, in the whole superstructure of administration and evaluation and governance finds its meaning and its justification in the pedagogical encounter. Teachers and students are the school and all else is not participation in schooling but assistance or preparation for the essential encounter.

The analogy with war need not, however, end where it did. It was based on old-style war, even with artillery replacing hand-to-hand combat. The picture changes with contemporary warfare. Now distinctions of front-line and behind-the-lines warfare become tenuous, civilian casualties tend to outnumber battle casualties; maintaining production is an essential part of the warfare, and factories are bombed. Guiding networks are of moment-to-moment significance and dictate not only general plans but specific action that determines the outcome. Even more, to take a longer-range view, industrial strength and military preparations determine the respective weight of the parties to such an extent that victory is in effect won before the war begins, or else that even victories in battle do not bring victory in the war. Under such changed conditions it becomes difficult to answer who did or did not take part in the war. Should we not similarly construct a concept of the educational process in which the pedagogical encounter, though obviously important, will no longer be isolated as the primary and controlling educational event? We would then realize that we are no longer dealing with an isolated or unitary set of interactions between two individuals, even though in the past this may have adequately captured what was going on.

A more holistic approach to education is therefore needed, one that will see it more comprehensively as a function of the character of our life. Whether this requires us to go as far as Mill did in urging that students learn to learn on their own, cannot be decided simply, even on the general formulation of the priority of learning. In effect it regards teaching as a learning aid that happens, on causal grounds, to be more important than some other aids at some levels. One would have to judge whether teachers continued to be more important at other levels than, say, intelligent classmates with whom one could have more continuous discussion, study and live together, and so on. Of course if the pedagogical encounter is a widely necessary means for a long enough period, it will add to its values from other roots. That would explain the tendency to think of it in an endlike way; it becomes less a means than a constituent part of education. In addition, the human being a social animal, the need for teaching expresses itself in social form, just as the need for maintenance of health expresses itself in doctor-patient relations. But the doctor-patient relation is no longer the primary focus in the maintenance of health, as other complex health support relationships enter on the modern scene. So too a comprehensive view of teaching and learning today sees lessons emerging in vastly broader areas of human experience and taking forms in which they can serve as resources for facing the future. As learning acquires a broader base, education in its traditional forms has to rethink its meaning and its emphases.

Notes

1. James E. McClellan, *Philosophy of Education* (Englewood Cliffs, N.J.: Prentice-Hall, 1976), pp. 53-54, 68-69. For his discussion of indoctrination, see pp.

139-51. His emphasis is on guaranteeing that the interactions between teacher and student will not circumvent the student's independent application of the appropriate criteria for what goes on in this interaction.

2. Paul H. Hirst, *Knowledge and the Curriculum: A Collection of Philosophical Papers* (Boston: Routledge & Kegan Paul, 1974), p. 101.

3. McClellan, *Philosophy of Education*, pp. 51, 139, adds convincing, conning, charming, beguiling, "brainwashing," and so on. Cf. Barbara Smart, "The Concept of Indoctrination," in *New Essays in the Philosophy of Education*, ed. Glenn Langford and D.J. O'Connor (Boston: Routledge & Kegan Paul, 1973). Smart cites Wilson's statement that we could teach "A"-level mathematics and physics electrically without objection, but if we did it for religion it would be indoctrination. This raises the question whether the significant factor in avoiding indoctrination is choice by the subject, cooperation by the subject, or the logical justification that appears in the content itself, as in mathematics. For a direct emphasis on rationality, see Israel Scheffler, "Concepts of Education: Reflections on the Current Scene," in his *Reason and Teaching* (Indianapolis: Bobbs-Merrill, 1973).

4. This, of course, had been Plato's view. In the U.S. scene it was influential in social psychology by stimulating investigation of patterns of authority in the classroom—for example, the comparative studies of authoritarian, laissez-faire, and cooperative-democratic structuring of children's play groups. See Kurt Lewin, Ronald Lippitt, and Ralph K. White, "Patterns of Aggressive Behavior in Experimental 'Social Climates,'" *Journal of Social Psychiatry* 10: 271-97.

5. Glenn Langford, "The Concept of Education," in *New Essays in the Philosophy of Education*, ed. Glenn Langford and D. J. O'Connor (Boston: Routledge & Kegan Paul, 1973), p. 3.

6. McClellan, *Philosophy of Education*, p. 31.

7. Michael Oakeshott, "Education: The Engagement and Its Frustration," *Proceedings of the Philosophy of Education Society of Great Britain* 5 (January 1971): 50.

8. Aristotle, *Nicomachean Ethics* 8, 1-3.

9. This picture of teacher-student bonds can be found in quite different outlooks. Compare Paulo Freire's conception of "co-intentional education" in his *Pedagogy of the Oppressed*, trans. Myra Bergman Ramos (New York: Herder & Herder, 1970), p. 56. Teacher and student, both subjects, are cointent on reality with committed involvement, unveiling it, coming to know it critically, and re-creating the knowledge. This is opposed to the prescriptive relationship between oppressor and oppressed, in which the consciousness of the latter is transformed by the former to conform with the prescriber's consciousness. Freire sees the latter process as a banking model, in which deposits are made in the student's mind and filed by the student.

10. Oakeshott, "Education," p. 51.

11. Jerome Bruner, *Toward a Theory of Instruction* (Cambridge; Harvard University Press, Belknap Press, 1966), p. 6.

12. Ibid., ch. 4, esp. pp. 74-75.

13. An excellent example is the uncertainty that prevails today about what in particular is supposed to replace the relation of university and student that used to be described as "*in loco parentis*." Granted that has gone by, is the relation of teacher and administrator to student that of chance strangers, seller and buyer, landlord and tenant, producer and consumer? Or is it to be spelled out in contract, taking whatever shape is agreed on? Or is the agreement to be between the univer-

sity and other urban bodies with respect to the students in residence? (For example, whether city police are or are not to come on the campus?) Or is the relation to be spelled out in some conception of a self-governing community with faculty and student and administrative participation? If the older ideas of authority and loyalty or obedience have given way to democratic ideas of participation and responsibility, it is perhaps responsibility that needs the most contemporary clarification.

Part IV
Some Central Problems of Curriculum

Introduction

There is no telling when a problem will enter the roster of significant educational issues, or will drop out. Curricular issues are fairly constant. Some problems are thrust in by crises of the time or by their ramifications in the practical conditions of life. Whether we should have movable desks becomes a serious theoretical issue when it is seen to implicate the quality of interpersonal relations. ROTC in the school gets caught in basic attitudes toward war and violence, patriotism, and international relations. Prayer in the schools is as much an issue of politics as of religion. That the significance of questions changes with alteration in the conditions of life, with the growth of knowledge and insight, is a common enough experience. A critic doubtless thought that he was making a good jest when he described Henry James's characters as undergoing torments of decision about whether or not to offer a cigarette. But look what happened to that very gesture: it used to be a familiar and trivial act of goodwill (and when prices rose, an act of generosity). To offer a woman one then became a sign of support for sexual equality. Today, to offer a cigarette to man or woman has become a hesitant act of enticing a fellow human into carcinogenic vice!

In the earlier parts we have had many illustrations of problems moving into prominence on the educational stage. Grading became an issue when certifying people became an important enterprise in economic life and when the merit of the concept of merit itself became controversial. Equality in education called for analysis when the succession of liberation movements was cast as removing basic discriminations. Mainstreaming entered the roster of educational issues when the needs of the handicapped took their turn in these movements. The compulsion in compulsory schooling was brought into question when a resurgent libertarianism reacted against the broadening of social controls. Voluble turmoil, however, is not itself enough to constitute a problem that calls on philosophy; Swift caricatured the big-endians and the little-endians who waged war on which end of an egg should be opened. But very often, when there is educational smoke, there is likely to be educational fire.

The listing of perennial and novel problems to which the perspective of this book might fruitfully be applied is legion. For example, we are fast reaching the point where questions of the scope, location, duration, and quality of education have become general and critical issues. "Who should be educated?" gets its importance not simply from the ideal of democratic education but from the pressure of many specific contemporary needs of a technological society in which a variety of changing skills imposes fresh demands. "Where should education take place?" is a natural query as a school system adds to its levels (nursery and day care from the hitherto preschool population and continuing education from the hitherto postschool population). It is asked whether education should not be an integral part of many different institutions (workplace, labor unions, cultural institutions, special associations) and modeled in many distinct ways; even major tasks that have hitherto been loaded on schools and colleges might be transferred to general community institutions. (An interesting contrast: ancient Athens had gymnasiums for its citizen population, and educational functions grew up there; we have gymnasiums for our schools and colleges, but not systematically for our general citizen population.) "How long should education last?" is an intelligible question when we compare the older idea that a few years' schooling was enough to last for life with today's emerging ideal of lifelong learning. (Now the distinction between education and schooling becomes critical!) "What can we do about the quality of schooling?" is perhaps the most complex of questions, for in it are enmeshed legitimate demands for excellence and traditional elitist mistrust of the capabilities of the masses; a sharp intellectual scalpel is required to separate the strands. (This question often takes a very practical form in the controversies over grouping: separation of "gifted students," the special schools versus the comprehensive school, and so on.) And beyond all such basic issues lie questions of organization and structure: for example, governance in and of educational institutions takes us into social issues of direction and control; they are not just technical issues like whether a municipality should have a city manager or an elected mayor but how far a democratic social philosophy is to be carried.

The fact that unusual problems may be brought to philosophical attention rather than only familiar issues of the philosophical tradition raises interesting methodological possibilities. Traditional modes of philosophical analysis, from Socrates to Ryle, have all been retrospective: they were analyzing concepts already built up, or at most they were engaging in surreptitious reconstruction. A philosopher facing a changing field may find that the materials call for the construction of fresh concepts as a result of the analysis of the problems and the breakdown of older concepts. This calls for prospective engagement in a kind of constructive analysis. Similarly we have to be on the lookout for problems of growing educational importance, or spot a broad problem in what appears to be just a local issue, and not wait until problems reach crisis proportions. In such times of change, philosophy in its relations to education is called on for active, even original, cooperation.

Part IV looks toward what is a desirable perspective in issues of curriculum. (Curriculum is here to be understood in the somewhat broader sense in which it covers not merely subjects taught but planned programs embodying educational intentions.[1]) Building or reconstructing a curriculum gets its importance not simply because it is a recurrent matter of educational decision, nor because there are disputes about it, but because cleavages of the humanistic and the scientific, the technical-vocational and the liberal, raise important issues of the nature of knowledge and attitudes to action. Similarly, in considering what the schools can do about moral and social education, we find a war being waged in terms of slogans of repression and permissiveness emanating from opposing camps on the social scene. We are thus led into the serious and recurrent problems of discipline that involve our understanding of the creative and the expressive in human life. Chapter 13 has proposals on how to look at the difference and relation between science and the humanities. Chapter 14 tries to bring some order into the conflicts about moral and social education. Chapter 15 scans the familiar range of sport and physical education, arts and crafts, and basic skills to show the depths underlying their complexity. Chapter 16 focuses on current issues in the confrontation of liberal and technical-vocational education; the chief effort here is to find a core in the idea of "liberal arts and sciences" that will avoid confusing it with the notion of the humanities as against the sciences, and so enable us to confront the issue of its total place in education.

Note

1. For different senses of "curriculum" varying in breadth, see Clive Beck, *Educational Philosophy and Theory: An Introduction* (Boston: Little, Brown, 1974), ch. 7.

13. Scientific Knowledge and the Humanities

The present curriculum is the residue of successive historical layers and struggles. Even parts that are standard today had trouble getting admitted. The entry of science itself, as we now know it, was not a simple matter, for an adversary relation developed between it and the older literary and classical culture. In England, the first timid suggestions to introduce physical science into ordinary education, Thomas Huxley tells us in his lecture "Science and Culture" (1880), were opposed by practical people on one side and classical scholars in the name of culture on the other.[1] The practical people eventually learned better as scientific technology became indispensable to industry in the twentieth century and ordinary life began to be lived in an ambience of technological products. The classical scholars had an ideal of culture that they pitted against science. Huxley makes reference to Matthew Arnold's conception of Europe as an intellectual and spiritual unity with Roman, Hellenic, and Hebraic sources, and he takes the fundamental theses to be that education should be directed to a criticism of life in the light of the best ideal and that literature provides the material for such criticism. Huxley accepts the first but questions the second; defending science against charges of narrow practicality, he portrays it as an equal or even superior source of human understanding. Interestingly, he points out, the Renaissance had to fight a battle similar to that faced by science's defenders to get Greek into higher education.

Huxley, of course, was involved in the wider philosophical battles in which his educational stand was enmeshed. Particularly after the impact of Darwinian evolution, science was associated in the mind of the older culture with materialism and a secular outlook in a challenge to what was regarded as the spiritual. In the century that followed, all sorts of analyses went on to sharpen the distinction between the scientific or the study of nature and the cultural and humanistic as insight into man. For example, science was precise, empirical, and devoted to measurement; the older culture dealt with the intuitive and the imaginative. Science was mathematical and aimed at universal laws; literature and the humanities were concerned with the individual, the unique. And so contrasts were intensified between the objective and the subjective, between the public and the private, between fact and value, between the outer material and the inner spiritual. Older influences of social status did not drop out even with social change. The older culture, having been aristocratic and elitist, was traditional and well established; it had no need to justify itself, it was almost self-justifying. Sensed as intrinsically valuable, it could almost boast of uselessness. Science, on the other hand, it became widely felt, was justified by its practical fruits in handling the world about us. By the time that C.P. Snow made popular the contrast of the "two cultures" in the midtwentieth century,[2] there was already a long history of not merely separation, conflict, and tension within the educational world, as well as in problems of curricular construction and decision, but also a great deal of conceptual adjustment.

In the United States, conflict had taken different shape. Huxley had doubtless underestimated the role that science had already been playing in Scottish education and its input into the middle Atlantic and southern states in Jefferson's America. And Snow's dichotomy was certainly more severe in twentieth-century England than in the United States of the twentieth century. But the United States had its own problems of the relation of religion and science, its perennial controversies of creationism and evolution, its own resistance to the development of secular colleges and universities. Nevertheless, where practice was concerned it readily sought the aid of science, early for agriculture and mining and then for technology as a whole. Schools of engineering went on a separate course from schools of liberal arts. Other changes were taking place under the rubric of science itself, for example, part of the older culture dealing with human beings had grown into the social and psychological sciences, modeled on the physical and biological sciences. In the lower schools the social studies had been tied to action and attitude and civic responsibilities, but in the colleges and universities they professed neutrality as sciences and became theory, not application. What was left of the older cultural studies—literature, history, language, the theory of the arts, philosophy, religion, and the value aspects of the social studies—came, in the United States at least, to be embraced under the term "humanities." This has become an official designation not only in curricular usage but for governmental grant purposes, as in the National Endowment for the Humanities. It is a convenient designation, if too tight a unity is not forced on the varied group that falls under the term. And so one basic issue within the curriculum is often seen to be the relation between the sciences and the humanities, involving a clarification of the underlying philosophical contrasts that have been involved in the development of the two.

Similar issues arise in other parts of the present curriculum, and they too rest on underlying philosophical contrasts and a long history of cultural patterning. Perhaps they can be briefly glimpsed in the common images that center on the specialists. The contrast of scientist and humanist presents the scientist as cold thinker or pure intellect and science as the realm of facts, the humanist as having a monopoly of value and the imagination. The artist is associated with the humanist in such sketches and art is seen as the realm of feeling and sensitive response. But there is also the third image of practical action, of responsibility, decision, typified in the business executive or the active politician. The scientist is neutral: when the scientist verges on social action it is "as a citizen"; when the poet has a social message the poet fears ceasing to be a poet and becoming a propagandist. The student preparing to be an engineer may be given a separate allotment of culture in a humanities course, usually having to do with some of the "great books" and some demonstration lectures on music, painting, and sculpture. This will be carefully set apart from the scientific work, and justified by the argument that life has a value beyond the work of science. Thus in the very attempt to give a rounded education the partition between science and the humanities is perpetuated, with culture regarded as an additional, separate consumption value. The practical is, of course, emphasized in the character of the engineer's work; that having to do with science concentrates on working out problems of application. Practice in that case means production or construction. Only more recently are moral and social aspects of engineering being raised as problems of practice within the curriculum, just as business and medicine and law are all becoming concerned with their ethical responsibilities.

In facing the basic relation of the scientific and the humanistic in this chapter, and the moral and social (the practical) in the next chapter, we are of course working out the thesis of the continuity of human experience discussed in part III. We are asking about the stark division in current curricular attitudes—the scientific, the humanistic, the practical—and whether we are to look for natural differences of structure so that each may be studied in its distinctive way, or whether we are to understand them as resting on relative contextual divisions within a comprehensive and integrated view of learning as a whole.

In such an inquiry it will be helpful in examining one division to pay attention to the presence of features that characterize the other divisions. This means, so far as possible and relevant, to stress the imaginative and practical and social aspects of science, the cognitive and practical aspects of the humanities and arts, and the cognitive and imaginative aspects of practice. Such an exercise can serve as a corrective, like bending the curved stick in the opposite direction to straighten it out. But it can do more: it can help us see the congealed categories at the root of many of these problems—in part suggested in chapter 11 above—such as the way in which the sharp separation of science and the humanities has invoked the separation of fact and value; or how the concept of practical action has been affected by the oversharp separation of theory and practice; or (later) how views of sport are affected by the hardened separation of body and spirit; or how the isolation of art is supported by a psychology of feeling that turns it into an epistemological category. The outcome should be not only a more integrated view of the curriculum as a whole but a clearer view of the continuities of experience.

Scientific Knowledge

The objectives in giving science so large a place in the curriculum are many: to prepare scientists, to give students some understanding of what the world is like in the light of scientific results, to convey (particularly through laboratory work) some sense of the standards and methods of scientific inquiry and the requirements of evidence, to encourage scientific literacy and so a greater ability to understand and deal effectively with the technological products that play so large a part in our present mode of life as well as to make more informed decisions. Selective focus on these objectives and the different weights given to them at various levels of schooling raises issues of their comparative value, i.e. precisely why it is important to teach science and what students really should get out of it. Especially for the mass of students who are not to become scientists, there are experiments on how science is to be taught—for example, on the college level, by selecting one particular science and working within it, by a history-of-science approach that traces the development of problems, by a sociological approach that looks to technological changes and their causes.

Our first concern is with the basic values appealed to in justifying the teaching of science. We have to go further and look into the values of knowledge as such, for science is a way of acquiring systematic knowledge. It is well to recall that etymologically "science" is simply knowledge; science became separated only with the rise of the exact sciences. Our second concern will be to show the continuities of science with other disciplines. Both of these concerns take us to the variety of attitudes found to knowledge as such, and to some extent to underlying problems about the relation of mind to knowledge and the nature and method of scientific knowledge itself.

There is even a prehistory to this inquiry. We are so accustomed to the pursuit of knowledge as a goal that we forget that the right to know had first to become acceptable. After all, Adam and Eve were expelled from Eden for eating of the fruit that would give them a knowledge of good and evil. Prometheus was punished for bringing fire and the crafts to mankind. In very practical situations it was debated whether people should flee before a plague or seek medical cures if plagues and disease were punishments inflicted by God.[3] To cure became respectable only when the activity and skills of doctors were themselves seen as somehow expressive of divine intent. The heritage of the old struggle is still to be seen in contemporary controversies over the possible accomplishments and limits of technology, especially where in recombinant genetics it raises the issue of generating fresh forms of life and altering existent forms. A different hesitation arises, of course, from fears of what technological development and its industrial uses may do to our environment and how they may affect the comfort and even possibility of continued life on earth.

The usual way of justifying the pursuit of scientific knowledge is to appeal to its intrinsic value or to call attention to its obvious instrumental values. The philosophical history of justifying knowledge shows that theories of metaphysics and method and the nature of man are involved, and it raises the doubt whether so simple an antithesis, though it may push aside hesitation in some practical contexts, is refined enough to cope with curricular problems. Classical analyses of knowledge (Plato and Aristotle and the classical tradition) relied on its intrinsic value as the contemplation of the order of nature, which was an ultimate human objective because the human being is a rational being and is fulfilled in such contemplation. The power of this outlook is suggested in Plutarch's picture of Archimedes: this greatest engineer of ancient times looked down on the very machines that he invented as merely utilitarian and remained overwhelmingly absorbed (to the neglect of his person and his life) in the splendor of his proofs.[4] The justification of science as power came with the rise of modern science and the growing control over nature it made possible. Bacon, to whom this vision is usually attributed, was more balanced than he is often pictured; he wanted experiments that would yield light as well as fruit.

Does the value of scientific knowledge then lie in the contemplation of the order of nature, in the anticipation of the fruits of industry, in the motivation of power and the satisfaction of domination and control, or in some sense in all of these? No doubt particular ages have selected different emphases, and different philosophical schools have looked for theoretical reasons to give priority to each of these strands. For example, a Platonist views mathematics almost in the fashion of astronomical or geographical exploration, as if new domains were being discovered like new constellations or new continents. On the other hand, a twentieth-century positivist regards the discoveries as imaginative constructions to be tested by their power in application, the more desirable being the ones that lead to greater knowledge and increased control over nature. A broad pragmatic approach attempts a synthesis of the various phases, but all within a naturalistic view of the human being as part of the evolutionary process. It may also make clear how a theory of knowledge ties in with an underlying theory of mind and with the shape of people's social and practical life. For example, Dewey presents a natural-social history of mind in relation to knowledge.[5] In classical and medieval times, he says, the individual was not regarded as the knower but as the focus in which a divine Reason operated. After the sixteenth-century rise of economic and political individualism, knowledge came to be seen as won through personal and private experience, and mind as wholly individual. The philosophical translation of the struggle for greater freedom of thought in action was philosophical subjectivism; mind, isolated from the world in this way, could yield only association of ideas or impressions. Such exaggeration, says Dewey, did not express adequately what people wanted: they sought greater freedom in nature and society, not to be free of nature and one another. A view of mind and knowledge consonant with this reality therefore suggests the role of the individual or self in knowledge as the redirection or reconstruction of accepted beliefs. The individual locus of knowledge is thus maintained in its function, but in a social and natural matrix.

This view fits in with Dewey's analysis of consciousness and the occasions of its occurrence, the upsetting of an equilibrium that generates a problem situation. Its implication for the question of the value of knowledge is that knowledge is no longer just contemplative, nor is it just practical. The function of knowledge is, as Dewey says, broadly, to make one experience freely available in other experiences.[6] He contrasts it with habit, which involves a modification of the individual through an experience, thus making it easier for the individual to engage in like action. The values of knowledge can then be of all types that the values of experience can be: intrinsic, instrumental, partial component of the satisfying whole, and so on. The desirable attitude to different parts of knowledge or to thinking and knowing in general would then be a specific normative issue: for example, whether it is better educationally to pursue knowledge to solve the problems it poses, to secure prestige or power, or to contemplate the beauty of the formulae. Instrumentalism, so often criticized as concerned with practical utility, is not incompatible with a recognition that the enterprise of discovering knowledge becomes a specialized undertaking.[7] Dewey can even say: "It is true of arithmetic as it is of poetry that in some place and at some time it ought to be a good to be appreciated on its own account—just as an enjoyable experience, in short."[8] And after noting the variety of uses of science—military, technological, commercial, philanthropic—he concludes: "All that we can be sure of educationally is that science should be taught so as to be an end in itself in the lives of students—something worthwhile on account of its own unique intrinsic contribution to the experience of life."⁹ He balances this with a comparable analysis of poetry, which, while it seems nowadays to have value chiefly in the context of leisure, has historically been allied with religion and morals and nationalism; he concludes that education should convey the sense of poetry as a resource in life. In both cases, education appears to have the task of bringing out that aspect that is likely to be neglected.

The sense of intrinsic value, or being simply a good, not a good for something beyond, is very straightforward if taken as signifying simply that the activity is attractive, that it is enjoyed. It does not tell us what precisely within the activity is attractive, unless knowing is treated as a unitary activity. If it is complex, the question is reopened within the analysis of knowing, and we have again to ask whether what attracts directly is the contemplation of the object of knowing, the sense of power or success or liberated energy in the act. Perhaps the difficulty lies in the theoretical content of the notion of intrinsic value itself. For the treatment of knowledge, it may not matter which of the aspects indicated is the precise locus of intrinsic value; any one or the combination of all may be, so long as they are within the act. Knowledge has such overwhelming value in sum that the fact that it can be attractive or enjoyable is enough.

Nevertheless, a strong anti-intellectualist attitude is often directed against science just when we would expect it to be welcomed as the most advanced achievement of the knowledge enterprise. Moderns can take in their stride the occasional medieval expressions of the view that a bit of piety or the love of God outweighs all knowledge and all thought, or even the suggestion among philosophers of an overarching insight or intuition better than knowledge. Yet the array of twentieth-century critiques is formidable. Surprisingly, G. E. Moore, in spite of his thorough intellectualism, assigns knowledge a low intrinsic value, though it is a necessary ingredient in wholes that are good in high degree; for the latter, he compares the low value of pleasure by itself with the high value of pleasure combined with a consciousness of its existence.[10] Bergson attacks intellectual knowledge as a secondary way of approaching reality; the intellect is an instrument developed in evolution for practical survival, and he calls for an intuitive method to give direct access to reality.[11] Martin Buber regards science or knowledge in general as turning away from the immediacy of direct dialogue in the I-Thou relation; knowledge stands outside its object and treats the object as an It.[12] We have noted the attack on science and knowing itself in the irrationalist strands of the counterculture (chapter 9); for example, as Roszak formulates the attack, science involves "distancing" from its object.[13] Now distancing is a very difficult notion. It is easy to illustrate it by the surgeon's treating the patient as an object, and to suggest that without aloofness there could be no science and technology. But distancing as it is presented in the attack is so broad as to be a mark of all consciousness; it must then be involved in appreciation of beauty as well. Easy contrasts between knowing about love and being in love are not helpful because being in love has an element of knowing in it. The leap to immediacy, advanced in the irrationalist attack as the alternative to science and knowledge, seems to be self-defeating. Even claims for immersion of the self secured by drugs often talk of expanded consciousness, and so in principle the drugs would do no more than microscopes and telescopes have done, though in a different area.

A ready alternative to sheer abstraction and sheer immersion may be described as shuttling. In the scientific process it is written large in the use of theory to guide experiment and the use of experiment to refine theory. But this involves a large temporal span. Immediacy may be regarded as simply the ideal of reducing the span. The notion of self-conscious action seems to fit such a model: drivers who know exactly what they are doing while doing it may be thought to be acting with automatic immediacy, but in principle the process is no different from airplane pilots with panels of instrument readings. So too in reflection on experience the reflection is itself an experience, and the experience reflected on embodies the knowledge structure of past experience. The notion of shuttling can be taken quite literally, for even in vision and thinking there is a time interval, however brief: the hand turns the steering wheel and the visual, tactile, and kinesthetic sensations provide the guides (in cooperation with the brain as storing past lessons) for the next movement of the hand. Where the shuttling occupies a long stretch, where it is almost a momentary episode, is an empirical question for the type of field and problem. It is not understandable, however, as sheer immediacy or sheer transcendence of the intellect, nor in turn as a dualism of isolated processes. Something like this is the answer in the long run to the current irrationalism based on the idea of distancing.

The other attacks may be disarmed in different ways, and their salutary warnings noted. Of course there are problems of attitude within scientific work and its application in technologies. An attitude of aloofness has its proper conditions and functions, it has its many types, and some types become callousness when misplaced. Buber's sensitive treatment of interpersonal relations is a sound reminder that knowledge is not the only central value, but he neglects the way in which interpersonal relations can become richer with mutual understanding, which is knowledge brought back into the relation. Bergson's appeal to intuition rests on the view that such insight can have no place in science. But it is quite possible that the phenomena to which the installation of insight as a metaphysical approach appeals may themselves fall within the range of scientific modes. When the imaginative character of scientific construction is recognized, this becomes a plausible answer. Moore's judgment alone we may postpone at this point. It raises the more serious question whether the concept of intrinsic value can really do the job for which it is being used in discussions of the value of different disciplines. We shall consider it with respect to the humanities, for there the claim to intrinsic value is more critical, particularly because the humanities usually reject instrumental justification.

We turn now to the second concern, how sharply science may be set off from other disciplines. The isolation of science has rested historically on a portrait of its method as a neutral presentation of the facts of the world. But even Bacon, who is often held responsible for a narrow inductive view of science, took the task of advancing science as more than sheer empiricism. His analogy of the ant, the spider, and the bee shows this: the ant gathers the data, the spider spins webs out of its own substance, but the bee both gathers and spins organizing frameworks. The bee is the hero of science.

The question of the continuity of science with other disciplines lies at the heart of twentieth-century movements in the philosophy of science. The early half of the twentieth century witnessed the rise and dominance of logical positivism. Reacting to what it saw as metaphysical obscurantism and irrationalism in the European milieu, the Vienna Circle presented a "rational reconstruction" in which science had a distinctive method: knowledge was preeminently the sort of thing the natural sciences carried out and the philosophy of science was the epistemological investigation of the method of science. Metaphysics rested on logical error; religion and ethics were fundamentally emotional expressions. Social science was possible insofar as it emulated the natural science model, and respected the sharp distinction of fact and value. The sociological history of science itself played no significant part in questions of the validity of science.

The revolt against the positivist philosophy of science is often dated with Thomas Kuhn's *The Structure of Scientific Revolutions* (1964).[14] By attending to great scientific turning points in which new models of the universe and new conceptions of the human being emerged, it became necessary to deal with fuller cultural and intellectual changes as well as their sociological background. In effect, there emerged a view of science in which its method involves value components as well as sensory and logical components, in which purposive activity of given time and place helps shape organizational structures of knowledge, and in which imagination plays a central part in the advance of knowledge and its scientific forms. In this respect the scientific enterprise, far from being the embodiment of the cold fact-gatherer, becomes assimilated to the imagination of the artist. While this general revolt against positivist philosophy of science has not yet settled into a fresh coherent model, it has broken down all sharp borderlines and compelled forbidden questions to be addressed afresh. There have been not only attacks on post-Kantian epistemology as a whole but even attempts to assimilate the character of discourse in science and in literature.[15]

Perhaps the general point about the continuity of disciplines can be made by looking back, before the controversies of the twentieth century gained force, to Santayana's approach in 1905. In *The Life of Reason* he thinks of science as a system of symbols.[16] His comparison of myth, science, and religion (suggested in considering whether religion was an independent form of knowledge, in chapter 11), treats all three as concerned with symbols but in a functionally different way. Myth is a kind of poetry. When it is used to intervene and order life, making distinctions of right and wrong, it is a religion. When it supervenes on human life, giving expression to our fantasy, it is poetry. But when it is reduced to its minimum—stripped, he says, to its fighting weight and valued for what it points to—it is science. Science is thus an imaginative enterprise, operative in liberating people within their world by extending the scope with which their experience may guide them. It grows as a social enterprise and so develops common concerns. It is a kind of common art directed to common practice.

A number of educational consequences flow from these considerations about the character of science in the contemporary world. Central among them is the recommendation that science no longer be taught as a provincial inquiry into one corner of human life but as integral to all human operations. We are not adjusted to this yet, except perhaps on the more obvious practical side. We recognize science as involved with our food, shelter, hygiene, and so on, but do not realize that growingly it has a place in our understanding of our human relations, our handling of our social and political life, and, more than we think, it takes a place in our thoughts and in our morality. It would then have to be taught as continuous with the rest of our knowledge, though with a due appreciation of its special refinement, technical precision, and the expertise of its method with systematic theory on the one hand and critical experiment on the other. The teaching of science would have to keep an eye on the broader range of knowledge than the sciences of physics and astronomy to convey the full nature of the creative quest for knowledge—particularly, for example, sciences that deal with temporal spans such as biological evolution or human historical development. In dealing with relations of science and technology it would have to overcome the oversharp separation of the pure and applied, not only in contemporary science but even in earlier science, and to recognize the role that technological problems (mining, navigation) played in setting questions and prompting scientific investigations as well as the manufacturing of instruments (microscopes, telescopes, measures) for scientific investigations. In dealing with the relation of science and economic life, recognition would be necessary not only of the past role of economic influences in encouraging scientific development but of the need for general rather than narrow vocational scientific education as a background: in a world of changing technologies, any specialized vocational training may be swept away by a technological shift whereas general scientific education gives learning a wider scope.

There are of course serious challenges involved in such changed attitudes to the teaching of science, but they would have to be faced in any case because of the position of science in the modern world. Students are both attracted by it and repelled by the lack of humanism often associated with it. Students in the sciences are often cut off as a special elite. If our moral agenda calls for a broader democratization, the demand here would be for an integrated understanding and a mutual responsibility. The historical parallel of science with literacy is suggestive. Reading and writing were once as mysterious and rare as mathematics still is. Educational imagination, whether utilizing logical devices, teaching machines, games, or simply improved communication, should be equal to developing techniques of wider intelligibility for the mastery of mathematics and so of scientific knowledge from within, not merely from an improved scientific journalism.

The educational challenge along such lines is to convey not simply scientific results but also the sense of the scientific enterprise. If teaching, even on the lower levels is kept abreast of changing frontiers to some degree, the idea of growing knowledge and changing ideas will be conveyed. Hence there may be some success in avoiding the greatest danger: installing science as a new orthodoxy in the public mind instead of cultivating a proper sense of fallibilism and humility about human ignorance. (At the present time, nature itself seems to have this teaching job by turning up rapidly unanticipated distressing consequences for almost every happy scientific remedy.)

With respect to the students who are to be the scientists, the challenge would be to cultivate a firm sense of social responsibility. This, though essential, leaves open the type of attitude involved. For example, responsibility may be expressed in authoritarian manipulation of people as well as in democratic cooperation. Hence the scientific study of human beings has to be brought well within the teaching of the social studies in order to clarify such issues in a critical manner.

In brief, the isolation of science in the curriculum from humanistic studies has to be overcome within the teaching of science itself and (as we shall see) within the teaching of these other "subjects"; it is not to be disposed of by reading a poem on science in the assembly, even if it be commissioned from a poet of the stature of an Archibald MacLeish or a Robert Frost.

The Humanities

The humanities in the curriculum are most easily discussed with an eye on the college level, where the distinction of "realms" is more fully articulated. In the liberal arts college the division is usually into science, social science, and humanities. Science includes physics, chemistry, biology, geology, and usually mathematics. Social science lists economics, political science, sociology, anthropology, psychology. Humanities embraces literature, languages, philosophy, religion, the arts, history. Sometimes history is found among the social sciences. Many of the subjects are discomforted by their classification. Psychology on its physiological side has affiliations with biology; philosophy through logic has a kinship with mathematics, and it is also more at home in the social sciences if they will not disqualify values. Linguistics is as much at home among the social sciences as among the humanities. Jurisprudence is found among the humanities as well as in political science.

The case of mathematics and that of the arts require special attention. Applied mathematics certainly belongs with the sciences, but pure mathematics has always been touchy about being ascribed direct empirical relevance. As part of the old culture, it could easily claim a place among the humanities. With respect to the arts, distinctions have to be made in the kind of activity. Criticism, appreciation, history—of art and literature— are humanistic studies. But creation—painting, musical composition or performance, writing poetry or a novel—is rather the ground-floor or first-order material on which the humanities are reflecting. The situation is sometimes unclear when practice of some art is regarded as the laboratory work of a course on appreciation. This rather reverses the relation: Shakespeare and Rembrandt are not laboratory specimens of principles developed in the study of art and literature but, rather, the primary materials on which those studies feed. For the most part the arts in their creation go with the crafts rather than the humanities. Some works of literature, however, seem to step directly into the humanities because of the reflections found within them. Thus Shakespeare—in *Othello*, for example— can be conceived as a reflective commentator on the passions of humans and the vicissitudes of life; and Tolstoy in *War and Peace* presents a philosophy of history within its story. Most of art and literature, however, requires humanistic interpretation to elicit such aspects. Indeed, inquiry into aesthetic ideas began with Socrates's reflection that the artists seemed to be acting under inspiration and could never explain what they had created. In our present discussion, the arts will be separated from the humanities and considered with the crafts.

Many asymmetries, even anomalies, can be found in the more detailed location of subdisciplines. For example, the history of drama may be found in an English department, but dramatic performance in a theatre department, although history of art and art appreciation as well as art theory be located in an art department. The appreciation of literature is usually merged in the history of literature, or goes with creative writing. Statistics may not be with mathematics but be scattered among economics, psychology, and so on. In general, the relation within any discipline of its theory, history, performance, and appreciation allows of considerable structural variety. The grounds for classification deserve careful study to see whether they vary with such intrinsic factors as the amount of theory needed for performance, or with contingent factors such as the size and power of departments and the chance traditional attitudes of a discipline. We shall here concern ourselves only with the relations of the broader classifications.

The difficulties in classification and the separation of the humanities from the social sciences suggest that in the attempt to understand human beings and their ways and their works a division is being made on methodological grounds. Where the study can be carried on in the manner of the sciences, it might be said, it is social science; the rest of the field belongs to the humanities, which originally occupied the whole field. Indeed on the European continental scene the study of human beings has tended to be more unified in the older tradition of classical cultural learning. The major contrast is between the study of nature (science) and the study of spirit (culture). If the concept of humanistic learning is employed for the latter, it would include the social fields but not conceived particularly as sciences. In the United States, both social scientists and humanists would probably object strongly to their being bundled in this way. Driven to find an inner unity, the humanists have centered on the idea of values as their common concern, while the sciences are relegated to fact.

We have suggested how the antagonism of the "two cultures" may be overcome from the side of science by recognizing the continuity of science with knowledge in general and by bringing out the place of values and purposes, imagination and construction, in the processes of science itself. The same lesson is needed for value, so that the characterization of the humanities as primarily concerned with values and so isolated from fact will be similarly relaxed. The dichotomy of fact and value has been a formidable one in the history of thought. The metaphysical view has been that fact and value are different categories of reality. This was bolstered with the psychological view that different faculties are involved—intellect and cognition for facts, imagination and feeling for values. Methodological approaches added contrasts, some of which we have noted: science concerned with universals, the humanities (like the arts on which they reflect) with individuals; the one with the outer, the other with the inner; the one with the objective, the other with the subjective; the one with the measurable, the other with the intuitive.

Most of these contrasts have by now worn thin. We see them to represent hardening of aspects or distinctions in earlier stages of the growth of different human activities or inquiries. Take, for example, the contrast of objectively measurable nature versus the nonmeasurable activity of spirit. This seemed in the early twentieth century to be an unbridgeable difference. But the progress of thought in mathematics and the philosophy of science showed first that measurement was simply a way of *ordering* things and comparing the orderings, and second that there were all sorts of complex orderings of different strengths. Statistical study and ingenuity in devising operations added to the story. The differences between simple and complex orderings remain as great as ever, but the gulf has disappeared and the continuity is no longer absurd. So too the continuities in value throughout all human experience have become clearer. Value is the selective aspect in all experience, not a special domain or a special activity. In fact experience itself is constantly selective in light of purposes and needs that guide attention and habits that have fashioned our view of the world and its characters. Hence there is a thorough permeation of all value and knowledge. We can properly contrast evaluation as an enterprise from description as an enterprise, but in each of them there will be fused knowledge and value. The relative contrasts we make of fact and value arise in situations of evaluation in which standards, predesignated as values, are being applied to a situation for choice or comparison or criticism.

Given such a perspective, there is no philosophical reason to make an absolute dichotomy between the social sciences and the humanities. They both have the same general aim—to give us an understanding of human beings, their nature and aspiration, their world and predicament, their sensibilities and relations, their hopes and dreams. The understanding we get through acquaintance with literature, religion, history, philosophy, language, and jurisprudence can be seen as continuous with that through psychology, sociology, and anthropology. Apart from technicality of method in the latter, there are of course differences in division of labor. *King Lear* is not a sociological monograph on the family problems of senior citizens, but reflections on it provide insights that gerontological studies do well to embrace. Not only are the initial problems of understanding human beings the same but in the end the desire to better their lot by making their world a more congenial place to live in is identical. Perhaps the social sciences think to end up more with control, while the humanists in their utopias have projected future possibilities more boldly.

Once the continuities of the humanities are established with the whole effort to understand human beings, then the fact that a great part of the humanities are engaged in evaluative processes and critical enterprises and in refining ideals of perfection no longer is the source of a profound break. Even the physical sciences have that aspect in their theoretical endeavors; Newton has devised a scheme for representing the motion of physical bodies, and Shakespeare in his historical tragedies has found a way of representing people's passions and their historical and political dilemmas, though the modes are different. And if the point is holding to values and ideals, not representing them, then seen in the evaluative enterprise Newton too has an ideal of science in relation to reality and how to proceed, and Newton too is concerned with the lessons of his science for people's crafts and businesses of life. The tendency of humanists to reject utility in arguments about justifying their pursuits and to insist on the intrinsic value of their activities seems to embody an unnecessary restraint or else a narrow conception of utility. The humanities, like the classics, are of broad human value. They awaken the mind, heighten consciousness, develop analytical and structural powers, sharpen the ability to express and communicate, and in a thousand ways broaden and delight the mind. They build an ideal community between past and present and between far-flung areas of the present. They enhance creative power in a way applicable to any field and so make people more able to grapple with change.

When philosophers of education sometimes describe education as the initiation into intrinsically worthwhile activities, they doubtless have the humanities in mind. Yet, as Peters points out in "Ambiguities in Liberal Education and the Problem of Its Content," the assertion that our appreciation of a great tragedy is of intrinsic value somehow does not capture the scope of the insight it gives us into vital problems of life and death, conflict and resignation.[17] What is happening to us is of importance; the growth and development of the self is part of the picture. Narrow utility is not sufficient to describe what is happening, but neither is the apprehension of something of intrinsic value sufficient to do so. The implication seems to be that the concept of intrinsic value is itself too gross or too narrow to handle the question. This is an important matter if we hope to break through the demand in large questions to pin an answer on the judgment of intrinsic value.

We can best deal with this issue by looking back to G. E. Moore's criticism of knowledge as of little intrinsic value, postponed from the discussion of the value of knowledge. How can we judge that something has intrinsic value? Moore's method was to isolate the object being judged as if it were a world by itself. In this way he expected to avoid confusion with instrumental relations as well as take care of the phenomenon that two objects together might have a value that bore no direct relation to the separate values of their parts. Now, very few things can submit to such a test, simply because very few things can be isolated as if they were a world by themselves. Only fairly unitary experiences admit of it, like being pleased. Perhaps that is why the concept is most useful in the arts, where appreciation can be directed to an object that has been framed or isolated. Surprise has sometimes been expressed at the fact that Moore found very few things of intrinsic value. Perhaps the conclusion should be that our idea of intrinsic value if interpreted in this way is not a very fruitful idea for most of the evaluations that we have to carry on—certainly in education where the objects to be evaluated are complexes in multiple relations. In our evaluation of knowledge, we saw it could tell us that knowledge is attractive and knowing is enjoyable, but if the activity was not unitary it gave us no clue to what in it was attractive or enjoyable. Perhaps we can get no further in applying the idea to the humanities. Additional theoretical components with which the idea of intrinsic value is laden require much more philosophical analysis than the idea has yet undergone. We may continue, of course, to speak of intrinsic values in science and in art, but it will be in the broad sense of the joy in an activity, no matter how extensive and complicated its object and no matter how enmeshed with utility the contents may be.

The educational consequence for the humanities of the continuities between the "two cultures" would be a greater recognition of the place of the cognitive in the appreciation of literature and the arts. To some extent this is happening. With the growing interest in the history of science we come to realize how different scientific world pictures have affected the arts and humanistic disciplines, just as we learn also of the dependence of science on larger cultural patterns. We also noted in considering the relation of different forms of knowledge (chapter 11) that the psychological theory of the feelings and emotions can seriously affect our ideas of the aesthetic. For a long time psychology was behavioristically oriented or concerned with the biological bases of the emotions. Their finer texture and differentiations as well as their situational variations were more likely to be ascertained from literature. A richer cognitive psychology that treats the emotions as registering an awareness of the world can integrate the scientific picture of the human being's sensory equipment and the humanistic analysis of the human being's sensibilities. The recognition of continuities in science and the humanities should open the door to fresh educational possibilities. Some directions in the teaching of the arts will be raised below.

Notes

1. Thomas H. Huxley, *Science and Education* (New York: P.F. Collier & Son, 1900), p. 122.
2. C.P. Snow, *The Two Cultures and the Scientific Revolution* (Cambridge: Cambridge University Press, 1959).
3. Immanuel Jacobovits, *Jewish Medical Ethics: A Comparative and Historical Study of the Jewish Religious Attitude to Medicine and its Practice* (New York: Bloch, 1959), pp. 13f.
4. Plutarch's picture is in his *Lives*, in the life of Marcellus, the Roman consul who conquered Syracuse; Archimedes was killed in the siege.
5. John Dewey, *Democracy and Education* (New York: Macmillan, 1961; original publication, 1916), pp. 291-96.
6. Ibid., p. 339.
7. Ibid., p. 190.
8. Ibid., p. 240.
9. Ibid., pp. 240-41.
10. G. E. Moore, *Principia Ethica* (Cambridge: Cambridge University Press, 1903), ch. 6.
11. E.g., Henri Bergson, *Introduction to Metaphysics*, trans. T. E. Hulme (New York: Liberal Arts Press, 1949).
12. Martin Buber, *I and Thou*, trans. Ronald Gregor Smith (Edinburgh: T. & T. Clark, 1937).
13. Theodore Roszak, *The Making of a Counter Culture: Reflections on the Technocratic Society and Its Youthful Opposition* (Garden City, N.Y.: Doubleday, Anchor Books, 1969), ch. 7.
14. Thomas S. Kuhn, *The Structure of Scientific Revolutions* (Chicago: University of Chicago Press, 1964; 2d. ed., enlarged, 1970).
15. For a sensitive treatment of values in science, see Jacob Bronowski, *Science and Human Values* (New York: Harper & Row, 1972); also his *The Ascent of Man* (Boston: Little, Brown, 1976). For a sweeping attack on epistemology in modern philosophy and for the assimilation of scientific and literary discourse, see Richard Rorty, *Philosophy and the Mirror of Nature* (Princeton: Princeton University Press, 1979).
16. George Santayana's five-volume *Life of Reason* (New York: Charles Scribner's Sons, 1905), includes *Reason in Science, Reason in Religion*, and *Reason in Art*. The depth of Santayana's insight is more remarkable when we realize that when he speaks of science he is still referring to the natural sciences. He regards psychology that is not physiological as simply literary psychology, and he makes no effort to see history as scientific. Since that time, of course, the roster of sciences has tremendously expanded; over and above the psychological and social sciences and historical sciences, we now speak of endeavors in extremely varied fields as sciences, for example, environmental science, regional science, decision sciences. Although in many cases these represent largely aspiration, the facts of usage work toward a view of continuity in disciplines.
17. In *Ethics and Educational Policy*, ed. Kenneth A. Strike and Kieran Egan (London: Routledge & Kegan Paul, 1978).

14. Social and Moral Education

Although social and moral education have not been as coherently organized as science and the humanities, it has always been a tacit objective of the schools to impart a moral outlook and a sense of social responsibility. Parents expect it, the community calls for it, and the main question is how to do it effectively. When there was social consensus on requirements and church and family bore the brunt of the task, the moral and social atmosphere in teaching was largely taken for granted. History classes drew lessons of civic responsibility and interwove patriotic themes, literature exhibited character and moral struggles, and even science had its heroic models of inventiveness, initiative, and industry. Assemblies and ceremonials reenforced the demands of duty and civic leadership, student clubs gave opportunity for training in the processes of democracy, and everywhere vigorous discipline with sanctions laid down firm lines of appropriate and inappropriate behavior.

Today the situation little resembles this idyllic past that doubtless never was.[1] Society at large is in confusion: in part a breakdown of old standards, in some areas a confrontation between emerging new standards and efforts to restore the old, in many (even apart from confrontation) serious doubts about the impact of changed conditions. An almost anarchic disregard of law and morality pervades old and young alike, an increase of crime, vandalism, drug use, collapse of traditional sexual standards, a lax attitude toward bribery and corruption, political cynicism, and so on. Durkheim's *anomie* describes this well—a situation in which there is no law and anything goes, no limitation on the pursuit of personal gain. Confrontation is clearest in the numerous liberation movements that seek a principled extension of the older ideals of equality and democracy and a major alteration in the older success ethic. In the strength and urgency of their demands they appear to be taking morality very seriously rather than ignoring it, but their demands call for many changes in older ways. They are met with a new militancy of a "moral majority" organizing for restoration of traditional moral beliefs. Unlike such struggles, typified by the battles over abortion, there are areas in which changed conditions are so obvious that older and simpler principles admittedly need qualification; for example, how far in a growingly interconnected world virtues of patriotism and the striving for superiority of one's own group should give way to a world perspective with altered virtues and all-human rights and well-being.

Historical changes lie behind these moral and social transformations: the general growth over past few centuries of middle-class commercial and industrial life patterns with their acquisitive, individualistic, and success-oriented values, and on the other side contemporary socialist revolutions of diverse sorts; secularization and the removal of older religious restraints; changes in the family—the impact of urban growth, the rise of the divorce rate, the decrease in familial moral influence on the young in favor of the peer group. Special factors have added their weight in different countries and localities; for example, in the United States the variety of ethnic groups and the intermingling of cultures helped promote a pluralism that in changing times could take a looser form of "moral relativism." Large-scale immigration reenforced this by creating a gap between the moral outlook of generations, and rapid social mobility had a similar effect.

Against this background in which pluralism undermined consensus, change produced conflict, individualism threatened group solidarity, it is not surprising that the schools have been called on to take up the slack in moral and social training to make up for the loss of authority in other institutions—especially as the greater part of the young have been brought within the school. This has led to more careful reflection about what the schools are actually doing in these matters, not merely in direct teaching and explicit activity but also in the secondary learning that comes from how teaching is carried on and the "hidden curriculum" of values conveyed by the way the school is organized and administered, its inner conflicts and inconsistencies, the relation of the values it imparts to those imparted outide the schools. (Cf. chapter 7 for the problems concerning the relation of the bureaucratic and the democratic, the competitive and the cooperative, preparing for the "outside" world and preparing for moral resistance to its pressures and temptations.)

In such an atmosphere of uncertainty and crisis, attention turns to the theory of moral and social education. Attitudes to discipline are directly involved because in many places turbulence and even violence invade the schools themselves. Different programs of moral education are projected and some are tried out. Issues of moral philosophy become implicated: what conception of morality underlies the programs, how far morality is inherently "relative," how far it is constant or changeable, and what is to be done.

A serious discussion of these questions has to bring historical sobriety into the tumultuous controversy. We have to discount at least a part of the despair that equates changing standards with deterioration and decadence, or conflict of standards with absence of standards. And we have to work through theoretical formulations that may hinder us from facing issues more directly. With respect to moral relativism preparatory work was done in chapter 8. It was suggested that the central issue was not really the conflict of two ethical theories, relativism and absolutism. It was, rather, the moral problem of how to approach a situation in which individual judgments (or group judgments) differ and no immediate way is known to resolve the difference though action is required. What appears to be a relativistic theory is really a particular morality of individualism (or in the group case, e.g. nationalism). Our age is experimenting with an extreme form of individualism (or group decision) and the moral issue is the assessment of this experiment. The discussion in chapter 8 considered how a broad historical view could provide leads for such assessment.

This chapter accordingly faces more directly the theoretical ideas that underlie controversy and proposals for moral and social education in the schools. We begin with popular formulations about discipline and the conflict of the permissive and the repressive, move next to leading contemporary approaches and programs, and finally ask what in the light of their critique may be offered for moral education.

Discipline and the Conflict of the Permissive and the Repressive

Discipline is popularly discussed in terms of a conflict between the permissive and the repressive. The schools, a ready scapegoat for the prevalence of social disorder, are blamed for being too permissive, for abandoning strict discipline, for trying to give students what they like rather than what is good for them. Some look back to the birch rod; more would be content with greater use of penalties if only to restore respect for authority and end the violence that disrupts order. Others, with no less love for peace and order, are firmly convinced that these are not to be secured by coercive methods or attitudes that exact a price in their effect on the students. They dream of conditions of schooling that make learning meaningful; they believe that repression is the mark of failure, not the unavoidable nature of things. Advocates of repression counter with the reflection that life and learning are a serious business that involves hard work and self-control, and to appeal to what will merely attract students may only strengthen a willful egoism.

Although the opposition in its sloganized form is doubtless oversimplified, it rests on two underlying serious issues. One is the interpretation of the present historical situation; the other is the almost perennial conflict over the theory of human nature.

In one view the world today is in an advanced stage of deterioration. For example, Robert Nisbet, in *History of the Idea of Progress*, presents the continual erosion of intellectual and spiritual beliefs that supported an ideal of progress;[2] and Alasdair MacIntyre, in *After Virtue*, traces the moral deterioration from Aristotle to the present day, where he is waiting for a new St. Benedict, presumably to guide us to small communal enclaves in which to shelter from the pervading storm.[3] An opposing interpretation is that the present is a time of change in which the older institutions have broken down and lost their constructive character so that new ones have to be devised; it does not discount people's basic aspirations and moral potential.

Opposing theories of human nature were examined in chapter 4 in the more limited context of social philosophies. The disparaging view was seen in Plato's and Burke's contention that the mass of men require constant restraint; discipline cultivates the habit of obedience, but only a few can achieve the true inner discipline that can be counted on to maintain self-control and self-mastery. The more hopeful theory regarded human nature as either plastic or affiliative; in a well-regulated society there need be no perpetual conflict with an inherently aggressive and acquisitive "dragon" of appetite. Let us track the course of these opposing theories separately.

Kant profoundly changed the theory of discipline by insisting that the basis of discipline lies in everyone.[4] No human beings require external direction to tell them what they ought to do, for they find within themselves respect for the moral law. Kant did not diminish the place of restraint, for the moral situation is essentially one in which desire is thwarted by the respect for the moral law. In effect, he democratized repressive discipline; it is self-discipline, and autonomy (cf. chapter 8) involves everyone controlling himself or herself.

Durkheim, whose work on moral education has been very influential, naturalizes Kantian ethics by subjecting it to sociological inquiry.[5] He shifts the object of respect from the moral law to the social group. Discipline is still to be central in moral education; it implies authority and regularity and expresses the command of society that we do our duty. Self-restraint is a necessary condition of self-mastery. He fears the rise of the anarchic spirit in a revolutionary period such as he regards his time. Self-determination or autonomy comes from understanding the connection between oneself and the group, which can ensure solidarity; this recognition entails consent to duty and so removes its bondage. Authority in education is thus of importance, and the role of blame and of punishment is to express reprobation for what has been done. He regards discipline as the core of moral education, not as a means to secure some ulterior moral condition. Stressing the need for concentrating one's energies to get anything definite accomplished, he focuses morality on providing limits that prevent dispersion. "Morality is a comprehensive system of prohibitions. That is to say, its objective is to limit the range within which individual behavior should and must normally occur."[6]

Many other theories, though differing with one another, end up by stressing the need for repression, external or internal. Biological theories of aggression, whether inherent or acquired, or death instincts that demand aggressive expression to avoid internal self-aggression, can call for a repressive discipline on social grounds to check social chaos. Even a behaviorism that denies instincts may prescribe discipline in conditioning to develop by reinforcement an automatic response. Psychological theories that trace the internalization of prohibitions and the emergence of guilt-feeling as a regulative mechanism shift the scene of repression from outside (e.g. the parents) to within the self, but whether this constitutes self-discipline depends on the character the theory assigns to guilt and its operations.

As opposed to the Platonic and in modern times the Kantian, the moral philosophy that supports more permissive approaches to discipline is best seen in the moral sense ethics of the eighteenth century—Adam Smith is a good example—which was later drawn on by the anarchist philosophers.[7] This posited sympathy or fellow-feeling as the basic phenomenon of morality, and derived all moral notions, including duty, from the complex of sympathetic reactions. Moral education consists therefore in providing opportunity for this natural sympathy to find a natural outlet. In the movements that develop such an approach, sympathy is not just a compassionate reaction to others' sufferings but a basically affiliative attitude to other people, a mutual and cooperative outlook that is close to the ideal of community. The anarchist writers who took it up focused on the need for action to remove the institutional barriers that hinder and distort natural cooperative tendencies. Because power is regarded by them as the chief source of distortion, the usual conception of discipline and the punishment that accompanies it is precisely the wrong path for moral education and the cultivation of self-control or genuine self-discipline. Pacifists like Tolstoy and Gandhi appeal to a basic mutuality or love-force that is stirred in others by the technique of nonviolence. Repressive discipline is therefore part of the problem, not part of the answer. (Interestingly, there are cases of delinquency that have been treated successfully by withholding punishment; in those cases at least, the need for punishment on the part of the delinquents was a significant part of the problem.)

Such approaches have to reckon with the aggressive and grasping behavior appealed to in justifying repressive programs. On one psychological theory, aggression is the reaction to frustration of one kind or another and so is socially modifiable. Much of traditional acquisitiveness has been attributed historically to a world living on the margin of bare necessity and rarely rising above scarcity. The disparaging view of human nature has itself been taken to reflect the individualistic competitive institutions of Western society in the last three hundred years. Darwin's approach to morality in *Descent of Man* assumes the sympathy background. He thought that sympathy had been such an advantage to animals living in groups that those capable of it naturally survived.

Freudian and Marxian theories helped furnish intellectual weapons against the repressive outlook. This is less true of Freud himself: his central theory gives the superego a repressive function, and his later view of the death instinct gives aggression a basic place in human nature. Subsequent psychoanalytic theorists, however, began to see cultural and historical influences at work in shaping internal regulative processes. Suggestions of this sort are occasionally found in Freud as well. For example, he compares Italian and German signs in warning against an exposed live electric wire. The Italian sign is advisory: something like "If you touch, you die." The German starts with a prohibition, "It is forbidden to touch this wire," and then goes on to explain why. (It is reminiscent of Marx's remark that every Prussian has a gendarme within his breast.) Erich Fromm distinguished a humanistic conscience that might replace an authoritarian conscience under different cultural and interpersonal conditions.[8] Marcuse suggested the idea of surplus repression, modeled on Marx's concept of surplus value, and tried to see how much of the repression of libidinal tendencies was due not to psychological necessity to get a sturdy ego but to historical necessities at an earlier stage in human development.[9] This view, which allows a greater scope for Eros than the strict customary discipline, was much invoked in the sexual liberalization of the 1960s. In this respect the critique of the puritan morality appealed to a psychological underpinning.

Dewey has often been associated with progressive education, which is alleged to follow a strongly permissive path. How he deals with the psychological theory underlying the issue is therefore of special interest.[10] He denies that the moral situation is basically one of desire versus reason or duty and hence calling for repression of desire. It may be short-range desire versus long-range desire, or more fundamentally—because the pattern of desire is itself socially molded—the entrenched habits of action versus the newer path of action demanded by the analysis of the problem at hand in the particular case. The intelligence that he wants cultivated is the human being's way of reconstructing the old in the light of new proposals to deal with problems of change; not only patterns of desire but also patterns of traditional conduct and institutional patterns are at issue in such processes.

Evidence from the schools on the consequences of permissiveness is not as helpful as might have been expected. There is far less permissiveness in public school systems than is alleged in attacks on progressive education. The schools have been too underfinanced to give progressive education as proposed in the texts a real tryout, and discipline has remained largely authoritarian. Some forms of punishment have been forbidden (often under roused parental pressure) and some limitations placed on what can be done to students. Where violence and chaos have been found in urban public schools, it is a function of the social conditions of the cities, not of school discipline policies. For genuine experiments in different forms of permissiveness one has to go to private schools, sometimes to nursery schools. And here the issue is likely to be less chaos than apathy. The extreme hypothesis that the child needs only opportunity to give expression to natural tendencies is itself far from established. The more modest hope of undercutting the issue of permissiveness and repressiveness by providing so attractive a school that children will be drawn by their interest into the work remains of course a constantly desirable objective. But the real issue between partisans of the repressive and the permissive lies in disputes about the presuppositions concerning human nature, the character of interests, and the self, and the influence of social and cultural conditions on their patterning. The surface antithesis can do little more than warn us that there have to be some limits in conduct and there has to be attention to the full consequences of different programs on pupils and their development. It should function more as a complementary than an antagonistic couple, plus an indication of underlying theoretical differences. In particular contexts it is quite different whether our concern is merely to keep down violence in the school building, to have a quiet classroom, or to contribute seriously to altering the tone of a city or country by educational dealings with the rising generation. We have, therefore, next to look at the kinds of moral education proposed.

Some Contemporary Approaches to Moral and Social Education

We examine briefly here four different approaches. One concentrates moral education in the limited task of what is labeled "Values Clarification." A second seeks basic agreement, within a contemporary diversity and conflict, on an ideal of rationality that imparts a method of inquiry and decision rather than a substantive moral and social content. A third bases moral education on a theory of the psychological development of moral maturity. A fourth channels the traditional modes of citizenship education into a broadened social-moral education attuned to changed conditions. These do not all address the same questions nor stem from the same disciplines. The first two are grounded in philosophical traditions, the third takes its origin from psychology and the fourth largely from political science and education. All end with directly normative conclusions.

Values clarification rejects persuasion, regulation, dogma, appeals to conscience, and the moral emotions as ineffective in helping children develop moral values. It finds even moral example to be unsuccessful. It seeks an internal base in the child so that he or she will be free to carry out an individual development. Much of the approach lies in detailed techniques for nondirective stimulation, putting students in situations in which they will be prompted to think about or do something that will encourage thought about value problems.[11] The approach thus explicitly adopts a policy of neutrality toward substantive morality: it does not prescribe or legislate, and is essentially Socratic in its spirit. Yet this neutrality is limited by the values in its initial formulation of the moral problem as well as by its method. It is avowedly concerned with the way the student is related to society and where he or she falls on a continuum of attitudes from one described as positive, purposeful, enthusiastic, and proud, to an extreme confusion in which people are apathetic, flighty, uncertain, inconsistent, drifting, overconforming, overdissenting, posing.[12] It also opts for special values in its techniques, for example, public affirmation of values or deliberate choice rather than slow growth. And its insistence that individuals make their own decisions embodies a salient individualism. Hence its total configuration is after all a substantive though minimal common ground, rather than a complete neutrality—the cultivation of a certain attitude to life. While many of its techniques may be effective and provocative, as a philosophical approach to morality it is a highly self-limiting conception that puts its total weight on a heightened individualism.

Unlike values clarification, which began with the view that no other mode of moral education is successful, the concentration on rational method is a response to acknowledged plurality of moral beliefs and the uncertainty of substantive conclusions. A comparison to science is sometimes offered. Scientific results change and disagreements are expected, but the method of science is dependable. So too moral education should impart necessary skills for making and acting on reasonable moral decisions rather than specific moral content.[13] When spelled out in detail, such skills go beyond the intellectual capacities that rationality connotes. They lead into a whole submorality of the processes of deciding that embraces cooperative discussion and the virtues of successful communication. This extends to affective attitudes, including an empathy that comes close to a general human sympathy, and a broadened view of the prudential and of individual mental health that comes close to commitment of community.

Nevertheless, in spite of such palliatives, the move to the formal and the methodological is at bottom unsatisfactory on several grounds that touch the nature of rationality, the relation of method and content, and (we shall see) the conception of morality itself. As we have seen in chapter 8, there is no wholly self-contained concept of rationality that does not build into itself materials from the growth of human knowledge in field after field and that in doing so carries along value selections about desirable human attitudes, hence is dealing with problems of content at every step. Second, the absolute distinction between form and content has been challenged in favor of a contextually relevant one (chapter 11). The identification of form in a given inquiry thus already marks a basic investment in the specific content that is being elevated to organize the particular inquiry, and so in the kinds of values it transmits. In any case, if the parallel between moral and scientific education be pursued, it does not follow that there is to be no teaching of moral content. The teaching of science does present the basic laws. The important thing is how they are presented, that is, with an understanding of their evidential base, and the grounds that are capable of change. Just to present scientific method without an understanding of the discipline of scientific work and the growth of scientific knowledge would be as meaningless as to present scientific results of the time without reference to the methods by which they were achieved.[14] So too students should become aware of the moral structures and practices within which they are living, their perennial elements and traditional elements, their emerging forms and problems, the forces working to support or oppose them, and so on. The tentative and the probabilistic, which are the features that keep science open to progress, are internal to its operations; they do not forbid acceptance of scientific results in a given time in an appropriate way, and the teaching of those results in an appropriate way. Emphasis should not thus be on avoiding moral conclusions of our day, but on the kind of evidence required, the spirit in which acceptance is held, an appropriate sensitivity to the possibilities of change, continued attentiveness to the conditions of stability and change.

Psychological data and theory have played a significant role in recent moral philosophy. One approach, directed to the problems of moral education, is the search for paths of invariant moral development. It tempts moral education with the shortcut of a succession of stages along which children are to be prompted toward greater moral maturity. Thus Kohlberg offers a scheme of development with three levels—preconventional, conventional, postconventional—that includes six stages, beginning with a punishment and obedience orientation and ending with an orientation in terms of universal ethical principles.[15]

It is, however, hazardous at the present stage of psychological theory to invest moral education in any particular thesis of stages. Too many controversial issues are involved in any one such scheme. In Kohlberg's case, apart from methodological questions psychologists have raised about the testing and statistical procedures, and apart from the possibility of alternative schemes suggested by attention to other phases of individual development,[16] there is question about the narrowness of the concept of morality employed. It focuses almost wholly upon justice and universal prescription in a Kantian vein, distinguishing sharply structure from content and focusing on the former.[17] This, however, embodies a latent content of individualism, in passing judgment upon the individual's act of will in preference to a cooperative effort to solve human problems. The way the test questions are formulated shows this: the isolated individual has to decide to do or not to do something that is already branded—e.g. as stealing—that is, as wrong, so that to do it is already to violate moral and legal law. In the background is a conflict, whether between duties or between duty and good. The lone individual has nothing else to do but make a choice between the two options. This view of morality lacks any concern with the possibilities of reconstructing the situation, of recognizing the injustice of a situation in which a person is faced with such limited options. Yet it is precisely the matter of reconstruction that is central for the youth of today in a world of profound social change. A further criticism is that the picture of the individual making the lone determination on universal principle conforms to traditional male values of isolated or aloof rational decision and domination as superior to more typical female values of care and mutual concern.[18]

Unlike the other three approaches, education for citizenship traditionally looks directly to the sociopolitical morality. In the United States such education related the obligations of the citizen to the state and so was permeated with concepts of patriotism, duty, allegiance.[19] In the social struggles of the twentieth century around problems of liberation from national oppression and class exploitation, redistribution of burdens, civil disobedience and dissent, individualism and individual rights, the ground has been cut from under the simpler forms of education for citizenship. Glorified conceptions of the state have been thoroughly criticized, particularly its distinctive and unitary eminence; it has come to be seen as one among many interacting institutions of a society attempting to meet a people's needs. Hence citizenship assumes an intermediate status: on the one hand it involves specific rights and obligations in detailed matters; on the other it takes on a more integral character, more than just role. It is geared to community in a society, rather than to the political state alone. A transformation has accordingly been going on in its basic categories.[20] Emphasis is moving away from the older categories of *ruling and authority* with its correlates of *obedience and loyalty*. Under these older conceptions civic education was concerned with producing intelligent leaders and disciplined followers. In place of this, in line with the surge of equalitarian and democratic ideas, the emerging categories seem rather to be *participation* and *responsibility*. It should be recalled that students in many countries played and are playing a pivotal role in the struggles that brought on the transformation; often they align themselves with ideas of a world in the making rather than the categories of what they see as the establishment, and so with a vision of the future rather than simply confrontation. Perhaps the chief victim in this transition has been the ideal of *community*, whose important place we have noted in the moral agenda (chapter 7). What loyalty remains tends to be directed to the partial groups engaged in the struggle rather than to the society as a whole.[21]

Civic education is therefore faced with the tasks of shepherding the transition from authoritarian to participatory categories in practice as well as theory, and of restoring a viable ideal of community. This involves ideals not merely for education but for the reconstruction of institutions, hence the task of conveying by education the moral character of institution-building and reconstruction. Education for cooperative institutional change under a sense of common well-being, with whatever personal sacrifices it may involve, is probably the democratic form—a redefinition of patriotism—to replace the older authoritarian education of unquestioning patriotism. In such shifts civic education should move from a narrow or partial concern with a limited aspect of morality to an almost total concern with a social morality and its vital contemporary structure.

What emerges from our critical consideration of the four approaches is clearly that moral and social education require a broad and integrated conception of morality. Indeed, it becomes difficult to distinguish moral and social education as if they were two separate "subjects." Moral education cannot be limited to the rudderless individualism of the values-clarification movement; nor to the sparse fare of method and rationality; nor to a reliance on an abstract notion of maturity; nor to the one-sided commitments of traditional civic education. A viable morality today cannot deal with the individual in isolation, as the first three of these cast their thought, nor with the social in itself, as the fourth is compelled to do. Individual and social are simply aspects of all conduct. A similar isolation with respect to the concepts of moral inquiry has also to be overcome. Morality has been cast at times exclusively in terms of one or another of three families of concepts, as if they were self-contained: right and wrong, obligation or duty as against interest; virtue and vice as traits of character; good and bad (or evil), value (intrinsic and extrinsic). Yet all of these are rooted in aspects of living, phases of the human makeup, problems of group life. Good and bad are associated with appetite or desire, or with aspiration, or with critical judgment of such strivings. Virtue and vice are associated with character formations, with affective response to or appreciation of persons and their actions. Obligation is associated with interpersonal claims, regulation, laws, or other ordering relations. As human life involves all of these in their complex interrelations, morality is correspondingly complex.

Finally, moral education cannot avoid facing issues of variety, change, and conflict. If moral education is to prepare students to understand variety, cope with change, and resolve or minimize conflict, it cannot concentrate solely on the abstractly universal or even the perennial but must attend also to what is necessary under the varied and changing conditions of human life, nor is it exempt from the tasks that lie in the moral agenda for education in general (chapter 7). Moreover, there is no shortcut through the belligerent customary confrontation of absolutism and relativism and the demand that we decide for one or the other (chapter 8). Neither of these theoretical formulations is helpful; there is just as much aggressive conflict and destructiveness possible under one as under the other, though it may be hidden in one case and flaunted in the other. Similarly, communal conciliation and compromise can take place under either. Instead, a morality developed in substantial detail requires complex differentiation of contexts and issues rather than general slogans. A moral conflict between generations is quite different from that between ideologically warring nations, and a moral problem of righting injustices or removing discriminations from that of working out settled principles of distribution. A methodology of conflict resolution and adjustment to change is itself a complex set of principles and techniques separating background disagreements from immediate issues, encapsulating isolable differences, substituting cooperation for belligerence, developing a longer-range vision that puts temporary conflicts into perspective and reformulates issues to remove rather than harden the conflicting bases, and in general establishes a morally positive attitude to compromise.

What Is to Be Done in Moral Education?

The task here is not to add a fifth to the four theories of moral education considered. It is rather to build on the strengths discovered, in full recognition of the complexity of morality. This means seeking a variety of footholds for moral education in place of a single theme: locating points of agreement often ignored because taken for granted; differentiating issues of basic principle from possibly varied implementation and compromise; separating institution-building from problems of conformity; working out how to live with moral disagreements; making place for tentative resolution and experiment; in general, building a cooperative attitude in facing problems that may provide a foundation of good will. A few of these tasks will be illustrated here; emphasis is not on completeness nor on developing a morality but on the way in which the education may proceed whether it goes on through classroom teaching, administrative structure and policy, or special moral instruction.

A background commitment in moral education is usually to a democratic equalitarian outlook, at least to the basic idea of respect for every person. Special value thus lies in the individual, and this implies a social concern for his or her development and expression of powers, interest, and happiness. The usual recognition that value does not lie in the group as such but in the individuals who compose the group is often confused with the view that it lies in each individual alone, that each person's concern is with his or her own value. The reference in the morality, however, is to *every* individual. Both the standpoint of the absolute group as having value and the standpoint of the lone individual (which would even allow the use of others as merely means to the individual's ends), if exalted into a morality, are deviations from the mainstream morality. The latter allows a reasonable pursuit of self-concern, a natural interest in those nearer (family, kin, nation), a philanthropic interest in all humanity, a generally cooperative attitude to others, and a helping hand to those in trouble. It calls for exercise of individual effort and initiative, which though often interpreted negatively as not depending on others for support is traditionally a readiness to engage in positive action in fashioning institutions cooperatively.

If we start with this mainstream commitment, schools have to ask whether they have not been cultivating something closer to the egoistic deviation. It is almost as if they said, "Basically, we are preparing you for the battle of life where there are few opportunities and those are to be secured by beating the other person. Hence you are to compete for grades, ribbons, stars, places, scholarships, favor of teachers, and maybe you will be selected by the system." Joys of learning and good fellowship are cast in the shade. There have been some attempts at diminishing the competitive element and letting students go at their own paces. There have been few attempts to interest the whole group in the advancement of everyone in it. For comparison, consider the following extreme example: Suppose the society were engaged in what seemed to be a perpetual war, and students were all to be drafted for a few years' service after graduation. Would the social morality of the school be geared to exalt killing because it was in fact the "normal" postschool occupation? Would it rehearse for it by constructing a model of sport in which victory at *any* cost and by *any* means was the paramount end? Or would it be even more important to keep the ideal of peaceful human relations central, in the hope that succeeding generations might get rid of the "perpetual" war instead of accepting it as the normal way of life? Similarly, the economy may be a competitive scramble for scarce places, but it does not follow that moral education in the schools is required to perpetuate a success-oriented social morality as a "preparation for life."

Many more special values will be associated with this basic democratic-equalitarian respect for people. The organization and regulation of a school requires rules and principles of conduct to govern use of material resources and mutual treatment of personnel and students. All such proprietary arrangements, authority relations, common goals, and prescribed sanctions offer an opportunity for moral education. They are not speculative matters but practical guides where definite arrangements of one kind or another are necessary. Now all of these have a moral quality, whether of justice or of well-being or of character formation. They are all, then, fit subjects for moral deliberation by teachers and students, a deliberation that if not denied to them cannot fail to have an educative effect. Working answers can be reached and acted on. The same holds for innumerable regulations about worth of effort and relations of means to ends. Such moral education can take in its stride the fact that there will be many more disagreements in the working out of morals than in science. But here, just as in science, emphasis can fall upon innovative ways in which disagreements can be resolved, their impact minimized, or issues reformulated to bring out the strengths of opposing positions in an inventive way for possible fresh synthesis or for constructive compromise.

That such moral construction is not simply a matter of imparting standard principles to an incoming generation but a call for a reconstructive attitude by both teachers and students can be seen in areas of school life in which there are inconsistencies between principles and practice and areas in which the principles themselves are entangled and have to be extricated. Issues of administrative structure may illustrate the first; issues of grading, which we discussed in chapter 2, illustrate the second.

With respect to the hidden curriculum in the administrative structure of the school, the direction of democratic reconstruction at least is clear: the need for ensuring a wider participation of students in the determination of school policy that will educate in purposeful initiative and serious responsibility. To draw careful lines not only between authoritarian and democratic attitudes but also between paternalistic and democratic attitudes is one of the most serious and difficult tasks of moral and civic education, for it is an area in which moral preaching is readily subverted by action that rings hollow.

Patterns and procedures of grading, we saw, convey important principles in social morality, namely, those concerned with merit and reward. Here we found entangled at least four separate themes: success in job performance, competitive position, certification, moral earnestness. Hence the grading system contains a whole hidden curriculum in moral education that has to be unraveled. How far are the students learning that school is where they get certified for jobs? Or are their degrees of accomplishment being constantly measured to impart a morality of success and achievement? Or how far are they urged on to develop an earnest outlook characterized by effort? How far are they entered in competitive battle with classmates and why? In sorting out these aspects of moral education and in a more differentiated attunement of means to ends and in a weighing of ends—for example, between job preparation and cultural development—the school will be confronting its own basic objectives, and without the confronting there is likely to be inner conflict in the school's moral teachings.

Such illustrations show the need in moral education, beyond the basic permanent values, to have a substantive consideration of perennial goals, patterns of human relations, institutional structures, and attitudes on procedures. Many of these in contemporary morality will have a fairly settled position, as we have seen in considering the moral agenda. Here emphasis in moral education falls on a common working out of their implications for particular areas of practice, and a concomitant refinement of ideas in light of the consequences of practice. Let us turn next to areas of explicit change and conflict to see what paths moral education may take in handling them.

Some changes may be largely jurisdictional, though they have profound effects. Thus many of the problems that in the past were faced by the individual alone are now handled by collective effort, often through institutionalized forms; others, however, that were once institutionalized, are being turned over to the individual. Examples of the former are the various forms of social security, health care, and education. Examples of the latter are sex, choice of vocation, and to some degree the determination of the pattern of one's life. It is becoming more important to distinguish morally questions to be handled cooperatively, those to be left to the sensitive determination of the individual, those that depend on the well-developed self, those that count on a refined sense of duty, and those that have to be enforced by collective obligations. A morality will need a full repertoire of its historical concepts, dealing with character and ideals as well as sense of duty, and will probably have to work out new concepts as understanding of human nature is deepened and broadened. (These aspects of moral education may admit of class discussion in history and political science as well as in special moral teaching where such is found practicable.)

With respect to major substantive problems in which conflicts in the community involve marked disagreement, the task of moral education in the schools is a particularly difficult one. As a community institution, the school has to express the community's need for deliberation, refinement of issues, search for inventive solutions, resolution of conflict. Its ideal is not to politicize the school by simply incorporating majority opinion or by yielding to dominant pressure (chapter 5). In short, the very recognition of an issue as a frontier problem in the life of the community subjects it to a special way of handling in moral education. What is being conveyed to the students is that controversial moral problems are not routine moral problems. Let us look briefly at two outstanding issues: economic systems on the one hand and sex and male-female relations on the other.

In the United States the pressure for a "free enterprise" social ideology in the schools continues strong, while the community is split in light of changes that have taken place over the last half-century. In such a situation of conflict and debate, the focus of a social morality in the schools should clearly fall on deliberative discussion. In this the schools should stand out as a long-range institution, committed to careful and realistic analysis of alternatives without ideological distortion, to advancing procedures for decision without hasty resort to dogmatism and violence. An important step in keeping open the channels of democratic discussion is to make room for differences. The schools have increasingly taken this hard step under the equalitarian pressures of the liberation movements and the hard knocks of the student revolts of the 1960s. Another, extremely important, step is to realize that the way of formulating present problems that results in antagonism may often be relative to contexts and conditions that are disappearing. Issues of present intensity may lose their vigor, and in a longer-range perspective effort could better be directed to emerging problems. This lesson has been strengthened by the very rapidity of change in the twentieth century and the way older conflicts have vanished. This point is often made in the remark that opponents struggling for a larger share of a limited good might better expend their energies in cooperating to increase the supply of the good. Such a forward-looking perspective is particularly appropriate for education insofar as in the schools education deals typically with an oncoming generation who will be operating in the future, not in the past. This does not entail an optimistic view that all problems will be solved, but that to be educated is to handle even insoluble problems with continued common effort.

The problem of sex and male-female relations has been particularly troublesome in the schools because of conflicting pressures in the community and the pace of social change. Here the school has rarely played more than a rearguard role. Today, precisely because this is an area of changing and conflicting views, its moral position is in one sense easier. It can draw back from promulgating a dogmatic sexual morality and instead play multiple roles. One is informative—providing the best available knowledge about sexual matters. This is more difficult than it seems because there is still conflict over the appropriateness of teaching about sex, stemming from traditionalist groups, but clearly some such teaching falls within the subjects of health and hygiene and general matters of the body. Second, on the moral outlook, there is the obvious importance of having a sexual morality that, with its full moral implications and alternative ideas, should be a matter of serious inquiry. Students should come to understand the present situation: that there are different choices that different groups and individuals are adopting; what reasons have been given for the differences and changes in attitude; what disagreements and conflicts involve; the seriousness of the choices and their ramifications in life. Third, there is the fundamental cultivation of the equalitarian outlook as between men and women, which is basic to the democratic conception and is only coming to be recognized. To help students carry this through the difficult domain of sexuality and face its ramification in traditional culture is itself a major task.

In general, it is not easy to read off the demands of contemporary moral and civic education from contemporary ideals without understanding and decision concerning the contemporary situation and its problems and development. The sense of community, for example, cannot be given shape without determining its scope in the relations of national and international society. Increasingly too, it involves a balanced attitude toward past and future, as problems of overpopulation and depleted resources have made too clear. These are, of course, frontier problems; on others, such as attitudes on racial quality and the removal of discrimination, or on preservation of others' civil rights, basic moral agreement has been established, though controversies remain about ways of implementation.

In sum, moral education is not handing over a code to be learned, nor imparting a method to be exercised, nor again habituating a set of virtues—although it may make use of all of these. It is an immersion in the complex dynamics of the moral life, with a broadened conception of the nature and tasks of morality itself.

Notes

1. There were, of course, different stages in the transition from the old to the contemporary situation. For example, B.E. McClennan in a brief sketch ("Moral

Education and Public Schooling: An Historical Perspective," *Viewpoints*, Bulletin of the School of Education, Indiana University 51 [November 1975]: 1-15) points out that when people lived their lives in one place under the institutional conditions of that time, there was no urgency to carry through moral education early or quickly. The situation changed with the growth of mobility at the end of the eighteenth century. Values then had to be taught and behavior shaped in the children before they left home. He attributes the preference for women teachers in the early grades of public schooling to the belief that they were particularly adapted for moral instruction. Changes in moral education itself—from a reliance on rigid rules and the equation of virtue with reward (as in the McGuffey readers) to a reckoning of social consequences in a complex altered world came with the emergence of a corporate and bureaucratic society, and precipitated a continuing battle between traditionalists and reformers.

For the prominence of character training in the early twentieth century as the essence of moral education, and the many programs that sought to carry it out, see Harry C. McKowan, *Character Education* (New York: McGraw-Hill, 1935). See also Barry I. Chazan, "The Moral Situation: A Prolegomenon to Moral Education," in *Moral Education*, ed. Barry I. Chazan and Jonas F. Soltis (New York: Teachers College Press, Columbia University, 1973), pp. 41ff.

2. Robert Nisbet, *History of the Idea of Progress* (New York: Basic Books, 1980).

3. Alasdair MacIntyre, *After Virtue: A Study in Moral Theory* (Notre Dame: University of Notre Dame Press, 1981).

4. Kant's account of moral education emphasizes that the child should become accustomed to acting in accordance with maxims whose reasonableness the child can see for himself or herself. Character is understood to consist in a readiness to act according to maxims. Contrary action—e.g. telling a lie—should not be punished but treated with contempt, and telling the child he or she will not be believed in the future. This is to direct the child to respect for the law, not to expectation of reward and punishment. See Immanuel Kant, *Education* (Ann Arbor: University of Michigan Press, 1960), ch. 5.

5. Emile Durkheim, *Moral Education*, trans. Everett K. Wilson and Herman Schnurer (Glencoe, Ill.: Free Press, 1961).

6. Ibid., p. 42.

7. Adam Smith, *Theory of the Moral Sentiments* (London: G. Bell & Sons, 1911). The anarchist use of this tradition is clearly seen in the ethical writings of Peter Kropotkin.

8. Erich Fromm, *Man for Himself* (New York: Rinehart, 1947).

9. Herbert Marcuse, *Eros and Civilization* (Boston: Beacon Press, 1955).

10. John Dewey, *Human Nature and Conduct* (New York: Modern Library, 1930); John Dewey and James H. Tufts, *Ethics*, (New York: Henry Holt, 1932), ch. 10.

11. See Louis E. Raths, Merrill Harmin, and Sidney B. Simon, *Values and Teaching*, (Columbus, Ohio: Charles E. Merrill, 1978). An extract from an earlier edition (1966), under the title of "Teaching for Value Clarity," is contained in Barry I. Chazan and Jonas F. Soltis, eds., *Moral Education* (New York: Teachers College Press, Columbia University, 1973), pp. 170-82. On the whole, the approach remains on a commonsense level; it does not raise questions about the psychology of our different attitudes, nor the social conditions that would have to be tackled to make the achievement of sounder attitudes more likely. Sometimes it sounds like genial

and looser Socratics, sometimes like nondirective therapy; it certainly embodies Deweyan problematics, and in its lack of fear about the patterns that individuals may end up with, it has a Jeffersonian faith in people.

12. Raths, Harmin, and Simon, *Values and Teaching*, pp. 5-6.

13. This approach is elaborated in John Wilson, Norman Williams, and Barry Sugarman, *Introduction to Moral Education* (Baltimore: Penguin Books, 1967). For a general criticism of Wilson's approach, see the review of the book by Barry I. Chazan in *Studies in Philosophy and Education* 9 (Summer 1975): 138-43.

14. This point is well made by Israel Scheffler, in "Moral Education and the Democratic Ideal" in his *Reason and Teaching* (Indianapolis: Bobbs-Merrill 1973). Scheffler stresses the role of present content as a basis for further development, and so the indispensability of present practice in making future refinements and revisions possible, and in providing a conception of what the moral point of view is. The last furnishes a second-order vantage point on practice (pp. 141-42).

15. Kohlberg's stages are: on the preconventional level, a *punishment and obedience orientation* and an *instrumental orientation*; on the conventional level, a *"good boy–nice girl" orientation* and a *"law and order" orientation* of authority; on the postconventional level a *social contract legalistic orientation* with a utilitarian character and a *universal ethical principle orientation* in which right is defined by one's conscience in accordance with self-chosen ethical principles of justice. For a summary of Kohlberg's approach, see his article "Moral Development," in the *International Encyclopedia of the Social Sciences*, ed. David Sills (New York: Macmillan and Free Press, 1968), 10: 482-94. For a later exposition, see his "Moral Stages and Moralization: The Cognitive-Developmental Approach," in *Moral Development and Behavior: Theory, Research, and Social Issues*, ed. Thomas Lickona (New York: Holt, Rinehart & Winston, 1976), pp. 31-53. For discussion of Kohlberg's approach and the problems of moral education, see also C.M. Beck, B.E. Crittenden, and E.V. Sullivan, eds. *Moral Education: Interdisciplinary Approaches* (Toronto: University of Toronto Press, 1971).

16. For an example of a contrasting scheme of psychological development, see E.H. Erikson, *Childhood and Society* (New York: W.W. Norton, 1950). This lends itself readily to a theory of virtues coming on the scene as successive challenges face the person in typical situations from infancy to old age and are successfully met. Thus trust as against mistrust begins when the infant achieves a willingness to let mother out of sight without undue anxiety or rage, and ego integrity comes much later with ultimate acceptance of one's life cycle without fear of death. Such a developmental approach would furnish a basis for a maturation of virtues rather than universal principles of justice.

17. Kohlberg's scheme was originally a development from that of Piaget—see Jean Piaget, *The Moral Judgment of the Child*, trans. Marjorie Gabain (New York: Collier Books, 1962; originally published 1932). Piaget himself traces the philosophical antecedents of his work from Kant through Durkheim and others. What has happened is, in effect, that Kant's special narrowing of morality to maxim-testing and law-following, centering on obligation as contrasted with the broader teleological tradition of pursuing the good life, was taken over for sociological and psychological research without any reckoning of alternative conceptions of morality in the history of ethics. Kohlberg does not move out of this tradition, and in later writings attempts to defend the view that justice is the whole or the greater part of morality.

18. This point is richly developed in Carol Gilligan, *In a Different Voice: Psychological Theory and Women's Development* (Cambridge: Harvard University Press,

1982). See also the special issue on moral development of *Ethics* 92 (April 1982), especially Owen J. Flanagan Jr., "Virtue, Sex, and Gender: Some Philosophical Reflections on the Moral Psychology Debate"; also Kohlberg's reply. Flanagan makes the interesting contrast of two biblical stories: the judgment of Solomon as to which of two contenders for an infant was the real mother, by ordering it to be divided in half and seeing which woman instantly gave up the child rather than win over her opponent through the child's death; and the readiness of Abraham to sacrifice his son Isaac at God's bidding. Flanagan sees these as epitomizing the difference claimed between female and male psychology.

19. For a comparative evaluative study, see Judith V. Torney, A.N. Oppenheim, and Russell F. Farnen, *Civic Education in Ten Countries*, International Studies in Evaluation VI (New York: John Wiley & Sons, 1975). Among the interesting findings were that "students who reported frequent participation in patriotic rituals were both less knowledgeable and less democratic in their outlook" (p. 18), and also that "in every country where student support for Democratic Values was above the mean for all countries, Support for the National Government was below the mean for all countries (and vice versa)" (p. 328). Tests covered more than thirty thousand students at three age levels and five thousand teachers in thirteen hundred schools in ten countries.

20. For a wide range of studies of contemporary problems in civic education, see *Citizenship and Education in Modern Society, Proceedings of the Symposium on Citizenship and Education in Modern Society*. The symposium was sponsored by the Mershon Center, The Ohio State University, April 1980. The general shift in categories is discussed in Abraham Edel, "The Good Citizen, the Good Man and the Good Society." Interesting suggestions for international education are found in Chadwick F. Alger, "Enhancing the Efficacy of Citizen Participation in World Affairs." See also Henry Giroux, "Critical Theory and Rationality in Citizenship Education," dealing with the impact of different philosophical approaches. Among other special topics dealt with are problems raised by ecology and ethnicity, as well as the hidden curriculum.

21. For a reassertion of the importance of loyalty in moral theory, see Andrew Oldenquist, "Loyalties," *Journal of Philosophy* 79 (April 1982). For a renewed consideration of civic education through the perspective of educating the teacher, see the essays on the theme "The Civic Education of the American Teacher," *Journal of Teacher Education* 34 (November-December 1983).

15. Complexities of the Familiar: Sport and Physical Education; Crafts, Arts, and Technology; Basic Skills

This chapter examines a number of components in schooling that are usually taken for granted, the result of which is that we miss their complexities, overlook their depths, and lose out on the sense of alternative directions they might be taking. The obvious lesson is that the familiar requires as much probing as the controversial.

Physical Education and Sport

Health activities could be a community concern through other institutions than the schools because they pertain to everyone; their location in the schools for students is only a matter of convenience, acceptable if there are no strong counterreasons—for example, if they do not draw too heavily from the learning budget. On the other hand, pupils in the classroom may very well need occasional stretching or exercise in the interests of learning itself. Learning about health and bodily activity is, however, another matter. It is an integral part of learning about the person. Now, if health activities are the laboratory work of such learning, health activities become thoroughly enmeshed with the educational program. We need then some principles about the body and the mind to guide the shape of this educational program.

The old advice about having a sound mind in a sound body does not help very much. It sets forth the admirable goal of achieving both but does not say whether the existence of one depends on the existence of the other. The theory of body-mind relations is extraordinarily complicated both in philosophy and religion, as well as in ordinary attitudes of people. Human beings have tried to mortify the flesh, to dominate the body, to build masterful bodily machines, to be almost purely minds. On the other hand, in spite of different interpretations of the facts, there has been a sober acknowledgment that the flowering of human capacities of the mind and the spirit requires some care for the body. The major opposing interpretations have been what we may call *dualistic* and *organic*. The dualistic separated body and mind and then offered all sorts of accounts about their interrelation or opposition. The organic took the mind to be in some way an expression of the total organism functioning in the world environment, though it had different views of the character of that world and its environment. It is a mistake to equate these opposing interpretations with other types of philosophical differences, for example a religious as against a secular or a materialistic world view. Religions themselves, and even a particular historical religion like Christianity, have divided sharply on dualistic movements and organic movements in their own careers. Theological analyses of matter have varied as have theological attitudes to the bodily.

An important consequence of a dualistic approach is that "bodily" and "mental" become basic categories for classifying experiences. Not only are qualities and affections parceled out but pleasures and satisfactions are bundled separately. The history of ethics shows the results clearly. Bodily pleasures such as food and sex are given the lowliest status. Pleasures of smell and movement and vision often (as in Plato's list) are intermediate. Intellectual pleasures of course belong at the top. This is not merely an aristocratic categorization; we find even a liberal like John Stuart Mill talking of the bodily pleasures and the intellectual pleasures and asking whether you would choose to be a dissatisfied Socrates or (almost) an ecstatic pig.[1]

Suppose, however, we are careful to abandon a conception of the intellectual that was shaped in a dualistic outlook and employ the notions of cognition and value explored in dealing with knowledge and the humanities. Suppose too we supplement that with an organic relation of mind and body. (Indeed Mill had no right on his own views of mind to be classifying pleasures the way he did.) Then the degree of the intellectual, the cognitive, the ideal, perhaps even the spiritual, might be less a matter of the content than of quality of life. Ordinary language and ordinary experience note the difference, whether we are engaged in a "bodily" or a "mental" context. We may line up the contrasts: in food, the glutton and the gourmet; in sex, lust and love; in vision, an inquisitive glance and an aesthetic beholding; in hearing, a casual hearing and informed listening; in motion, a sluggish pace and a graceful step; in the imagination, an idle daydream and the creative fantasy; even in science the pursuit that is ego oriented and the pursuit that is task oriented. In general, then, the distinction lies in the extent to which the ideal penetrates the material and fashions its character. In evolutionary terms it is probably the distinction between the purely animal and the form that the act takes as a human act when it is transformed in human purpose and human consciousness. It becomes a social act in a human community altered by speech and intercommunication and common life.

The schools have seldom had an explicit philosophy of the body for health education, and whether the individual regarded his or her body as a slave (an early ancient conception), a machine to be kept in good order, a part of the self, or his or her very identity was not really faced. No doubt the actual teaching of hygiene was the channel through which some conception was formally conveyed. Such teachings have probably not been decisive for two reasons. One is that a vital part of the area of attitude to the body concerns sex and the schools have traditionally avoided dealing with this. The other is that the students' ideal feelings have probably been focused on sport rather than on what they have been taught about their bodies.

As for sex education, it is clear that the schools sooner or later will have to deal with this as part of health education. As indicated in the previous chapter, it does not mean that they have to set down a specific line. They can provide the knowledge that a contemporary needs to avoid blunders in life, and to be able to make his or her own decisions on questions that our social morality is coming increasingly to recognize as falling within the individual's informed decision. It was suggested therefore that the school's role here may soon become easier than when it was expected to transmit a specific sexual morality. The school may have the task of transmitting agreed-on virtues of the spirit, and agreed-on attitudes of sincerity and responsibility, of deliberate decision, of awareness and self-consciousness. Sexuality is a clear case of what we were discussing about the effects of a dualistic attitude. Long treated as purely bodily, it suffered from the opposite tendencies of being treated as purely physical or being overromanticized. Its traumatic history in the process of liberation is too well known to need recounting, and the achievement of a sound sexual morality is still one of the serious problems, not as an isolated matter but as part of the whole of social morality and institutional construction, and indeed the quality of life.

Sport, if we attend to it carefully, stands out as one of the most revealing areas for understanding the aspirations of students and the relations of body and spirit. We must look at it broadly, not simply in terms of stellar events. Surprisingly, little philosophical attention has been paid to this area. There is by now philosophy of religion, of science, of law, of education, of medicine, but only beginning of sport. And yet in the United States, sport engages the interest and enthusiasm of masses of people. It is sometimes compared to a religion because of the devotion it wins and the ritual character it has. Much of it in the schools and in professional sport is spectator sport. The schools have complained of this and tried to encourage participant sports. In the country at large, however, athletic participation has spread. There has always been cycling, then increasingly swimming, skiing, motorcycling, and now tennis and almost an epidemic of jogging. Of particular interest is the literature that has grown up alongside some of these sports. What often strikes one is the spiritual quality of the feeling aimed at. In jogging, as indeed in skiing and motorcycling, the description is that of being, as it were, in a high gear of the spirit, a sort of full actualization, reminiscent of the complete actuality that the ancients found in the contemplative act when the agent became one with the object of his contemplation, almost the mystic's absorption. It is the sense of the full use of one's disciplined capabilities. And, as the practice of the sport or the exercise shows, it requires constant effort, constant self-discipline, and constant care of one's equipment as well as one's person.

Integrating sport in this sense within the curriculum in a well-thought-out philosophy of the organic relation of mind and body would probably be a solid basis for much of character and attitude within the educational process. It would include a moral critique of sport, not merely the acceptance of whatever tendencies were found in sport: for example, of the patterns of teamwork in the light of ideals of community (the familiar critique of the star system), of the organization of training, of any isolating tendencies in some sports (as has been suggested about jogging), and so on. Bringing sport within the curriculum in this way would make possible the transfer of standards of discipline from sport to other areas of work, and the readier understanding of quality in performance and its relation to discipline in intellectual labors. The isolation of sport from the rest of the work of the schools means that a model that has a strong hold on the youth is largely wasted as an educational force.

Sport too suffers by its isolation. It has been permeated by a loss of civility and what used to be essential to "sportsmanship," by an intensified competitiveness and a consequent aggressiveness, all geared to ways of the marketplace. There is no longer any appreciation of what it means to be a good loser, for (as is often said) winning is not the most important thing, it is everything. And the line between amateur sport and professional high-powered earnings becomes a tenuous one. How far-reaching these tendencies have been is most evident in a game like tennis, which today little resembles the gentlemanly sport of earlier times.

Occasionally colleges have eliminated competitive sport in the light of its growing evils, but some come back to it under alumni pressure. Such episodes suggest that only by an educational integration of sport within the schools, with a conscious theory of educational objectives, can its deterioration be checked.

Crafts, Arts, and Technology

The Greek world had an inclusive ideal of *techné* that embraced both arts and crafts. The sculptor, the builder, the rhetorician, and even the ruler were examples of the craftsman or craftswoman or artist. The underlying idea was one of making or producing, in which experience was required, definite standards governed the production, and knowledge was implicit. There were distinctions of social prestige among the crafts. Craft, art, and *techné*—if we read the third now as technology—have moved along different paths. The fine arts took a select few out of the bundle and became an independent, more prestigious realm. The rest of the crafts multiplied with division of labor and growth of knowledge. Some achieved the status of professions. Those imbued with advanced science turned into technology and were thought of as applied science. The remainder were left to shift for themselves; if they were full-time occupations, they might be thought of as *vocations*, although originally that term carried the sense of being called to a task or career. Eventually nearly all these kinds of making found some place in education. The fine arts, or some rudimentary sample, are in the schools and studies of them are among the humanities. The professions occupy whole schools or colleges, as do the more prominent technologies. Vocations that required learning beyond merely association with craftsmen and craftswomen, and apprenticeship became the subject of vocational training, and some are now working their way up into quasi-professional status. Let us consider separately the crafts, the arts, and technology.

From an educational point of view the focus is on knowledge, the extent and kind of knowledge involved in the production, and the degree to which it becomes systematic and plays an important part. The rise of the crafts in the history of humankind came with the discovery of agriculture, the domestication of animals, the making of pottery and clothing. The organization of crafts had a definite shape: individuals or groups of individuals engaged in production; the productive process was directed to a definite goal or product; steps on the way consisted of gathering the relevant material, changing its form through the action of the person exercising a set of skills; knowledge was acquired through the experience of previous craftsmen and craftswomen and handed on by learning through association and practice.[2] For the most part the mastery of the whole process was in the hands of the individual. This pattern of looking at making furnished a definite model for interpreting activity.

The lower-school curriculum has generally included some craft skills. The governing idea may be that they are useful skills in ordinary life, or that they point to a possible way of supporting oneself, or that not all learning should be book learning. An old-fashioned selection was manual training (carpentry) for boys and cooking for girls. When social production became more complex, and division of labor more intensive, there was some shift from craft to isolated skill—for example, for girls from cooking to typing. Job preparation plays a large part, but the difference in type of activity itself is marked. Cooking is taught in a craft spirit, with the person in charge of the whole enterprise, while typing is taught as a skill to be fitted into some other complex enterprise.

The craft spirit is a congenial one for education. Learning a craft may unify different skills in a single process; it provides an understanding of the whole set of activities, and it furnishes an inherent motivation in the clear relation of activity and product and often in the joys associated with a sense of achievement and mastery. The spirit can be applied to projects that are not part of traditional crafts. A photography club in the school may be carried on in the same way. Driver education may be offered as an isolated skill, but when taught in relation to understanding the machine, its care and repair, then it moves toward a craft.

The craft spirit stays close to practice and production. Because it has an eye on what will actually be produced, or more generally on what will actually be the result, it develops sensitivity to contingent factors in the particular situations. The craftsman or craftswoman rarely is simply following a rule but, more likely, is seeing how the advice of the rule as a lesson of experience works out in the case at hand. The use of a case method in teaching—whether in law school or medical school or business school—reflects the same spirit.

The craft approach has much to recommend it in the schools, as against simply teaching a skill. Typing could, for example, be taught nowadays as part of the whole craft of replication. Printing was an important craft, at some times verging on an art. Replication by machine, by photograph and microfilm, by Xerox, and now by word processor, has broadened into a whole discipline. In this kind of transformation, advancing technology actually humanizes a skill by bringing out the underlying purposes and associating them with variety of techniques. Adapting technique to purpose overshadows the mechanical character of the skill. Which crafts at what levels of the school curriculum is, of course, a specific question of educational evaluation, taking into consideration time and place, the state of the productive economy and attractive pursuits, as well as specific educational costs and outcomes. The importance of a craft is not merely that it is more humanistic than a skill, but also that it is taking the stance of the particular and the practical; it aims at an individual product, not universal knowledge. This is its virtue but also its limitation. In this stance, craft is quite other than science.

The professions find their way into higher education, not because they require a great deal of preparation—this could be done by a required apprenticeship in the case of medicine or law or teaching, in hospitals or courts or schools (just as for electricians and plumbers)—but because that preparation involves a large body of knowledge. This knowledge may be either specific to the field, or selective from various sciences and disciplines. An important further factor is also involved: professions are often self-regulating in the sense that the professionals or a representative body set the standards for the practice and judge the practitioners. With this combination of knowledge and judgment involved, the education of the professional in general is likely to be improved by association with broader liberal education. Wolff points out that a businessman need not be certified by other businessmen to start a business.[3] If this excludes business from the professions, then a school of business requires a different justification—unless its constituent professions, such as accountancy and economics, qualify it. Perhaps the fact of being an activity of serious consequence in society may be enough to justify attempts to raise its level of performance through university education. But if so, some clear principle is needed to decide where to draw a line.

As for the arts, they are long to some degree a recognized part of schooling. Traditional curricula have generally included art appreciation, but increasingly some opportunity for work in at least one or another of the arts themselves.

Contemporary teaching of the arts is in an advantageous position because the field has broadened in many directions, compared to the older set of limited fine arts. Opportunities for experimentation are increased. One factor has been the addition of materials and devices: fresh uses of concrete and glass in architecture, new kinds of material in paints, improved modes of composition and distribution of books, electronic recording for music, film and notation for dance. Fresh arts of photography and film and the media of radio and television add to possible avenues of artistic creation and expression. Greater communication has brought in influences from other cultures, particularly African and Eastern. To some degree the antagonism of pure and applied art has broken down. After all, church art in medieval times was applied and decorative. The objection to commercial art today is less to its being applied art (as in textiles or household pottery and utensils) than to its being subordinated to selling and advertising.

Conflict over the role of art in society is an old matter. Tolstoy in *What Is Art?* almost turns statistician, calculating how many hours are spent by masses of the young in moving muscles, pounding keys, dabbing on canvas. He asks what is it all for. His emphasis is on the communication of basic human feeling as the key to the moral character of art.

The controversy over whether art should convey a social message is usually cast as a distinction between art and propaganda or didacticism. If art and literature give us insight, why not insight also into social problems? The persons to whom this insight is conveyed may alter their conduct. Drama is a great teacher. The objection to propaganda is to bad art; it is like teaching by rousing emotions instead of bringing understanding.

Just as science had to realize the role of the imagination and of value as selection in its processes, so art had to become conscious of the role of cognition in aesthetic sensibility both in production and appreciation. In controversies about production and expression this has sometimes appeared as the conflict of a restraining art tradition and a creative free expression. Every artist and every teacher knows that this is a false dichotomy. Creativity more often means going beyond a disciplined mastery of some tradition rather than starting from scratch. The same is true of appreciation. Too often there is the attitude of the consumer who simply looks at the surface and likes or dislikes—asks to be turned on or turned off. This is the spirit of the false front, whether in architecture or in car design. Many aesthetic values are missed if there is no understanding of the construction and the design. It is almost as Santayana says of music, that listening to it may be merely a drowsy reverie.

The problem facing the teacher is therefore to find an appropriate way of bringing an awareness of production to enhance appreciation. Aristotle, in the section of the *Politics* that deals with education, asks how far the student of music should learn to perform on an instrument. He decides it should be just enough to be a good critic. Without entering into his arguments (which are partly biased against performance as too lowly for a gentleman), we may note the merit of his criterion. The ideal of a good critic can fuse knowledge or understanding with that of refined experience, and it embodies some awareness of the problems of production, not merely the standpoint of consumption. It has the appropriate relevance to the general problem of today's education—the need for critical·consciousness grounded in knowledge, and the independence of spirit and creative imagination required for reconstruction.

Freed of a narrow view of art, education finds itself with a number of serious challenges. One is to convey the sense of art as a great bulwark of imaginative experimental freedom; this is as true of social utopias as it is of the visual arts. Another is to convey the sense of the importance of knowledge and tradition *in* art—not merely *of* art—both in creation and appreciation. Another is to cultivate a sensitive or refined creative experience in a diversity of media. Accompanying such experiences there is need to develop a sense of responsible appreciation and criticism that is not sentimentalism, inarticulate feeling, selective inattention, pleasurable response on a low level, nor a pedagogic binding of taste, nor again a verbal limitation to such ejaculations as "fabulous" or "thrilling" in a language so rich with distinctions. Opportunities also exist to utilize the increasing volume of materials from other cultures, not as exotic products but to help us understand the integral character of art in human living. Because art has been recognized as the realm in which one encounters intrinsic values, experience of art should also be an opportunity for coming to understand the complex relations of intrinsic, instrumental, and structural or systemic values. Such arts as architecture may teach these lessons more readily than sculpture, and the relations of beauty and utility in practical arts such as pottery, clothing design, and so on will readily involve them. In the contemporary broadening of the fields of art, the teaching of art will have to elicit and perhaps convey an underlying aesthetic theory.

The remaining question concerns the character of technology. Where does it find its place among the crafts and the arts on the one side, and science on the other? Or is it *sui generis*? The frequent characterization of technology as applied science allies it with practice but looks at it from the side of science as theory: technology is science getting practical. If we look at it from the side of practice instead, what we see rather are various crafts being altered and repatterned through the use of instruments and mechanical, chemical, electrical, and, more recently, biological devices. We need not pursue the internal changes in the crafts that the historian of growth of technology finds,[4] such as the shift in the fine-tuning of production from the operating craftsman or craftswoman to the machine designer, or the way in which new crafts grow out of old ones from the possibilities that new instrumentation opens up. From the perspective of practice, then, to think of applied science is to turn things upside down. What is happening, rather, is the appeal by an ongoing practice to the resources of science, and from the perspective of science an intervention in the ongoing practice. The separateness of technology comes where the instrumentation spans several crafts. The manufacture of the instruments then becomes a separate process, economically viable in the light of the multiplicity of uses. Thus devices developed for war are used for the work of peace, and machinery is deliberately designed so that it can find many uses. Sometimes we find—parallel to art for art's sake and science for science's sake—an attitude of tools for tools' sake. Then we are left with inventions looking for possible uses and there is the temptation to try out what has been invented without reckoning its manifold consequences.

Educational lessons from such an analysis of technology call for recognizing both the continuity and separateness of science and technology. Practical problems have played an important part in stimulating the growth of science, and the influence of technique and instrumentation has been internal to its development. Hence cooperative relations are desirable. But basic research should not be geared to or controlled by local demands of practice. (It is almost as if the pursuit of science were a separate craft, with its own practitioners and its own rules of operation.) A second lesson is that technological education cannot be divorced from the moral questions of the uses of its instruments. This is a lesson that engineering schools are beginning to take to heart under the impact of problems of nuclear energy, pollution, resource depletion, and growing fields such as recombinant genetical engineering. It was always inherent although put aside under slogans of scientific neutrality. The character of moral education in relation to technology is still a matter to be worked out in contemporary education and in society. Even more, the same moral problems of responsibility are now increasingly marked in basic science itself, as problems of recombinant genetic research and its dangers have dramatically shown. These go beyond even nuclear issues because the dangers come from research itself, not the applications.

Basic Skills

That the schools teach elementary skills from the start is taken for granted. Reading, writing, speaking, and calculating are generally regarded as the basics. What the skills are that are to be taught is not, however, so simple a matter. The more the question is explored, the longer grows the list; and the more each skill is analyzed, the larger is the brood of constituent skills that nests inside it. The four basics are only the central cognitive skills in a mass of skills verging on attitudes that the child acquires: to speak clearly, to keep quiet as well as speak, to engage in discussion with others, to take care of one's own things in an orderly way, to help clean up generally, to respect others' space and property, and so on. Skills contain attitudes and attitudes involve skills. We become conscious of the need for cultivating them or explicitly teaching them when we are brought short by inadequacies in performance. As long ago as 1876 Thomas Huxley complained that students entering medical school did not know how to observe and time had to be wasted teaching them how to look.[5] Why should not a contemporary curriculum find place for teaching looking in the early years, not only in practicing what one has observed by describing the scene (which would bring in skills of retention and visualization in recall) but by acquaintance with microscope and telescope, and with collateral realization of the extent to which selection and interpretation enter observation?

(Whether motivation requires connection with games, science, problems of crime detection, or whether the sheer instruments will themselves be attractive enough is a separate matter.) Again, little attention to conversation and arguments is needed to reenforce the conviction that people need more instruction on how to listen; so frequently discussions turn into successive monologues. The suggestion has been offered (I do not recall where) that to practice listening a rule of discussion might be: before A presents an argument against what B has said, A has to summarize what B said to B's satisfaction. As for talking or the improvement of speech, while it has not the current notoriety of reading problems, there is much in general verbal patterns to suggest that it requires attention—for example, the use of standardized words where the language has subtle differentiations, or the current use of "you know" as if it were a comma.

Problems arising in other educational tasks constantly call attention to skills and to dormant powers that need awakening. Moral education, taken seriously, rapidly shows that a fundamental hindrance is the lack of empathy with others' situations; if only A felt what it was like to be in B's shoes, we constantly say, A would not take this (selfish) stand. Now empathy is something that admits of training. Games involving role playing are a recognized mode of increasing sensitivity to different predicaments, and often after playing a role the person is given the reverse part to play. (In principle it is no different from the law school practice of having the student take successively opposite sides of a case.) An extreme example was furnished by a teacher who, wishing to have the pupils empathize with victims of discrimination and to show the arbitrary character of discrimination, selected members of the class at random to be shunned, abused, and (within limits) tormented for a day. The students were said to have been much affected. When we move on from interpersonal abilities to cognitive skills, the variety of candidates for mental training are legion: distinct abilities can be marked out in classifying, noting analogies, analyzing, structuring, comparing.

The breakup of skills into constituent skills is advanced in two important educational contexts—testing and remediation. For example, broad discontent with achievement in basic skills has precipitated in the United States a demand for competency testing; in many places a pupil has to pass a test in such fundamentals to secure a high school graduation certificate. In the construction of the actual tests, each item has to be directed responsibly to testing some specific competency; otherwise the results would not be meaningful. First an interpretation of competency is required; for example, this is restricted to functional literacy and computation, that is, to being able to understand sufficiently for purposes of ordinary life procedures—to fill out an application form for a job, to balance a bank account, to answer questions for securing a license, to calculate costs and change in purchasing, and so on. Then the separate questions have to be checked to make sure they pertain to the objectives and do not depend on other factors, such as experience in a specialized class or environment. In remediation the effort naturally arises to discover the exact point at which the learning process was blocked or frustrated. In the obvious case of reading difficulty, which has been much studied, a block may have concerned vision (e.g. confusing direction of letters or reversing letters), hearing (distinguishing sounds and syllables), the orderly relation of parts, the significance of symbolizing, speed of reaction, and so on. Each of these admits of separate practice or instruction possibly using contexts other than reading: for example, direction can be practiced in terms of facing one way or another, order in terms of arranging objects, discernment of shape by looking for embedded figures.

The sense in which cooperating skills are analyzed out of a complex skill by studying where failures have occurred does not mean that the complex is composed out of elements that have to be separately learned and put together in some way. The order of learning does not necessarily correspond to the analytic order. The plight of the centipede in the familiar story is a case in point: when asked which foot it moved first, it became paralyzed. Whether the normal learning is first of separate elements or takes place in some synthetic grasp, whether it goes through stages dependent on some maturational process or can follow different orders, is a matter of separate empirical study. The planning of a curriculum to embody learning the basic skills requires psychological knowledge of where the child is at that time and at which point the skills may be prepared for, cultivated, matured, or sharpened. For one thing, the child usually comes to school with some learning of skills. Language has been acquired, and it is by no means easy to know what that has involved. Certainly there is an implicit learning of rule-following insofar as the child utters grammatical sentences. Other situations involving social restraint have shared in developing a certain attitude to rule-obedience as well as rule-following. Piaget, for example, traces the child's attitude to rules from an early stage of belief in there being a fixed order of things to a later stage of recognizing their constructibility.[6] Bruner points to stages in the cognitive differences of interpreting a phenomenon:[7] for example, a young child sees a ball bouncing off a wall as traveling in an arc, touching the wall on the way; a ten-year-old sees the angles related, as one changes the other does; a thirteen- or fourteen-year-old basketball player comes to see the two angles as equal. Our ideas about stages, just as the relation of elements to wholes, have to be treated with caution. Not only may they reflect a biased sample but, even if found to be stable, they may reflect local habits of greater attention to certain types of phenomena, special culturally influenced interests, and so on. Educational experiment is therefore part of the evidence because education is itself one form of cultural influence. It is not always easy, once we get beyond areas of authentic knowledge of maturation to distinguish where attempting to teach something will be vain because the capacity for its acquisition is not yet developed and where not to attempt to teach it is to leave capacities dormant. In constructing a curriculum on assumptions about stages, educators are often between the Scylla of futility and the Charybdis of procrustean coercion. Education must then make its own decision in different areas about where a man's reach should exceed his grasp.

What are the capacities we are trying to bring to fruition in the teaching of reading? Reading is not just matter of receiving a communication through symbolic marks. At a minimum it is receiving information, and that accounts for the interest in speed reading. No special significance attaches to information coming through reading rather than another source. But serious reading bears the same relation to reading as discussion bears to listening to a lecture. Serious reading is a kind of internal discussion, whether the book is a novel or essay. It involves an activated self. It allows of leisurely repetition, going back over material, meditating. It sets the imagination going for critical response, for envisaging alternatives, tracing implications. Reading in this fuller sense is a special experience that is intellectually creative. Reading is frequently contrasted with watching television. It is more than the fact that the reader is active and the television viewer is relatively passive; nothing prevents television from encouraging questions, posing alternatives, accompanying presentation with multiple commentary and discussion. But because television gives determinate visual shape, say to the characters in a play or story, and to the setting, it constrains the imagination. The constraint is not of course complete. The viewer may wonder why the character reacts in one way rather than another, but the viewer cannot wonder what the person looks like or how the person expresses emotion. The same objection may be made to a performance of a play: it is channeled along one interpretation. There is compensation in that the performance, whether on stage or television, can be richer than what the average reader is likely to envisage. And different performances of the same play are of interest precisely in that they break the constraint. For the same reason, reading the play first results in a richer experience: the performance is now in association with anticipated possibilities that arose in the reading.

If such considerations are educationally significant, then reading is not in the longer school stretch to be taught as simply a matter of speedy or convenient acquisition, although it may be reduced to that in some contexts. It is an experience in its own right, an exercise of the critical interpretive imagination. It merges with reflection, explication of meaning, and the full range of mental activities. Such an understanding of reading fits the familiar humanistic emphasis on the importance of careful study of books as an essential discipline. It need not lead to the exaggerated claim of some college curricula that would make the whole curriculum consist of the study of the great books, for reading as we have pictured it exhibits equally the capacities that issue in scientific activity or in practical life. And as writing is mastered, it magnifies the active and creative side implicit in reading. Perhaps the richer interpretation of reading might be expressed by saying that the expression of capacities usually sought in teaching writing ought also to be taking place in reading.

We have wandered far from the teaching of the basic skill, but let us go a little further before turning back. It looks as if the traditional philosophical concerns about insight, inductive generalization, and modes of analysis may be very close to the problems of teaching the basic skills. If so, different philosophical views in these matters could be a useful resource for educational practice, for ultimately they are concerned with the character of experience and learning from experience. Let us take, for example, the usual differences in inductive theory. Classical views stressed insight, the way in which the lining up of particulars yielded an active grasping of a structure or pattern or essence. Contemporary phenomenological views reach the same result even more strongly because the pattern is often seen as directly grasped in the phenomenological field and less dependent on multiple particulars. On the other hand, a traditional narrow empiricism simply regards induction as the process in which the relative frequency of different paths of particulars registers their weight in our habit formations, or more consciously we use the equipment of probability to take measures and make forecasts. A pragmatic turn to empiricism raises the still deeper question of how we get the particulars that we are lining up. Whitehead says somewhere that one of the greatest geniuses was the person who first saw the similarity of seven fish and seven stones; and James says that we are set down in the middle of the world and we go about finding likeness in what we thought to be different and differences in what we thought to be like. The hidden curriculum of experience is that purposes and values in selecting from the flux create different orders and different patterns of stability. With this key both the traditional empiricist view and the classical insight view are seen in a new light. Induction is rarely sheer counting of particulars; it involves the existent base of theory and interests about the particulars themselves. For example, the statistical study of specific human behavior (say, election behavior) requires some knowledge of what people are after in their behavior; it is reflected in the selection and formation of subclasses or subgroups that the statistician regards as significant for gathering further data. Insight is now seen not as the direct grasping of truth in structure but as the proposal of a possible structure. This shifts the problem to possible alternatives. To take an oversimplified example, if we start with a set of integers 1, 2, 4 . . . and ask what to expect next, the usual answer of insight might be 8; the viewer has tacitly taken the relation of a successor to a predecessor to be one of multiplication and by a constant multiplier. But suppose it is taken as addition in a different orderly way, then the next item could be 7, if the order of what was added itself followed the series of integers. Of course numerous other possibilities could be generated by different formulae. (Our two follow 2^n and $[(n^2 - n)/2] + 1$ respectively.) In any empirical matter, therefore, any insight acts as a proposed hypothesis to be tested against alternatives.

How does such a philosophical conclusion affect the teaching of reading—both the earlier teaching as well as the later concern with serious reading? It might in fact have suggestions even for the preparatory practices preceding reading. Such exercises include practice in discerning an order in given materials, such as the pattern of arrangement in successive objects. Why should not the acquisition of the habits of discerning an order be accompanied or followed (choice here depends on psychological and other educational considerations) by exercises that call for seeing alternative possible patterns, unusual rather than standard ones, and stimulating inquiry about what difference the alternative patterns would make or under what sort of conditions they would be useful. The lesson that a standard order or interpretation is only one among many, that different ones are being constructed in the light of different implicit interests and purposes, would be an important one for encouraging an active and creative insight or intellectual imagination. It could be carried out in simple terms on a quite early level.

Comparable lessons and suggestions could doubtless arise from considering different analytic modes. An extremely important one is the contrast between the interest in formulating and systematizing universals and that in tracing the development of an existent process that is going on with the full impact of contingent factors. This lies at the root of claims for different modes of experience in science and history, and we have seen the divergence in science as theory and crafts as practice. If these are to be construed as division of labor in the exercise of basically the same capacities, then it is an educational challenge to work out learning procedures as early as possible in which in an elementary way such divergence and relations may be exhibited and understood. Perhaps this would come in the understanding of arithmetic in its relation to practical problems.

Our examination of basic skills has emphasized the underlying assumptions and how these when probed may lead to a reassessment of practice. But of course such reassessment also calls for attention to the technical and social conditions of the given period. For example, memory used to be emphasized as basic in older learning, and more systematic attention to it as a skill would doubtless still be valuable. Today it may seem equally important to teach the child the use of libraries and techniques of efficient recording and computer resources, as extended social memory systems.

A more general question is the role of play and games in relation to the development of skills. The many faces of play have long been explored: its role as relaxation, its stimulation of the imagination, its character as the precursor of art in its fantasy and of skill in its imitation of grown-up activity, its relation to entertainment and to work. How deeply philosophical issues enter educational judgment here can be seen from the contrast of W. T. Harris and John Dewey on the question of the difference between work and play. Harris thought the ideas of work and play should be kept strictly apart in the mind of the child, for the former must be associated with authority and responsibility, the latter with fantasy and the capricious will.[8] Dewey finds them by no means antithetical and assigns the sharp contrast to undesirable social conditions; the difference is rather that in play the element of interest is more direct, while in work there is a greater span in the relation of means and end.[9] Behind this disagreement lies their attitude to the role of interest in education. Harris regarded the authority of the school as essential in the development of a cultural self, as contrasted with the undisciplined play of native instincts and desires of a child that need to be socialized. Dewey saw interest not only as the motive force that makes success in teaching possible but as ultimately identical with self; the two terms denote the same fact and the kind of interest that a person actively takes in something shows the quality of selfhood existing.

The forms of play and the instruments of play raise the same kind of issues as the analysis of reading and are faced with the same dangers. For example, toys often constrain the imagination (as television performances do), although they may also offer a richer specificity of detail than might have been independently conceived. Almost a whole philosophy of children's toys is required to thread one's way among the welter of offerings. It is particularly necessary to distinguish toys oriented to a special skill, those addressed to a specific mood or appealing to a particular interest, and those opening a broader road to imaginative play. Similarly, the role of games is varied. All teach the idea of rules and rule-following, and some the necessity of self-discipline. Some heighten competition while others heighten the sense of construction. And there are the familiar toys designed to develop specific skill in an entertaining way—for example, teaching logic or the basic moves of set theory. And some, as is too evident in sport, become themselves work for the players, a work of entertaining large masses of people.

Notes

1. *Utilitarianism*, ch.2.
2. The structure of the craft is expressed philosophically in the teleological model, noted above ("Introduction to part II") in relation to the means-end scheme of evaluation.
3. Robert Paul Wolff, *The Ideal of the University* (Boston: Beacon Press, 1969), p. 10.
4. Cf. Hunter Dupree, "The Role of Technology in Society and the Need for Historical Perspective," *Technology and Culture* 10 (October 1969): 529-34. I am grateful to Professor Dupree for an illuminating discussion of the relation of crafts, technology, and science, as seen in historical perspective.
5. Thomas H. Huxley, "On University Education," lecture at the opening of the Johns Hopkins University, in *Science and Education* (New York: P. F. Collier & Son, 1900), p. 215.
6. Jean Piaget, *The Moral Judgment of the Child*, trans. Marjorie Gabain (New York: Collier Books, 1962).
7. Jerome Bruner, *The Process of Education* (Cambridge: Harvard Univerity Press, 1960), p. 35.
8. W. T. Harris, *Psychologic Foundations of Education: An Attempt to Show the Genesis of the Higher Faculties of the Mind* (New York: D. Appleton, 1898), pp. 283ff. (work and play and the significance of play, pp. 317ff, (child revelation through play, p. 331; manual training).
9. John Dewey, *Democracy and Education* (New York: Macmillan, 1961; originally published 1916), ch. 15 ("Work and Play in the Curriculum"), and pp. 351-52 (on duty and interest).

16. The Confrontation of the Liberal and the Vocational-Technical

The contrast between the liberal and the vocational-technical (including the professional) has become a serious contemporary conflict in education. It concerns not merely curricular requirements but the structure of institutions. The relative position of the two has a long history in which marked shifts have taken place and different aspects of their relation come into view. The liberal, once the mainstay of education, especially higher education, now finds itself increasingly on the defensive. We have therefore, with an eye on that history, to untangle the several strands in the two concepts and move toward decision on specific curricular and structural issues. In this chapter we want to look at the meaning of the ideas of liberal and vocational-technical, how the confrontation changed in the ascent of the vocational-technical, and the case for the independence of the liberal today. The subject was previewed in discussing Dewey's view (chapter 3); here it is to be considered as a normative issue of our day, in the light of the discussions of learning and knowledge (chapters 11, 13).

Meanings of "Liberal" and "Vocational-Technical"

The idea of the liberal has many shades and has been involved in different antitheses. Sometimes the contrast is between the liberal and the narrow or technical; here the liberal involves a broader background of knowledge. Sometimes the liberal is itself narrowed to a set of subjects; it may then refer to the humanities as against the sciences, or more frequently to the liberal arts and sciences as against their application in engineering or business. In this usage, liberal education is sometimes assimilated to general education. Often liberal is contrasted with useful: the intrinsic value of liberal studies is stressed, sometimes perversely its lack of utility. (If the liberal arts and sciences are central to understanding people and their aspirations, to find them of no use is to take an illiberal interpretation of utility.) In a quite different usage, social ideas cluster around the idea of the liberal. While the political notion of the liberal as against the conservative is an unrelated one—except perhaps in the view of the liberal mind as broad and experimental or receptive to new ideas—the notion of liberal as elite and superior to the useful has also been pervasive. Hence the component of status that enters into the contrast of liberal and vocational is something to reckon with seriously in educational judgments. Finally, there is an increasing tendency to regard liberal as the opposite of illiberal, and to refer both to a way of treating ideas or material in thought and discussion, and so in teaching. The difference here is in spirit rather than subject matter or utility. A liberal treatment is more philosophical; it goes into wider meanings and assumptions and implications; it deals with human meanings as well as technical aspects, and with consequences as well as immediate relations. In this sense, there could be a liberal teaching of engineering or business, not only of English or history or science or philosophy. And there could be an illiberal teaching of literature or of Plato and Kant, as well as of calculus, if it focused on narrow detail.

While context will generally show which contrasts are intended, our major concern is with liberal in the sense of the liberal arts and sciences, both as subjects and as taught in a liberal rather than an illiberal spirit. It is most important therefore not to equate the liberal arts with the humanities alone. (Such a narrowing would exclude the scientific from the cultural and undo the perspective achieved in chapter 13.)

The idea of the vocational also has many components. A central one is the orientation to practice, and associated with that the reference to utility. Another stems from the idea of vocation as a chosen kind of occupation or work, hence vocational education as training for a particular form of work, as against general education. The vocational is sometimes associated with a different range of abilities and interests, those involved in applying and utilizing rather than the ones more oriented to knowledge and research. And sometimes the vocational is even identified with the insistence on utility and so contrasted with the spirit of general inquiry. The assumption that education is to be to some degree vocationally directed finds general expression in the widely held idea that education includes some preparation in one way or another for getting and being able to hold a job.

On the other hand, nothing in principle prevents the practical and the vocational from being taught in a liberal spirit. And the very notion of a vocation sometimes assumes an exalted character, for example, when a philosopher writes (as Fichte did) of the vocation of man. Moreover, as professionalization grows in all disciplines (including philosophy itself), all disciplines appear to assume a vocational character.

With such varieties of usage for both liberal and vocational-technical, clearly any problems of confrontation have to be addressed with attention to their special and particular historical contexts.

The Ascent of the Vocational-Technical Emphasis

What makes the idea of liberal versus vocational-technical education particularly serious is that education is at a crossroads, and moreover that it has inherited the shifts of many generations on the question. The problem of their relation has to be understood in historical perspective. It is well known that the classical-cultural education was limited to the upper stratum of society and that preparation for trade and special forms of work was introduced as an inferior kind of education. In the United States, during a period of great expansion (from roughly 1890 until after World War I), the place and character of vocational education became a serious philosophical issue. In chapter 3 we compared the views of W.T. Harris and John Dewey and suggested that while Dewey's position fitted more adequately the conditions of that period, a case could be made today for Harris's insistence on a common core of cultural education and self-formation for all, on the basis of Dewey's own philosophical position and the recognition of changed conditions. It is this view of the relation of liberal and vocational-technical that we want now to explore.

At the time Dewey was writing, the era of technological expansion was under way. Engineering, not merely natural science and mathematics, had to engage wider educational attention. Applied work in agriculture had already won a place, law was an old profession and moved more and more into schooling systems; eventually with the growth of corporations, schools of business administration were established. Doubtless much of this did not follow the lines that Dewey envisaged, and certainly he did not intend the separate vocational high schools of the many large cities in which, as late as the 1930s, students branded as not academically minded were set apart to complete compulsory schooling. Nevertheless, in one way or another, the technical and the vocational, the applied and the useful, entered the regular work of the schools. By midtwentieth century changes in the character of industrial production began to have an educational effect. The rapidity of technological change shifted focus from training for specific jobs to more fundamental training that would equip the student for a wider range of jobs and for shift of skills. This has obviously been accentuated by the electronic and computer revolutions in industry, which are extending automatization and robotic control of many productive processes. Comparable changes in social matters, requiring a broader educational perspective—for example, teacher training, social work—have a similar effect.

While in some of the European countries the technical and vocational are still struggling for educational equality, in the United States liberal education is on the defensive. Because the democratizing process has been carried further in U.S. education, the confrontation stands out there in sharper terms and is tied in with active movements in curricular and structural change. Hence the central issue may be fruitfully explored in this context. We deal then largely with higher or tertiary schooling in the United States.

From the time of the founding of the American republic, education was looked upon as a way of moving toward a better life for people, of understanding humankind and designing appropriate institutions. It played some part in social mobility, especially of immigrant groups. It provided the skills necessary for expansion of industry in the twentieth century. In the rapid expansion of the second half of the twentieth century, the job motif in vocationalism came to the fore. Statistical reports that those who had more and better schooling got more and better-paying jobs were often translated from a correlation into the instrumental judgment that the purpose of more education and particularly higher education was to ensure getting a good job. With the recession of the 1970s and the overcrowding of the favored professions, the value of higher education—cast in job terms— was increasingly brought into question. Student shifts to vocational studies became very marked, and within liberal arts itself from humanities to social science (for example, to fields with vocational possibilities, like psychology and economics). The concept of "career education"—that one's education in general after fundamentals should be oriented in a broad career direction and general education should come within that scope— has been periodically launched and relaunched under different names.[1]

The practical curricular form that such tendencies take may be seen in the various structures in higher education and in proposals concerning the future of liberal arts. Many colleges or schools of engineering, business, education, and the like have long taken in students from the beginning of their undergraduate work and given their own liberal arts subjects, though sometimes sending students to the associated liberal arts college in the university for those courses instead, while controlling requirements. Increasingly there are proposals that liberal arts colleges gear their own work in specialized career directions. They have long done this with respect to premedical and prelaw sequences, and in science departments the pressure to do advanced specialized work has often prevented students from getting a wider liberal education. The very demand for higher quality and more advanced work has at times itself had this narrowing effect; it is reenforced by the proliferation of specialities in advancing knowledge. The result is a transformation in the way of looking at liberal arts itself: it becomes seen as preparation for a teaching career or a research career. As new areas emerge and new professional fields take shape—for example, communications, urban problems and city planning, governmental and social services, nursing and health sciences, ecology, even curatorships for cultural institutions such as libraries and museums—the career orientation begins to cover and capture the liberal arts subjects in a new configuration.[2]

Let us take an extreme case of the argument. In a controversy over the status of the school of liberal arts vis-à-vis the professional schools at the University of Hawaii, Manoa, reported in the press, Chuck Gee, dean of the School of Travel Industry Management is quoted for the view that liberal and vocational education can be merged:

> Strangely enough, it is perhaps in a "professionally tainted" discipline like TIM which combines a liberal education foundation with a business management core, a specialized body of knowledge applied to tourism, and a practical internship to bridge classroom theory with industrial practice, where students can truly appreciate the relevance of liberal arts courses and meaningfully apply the substance of what is learned from art, music, literature, philosophy, sociology, geography, physical and natural sciences and the like put to real world use in hotel architecture, landscaping, environmental planning, management and organizational development, international marketing systems, food service planning and concern for public health, etc.[3]

He adds that in our economy today two out of three jobs are service based and the orientation of education to the service industries makes special sense. Polarization over the vocational-liberal issue here is futile.

This brief historical survey of the maturation of the problem brings us to a formulation in which it is no longer vocational education that is at issue. The question is rather the independence of liberal arts education in an age in which vocational and professional education have already solid institutional form and almost entrenched academic position, and in which the needs of society call for vocational education and the necessities of the larger numbers who have come into expanded schooling call for economic concern. Let us scan some of the arguments, old and new.

The Case for the Independence of Liberal Arts Education

One type of argument centers on whether application as such is inimical to the awakening of the intellect. Plato urged it long ago in extreme form (cf. chapter 3): he objected even to any idea of motion or construction in geometry as too earthy or too sensory. An angle would not be conceived as the rotation of one line away from another while maintaining a common end point but as a segment of a circle. Even such concepts would not be pure enough because they have a spatial reference. Plato would have been delighted by the formalization of abstract geometries and by programs of the logicization of arithmetic. On the other side have been the psychological claims for the concrete as stimulating interest, for the purposive as providing motivation that charges the intellect and provokes its exercise until broader problems take over. In addition, we may question whether intellectual interests and human interests are to be compartmentalized. Ideal energies wherever roused can carry throughout. Such themes characterized the movement of progressive education, which found nothing demeaning in teaching arithmetic by making change as a storekeeper, or learning geometry through carpentry, or an early introduction to science through the technical devices of the ordinary environment, or logic through computer programming.

Such issues, while important for pedagogy, are not most fundamental for our question of liberal versus vocational education. They probably require a complex rather than a single answer, with measured differences for personality types (for example, there appear to be at least two types of mathematical imagination, one inclined to abstraction, the other to spatial-topological imagery), or for different levels in the educational process. Certainly, if a particular approach through applied problems fits nursery school, it does not follow that it is required for introducing new subjects in college. Answers depend on psychological assumptions and call for educational experimentation.

A quite different argument for the independence of liberal education questions whether practice can come up to a professed ideal of encompassing the liberal arts. Pressures of the real world are such that if there are no strict rules or separate institutional forms irretrievable inroads will be made on basic liberal education. It will be sacrificed by degrees in a professional school as less important to the real business of life, whatever the formal requirements. If some years of liberal arts are required *before* vocational or professional school, they are treated seriously in fact as well as in name. If they are scattered during vocational school *within* its processes, they become second-class subjects. Whether this is in fact so, or unavoidably so, is a sociopsychological issue of contemporary life and schooling that requires empirical investigation. It is relevant to policy decision about the scope to be given career or vocational education. Evidence may be offered from even science teaching, not only from what happens to the humanities; for example, an introductory physics course in engineering schools may concentrate more on doing problems, while those in liberal arts schools more on the theoretical issues. Engineering and science courses in the universities may be compared to those in in-service educational programs run by such corporations as American Telephone & Telegraph: the latter are constantly monitored for their immediate relevance to the problems faced in daily work.[4] On the other hand, schools of business may insist on more general humanities courses—for example, not business ethics but ethics as a basic philosophy course. While the outcome of such investigation is interesting, the distance of the liberal from the practical could be set with conscious policy. The question would be whether that remains a hopeless ideal.

In the present situation, some defenders of the independence of the liberal arts continue the older arguments about the intrinsic values of the liberal arts. This conceptual approach was discussed earlier in dealing with the humanities (chapter 13), and it was argued that the concept of intrinsic value was inadequate to capture the fundamental issues. Moreover, the argument would not meet the question of independence, if indeed vocational and professional schools could encompass liberal arts teaching, just as they have in many cases embraced scientific research with success; for example, high-order research in basic fields is done in medical schools and in veterinary schools, and for that matter in laboratories of business corporations. This line of defense for separate liberal arts education often lapses into the older ideal of selecting and isolating an intellectual elite, as alone capable of the life of the mind. In some cases it is a conscious reaction against the progress of democratization and equalitarianism. Discounting the values of educational expansion and practical progress, it hopes at best for enclaves of the spirit in a largely hostile world.

I should like to suggest a quite different argument for the vigorous independence of the liberal arts and sciences. It takes us back through curriculum and the objectives of the curriculum into the relation of research and teaching. To focus on it separately, let us assume that the vocational and professional schools could achieve the professed ideal of imparting a liberal arts education to their vocationally oriented students. There is still something missing, which a liberal arts college can capture. The reason we do not see it immediately is because most of the accounts of the objectives of the curriculum are cast in terms of what they bring to the student. He or she acquires information and knowledge needed in the modern world, appropriate attitudes, interpersonal relations, ability to adjust and adapt, appreciation of the cultural heritage, and so forth. Certainly the statements of objectives by this time are written by educational experts, and they include all the latest progressive ideas as well as traditional values that are worthy of preservation. But strangely, they are all consumer oriented. They do not include attention to production, that is, to the objective of educating for the advancement of knowledge, for creation of new ways in society and art and progressive development in human life. It is just as in economic life: there is tremendous expenditure of energy and resources on technology that applies basic knowledge in production, but basic research that creates new knowledge from which future application may come is advanced only where it impinges fairly directly on some relatively immediate problem. This is true even in government expenditure of funds, not only in grants from private corporations. It is steered largely in terms of the problems facing health or agriculture or climate at one time or another, or even more, military preparation.

In the United States, if professionalism expanded to the extent indicated, the graduate school associated with the college of liberal arts and sciences would probably remain the chief center for basic research. It would, however, be under all the pressures of the professional schools to work on projects that concern them, just as industry or government has attracted science departments through grants into areas of its interest. Only independent and secure funding under the control of the researchers as a body can ensure the continuity of a balanced program of research.

The problems of basic research in relation to technology and industry are essentially parallel to those of liberal arts in relation to vocationalism, and can help our understanding of the latter. In both cases the danger has been a neglect of the role of intellectual work in advancing knowledge. In the past the venerated figures were an Edison or a Bell, who developed technologies out of the new basic research. Today an Einstein moves into the symbolic role. This reflects the change that has taken place in the relation of basic research and application; for the interval between basic discovery and application has diminished markedly and the connection is more evident, particularly after the discovery and application of nuclear energy. So too for liberal education: a freely exploratory education carried on at leisure with a primary interest in the materials and traditions and inner problems of the sciences and arts and humanities is the basic education out of which advancing knowledge and creation emerges. The various professions and vocations are then in a position to utilize it.

Such an understanding explains why liberal arts should not be viewed through the eyes of potential vocationalism. For example, work in philosophy may be looked at from the point of view of a future teacher, librarian, journalist, minister, book publisher, and even research as a profession. But none of these, even the last, captures the creative character of the work. This is not the previous appeal to intrinsic value or attractiveness of the work and its enjoyment, for that can happen in any field or any profession as giving scope for human energies; a business executive is proverbially functioning with zest and enjoyment, and a production manager could share in the delights of a craftsman or craftswoman. That every pursuit should be so arranged as to provide scope for free human abilities has been a long-standing ideal. It might be thought of as the democratization of intrinsic value. But there still remains the previous question whether in the long run the aim of advancing knowledge and creation is to be furthered through a selective process by which a more or less elite group is gathered in the liberal arts college and graduate school, while others in the professional fields are concerned with the knowledge-in-use. (There is, of course, no implication that creativity is excluded from knowledge-in-use, or from all practice, but this is not our present concern.)

This question marks a clear watershed in contemporary educational theory. We have noted the contrasting attitudes to the abilities and possibilities of people, in considering conservative and liberal critiques (chapter 4). A frankly elitist approach would gear the schools to a search for gifted children to be steered into liberal arts. It would regard the liberal arts school as the sun, with the other schools as planets. In brief, it would reproduce on the level of higher education the old dichotomy of the cultural schools and the trade schools. And it would do this on the underlying assumption that only a small part of the population is, after all, capable of the heights. The antielitist or democratizing view appears to come in three different strengths. The weakest is the insistence on equality of opportunity, the belief that many more creative spirits will be found and not lost if liberal education is the general path for all before the divergence into vocationalism of different sorts. This rests on the belief that antecedent testing does not really serve for adequate selection. (Even Einstein was not admitted to the technical institute to which he sought entry.) The widest liberal education will in fact raise the general intelligence. Statistical study of the effects of selective school systems and comprehensive school systems on the production of mathematicians suggests that there is no loss through the latter and in fact some are produced who would not have emerged under the selective system.[5] A stronger form of the democratizing view holds that a more educated general appreciation of creative work is necessary if society generally is to support and stimulate it. A larger critical audience, not a venerating populace that makes father figures out of scientists and Nobel prize winners is not only necessary but possible through more freely extended liberal education. The third or strongest form puts forward the ideal of extended creative participation—sometimes in almost rhapsodic tones, as in Walt Whitman's *Democratic Vistas*. There are all sorts of degrees of creativity in all sorts of media. An atmosphere of creativity is possible that draws the best from people; it has never been sufficiently tried. What some people do in dance and others do in music—as a widespread phenomenon—all could do more broadly if it were more broadly nourished and cultivated. What many do in bird-watching or in fish-tracking, many could do in matters of health, environmental science, social science, gathering of historical materials, and vast areas of intellectual and artistic expression if a generally educated population for the first time were to be the rule.

The necessity for the advancement of knowledge and culture, and for educating for it, seems then the crucial argument for maintaining the centrality of the liberal arts school in the contemporary curriculum, as independent and prior to vocational work. This means what is sometimes called, in the analogy of the tree, a "common trunk" before branching off. It should mean also the possibility of retracing steps for any who want to come back, but this should also hold for change from one profession to another. The question of how long a period is involved—whether two or three years—is a further one. This partly varies with the ability of the country to support education. In our consideration the work was assured in any case by the claim to include liberal arts materials in the professional schools.

The task of revising the curriculum to cultivate an aim of creativity in advancing knowledge and culture is no easy one. Some indications of such a movement are seen on the theoretical level. Fallibilism in the theory of science was an initial large step—the lesson increasingly evident in the history of science as well as in philosophy that scientific results at any time are open to subsequent revision and are not absolutely certain. In the contemporary world the rapid succession of unanticipated consequences and side effects of beneficial drugs and industrial products has made this point dramatically. Contemporary statements of the objectives of the curriculum have begun to include the formulation that students should not only learn to adapt to a changing world but also learn to criticize the institutions of their society and come to understand what needs to be changed. A critical attitude is the precursor of a creative attitude that suggests what might be a desirable change.[6]

Experienced teachers at all levels, once they focus on the problem of encouraging inventiveness and creativity, will doubtless have numerous ideas for revision. For example, in laboratory science work, how far is it really necessary to repeat old experiments, and how far can new (limited) problems be set so that genuine discovery will be involved? In social psychology this can readily be done because the gathering of data for statistical treatment (among the student body or in the neighborhood) often constitutes a ready field for a freshly devised study. Even in the library history studies of the lower grades the sense of fresh work to which the teacher does not know the answer and the class awaits what the student will bring (not whether it is the correct account to be judged so by the teacher) has a quite different impact. Focus on the advancement of knowledge could also characterize the study of bodies of knowledge themselves.

The case of knowledge has been used as the clearest, but obviously the same points apply to art and literature and culture generally. A focus on creativity as well as appreciation of great works will elicit more definitely the powers of the more gifted and enhance the powers of appreciation on the part of all. It will enable them to take part in a common culture rather than to be only spectators of it.

We are not, however, finished with our problem. The idea of advancing knowledge may be decisive for practice and for structuring contemporary education: it represents a consensus on a basic need. Behind it lie the different philosophical interpretations of knowledge and culture generally. We have partly glimpsed the diversity in considering the various attitudes to knowledge (chapter 13). The minimal one is in terms of utility: education by preparing people to exercise critical initiative and by stimulating inventiveness and creativity is constantly improving the great instrumentalities of our common well-being. This is, of course, no mean achievement. A more comprehensive account looks into the quality of life that knowledge and culture involve. Education for their advance makes possible a different kind of life. For example, Broudy sees the contemporary ideal of humanistic education as looking to "the mastery of the major intellectual disciplines to fashion the mind of man. To think the way the scientist does, to perceive and imagine as the artist and poet do—these are the contemporary goals of the humanities."[7] Once knowledge and culture are viewed in this way, Broudy finds, the idea of an academically overqualified population—so disturbing when education is tied to jobs—disappears. This vocational orientation speaks "a language in which a workingman reading Proust or Plato is a freak, and a plumber participating in a debate over space exploration is an eccentric. In a society in which philosophical plumbers are not oddities, academic overqualification will have to mean something other than not getting the job that corresponds to so many years of schooling or a specific degree. It will mean failure to use schooling to determine one's life by the resources of the cultural heritage in a society where such fulfillment is not inexorably tied to a particular kind of job."[8]

A broader account aims at a historical vista of humankind. In the older dream of Davidson, "Education, in the widest sense, may be defined as the upbuilding of a world in feeling or consciousness."[9] Education is self-making, and the fullest consciousness is not merely in tune with the advanced state of knowledge and culture in the progress of civilization, in the sense of finding a place within that world, but participates with full awareness in its community.[10] In shying away from the older moralistic language, and in realizing the conflict of values in the development of a complex world, we have sometimes forgotten the insights into human aspirations and the concept of a common humanity that these views expressed.

If liberal education remains associated with the ideal of building a community of persons, then it stands beyond the functional analysis in terms of roles and vocations—even where the role is itself that of preparing for research and the advancement of knowledge as a career.

Notes

1. For a searching exploration of the meaning and ambiguities of "career education" in relation to concepts of work, see Thomas F. Green, "Career Education and the Pathologies of Work," *Ethics and Educational Policy*, ed. Kenneth A. Strike and Kieran Egan (London: Routledge & Kegan Paul, 1978), pp. 211-22. Green distinguishes education for careers or work and education for jobs and employment.

2. E.g., Robert E. Marshak (then president of the City College of the City University of New York), "Problems and Prospects of an Urban Public University," *Daedalus* 2 (Winter 1975). He fuses liberal arts and professional studies in an urban educational model. He illustrates with career objectives of medicine, law, communications, and architecture, and suggests how an educational program of several years may be worked out, the earlier part of which will be carried through at the college and will embody an education that is liberal and career-minded and makes the student sensitive to the needs of an urban community. He stresses the way the motivation of the student would be optimized in such a program.

3. *Honolulu Star-Bulletin*, 23 May 1978.

4. *New York Times*, 7 January 1979, education sec., p. 15. Some of the courses at the company's center for technical education train for specific tasks; others are said to resemble university education, "except that they must be strictly aimed at problems of the phone company." A course modeled on university courses was dropped because "none of our engineers really needs the theory in the depth we were teaching." On the other hand, the relation to current problems of practice is immediate: "A.T.&T. classes change constantly. Instructors sometimes receive lengthy memorandums from research and development people and incorporate the material immediately and will change a class overnight to reflect it." There has been some development since then, as such centers have sought a status more comparable to formal schools.

5. See above, ch. 6, n. 3.

6. Cf. J. Passmore, "On teaching to be critical," in "Education and Reason," part 3 of *Education and the Development of Reason*, edited by R. F. Dearden, P. H. Hirst, and R. S. Peters (Boston: Routledge & Kegan Paul, 1972). Passmore notes how, as knowledge grows, instruction becomes greater and criticism is postponed to the university and graduate work. He proposes an earlier emphasis on critical and original or creative work—for example, using problems instead of exercises, dealing with cases in which we do not know the answer, and in general more critical discussion.

7. Harry S. Broudy, *The Real World of the Public Schools* (New York: Harcourt Brace Jovanovich, 1972), p. 49. Contrast this conception with the picture of scholarship as endearing eccentricity that we are too fond of to abandon, in Robert Paul Wolff, *The Ideal of the University* (Boston: Beacon Press, 1969), pp. 5-6.

8. Broudy, *The Real World of the Public Schools*, p. 215.

9. Thomas Davidson, *A History of Education* (New York: Charles Scribner's Sons, 1900), p. 5.

10. A reference to life as a whole is central. Dewey warns (*Democracy and Education* [New York: Macmillan, 1961; originally published 1916], pp. 246f.) that the demand for a variety of experiences may easily become simply a "check and balance theory of experience" in which a multitude of interests clamor for a place, and in the congestion education is forgotten.

Appendix A
The Social Character of Dewey's Philosophy

A synoptic view of the social depth of Dewey's philosophy calls for his view of *society and institutions*, of *human relations*, of *history and development*, of *the human good and justice*.[1]

Dewey's basic outlook is institutional and societal rather than exclusively individualistic. In this sense he is linked to the Continental tradition that looked to cultural and sociohistorical patterns to understand the individual and the individual's ways, and he shares the common effort with U.S. social theorists in the early part of the century who—in their concern with habits and customs, institutions and ways of life, the influence of environment and occupation and tradition and opportunity—shaped modern social science. For the most part, however, philosophy followed the individualistic model generalized from the leading noninstitutional economics in which social forms were to be reduced to the behavior of individuals acting out of personal desires and preferences. It has taken moral and social philosophy a long time to realize that many of its perplexities and impasses were the consequence of the individualistic model it used rather than any inherent puzzles in the problems. To take a familiar and striking example, the long debate in moral philosophy about why I am obliged to keep a promise became mired in the antithesis of utilitarianism and intuitionism—whether it is an overall advantage to keep a promise or it is intuitively or self-evidently obligatory. Only recently have moral philosophers begun to analyze promising itself as a *practice*, that is, as an institutional form in which obligations are constitutive.[2] To ask why a person ought to keep a promise is like asking why a bank cashier should process a check (whether or not the cashier likes the handwriting but not whether or not the cashier finds its numbers illegible) or whether a bus driver should continue on the route in a bus labeled "Center City" when he or she would much rather go toward the suburbs. Neither intuition nor utilitarian calculation is required to discern the obligation, though the reckoning may enter into justifying one institution or practice against another. But that is institution-making; it is not the discovery of personal obligation.

Dewey's institutional focus does not stop with the separate institutions themselves. No institution stands alone or has an isolated history and justification. It constitutes an ongoing enterprise of the society, more or less responsive to its problems and needs and the degree to which people have become sufficiently conscious of these to organize constructive efforts—they have become *publics* operative to express their interests and concerns.[3] Today the needs, concerns, problems, interests, and publics have begun even to transcend the national society. In many cases, to understand our institutions we have to think in terms of a world society and what is going on there.

Now, Dewey's view of society and its institutions even as suggested so far has an obvious bearing on his educational approach. Education is necessary because of the birth and death of members in a social group. It transmits the shared experience and ways of the group. Schooling or formal education arises as societies become more complex in structure and resources; there are continuities between socialization, enculturation, and schooling. Education operates in an environment to call out certain responses, the environment involving the social as well as rearrangement of the physical. It is extended through use of language to transmit ideas, as things gain meaning when used in shared experience or joint action. When accumulated experience in considerable part is written and transmitted through symbols, schools come into existence and become a special environment. Teaching takes shape as stimulus, learning as growth. The nature of children—their active interests and capacity to learn—shapes what guidance can accomplish. Dewey thus integrates questions of origins, motivating factors, general possibilities and limits, and dominating normative perspective.

Dewey's view of human relations is basically transactional rather than contractual. The individualist-voluntarist approach presupposed an isolated individual of a given inner nature who gradually builds up external relations to satisfy inner needs and desires, distinguishes by experience (in the association of its ideas) what to accept or reject. The voluntarist element, that obligations or commitments arise only from the individual will or from agreement among individuals, has remained central in ethics and social theory. On the other hand, in a transactional orientation the development of the self or the individual is dependent on the kind of transactions, that is, organism-environment-other persons, that are constantly taking place. Lungs and breathing are part of a homeostatic system that includes the air and the rest of the human body; there is a functional interdependence and constant interactive changes. So human life manifests qualitative and functional dependence on the transactional processes of persons, environment, and societies. This transactional orientation is grounded in a specific psychology of human action that Dewey worked through early and that once and for all made it impossible for him to analyze any issue simply in terms of abstractions or feelings or will-acts or inborn instincts—the run-of-the-mill counters of the philosophical tradition. In the famous essay "The Reflex Arc Concept in Psychology" (1896) Dewey criticized dualisms as well as atomistic and simplistic reductions; human behavior is the integrating reconstruction of a field in which a conflict has arisen and a reintegration is demanded.[4] It is a kind of protocybernetic conception that denies the isolation of stimulus, central process, response, and that insists on the description of what ensues in behavior as a function of the total organism interacting in environment. This early schema was rounded out in Dewey's subsequent contact with the social sciences. It has at least three vital consequences. First, it generates the idea of a problem situation as underlying inquiry, so that we may never rest content with a merely surface description nor with an abstract treatment of an answer; we have to see both question and proposed answer in the full context of what is going on and what problems generate the inquiry and what specific criteria for satisfactory solution are implicit. Second, the psychological schema turns us quite directly to the development of a self as the outcome of a social-transactional process, supported by the whole structure of the common life and its patterns. Third, it warns us against taking as absolutes the innumerable dichotomies that have beset philosophical inquiry, whether mind and body, stimulus and response, means and ends, intrinsic and instrumental value, theory and practice, work and leisure, liberal and vocational, and others in endless succession.

These three consequences are directly relevant to education.[5] For example, instead of listing aims of education as an institution—a favorite occupation in abstractions—Dewey examines institutional functioning in the total interpersonal learning context. Again, on a topic like that of discipline, he rejects the repressive processes that rest on assuming an inherent recalcitrance in the nature of the child. This does not license the permissiveness of, he says, a pleasant bait hitched to an alien material. It is the self-discipline that comes from uniting learning with interest in the sense of the intelligent carrying forward of purposeful activity; self-discipline is a function of appropriate self-development. As for the caution against dualisms, this is to be found in numerous educational topics. It underlies the integration of the intellectual and the practical, that is, of thinking and doing, in education; the distinction emerges as rather one of enlightened and unenlightened activity than of two separate activities. The continuum of ends and means that he elaborates in his ethics saves him from dividing learning into the occupations of leisure and culture on the one hand and of work and instrumentality and vocation on the other. Indeed, he sees the conflict of the liberal and the vocational as the expression of class-divided society, with a presumably superior education reserved for the upper class. Yet it is a mistake to see Dewey as submerging all education in instrumentalities; he is perfectly ready to affirm that both arithmetic and poetry ought to be appreciated at times as enjoyable experiences. Value and enjoyment, as in his treatment of aesthetic experience, are not limited to so-called ultimate ends but can characterize all successful energies.

Another important aspect is the centrality of change.[6] It is not merely that everything changes—the important point is not just Heracliteanism but the coefficient of Heracliteanism, the rate of change. The rate of change affects not merely the content and feeling of human life but the concepts appropriate for dealing with it. The emphasis on method and on intelligence, whether in dealing with the growth of science and technology or with ethics and social change, and the attack on fixed goals and rules in favor of principles of analysis presuppose a rate of change (and an accompanying complexity) such as to make fixed modes impossible. But even method presupposes some degree of constancy. If the rate of change were too great, the best we could have would be slight clues, broad virtues, abstract ideals. Dewey's coefficient of Heracliteanism is thus a middling one. Institutions are not amorphous, for they correspond to dependable stabilities for given periods. But the sense of change is strong enough to ensure that eternal vigilance is required, the view of present experience is never smug, categories are always on trial, and the refinement of method is never at an end. The recognition of change is not, however, to be a passive witnessing of events. It is guided by an activism that seeks intervention and control.

All this is obvious enough in education today. A century ago formal schooling was limited to a small part of the population, and most people got what learning they needed in practical techniques in work or through apprenticeship. Today, in the industrially developed countries of Europe and North America, mass schooling has been instituted, extending in the last thirty years on a broad scale into higher education, to keep the society going—in production, economic regulation, political and social life. Even that is not enough, and the pace of change calls for constant reeducation in professions, crafts, and social relations. Continuing education is added to earlier schooling; education through out-of-school procedures—books, television, newspapers, on-the-job training, and all the rest—now furnishes a large segment of the needed learning. In schooling itself new devices, such as computer-based teaching and improved tape recording and visual methods, are making inroads—not to speak of the constant change and growth in the body of knowledge itself. To deal with all this requires an educational outlook that can accommodate change and actively attempt to direct it without being thrown into turmoil. Dewey developed this outlook at a time when rapid industrialization was having a serious impact on the rural setting, and he called for an active participation of people rather than the passive reception of older ways. Technical development itself seemed to him a concrete embodiment of a growing social intelligence, a kind of knowledge institutionalized in social practice, that furnishes instruments for greater historical self-management.

Finally, there is Dewey's conception of the good and of justice. In his ethical theory[7] the good is a concept for critical evaluation of appetite and desire, of ends and means and the quality of the life that is lived, the human capacities and interests that are given harmonious expression in a community, the shared experience of people. Justice, like right, is a concept for evaluating the claims and mutual pressures of people in the groups and organizations in which life is carried on. The ideal of justice involves a society that supports the full achievement and expression of the capacities of individuals. The category of justice is thus distinct from that of the good, but the content of justice requires evaluation in terms of the good life. This approach differs from a contemporary rights framework, which treats of any ethical problem by ferreting out first the rights of the individuals involved. The latter is congenial to the older concept of the atomic individual with natural or human rights. But Dewey employs a social concept of individuality—an ideal of character that we seek to cultivate with our social resources, primarily education in the broad sense of that term. It embraces both the good and justice: good in the sense of a total social effort to bring to fruition the distinctive powers of human beings, and justice in the sense that this is an effort for all human beings. Such a concept of individuality, so fashioned, is not alien to that of community; shared experience is an integral part of it.

Notes

1. Dewey's collected works are being published by Southern Illinois University Press under the editorship of Jo Ann Boydston. Among the works relevant for his ideas discussed in this appendix are *Middle Works*, vol. 12, *Reconstruction in Philosophy* (1920); vol. 14, *Human Nature and Conduct* (1922); and his most important work in educational philosophy, vol. 9, *Democracy and Education* (1916).

2. The treatment of promising as a practice is found in John Rawls, "Two Concepts of Rules," *Philosophical Review* 14, no. 3 (1955): 3-32. For a similar social approach to other ethical ideas, see Philippa R. Foot, "Approval and Disapproval," in *Law, Morality and Society: Essays in Honour of H.L.A. Hart*, ed. P.M.S. Hacker and J. Raz (Oxford: Clarendon Press, 1977), pp. 229-46.

3. Dewey, *The Public and Its Problems* (1927).

4. Dewey, "The Reflex Arc Concept in Psychology," *Psychological Review* (July 1896): 357-70 (in *The Early Works* 5:96-109).

5. These are discussed in Dewey's *Democracy and Education*; see, for example, chs. 1-4.

6. For the role of change in relation to ideas, see Dewey's *Reconstruction in Philosophy* (1920); for the methodological consequences, see particularly, *The Quest for Certainty* (1929).

7. For the systematic presentation of ethical theory, see Dewey and Tufts, *Ethics*, rev. ed. (1932), particularly part 2, "Theory of the Moral Life."

Appendix B
"Aims of Education"—a Comparison instead of a Controversy

Usually writers who discuss the aims of education do not feel called on to discuss what an aim is. For example, A.N. Whitehead entitles a leading paper in a collection devoted mainly to the intellectual side of education "The Aims of Education," but he does not ask what an aim is nor say why he introduces normative questions by means of aims; he says immediately that we should aim at producing men of a certain sort, and warns against inert ideas.[1] Compare this with John Dewey's chapter "Aims in Education" in *Democracy and Education*.[2] To speak of aims "in" education rather than "of" education is doubtless intentional; Dewey does not believe that institutions have aims, only persons, for an aim directs activity with foresight of results. With an eye on the pupils, Dewey asks how there can be the continuity of aims rather than just a serial aggregate of acts: "To talk about an educational aim when approximately each act of a pupil is dictated by the teacher, when the only order in the sequence of his acts is that which comes from the assignment of lessons and the giving of directions by another, is to talk nonsense."[3] In short, to talk properly of aims is to talk of the kind of order in the activity of the pupil. If Whitehead does not want inert ideas, clearly Dewey does not want inert pupils; it is not the business of education to coerce inertness. But Dewey is not simply using the concept of aim as a vehicle for value judgments about personality. Where Whitehead was prepared to take "aim" in the ordinary sense, Dewey looks to the psychology behind it. In short, "aim" is a theory-laden term grounded in a psychological theory of thought and action; and inasmuch as such a theory tells what humans are up to and under what conditions they are functioning successfully, it has normative bearings for ethics, social theory, and education. "Acting with an aim is all one with acting intelligently. To foresee a terminus of an act is to have a basis upon which to observe, to select, and to order objects and our own capacities. To do these things means to have a mind—for mind is precisely intentional purposeful activity controlled by perception of facts and their relationships to one another."[4] Dewey examines what is involved in having a plan and discerning means and obstructions, and in taking account of resources and difficulties; all this is what is meant by "having an aim or purpose." If such a schema of relationships for the concept of aims is employed, to tackle Dewey on the use of "aims" would require an account of his psychological theory, apart from any proposal to deal with the normative consequences in some other way.

R.S. Peters reports that he has had a long-standing puzzlement about the concept.[5] He finds that talk of aims makes us too target minded. Contrasted with Dewey, whom he criticizes for taking aim to be equivalent to purpose, he limits the notion of an aim to a situation in which we concentrate on an effort to hit some distant target;[6] but he does not, like Dewey, see the target as an end-in-view that is serving to solve some underlying problem and that is to be evaluated and altered as it does this successfully or unsuccessfully. By narrowing "aim," in effect, to a phenomenon of consciousness, Peters sidesteps the bulk of the Deweyan analysis that relates the consciousness to underlying conditions. He is turning to another question—certainly legitimate—of what are the conditions under which we raise questions of aims in the narrower sense. And here he concludes that to ask what a person is aiming at is not to demand an explanation for what the person is doing but to ask the person "to specify his objective more precisely and to concentrate his efforts accordingly."[7] Peters is thus using a different psychological approach from Dewey's; as presented in his *Concept of Motivation*, it is an approach through the analysis of ordinary language in relation to behavior.[8] In spite of these differences, it is interesting to note that Peters's rejection of the concept as yielding too external an objective for education parallels Dewey's insistence that educational process has no end beyond itself.

Like "aim," the notions of purpose, interest, task, and so on seem to be theory laden, and psychology is in little position today to give a definitive theory in terms of which psychological language might be standardized. It follows that where there are varying usages, there are likely to be varying theories; hence a certifying theory for a particular usage needs to be explicit.

Notes

1. In A.N. Whitehead, *The Aims of Education and Other Papers* (New York: Mentor, 1949; originally published 1929).
2. John Dewey, *Democracy and Education* (New York: Macmillan, 1961; originally published 1916), ch. 8.
3. Ibid., pp. 101-2.
4. Ibid., p. 103.

5. R.S. Peters, "Aims of Education—A Conceptual Inquiry," in *The Philosophy of Education*, ed. R.S. Peters (New York: Oxford University Press, 1973), p. 40. See also his *Authority, Responsibility and Education* (New York: Eriksson-Taplinger, 1959), pp. 83-95, and *Ethics and Education* (London: Allen & Unwin, 1966), pp. 27-30.

6. Peters, "Aims of Education," p. 13.

7. Ibid., p. 14.

8. Cf. R.S. Peters, *The Concept of Motivation* (London: Routledge & Kegan Paul; New York: Humanities Press, 1958). Peters is explicit about the importance of approaching psychology initially through ordinary language: "Ordinary language enshrines all sorts of distinctions, the fine shades of which often elude the clumsiness of a highly general theory" (p. 49). And again, "The point of looking closely at ordinary usage, if one is a psychologist, is that it often provides a clue to distinctions which it is theoretically important to take account of. We know *so much* about human beings, and our knowledge is incorporated implicitly in our language. Making it explicit would be a more fruitful preliminary to developing a theory than gaping at rats or grey geese" (p. 50).

Index

Absolutism in relation to relativism, 169-70
Academic freedom, 101
Affiliation needs, 145-46
Affirmative action in education, 123-26
Africa, 17. *See also* South Africa
Aims of education, 331-33 (Appendix B); senses of "aim," 331-32
Alger, C.F., 294
American Civil Liberties Union, 78
Analytic philosophy, 4-5; ordinary language and, 333n.8
Anarchism, 72; critique of schools, 79-81; governing ideal, 81; in the counter-culture, 197; on mutuality and discipline, 279
Anthropological approach, 7-21 (chap. 1); advantages, 7-8
Appadurai, Arjun, 12
Archimedes, 261
Aristophanes, 185, 186
Aristotle, 35, 65, 154; on relation of agent and patient, 205-6; 219, 222, 235, 242-43, 248, 261, 278, 302
Arts in the curriculum, 301-3
Augustine, 13
Autonomy, 158-65; and individualism, 158-59; of morality, 159-60; Moore's formulation of, 159-60; and freedom, 160-61; as social experiment in individualism, 162-63; criteria for assessing experiment, 164-65

Bacon, Francis, 261, 265
Baier, Kurt, 173
Basic research, 15, 51, 304; and liberal education, 319-21
Basic skills: in the curriculum, 304-5; testing and remediation, 305-6; order of learning and analytic order, 306; reading, 307-8; philosophic concerns in, 308-10; play and games, 310
Bateson, Gregory, 11, 20

Beck, Clive, 255
Benedict, Ruth, 19, 167, 174
Bentham, Jeremy, 31, 115, 135
Bergson, Henri, 223, 235, 264, 273
Billington, David, 226, 236
Biological basis of education, 326
Bird, Caroline, 201
Bloom, B.S., 38
Body-mind relations. *See* Mind-body relations
Bosanquet, Bernard, 67, 68
Bowles, Samuel, 86
Bradley, F.H., 67
Bronowski, Jacob, 273
Broudy, Harry, 69, 86, 181, 201, 323, 324; defining education, 178
Brown decision, 19, 119
Bruner, Jerome, 243-44, 248, 306, 311
Buber, Martin, 223, 235, 239, 263-64, 273
Burke, Edmund, 73-74, 82, 86, 278

Carnoy, Martin, and Levin, H.M., 86
Cartesian rationalism, 11
Certification, 25
Change: Dewey on its centrality, 328
Chazan. B.I., 292, 293
Christianity, 17, 115, 135, 296; Catholic, 97; early Protestant, 162
Citizenship education, 284-85
Cold War, 19, 81, 106
Coleman, James, 126
Community, need for sense of, 145-47
Comparison as modern consciousness, 35-36
Competency tests, 305-6
Competitiveness, 24, 31-33; need to mute, 143-45; and free enterprise, 144-45; and moral education, 287-88
Compulsory schooling, 56-59
Conant, James, 81
Conditioning, 217, 238-39

335

336 Interpreting Education

Conservatism: critiques of schools, 72-77; New-Conservatism (or Libertarianism), 81-83; comprehensive types (Hogg, Nisbet, Oakeshott), 15, 21, 38, 75-77, 86, 127, 241-44, 248, 278, 292
Counts, George, 18, 21
Crafts in the curriculum, 299-300
Creativity: in art, 302; as educational aim, 322
Criticism: and social action, 3; of schools, 61-87 (chap. 4); importance of underlying social outlook in, 72; in art education, 302
Crittenden, Brian, 173
Cyrenaics, 164

Dante, 37, 115
Darwin, Charles, 280; Darwinism, 257; Social Darwinism, 95
Davidson, Thomas, 51, 61, 323, 324
Dearden, R.F., 173, 236, 324
Democratization, 138-41; concept of democracy, 139; democracy and students, 199-200; cultivating democratic attitudes, 239; democratic equalitarianism, 287-88
Democritus, 41
Deutero-learning, 11
Dewey, John, 4, 5, 12, 43, 60, 83, 87, 99, 161, 173, 181, 217, 236, 239, 262, 273, 280, 292, 310, 311, 315, 324, 331-32; compared with Plato, 44-49; on change and educational policy, 49-51; defining education, 177, 179; on the psychology of consciousness, 231-32; social character of his philosophy, 325-30 (Appendix A)
Dichotomies: formal-material, 228-29; sensory-intellectual, 229-30; fact-value, 230; cognitive-affective, 230; in the separation of science and humanities, 269-71
Discipline. *See* Permissiveness
Division of labor, 29
Driberg, J.H., 12, 20
Dupree, Hunter, 311
Durkheim, Emile, 275, 278, 292

Eddy, Elizabeth, 86
Edel, Abraham, 105, 126, 127, 151, 220, 236, 294

Education: variable content of, 9; character patterns, 10; orientations, 10-12; definitions attempted, 177-81; Dewey's formulation, 177-78; Broudy's, 178; McClellan's, 178; Peters's, 178-79; issues in the different formulations, 179; why the differences, 179-81; policy role of definitions, 180-81; changes in educational questions, 253-55; philosophical responsibilities of educators different from those of philosophers, 42-43
Empathy, 305
Enculturation and schooling, 13
Ends and means, 65
Engels, Friedrich, 68
Ennis, R.H., 126, 235
Equality: history of ideal, 112-18; in educational theory, 118-26; alternative patterns of, 119-21; of opportunity and results, 121-23; and affirmative action, 123-26; expanding equality, 136-38; and student treatment, 199
Erikson, E.H., 293
Evaluation, modes of, 66-67
Existentialism, 5

Ferrer schools, 80
Fichte, J.G., 314
Firth, Raymond, 20
Flanagan, O.J., 294
Flew, Anthony, 39, 126
Flower, Elizabeth, and Murphey, M.G., 60
Foot, Philippa, 329
France: technical education in, 50, 200; press in, 96
Franklin, Benjamin, 34
Freedom, 161
Freire, Paolo, 248
French Revolution, ideals of, 79, 147
Freud, Sigmund, 73, 92, 218, 280; Freudian psychology, 91, 161
Friedman, Milton, 82, 86
Fromm, Erich, 280, 292

Games, 310
Gandhi, M.K., 110, 279
Gee, Chuck, 317
Gilligan, Carol, 164, 174, 293
Gintis, Herbert, 86, 87
Giroux, Henry, 294

Global perspective, 135-36
Goldschmidt, Walter, 20
Goodman, Paul, 25, 81, 86
Grading: 23-39 (chap. 2); and evaluation, 23-26; and meritocracy, 26-28; and certification, 28-31; educational distortions in, 30-31; competition and credentialing, 31-33; and effort, 34; and achievement, 34-35
Graubard, Allen, 86
Great Books movement, 47-48
Green, T.F., 205, 220, 225, 236, 324
Greer, Colin, 86
Griffen, W.L., and Marciano, John, 105
Gross, Beatrice and Ronald, 86

Hallowell, A.I., 10, 20
Hansot, Elizabeth, 201
Harris, W.T., 50, 61, 310, 311, 315
Hegel, G.W.F., 229
Heraclitus, 41, 45, 48
Hidden curriculum, 71; in administrative structure, 288-89
Hinduism, 97
Hirst, P.H., 173, 205, 207, 220, 223-24, 227, 229, 235, 236, 248, 324
Hobbes, Thomas, 146
Hogg, Quintin, 75, 86
Human nature theory: in Plato, 73 ff.; in Burke, 73 ff.; in Liberalism, 77-78; in Anarchism, 79-80; in views of discipline, 277-81
Humanistic quality, 147-50; in education, 148-49; not necessarily elitist, 149; relation to equality, 149-50. *See also* Naturalistic humanism
Humanities, 258-59, 268-72; subject-matters, 268-69; relation to social science, 269; contrasts of scientific fact and humanistic value assessed, 269-71; Newton and Shakespeare compared, 271; intrinsic value and utility, 271-72
Husén, Torsten, 126
Hutchins, R.M., 47-48, 60
Huxley, Julian, 68
Huxley, T.H., 68, 257, 273, 304, 311

Ideals: and their assessment, 107-27 (chap. 6); defined, 108; criteria for assessing, 108-12; evaluation of equality, 112-18; equality in educational theory, 118-26; drive toward ideal analyzed, 36-37; ideal and the workable compared, 37-38; the ideal in pedagogical encounter, 242
Ideology, 89-95; corrective view of, 90-92; relativist view of, 92-93; comparison, 93; evaluation from perspective of advancing knowledge, 94-95; corresponding institutional structures, 95ff.
Illich, Ivan, 31, 38, 69, 80-81, 85, 86
Immediacy in cognition, 263-64
Impartiality: as educational objective, 99-100; differentiated from neutrality, 100
Indeterminacy in science and morals compared, 168-70
India, literacy in, 18
Individualism: inroads on community, 145-47; and autonomy, 158-59; and relativism, 170
Indoctrination, 219-20, 237-38
Intellect, 44-45; different interpretations of, 48
Intent vs. causality, 217-20
Intrinsic value, 65-66
Islamic fundamentalism, 110, 164, 167

Jackson, Jesse, 34
Jackson, P.W., 86
Jacobovits, Immanuel, 273
James, Williams, 217, 218, 222, 235, 308
Jefferson, Thomas, 81
Jencks, Christopher, 127
Job performance as educational objective, 24

Kant, Immanuel, 67, 104, 115, 135, 153, 157, 159, 230, 278-79, 284, 292, 293
Kirk, Russell, 86
Kleinberger, Aharon F., 126
Kluckhohn, Clyde, 10, 20
Kluckhohn, Florence, 10; and Strodbeck, F.L., 20
Knowing: Ryle's analysis of two types, 221-22; multiplication of types, 222-23; thesis of radically different forms, 222-23; Hirst's version, 223-24; opposing continuity thesis, 224; importance of the issue, 225; how stable are forms, 225-28; varying classification, 227; educational

evidence unreliable, 228; underlying assumptions, 228-32; social character of knowledge, 232-35; advancement of knowledge as basic educational aim, 142, 319-21
Kohlberg, Lawrence, 283-84, 293-94
Kozol, Jonathan, 86
Krige J.D., 21
Krimerman, L.I., 56-58, 61
Kropotkin, Peter, 292
Kuhn, T.S., 93, 265, 273

Langford, Glenn, 209; and O'Connor, D.J., 220, 248
Latin 14
Lazarsfeld, P.F., and Thielens, Wagner, 21, 106
Learning and teaching. *See* Teaching and learning
Leeds, Anthony, 11, 17, 20, 21
Leeper, R.W., 236
Levellers, 114
Lewin, Kurt, Lippitt, Ronald, and White, R.K., 248
Lewis, C.I., 217
Liberal education: meanings of *liberal*, 313-14; independence of, 317-23; and vocational, 49-51; conflict with vocational as expressing class division, 238
Liberalism: critique of the schools, 77-79; present difficulties, 78-79; traditional values, 79
Libertarianism: critique of the schools, 81-83; in critique of compulsory schooling, 56-59
Linton, Ralph, 12, 20
Lippmann, Walter, 100, 106
Locke, John, 15, 97, 115, 229
Love, conditional and unconditional, 27-28
Lucian, 41, 60

McCarthyism, 4, 99, 103, 189
McClellan, J.E.: defining education, 178-79, 181, 220, 237, 241, 247, 248
McClennan, B.E., 291
Machiavelli, Niccolo, 15
MacIntyre, Alasdair, 278, 292
McKowan, H.C., 292
Magaino, R.F., 106
Maine, Henry, 151

Mainstreaming, 52-56; building community in, 55; activist attitudes, 55-56
Mannheim, Karl, 91, 92, 105
Marcuse, Herbert, 280, 292
Marshak, R.E., 324
Martin, J.R., 222, 235
Marx, Karl, 92, 194, 280; Marxian theory (Marxism), 5, 6, 7, 51, 68, 72, 76, 79, 91, 110; critique of the schools, 83-85; historical emphasis, 83; two lines, 84
Mastery learning, 38n.5, 127
Mathematics: Plato's vs. Dewey's views, 45, 48-49
Mead, Margaret, 10, 13, 18-20, 193-94, 201
Meritocracy: and grading, 26-28; equality of opportunity and equality of results, 117, 122-23
Michels, Robert, 47
Mill, J.S., 38, 65, 99, 162, 164, 174; on merit, 27; on the priority of learning, 208-9, 220, 296
Montefiore, Alan, 105
Moore, G.E., 67, 68, 159-60, 263, 265, 271-73
Mind-body relations, 295-97
Moral agenda: the concept and search for criteria, 129-30
Moral development: Kohlberg's theory, 283-84, 293n.15, 17; Erikson's pattern of development, 293n.16
Moral education: moral standards confused, 275; underlying transformations, 276; four current approaches, 281-85; conception of morality required, 285-86; proposals for today, 286-91; treatment of controversial areas, 290-91

Naturalistic humanism, 53-56
Nazism, 91, 110, 164, 167
Neo-Hegelians, 66, 75
Neutrality, differentiated from impartiality, 100
New York Times: policy on impartiality, 96
Newspaper, contrasting forms of, 96
Nietzsche, Friedrich, 113
Nisbet, Robert, 38, 75, 86, 127, 278, 292
Normative: in educational theory, 17-19; establishment of norms in education, 65-174 (part II)
Nozick, Robert, 82

Oakeshott, Michael, 15, 21, 75-77, 86, 241-44, 248
Oldenquist, Andrew, 294

Parsons, Talcott, and Shils, Edward, A., 20
Passmore, John, 324
Permissiveness: and the repressive, 277-81; opposing interpretations, 278-81
Persons, respect for, 27, 53, 56, 287
Peters, R.S., 173, 181, 218, 220, 223, 235, 236, 271, 324, 332-33; defining education, 178-80
Pettitt, G.A., 8, 13, 19, 20
Phenomenology, 5, 308
Philosophical systems: commitment to, 41-43; contrasting philosophies and their implications, 44-47; under changing conditions, 49-52; benefits and cautions, 52-60
Physical education, 295-99
Piaget, Jean, 113, 293, 306, 311
Pincoffs, E.N., 191, 201
Plato, 29, 38, 43, 159, 261, 278-79, 296, 317; and Dewey compared, 44-49, 54; theory of human nature, 73
Play, 310
Pleasures, classification of, 296
Plutarch, 261, 273
Politicization in schools, 89-106 (chap. 5); case for nonpoliticized schools, 101-5
Politics and social control, Plato's vs. Dewey's views of, 46-48
Positivism, 265
Practices as social. *See* Social
Pratte, Richard, 151
Priestley, Joseph, 161
Professions, 301
Progressive education, 19, 47, 281
Pugh, G.E., 39
Purpose. *See* Intent
Pythagoreanism, 41

Quality: in learning, 240-41; of life, 148; role of knowledge in, 323. *See also* Humanistic quality

Raths, L.E., Harmin, Merrill, and Simon, S.B., 292-93
Rationality, 153-58; unpacking the concept, 154ff.; how extended, 155-56; value components in, 156-57; and universality, 157; possible directions of growth, 158; rational method in morality, 282-83
Rattray, R.S., 20
Rawls, John, 26, 38, 329
Raywid, M.A., 103, 106, 151
Reading, 307-8; Oakeshott on, 76; reading readiness, 219
Redfield, Robert, 10, 20
Reimer, Everett, 31, 38
Relativism: moral, 165-72; formulation of, 166; stance of giving an account and evaluating, distinguished, 166-67; indeterminacy in science and in morality compared, 168-69; on diminishing indeterminacy, 170-72
Religion: institutional forms contrasted, 96-97
Repressiveness in morality. *See* Permissiveness
Rhodes, Cecil, 36
Rorty, Richard, 273
Roszak, Theodore, 263, 273
Rubinstein, David, and Stoneman, Colin, 126
Russell, Bertrand, 136, 222, 235
Ryle, Gilbert, 221, 223, 225, 231, 235, 254

Sagoff, Mark, 39
St. Louis Hegelians, 50-51
Salvadori, M.G., 226, 236
Sanctions in schooling, 12-13
Santayana, George, 60, 225-26, 236, 266, 273
Sartre, Jean-Paul, 236
Schachter, Oscar, 151
Scheffler, Israel, 248, 293
Schooling: differentiated from education, 8; social functions, 14-16
Schurz, Carl, 136
Science: entry into curriculum, 257-58; contrasted with humanities, 258-59; objectives in teaching, 260-61; values in scientific knowledge, 261-63; revolts against, evaluated, 263-65; historical approach to, 265-66; continuity with other disciplines, 265-66; Santayana on relations of myth, religion, and science, 266; student attitudes to, 267
Self in teaching models, 239-40

Sex education, 297
Skinner, B.F., 238
Smart, Barbara, 248
Smith, Adam, 161, 279, 292
Snow, C.P., 228, 258, 273
Social: practices, idea of, 325; character of knowledge, 232-34; character of Dewey's philosophy, 325-30 (Appendix A)
Socrates, 185, 242, 254, 268, 282, 296
Soltis, J.F., 292
South Africa, 17, 98, 167
Spencer, Herbert, 82
Sport, 297-99
Stoicism, 115, 135
Strike, K.A., 105; and Egan, Kieran, 106, 126, 151, 173, 273, 324
Students: and the generation gap, 193-94; alienation of, 194; movement of 1960s analyzed, 195-98; and equality, 199; and democracy, 199-200; and technology, 200; and excellence, 200
Summerhill school, 80

Teachers: self-image of, 183; nature of job, 184; responsibilities, 184-86; organization of, 186; economic concerns of, 187; unions of, 187-88; accountability of, 189-90; improvement of teaching, 190-191; models for teaching, 239; relation to students, 191-92, 241-44; contextual use of models in teacher-student relations, 244-47
Teaching and learning: phases of learning process, 12; learning prior, 204-10; whether relation causal, 205; Aristotle's model developed, 205-7; Hirst's account, 207-8; Mill's focus, 208; older models over-simple, 208-9; concept of studying added, 209-10; schema for variety of relations, 210-11; variety examined, 211-14; problems generated, 215-18; purposive vs. behavioristic models, 218-19, 239; pedagogical encounter, 237-49 (chap. 12); replacing "in loco parentis," 248n.13
Technology: relation to crafts, arts, science, 303-4; development of, 141-43; intermediate, 142
Tocqueville, Alexis de, 75, 164, 174
Tolstoy, L.N., 279, 302
Torney, J.V., Oppenheim, A.N., and Farnen, R.F., 294
Tracking. *See* Mainstreaming
Transactional compared with contractual, 236-37
Trow, M.A., 151
Tyack, David, 201

Valuational base: constituents, 130-34; for normative judgments in education, 134-35
Value: as selection, 270; patterns, 66
Values clarification, 281-82, 292-93n.11
Veblen, Thorstein, 15, 20
Vienna Circle, 265
Vilikazi, Absalom, 16, 21
Virgil, 13
Vocational-technical education: meanings of "vocational," 314; growth of, 315-17
Voucher system for education, 82

Warner, Lloyd, 16, 21
Whitehead, A.N., 308, 331-32
Whitman, Walt, 321
Wilson, John, Williams, Norman, and Sugarman, Barry, 293
Wolfenstein, Martha, 20
Wolff, R.P., 39, 106, 311
Women's Liberation movement, 83-84
Wylie, Laurence, 11, 13, 16, 20, 21

Zborowski, Mark, 19

www.ingramcontent.com/pod-product-compliance
Lightning Source LLC
Chambersburg PA
CBHW031231290426
44109CB00012B/254